California

Real Estate Principles

Bryan P. Church   **Schyler B. Church**

California Real Estate Principles
Authors: Bryan P. Church and Schyler B. Church

This textbook is written to provide accurate information on the covered topics. It is not meant to take the place of professional advice.

Website: www.accreditedtextbooks.com
Phone: (916) 966-9300
Fax: (916) 966-9305

Order textbooks directly via Accredited Textbooks
www.accreditedtextbooks.com

ISBN-10: 1-7338808-0-1
ISBN-13: 978-1-7338808-0-0

ISBN 978-1-7338808-0-0

54995

9 781733 880800

About the Authors

BRYAN CHURCH

Bryan Church has been a real estate broker for over thirty years and has sold, exchanged, and purchased many properties, including single-family homes, apartment buildings, commercial leased investments, and parcels of land. Clients have included individuals, partnerships, corporations, real estate investment trusts, the Federal Bankruptcy Court (asset dispositions), and foreign investment groups. Furthermore, he has been a custom home builder and developer.

He holds both B.S. and MBA degrees; and has completed a one-year course in substantive law. He has a Community College Teaching Credential that is valid for life and has taught real estate courses at several California community colleges. In addition to his community college teaching experience, he has taught many undergraduate and graduate-level real estate courses at Golden Gate University. He founded Accredited Real Estate Schools, Inc. in 1995 and is currently Chairman of the Board of Directors.

SCHYLER CHURCH

Schyler Church is a practicing real estate broker licensed in California and Hawaii. Alongside her father, Bryan Church, Schyler has co-authored *California Real Estate Principles* and *California Real Estate Practice* textbooks. She is experienced listing and selling both single-family homes and multi-unit residential properties. In addition, she has been a residential property manager and a contributor to Bryan Church's *California Real Estate Property Management* textbook. She holds a B.S. degree in Accountancy and is a member of the real estate faculty at Cosumnes River College.

Other Textbooks

Textbooks by *Bryan Church* and *Schyler Church*:
- ❖ California Real Estate Principles
- ❖ California Real Estate Practice

Textbooks by *Bryan Church*:
- ❖ California Real Estate Property Management
- ❖ California Real Estate Exam Preparation Workbook
- ❖ California Continuing Education Courses
  - Real Estate Update
  - Agency
  - Ethics
  - Trust Fund Handling
  - Fair Housing
  - Risk Management
  - Management and Supervision

Order directly via
Accredited Textbooks
www.accreditedtextbooks.com
(916) 966-9300

Preface

PRINCIPLES

The best way to learn the principles of real estate is through an actual real estate transaction. Fundamental real estate concepts are discussed while they occur during the purchase of an existing single-family home, so students learn **why** they are learning the concept along with **when** and **where** it fits into an actual real estate deal. The principles of real estate are presented in the order they appear during a normal single-family home purchase transaction, so students can relate new terms and concepts to the actual real estate brokerage business. The book is organized around five main sections:

I. **Overview** is a brief look at the entire real estate transaction process, including before, during, and after the real estate transaction.

II. **Before the Real Estate Transaction** considers activities that occur prior to the real estate transaction. They include starting a career in real estate, working with buyers and sellers prior to the real estate transaction, agency relationships, ethics, and fair housing, property and estates in land, and real estate contracts: offer and acceptance.

III. **During the Real Estate Transaction** discusses the important activities that occur from the opening of escrow until escrow closes. They include opening escrow and the escrow process, disclosures, physical inspection contingencies, appraisal contingencies, financing contingencies, taking title to real property, and close of escrow.

IV. **After the Real Estate Transaction** covers what happens after the close of escrow. It includes how real estate brokers and salespersons get paid, interim occupancy agreements, seller occupancy addenda, agent follow-up techniques, and how title insurance protects buyers, sellers, and lenders from title defects discovered after the close of escrow.

V. **Other Important Real Estate Areas** include real estate income properties and real estate taxation.

Table of Contents

SECTION I: OVERVIEW

CHAPTER ONE:

SECTION II: BEFORE THE REAL ESTATE TRANSACTION

CHAPTER TWO

Starting a Career in Real Estate   28-51

CHAPTER THREE

Working with Buyers and Sellers Prior to the Real Estate Transaction 52-83

CHAPTER FOUR
Agency Relationships, Ethics, and Fair Housing 84-113

CHAPTER FIVE
Property and Estates in Land Chapter   114-153

CHAPTER SIX

Real Estate Contracts: Offer and Acceptance | 154-179

SECTION III: DURING THE REAL ESTATE TRANSACTION

CHAPTER SEVEN

Opening Escrow and the Escrow Process — 180-211

CHAPTER EIGHT

Real Estate Disclosures Part I 212-245

CHAPTER NINE

Disclosures Part II   246-265

CHAPTER TEN

Physical Inspection Contingencies   266-287

CHAPTER ELEVEN

Appraisal Contingencies   288-317

CHAPTER TWELVE

Financing Contingencies   318-363

CHAPTER THIRTEEN

Taking Title to Real Property   364-391

SECTION IV: AFTER THE REAL ESTATE TRANSACTION

CHAPTER FOURTEEN

After the Real Estate Transaction   392-409

SECTION V: OTHER IMPORTANT REAL ESTATE AREAS

CHAPTER FIFTEEN

Working with Real Estate Investors and Real Estate Taxation   410-451

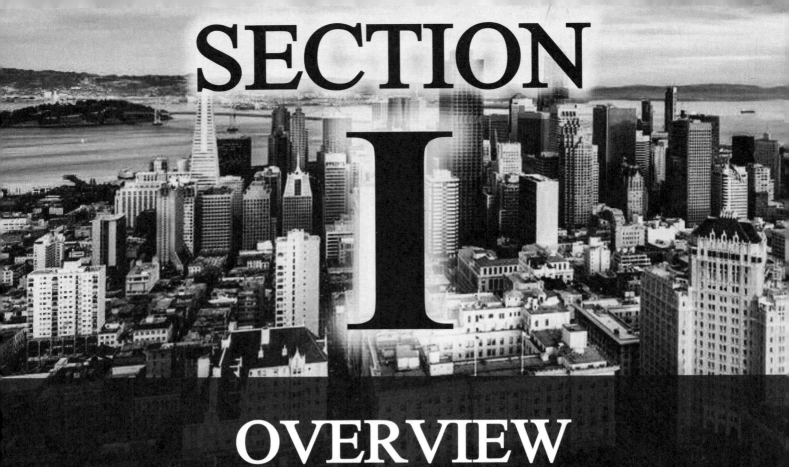

SECTION I

OVERVIEW

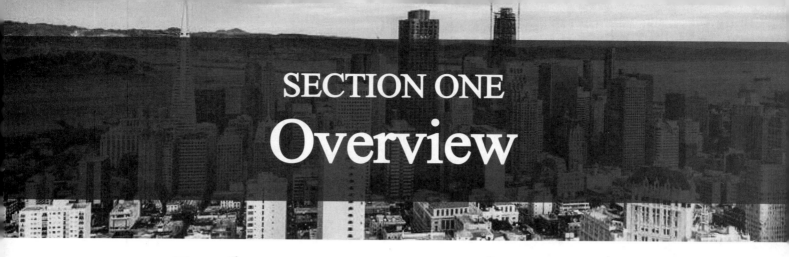

Real Estate Transaction Overview

BUYER'S AGENT
(SELLING AGENT)

Obtain Buyer and Discuss Objectives

Submit Offer(s)

Prospect for Buyers

Show Properties

Buyer Reviews Disclosures and Inspects Property

Buyer Makes Request for Repairs to Seller

Buyer Signs Escrow Instructions* and Loan Documents

Buyer Places Earnest Money Deposit into Escrow

Buyer Receives Preliminary Title Report from Title Company

Buyer Removes Contingencies

Final Verification of Property Condition

Loan Funding

OFFER & ACCEPTANCE

OPEN ESCROW

CLOSE ESCROW

Agent Follow-Up

Prospect for Sellers

Prepare Property for Listing

Review and Respond to Offer(s)

Obtain Listing

Seller Provides Disclosures to Buyer

Seller Responds to Buyer's Request for Repairs

Seller Signs Escrow Instructions* and Grant Deed

SELLER'S AGENT
(LISTING AGENT)

* According to escrow signing customs in California, properties located in Southern California may sign escrow instructions <u>early</u> in the escrow period just <u>after</u> opening escrow. In Northern California, however, escrow instructions may be signed <u>late</u> in the escrow period just <u>before</u> close of escrow.

Albert Einstein
"If you can't explain it simply,
you don't understand it
well enough."

1

Chapter
ONE

An Overview:
Before, During, and After the
Real Estate Transaction

When a person receives a real estate salesperson license and places it under a real estate broker, the first transaction is usually with a buyer rather than a seller. This is because buyers are easier to work with and usually provide commission income (e.g., closed deals) faster than listing homes for sale. Sellers usually require a significant amount of time to list the property for sale, find a qualified buyer, and close escrow.

Real Estate Agent: A person who is licensed as a real estate broker and under whose license a listing is executed or an offer to purchase is obtained.

As a **real estate agent** becomes more experienced, the agent will probably move into listing homes for sale because listed homes market themselves twenty-four hours per day, seven days per week and are a good prospecting base to find both buyers and sellers. Although, some experienced agents specialize in working only with buyers and are called buyer's agents.

Figure 1.1

> **PLEASE NOTE:**
> It should be noted that whenever a real estate agent is mentioned in the book, the real estate agent is a licensed real estate salesperson who has placed their real estate salesperson license under a licensed real estate broker who is responsible for the real estate salesperson's actions. Therefore, the real estate broker is included whenever a real estate agent (who in this case is a real estate salesperson) is mentioned throughout the book.

1. Before the Real Estate Transaction

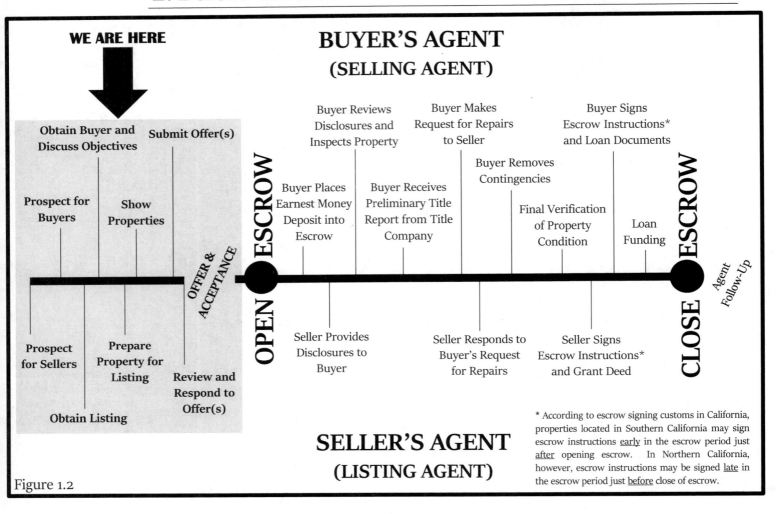

Figure 1.2

A. Transaction Part 1
(1) Prospecting for and Obtaining Buyers

There are many ways to prospect for buyers. A new real estate salesperson is well-advised to listen to their real estate broker regarding the most successful ways to find buyers. One of the best ways to prospect for buyers (and sellers as well) is through an agent's sphere of influence—which is everyone the agent knows, including friends, neighbors, and relatives. Consequently, most real estate agents will immediately tap into their sphere of influence and ask them to use the real estate agent's services to buy or sell a home.

Social media is a good way to notify and remind a real estate agent's sphere of influence that the agent is in the real estate brokerage business. This is a powerful way to reach a sphere of influence on a consistent and continuing basis.

(2) Buyer Objectives: What Buyers are Looking for

A real estate agent should determine what type of property the buyer is looking for and their timeframe in making the purchase. Buying parameters are frequently based on the buyer's existing family situation. For example, a husband, wife, and two children may be looking for a three-bedroom and two-bathroom home in the suburbs with a good public school system. In contrast, a single person may want a well-located home near restaurants, cafes, shopping, and work sources.

(3) Buyer Loan Preapproval vs. Prequalification

There are many people who are *ready* and *willing* to buy a home, yet a much smaller number who are actually *able* to purchase one. Most buyers will need a loan to purchase a home, so getting pre-approved with a lender is critical to finding a home and closing the transaction. The difference between being preapproved and prequalified is significant.

Preapproval means a borrower has contacted a real estate lender and the lender has reviewed the person's credit report, obtained employment and income information, and submitted the loan package to underwriting. Underwriting provides tentative loan approval–subject to certain funding conditions such as the property appraising for at least the purchase price and the borrower's credit score not changing during the escrow period prior to loan funding. A pre-approval letter is solid proof of a borrower's ability to qualify for the loan and can be used like cash when negotiating the purchase of a single-family home.

Conversely, **prequalified** merely proves the borrower has contacted a lender and provided basic loan information to allow the real estate lender to write a letter that states, "Based upon unconfirmed information we may be able to make a loan up to a certain amount."

> **Loan Preapproval:** Borrower has provided all documentation to the lender and the lender has run the borrower's credit report. The lender then issues a loan preapproval letter stating the borrower is preapproved for a loan to purchase the property.
>
> **Loan Prequalification:** Borrower has merely started the loan process and has not been preapproved for a loan.

PREAPPROVAL	PREQUALIFIED
Solid proof of borrower's ability to qualify for the loan	Not substantial
Submitted to underwriting for tentative loan approval with conditions	Only shows borrower contacted a lender

Figure 1.3 Preapproval vs. Prequalified

Sellers may not understand the difference between a potential buyer being preapproved for a loan versus being prequalified, so the real estate agent may need to explain the pros and cons of each type of loan letter. A wise seller may consider a preapproved buyer as having a high probability of obtaining a loan and closing the transaction. In contrast, a seller who accepts a prequalified buyer is accepting a buyer who may not be able to obtain a loan and close escrow.

B. Transaction Part 1

Seller

(1) Prospecting for and Obtaining Sellers

Prospecting for sellers is different than prospecting for buyers. When prospecting for sellers, the real estate agent is asking the seller to sign a listing agreement that will allow the agent to place the property on the market, find a suitable buyer, and receive a commission when the property sells. A seller who is willing to list their home with a real estate agent, does so because there is confidence the agent will sell the property for the highest possible price and within the shortest possible marketing time.

An effective method of prospecting for sellers is to contact the agent's sphere of influence and constantly remind them of the agent being in the real estate brokerage business.

Figure 1.4

(2) Seller Objectives

A real estate agent will need to determine *why* the seller is selling the property and its market value.

a. Why are They Selling the Property?

Understanding a seller's reasons and motivations for selling a property is one of the most important areas to determine during the selling process. By understanding the seller's motivations, the real estate agent can adjust the listing presentation and subsequent marketing plan to fit the seller's reasons for selling the home. For example, a seller may want to find a home to purchase *before* selling their existing home. The agent may suggest a 72 hour contingency that will allow the seller to obtain a signed contract for their new home, while the agent markets the existing home in an effort to sell the property for the highest price in the shortest marketing time.

Possible motivations may include:

1. Sell and move up to a larger home. This could be caused by a new child on the way or an older parent moving in with the family.

2. Sell and move down to a smaller home. This may be caused by retirement and empty nester status when the children have moved out of the family home and are living on their own.

3. Sell and become a renter. Some sellers may want to cash out and take the price appreciation (increase in value) from their home. This is especially true when market timing is near the top of an upward-trending sellers' market and property values are projected to decrease in the future.

4. Financial problems can cause a seller to sell their home to get out from under the monthly debt obligation (home loan payments).

b. What is the Market Value of the Property?

Market value is the price the market will pay for a parcel of real property. It is what a willing buyer will pay and a willing seller will accept for a property in an open and competitive real estate market. In other words, market value occurs when a buyer and seller–who are not under any duress (pressure)–come to agreement on the price and terms for the purchase of the property.

Real estate agents usually provide sellers with a comparative market analysis (CMA) that considers the sale prices of similar houses surrounding the property being listed for sale. These properties are called sales comparables (sales comps) and indicate the current market for similar properties that have recently sold near the subject property.

It is important to price the property near its market value to be able to find a buyer to purchase it. Buyers usually will not buy an over-priced property. Accordingly, if the buyer is using a loan to purchase the property, the lender will normally require an appraisal performed by a professional appraiser to verify the property's market value is sufficient collateral to cover the loan amount. If the lender must foreclose in the future, the lender will attempt to recoup as much of the loan amount as possible from the sale of the property.

(3) Comparative Market Analysis (CMA) to Help Determine the List Price

A real estate agent will need to determine the intended list price for the property. Initially most sellers have no idea what their property is worth on the open market, so they usually go onto publicly-accessible websites and look at properties that are listed for sale. The problem with this type of pricing analysis is that it considers the asking prices for properties that are listed for sale and not the prices for which they are selling on the open market. In addition, seller's may have a difficult time comparing sold properties to their own property.

This is where a real estate agent's expertise becomes important to a seller of real property. The agent can help the seller determine the appropriate list price that will provide the highest possible price within the shortest marketing time. For buyers, the agent can help determine a reasonable purchase price based on the existing real estate market for a property they are interested in purchasing.

A **comparative market analysis (CMA)** uses appraisal techniques used by professional appraisers to help determine an appropriate list price for a property. This is important because the buyer will most likely use a loan to purchase the property and lenders usually require a formal **appraisal** before they will make a loan on a property. This is to assure the lender that the property's value is high enough to provide sufficient **collateral** if the loan must be foreclosed in the future.

When buyers obtain a loan for a property, they place the property as collateral for repayment of the loan, so if the buyer stops making loan payments in the future, the lender will foreclose the loan, sell the property (through the trustee in a trustee's sale), and hopefully get most of their money returned to them. Therefore, when a real estate agent helps a seller price a property for sale using the same appraisal techniques used by professional appraisers, the appraised value of the property should be close enough to the purchase price to not become a loan underwriting and funding problem just before close of escrow.

In other words, many real estate transactions will require a loan plus a **down payment** by the buyer to be able to purchase the property. The lender is going to require a formal appraisal before funding the loan. Again, this is to ensure the property's value is sufficient collateral to cover the loan amount in the event of foreclosure. Therefore, the **listing agent** (also called the seller's agent who is the real estate agent representing the seller) must help the seller price the property as close to its true market value as possible to provide enough collateral (value of the home) to allow the lender to fund the loan and the buyer to close escrow.

(4) Obtain Listing

A real estate agent will ask the seller to sign a **real estate listing agreement**, along with an agency disclosure form. The listing agreement is a contract allowing the listing agent to list the property for sale, accept an earnest money deposit from the buyer and on behalf of the seller, and receive a **commission** when the property sells (usually after confirmation of recording of the grant deed after close of escrow).

Comparative Market Analysis (CMA): Analysis performed by a real estate agent to help the seller price a property for sale.

Appraisal: A formal report on the value of a parcel of real property.

Collateral: Placing something as security for a loan.

Down Payment: The amount of money a buyer pays out of his or her own pocket when a loan is used to purchase the property.

Listing Agent: Real estate broker who is representing the seller.

Real Estate Listing Agreement: Contract used by a real estate broker to list a property for sale.

Commission: Usually a percentage of the property sale price. Paid to the real estate broker who then pays the real estate salesperson working under their license.

A warranty of authority is given by the seller to the real estate agent. This allows the agent to place the property on the market and accept an earnest money deposit from the buyer. The seller normally gives the real estate agent a warranty of authority in the real estate listing agreement.

Once the listing agreement and agency disclosure forms have been signed by the seller and real estate agent, then the real estate agent can start marketing the property for sale. This may include a "for sale sign" in the front yard, entry of the property into the local multiple listing service (MLS), and the installation of an MLS lockbox in the front yard of the home. The lockbox usually holds the keys to the front door, along with those to any other exterior doors, and is used by real estate agents to help their buyers access the inside of the home. Lockboxes are generally attached to the front yard water faucet, gas meter, or front door handle.

Figure 1.5

With the common use of mobile devices in today's real estate market, paper flyers and flyer boxes are not as important as they were in the past. The internet has also provided buyers with easy access to listed properties, so real estate agents are having to find more ways to provide valuable services to their clients.

C. Transaction Part 2
(1) Show Appropriate Properties (that Meet the Buyer's Requirements) to the Buyer

Real estate agents usually preview several listed properties for sale and select the ones that meet the buyer's requirements. The agent then schedules six or seven of these properties to be shown to the buyer each day. Any more than this number will usually cause the buyer to not remember one property from another.

One of the key benefits of buyers working with a real estate agent is the agent's ability to access the inside of properties. Anyone can drive by a property and look at the outside, but it takes a special person to get inside the property. It takes a licensed real estate agent to garner the trust of the seller to allow access to the inside of their home. A person's home is their castle, and a random buyer who is not being represented by a licensed real estate agent may be casing the place for a future burglary.

Real estate agents go through an extensive screening process before they are licensed by the **California Department of Real Estate (DRE)**. Real estate agents are required to complete three college-level courses (Real Estate Principles, Real Estate Practice, and one elective course), pass an all-encompassing state

California Department of Real Estate (DRE): Regulates real estate brokers and real estate salespersons.

Figure 1.6

examination, and pass both California Department of Justice (DOJ) and Federal Bureau of Investigation (FBI) criminal background checks.

After all the above requirements have been completed, a person is entrusted with a real estate salesperson license. This license must be placed under a real estate broker who is responsible for the real estate salesperson's actions. On top of this, a portion of a real estate salesperson's license fees goes into the California Department of Real Estate's Consumer Recovery Account. This account is used to help buyers and sellers who have uncollectable judgments (caused by unscrupulous real estate salespersons and brokers) to collect limited damages (money) from the Recovery Account and attempt to return the consumer to the same position the consumer was at before the incident occurred.

For these reasons, real estate agents (real estate salespersons and brokers) have a special trust that can be used to get buyers inside properties. Thus, buyers rely on the real estate agent to do this for them. Access to the inside of properties is one of the key benefits real estate agents provide to buyers who are looking to purchase a home.

Sellers can be confident that the real estate agent who is going through their home has been vetted by the DRE, DOJ, and FBI. However, the buyers have only been vetted by the real estate agent. For this reason, requiring buyers to get preapproved for a real estate loan prior to showing them properties provides the lender with an opportunity to examine the buyer's finances, run a credit report, and find out if they are real buyers or criminals posing as buyers. Lenders verify buyers are who they say they are and are not merely looking to steal something from a home.

Getting inside a property cannot be replicated by the internet and is the key reason why real estate sellers list their properties for sale with real estate agents. It is also the reason why sellers are willing to pay a 5% or 6% commission for a real estate agent's services.

D. Transaction Part 2
(1) Make Property Available to Prospective Buyers

Depending on a property's price range and whether it is occupied by an owner, tenant, or is vacant; the seller may want to consider staging the home for sale. A professional staging company can be used to place tasteful furniture in a vacant property to help buyers visualize what the property will look like after the purchase. For owner-occupied homes, in which the seller is living in the property, staging the home is usually not practical, but it is important the seller presents the home in a condition that interests buyers and generates offers.

(2) Showing Instructions

The easier it is to get inside a property, the more buyers it will attract, and the greater likelihood it will sell for a good price and within a reasonable marketing time. Accordingly, a vacant property, with an MLS lockbox attached to it, tends to be the best showing instructions because no one is living there, thus making it is easy to show to prospective buyers. Moreover, a vacant property that has an existing loan on it may cause the seller to be more motivated to sell the property at a lower price because the monthly loan payments continue to be a cost incurred by the seller until the property is sold. Existing loan amounts can many times be found in the public tax record database.

In contrast, tenant-occupied properties are usually the most difficult to gain entry because a tenant is living in the property. The least effective showing instruction is calling the tenant to make an appointment to see the inside of the home. Tenants usually do not want to be bothered showing the inside of a property and will typically make it very difficult to get inside. For this reason, real estate agents may need to schedule showings 24 hours ahead of time and continue to follow-up with the tenant to confirm access is provided to the inside of the property at the appointed time.

Tenants who have lived in a property for less than a year must be given a 30 day notice by the property owner or manager to vacate the property. In contrast, tenants who have lived in a property for a year or more must be provided with a 60 day notice to vacate the property. Tenants typically are not motivated to help the landlord show the inside of the home because, after all, they are being moved

Figure 1.7 Lockbox

out of the property and must deal with the aggravation of finding a new place to live, going through credit checks, and all the hassles of moving into a new home.

For this reason, "Appointment with Tenant" showing instructions may sit on the market for sixty days or longer, even though the property is in good condition and correctly priced. Sitting on the market for sixty days, while the owner deals with an uncooperative tenant, will give the property a "shopped" image (on the market for a long period of time without offers) and may reduce showings even further. Once the tenant has moved out of the property, it can be shown as vacant/lockbox and finally get some prospective buyers inside it and subsequently sold. For this reason, some sellers like to wait until the tenant is out of the property before placing it on the market.

This is where real estate agents can be very valuable to their buyers. By persistence and hard work, a real estate agent may be able to gain entry to a tenant-occupied property, discover that it is a good deal, get their buyers into the property to see it, and negotiate a good purchase price. After the property has been on the market for sixty days or more, the seller may be motivated to reduce the price or accept a below list price offer from the buyer. It really depends on market conditions and motivation level of the seller.

Tales from the Trade

THE STORY OF THE UNCOOPERATIVE TENANTS

A single-family home was listed for $320,000 for sixty days and had very few showings and no offers. The selling agent (buyer's agent) had to fight her way into the property because the tenants were not being cooperative showing the inside of the property to prospective buyers. This is a common occurrence with tenant-occupied properties and is the reason some experienced sellers wait until the tenant is out of the property before placing it on the market. This is especially true when there is an upward-trending sellers' market and real estate prices are increasing during the required thirty (30) day or sixty (60) day termination of tenancy period given by property owners and property managers to tenants. The seller was a licensed real estate agent and lived two hours away from the property. Plus, there were seven other owners on title to the property—so everyone needed to agree to the price and terms of the deal.

The tenant had been given a sixty day notice to vacate the property and then it was immediately placed on the market while the tenant continued to occupy the home. In California, if a tenant has been living in a rental property for one year or more, the owner must give the tenant a sixty day notice to vacate it. In this case, the tenant had lived there for over a year and received a sixty day notice from the owner to vacate the property. The selling agent (agent representing the buyer) was finally able to get inside the property sixty days after it was listed.

Since the owner was a licensed California real estate broker, he listed the property in the MLS himself, thereby saving a 3% listing commission. He agreed to pay the selling agent a 3% commission upon the sale of the property. The owner's problem was that he lived too far away to easily help selling agents and buyers get past the uncooperative tenants and see the inside of the property. This caused the property to take longer to market and sold at a lower price than would have occurred if the property had been vacant and/or the property owner/listing agent lived closer to the property.

The buyer was made aware of this fact by the selling agent, so the buyer offered only

THE STORY OF THE UNCOOPERATIVE TENANTS

$305,000 for the property – $15,000 under list price. The sellers accepted the offer, thinking they were lucky to finally find a buyer after sixty days on the market and no offers. The reality, however, was very different. The real estate purchase market had increased in value during the sixty days the property was sitting on the market with no showings and no offers.

The buyers closed escrow for a home with a market value of $340,000 and had paid only $305,000. The buyers were moving into the property with $35,000 of "built-in" equity.

Another major consideration for the buyers was the local public school system. Elementary, middle, and high schools can affect the desirability of a property and therefore, its value. In this case, the entire school district was highly rated and therefore, added value to the home. The buyer's children were seven and five years old, so they could take advantage of the fine elementary school in the area. Over time, the family could continue to live in the home with a solid middle school and high school available to their children in the future.

E. Transaction Part 3

(1) Buyer Submits Offer to Seller

When a buyer finds the right home to purchase, the buyer's agent, also known as the **selling agent,** will write an **offer** to purchase the property. This is accomplished with a **Real Estate Purchase Agreement and Joint Escrow Instructions** (purchase agreement) that will specify the price and terms of the property purchase. At the same time, the buyer will sign a Disclosure Regarding Agency Relationship form (agency disclosure form) that discloses "who is representing whom" in the real estate purchase transaction.

The agency disclosure form is used to help disclose, elect, and confirm the agency relationship that exists between the buyer and the real estate salesperson (and of course, the real estate salesperson's real estate broker). The agency disclosure form discloses and explains the nature of agency relationships in California, requires the buyer to elect who is representing them in the real estate transaction (usually the real estate salesperson and their broker), and then confirms who is representing them in the transaction. Disclosing who is representing whom and electing this relationship is usually accomplished with the agency disclosure form. However, the confirmation of the agency relationship is usually made in the purchase agreement.

Selling Agent: Real estate agent who is representing the buyer.

Offer: Buyer makes an offer to the seller to purchase real property.

Real Estate Purchase Agreement: Contract used to purchase real property.

Seller

F. Transaction Part 3
(1) Review Offer Made by Buyer

Once the buyer's agent/selling agent has furnished the offer and the buyer has signed it, it will be presented to the seller. This is usually accomplished by the buyer's agent/selling agent submitting it to the seller's agent/listing agent. The seller's agent/listing agent then presents the offer to the seller. The seller has three possible responses: (1) accept the offer, (2) reject the offer, or (3) make a **counter offer** back to the buyer.

> **Counter Offer:** Seller makes a counter offer back to the buyer for the sale of real property.
>
> **Contract:** Agreement to do or not to do something.

(2) Accept, Reject, or Submit Counter Offer #1 to Buyer

If the seller accepts the buyer's offer, then there is a **contract** (agreement) between the buyer and seller when the buyer is notified of the seller accepting the buyer's offer. If the seller rejects the buyer's offer, there is no contract formed between the parties.

If the seller submits a counter offer to the buyer, this is an offer from the seller to the buyer and is normally at a higher price or better terms than the buyer's original offer. The buyer can accept the seller's counter offer, reject it, or submit a counter offer (counter offer #2) to the seller. The process continues back and forth until the buyer and seller come to mutual assent (complete agreement) regarding the price and terms of the real property purchase and a contract is formed between the two parties.

Real estate transactions that have several counter-offers between the buyer and seller tend to stay in contract more often than ones that are easy to get into contract and have few counter offers. Buyers and sellers who use several counter offers are usually negotiating from a position of strength and each is serious about making the deal.

Figure 1.8

G. Transaction Part 4
(1) Offer and Acceptance

If the seller accepts the buyer's offer, the seller will sign the purchase agreement. The buyer is then notified of the seller accepting the buyer's offer and a contract is formed. The buyer must be notified of the seller accepting the buyer's offer before a contract is formed by the parties. The buyer signs the notice of acceptance portion of the purchase agreement and a valid contract has been formed between the buyer and seller. The buyer keeps a copy of the executed (signed) purchase agreement, along with a copy of the agency disclosure form used to disclose, elect, and confirm the agency relationship between the buyer and the buyer's agent/selling agent.

If the seller rejects the buyer's offer, then the seller's rejection of the offer is delivered to the buyer and there is no contract formed between the buyer and seller.

H. Transaction Part 4
(1) Seller Counter Offer

If the seller executes (signs) a counter offer (called counter offer #1), it must be presented to the buyer. If the buyer accepts counter offer #1, then the buyer's acceptance must be communicated back to the seller. Once the seller has been notified of the buyer's acceptance of counter offer #1, there is a valid contract between the buyer and seller.

If the buyer does not like counter offer #1 from the seller, then the buyer will have the buyer's agent/selling agent write counter offer #2. This is a counter offer to the seller's counter offer #1 and must be signed by the buyer. Counter offer #2 is then presented to the seller and if the seller accepts counter offer #2 (and this acceptance is communicated back to the buyer), then there is a valid contract.

However, if the seller would like to change more items in the contract (usually price or terms), then a counter offer #3 is executed and the process continues until the buyer and seller reach mutual assent (mutual agreement).

Each time an offer or counter-offer is accepted, rejected, or a counter-offer is made, this fact must be communicated back to the party making the offer or counter offer. For example, if the buyer makes an offer to the seller and the seller accepts the buyer's offer, this acceptance must be communicated back to the buyer before there is a valid contract formed.

Even though the real estate agent is an agent of the buyer and/or seller and helps facilitate the real estate transaction, the agent is *not* part of the real estate purchase agreement (except for payment of commissions). The purchase agreement is between the buyer and seller.

2. During the Real Estate Transaction

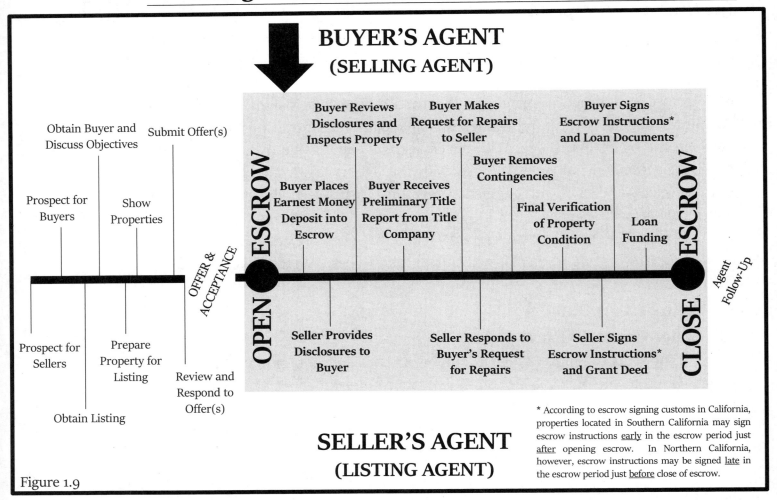

Figure 1.9

* According to escrow signing customs in California, properties located in Southern California may sign escrow instructions <u>early</u> in the escrow period just <u>after</u> opening escrow. In Northern California, however, escrow instructions may be signed <u>late</u> in the escrow period just <u>before</u> close of escrow.

A. Transaction Part 5
(1) Escrow Opened

Escrow is the process in which money or other documents are held by a disinterested third party (stakeholder) until satisfaction of the terms and conditions of the escrow instructions have been achieved. In other words, the buyer would like to take a serious look at the property before purchasing it. Therefore, an escrow agent is used to hold the buyer's **earnest money deposit** (used by the seller to ensure the buyer is a serious buyer) until the buyer inspects the property and decides to move forward with the purchase or terminate the transaction. If the buyer decides to terminate the purchase transaction, the escrow agent will usually be directed to return the buyer's earnest money deposit under the terms of the purchase agreement. This is accomplished by both the buyer and seller signing an escrow rescission form directing the escrow agent to return the buyer's earnest

Earnest Money Deposit: Used to ensure the buyer is serious about purchasing the property.

money deposit. Earnest money deposits for resale single-family homes are usually between $1,000 to $5,000.

When escrow is opened, the escrow agent (also called escrow officer or escrow holder) is the agent of both the buyer and seller during the escrow period. After close of escrow (when all the terms and conditions of the escrow have been met), the escrow officer becomes the independent agent of the buyer and independent agent of the seller separately. In other words, during the escrow period the escrow officer must have agreement between both the buyer and seller before the escrow officer can carry out any instructions from the buyer or seller under the escrow. This includes disbursing funds, paying invoices, or completing anything else contained in the escrow instructions. However, after close of escrow, when all the terms and conditions of the escrow have been satisfied, the escrow officer becomes the independent agent of the buyer and independent agent of the seller and can disburse funds and perform any other items individually to either the buyer or seller without the other party's agreement.

Prior to opening escrow, the buyer and seller must both agree which escrow agent to use for the transaction. Since most buyers and sellers do not have a preferred escrow agent, the real estate agents who are representing each party may suggest escrow agents they have worked with in the past.

If a buyer and seller are in an escrow dispute and both parties demand payment of the buyer's earnest money deposit, the escrow agent must receive a court order prior to disbursing funds. This court order is the result of an interpleader action in which the escrow agent asks the courts to determine what to do with the buyer's earnest money deposit.

(2) Escrow: Northern vs. Southern California

Northern California and Southern California have traditionally used different techniques for escrow and title insurance services. Northern California has used one entity to perform both escrow and title insurance. For example, a buyer and seller decide to use ABC Title Company to handle their transaction, so ABC Title Company will provide escrow services and title insurance for the property purchase.

Southern California, on the other hand, has traditionally used a separate escrow company and a separate title insurance company to perform the same services. Escrow companies have been very strong in the Southern California real estate market, so they have been able to maintain this separation of services over the years.

Northern California typically has buyers and sellers sign escrow instructions *late* in the transaction, usually a few days prior to the close of escrow. Conversely,

Figure 1.10

Southern California may have buyers and sellers sign escrow instructions *early* in the transaction, usually a few days after escrow is opened.

(3) Buyer Starts the Process of Obtaining Financing

At this point in the transaction, the buyer will start the process of obtaining a real estate loan to help with the property purchase. This will require the buyer to provide current pay stubs, verification of income, W-2s, 1099s, along with other information the lender will need to make a lending decision.

The lender will have already run the buyer's credit report at the time the buyer was preapproved for a loan, so this part of the loan package will already be in place. The lender may collect an appraisal fee from the buyer to pay for the appraisal of the property. The lender will require an appraisal to ensure the property being purchased, and used as collateral for the loan, will appraise for the agreed upon purchase price. If not, the buyer may be required to increase the down payment for the loan or ask the seller to reduce the sale price. The loan approval process usually takes between fifteen (15) and forty-five (45) days to complete.

(4) Disclosures Provided to Buyer

Real Estate Transfer Disclosure Statement (TDS): The primary disclosure for one-to-four unit residential properties in California and asks the seller to provide information regarding the condition of the property.

The seller is required by law, with a few exceptions, to provide a **real estate transfer disclosure statement (TDS)**, along with several other mandatory disclosures that are discussed in Chapters 8 and 9.

The TDS asks the seller to provide information regarding the condition of the property. In addition, both the seller's agent/listing agent and buyer's agent/selling agent must make a visual inspection of accessible areas of the property and report their findings on the TDS disclosure form.

The TDS is required for most one-to-four unit residential properties in California. There are several exceptions to this requirement. For example, foreclosed properties typically do not require the seller to provide a TDS disclosure; however, the real estate agents are each required to make a visual inspection of the property and note their findings on either the TDS disclosure form, or the agent's visual inspection disclosure form (AVID) if the TDS is not required.

During the buyer's due diligence period prior to close of escrow, the buyer will normally examine the property to see if it is in good physical condition, review the condition of the title, and then decide whether to move forward with the purchase. This is during the buyer's physical inspection contingency period that is negotiated in the purchase agreement. In California, single-family homes commonly use seventeen (17) days from the effective date of the contract (when it was signed by the buyer and seller—and acceptance communicated back to the person who made the offer or counter offer) to the end of the physical contingency removal period. Since most single-family home escrows are from fifteen (15) to forty-five (45) days in duration, the physical inspection contingency will be removed somewhere in the middle of the escrow period.

Furthermore, just after opening escrow the buyer normally receives a copy of the preliminary title report from the title insurance company. A preliminary title report ("prelim") is an offer by the title insurance company to issue a policy of title insurance. **Title insurance** is used by buyers to ensure they are receiving clear title to the property. A title insurance company searches a property's chain of recorded title and then issues a policy of title insurance insuring the title to the property. If an existing claim against the title (that is covered by the title insurance policy) appears after the buyer has closed escrow, then the title insurance company may be required to pay for the buyer's loss. An example is a cloud on the title to real property that results from a mechanic's lien that existed before the buyer purchased the property. If the lien appears after close of escrow, the title insurance company may be required to pay for the buyer's loss.

> **Title Insurance:** Insurance that protects a buyer from title defects existing on a property.

Just after opening escrow, the escrow officer may provide a copy of the covenants, conditions, and restrictions (CC&Rs) to the buyer and buyer's agent/selling agent. CC&Rs restrict the use of the property and can impact its usability and valuation. The buyer's agent/selling agent should review the CC&Rs, along with the preliminary title report, to determine if there are any unreasonable restrictions or defects on the title to the property.

Concurrently, this is the time in some Southern California counties that the seller is required to provide a pre-sale report that determines whether the property has any unpermitted additions or building code violation. The pre-sale report is provided to the buyer for review.

> **Addendum:** Additional pages of material that are added to and become part of a contract.

B. Transaction Part 5

(1) Seller Orders Pest Report (If Required in the Purchase Agreement and/or Accompanying Addenda)

Seller

A pest inspection is performed by a pest inspection company to look for subterranean termite infestation and damage, along with dry rot (fungal decay). The buyer may ask the seller to order a pest inspection and provide a pest report, which is usually accomplished in the terms of the real estate purchase agreement or with an addendum to the real estate purchase agreement. An **addendum** is used to include additional terms that are added to the purchase agreement.

Figure 1.11

Mark Moz/Flickr

C. Transaction Part 6
(1) Physical Inspection Contingency

During the physical inspection contingency period, the buyer may hire a home inspector to inspect the home and provide information regarding any major items that may affect its usefulness, desirability, and value. The buyer may decide to schedule one or more subsequent inspections resulting from the home inspector's findings. This may include an inspection of the Heating, Ventilating, and Air Conditioning (HVAC) system by an HVAC company that specializes in HVAC systems for single-family homes. Accordingly, if the home has a built-in swimming pool, the buyer may decide to obtain a pool inspection of the pool itself, along with an inspection of the pool equipment. The buyer may need to hire two different inspectors to accomplish this task: a pool inspector and a pool equipment inspector.

(2) Appraisal Contingency

The buyer may have negotiated an appraisal contingency in addition to a physical inspection contingency to the purchase agreement. If the property does not appraise for the purchase price, then the buyer may be able to back out of the transaction by not removing the appraisal contingency. When this occurs, the buyer will most likely be reimbursed for their earnest money deposit. If the seller does not agree to return the buyer's earnest money deposit by not signing the escrow rescission form, the escrow officer may have to file an interpleader action in court to allow the courts to determine what to do with the buyer's earnest money deposit. If the purchase agreement has a liquidated damages clause, it may affect the return of the buyer's earnest money deposit.

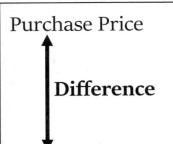

Figure 1.12 Appraisal Lower than Purchase Price Example

If the appraisal comes in less than the purchase price, the buyer may be required by the lender to either:

a. Increase the down payment to cover the difference in the appraised value and the purchase price—thus maintaining the lender's minimum loan-to-value (LTV) ratio. Of course, any changes to a contract require the approval of *both* the buyer and seller; or

b. Reduce the purchase price (with agreement of the seller)

Moreover, the buyer (with help from the buyer's agent/selling agent) may attempt to challenge the appraisal if the existing sales comparables justify a higher property value than the appraiser's opinion of value in the appraisal report.

The buyer usually pays for an appraisal when using a loan to finance the purchase of a home. If the purchase is with all cash and no loan, then an appraisal contingency is generally not used because a lender is not making a loan to help the buyer purchase the property. In other words, an appraisal is not required because a loan is not being used to close the transaction.

(3) Financing Contingency

Most owner-occupied single-family homebuyers will use a loan to purchase a home. In contrast, many investors may use all cash and no financing to purchase non-owner occupied investment (rental) properties. The owner-occupied homebuyer continues working with the lender during the escrow period to obtain financing for the property.

Real estate purchase agreements in California usually allow the buyer to add a financing contingency to the contract. The financing contingency for a single-family home purchase in California is usually approximately twenty-one (21) days or until the loan is funded. A financing contingency that is in effect until the loan is funded tends to benefit the buyer by allowing the buyer to not remove the contingency and not move forward with the transaction up until the loan is funded just before close of escrow.

The loan process begins with loan origination through a loan originator. After the loan has been originated, a loan processor will verify all supporting documents are in the correct order in the file. After the loan has been processed and all the documents are in the file, a loan underwriter will examine the file and make a lending decision. This decision may be loan approval, loan approval with conditions, or a rejection of the loan altogether. After loan approval, the lender draws the loan documents and submits them to escrow for the buyer's signature. The loan documents are returned to the lender for review and the lender then wires funds to escrow. However, before the above can occur, the seller must respond to the buyer's request for repairs (if any) and move forward with the transaction.

D. Transaction Part 6
(1) Seller Waits for Buyer to Remove the Contingencies to the Purchase Agreement

During this period the seller is waiting for the buyer to remove the physical inspection, appraisal, and financing contingencies to the purchase agreement. This is usually accomplished with the active removal of each of the contingencies. The buyer signs an active contingency removal form that is submitted to the seller for signature. After the seller signs the contingency removal form, copies of the signed removal are provided to the buyer and seller, and the contingency is formally removed from the purchase agreement. A buyer cannot use a removed contingency as a reason not to go forward with the purchase.

a. Buyer Requests that Seller Repair Items in the Property

After the buyer has received a home inspection report detailing the condition of the home, the buyer may ask the seller to repair some items prior to removing the physical inspection contingency and moving forward to purchase the property. A home inspection report will usually list the items of concern that should be addressed by the buyer and buyer's agent/selling agent. The most common items requested to be repaired are related to health and safety issues and may include broken windows, missing window screens, and other items that are not working properly and affect the overall value and desirability of the property.

The buyer's agent/selling agent usually notes the requested items on a **Request for Repairs Addendum**, has the buyer sign it, and then submits it to the seller's agent/listing agent. The seller's agent/listing agent then presents it to the seller. The seller can decide to go ahead and repair all the items on the Request for Repairs Addendum or repair only those items the seller believes are legitimate health and safety concerns. Of course, the seller can also say "no" to all the requested repairs and this must be communicated back to the buyer's agent/selling agent, who then presents it to the buyer. The buyer can either accept the items the seller is willing to repair, submit a revised list of items to be repaired, or not remove the physical inspection contingency and not move forward with the purchase. Most of the time the buyer and seller will come to agreement repairing the most important health and safety items and the transaction will continue until close of escrow. However, it is common for a seller to give a buyer a monetary credit in lieu of making repairs to the property.

Request for Repairs Addendum: Used to ask the seller to make specific repairs to the property prior to close of escrow.

b. Buyer Requests a Price Reduction

If the property's condition indicates it is worth less than the purchase price, the buyer and seller must agree to reduce the price, or the deal may fall apart. The buyer will usually send the seller an addendum asking for a price reduction and the seller will respond by accepting, countering, or rejecting the price reduction. If a meeting of the minds cannot be met, then the buyer and seller both must sign an escrow rescission form to terminate (cancel) the escrow.

c. Buyer Decides to Cancel Purchase Agreement and Withdraw from Escrow

If the buyer decides not to go forward with the transaction, the buyer will sign an escrow rescission form instructing the escrow officer to terminate the escrow. The seller must also sign an escrow rescission form before the escrow officer can return the buyer's earnest money deposit.

E. Transaction Part 7

(1) Buyer Performs a Walk-Thru Inspection (Final Verification of Condition)

According to DRE, "The agreement will specify that the buyer has the right to make a final inspection of the property within five (5) days prior to closing, not as a contingency of the sale but solely to confirm the property is in the same condition, any repairs have been completed as agreed between the parties, and the seller has complied with all other contractual obligations."

Unless otherwise agreed, the property is usually sold in its present physical condition on the date of acceptance. The seller is usually required to maintain the property in substantially the same general condition as on the date of acceptance. All debris and personal property are normally required to be removed prior to close of escrow.

Figure 1.13

(2) Buyer Vesting

Forms of real estate ownership include severalty (sole ownership), tenants in common, joint tenancy, community property, tenancy in partnership, co-ops, limited liability companies (LLC), domestic corporations, foreign corporations, joint ventures, and nonprofit/not-for-profit organizations. Buyer vesting is discussed in Chapter 13.

(3) Buyer Signs Escrow Instructions

In Northern California, the buyer and seller usually sign escrow instructions (with the escrow agent) just before close of escrow. In Southern California, escrow instructions may have already been signed by the buyer and seller early in the escrow period.

At this point, the buyer will decide how to take title to the property. This is an important part of the closing process and both the escrow agent and the buyer's agent are not allowed by law to give the buyer advice regarding how to take title to real property.

(4) Escrow Prorations

The escrow officer prorates items the seller has paid ahead of time. To accomplish this the escrow officer will use the buyer's money to reimburse the seller for items that were paid ahead of time. Since the seller will no longer own the property, the seller should be reimbursed (for the amount paid) and not pay for any costs that are incurred after close of escrow.

For example, if the seller paid the property tax bill for the entire year and the property closes escrow halfway through the year, the seller will be reimbursed for the half year that the seller does not own the property. This is called an escrow proration.

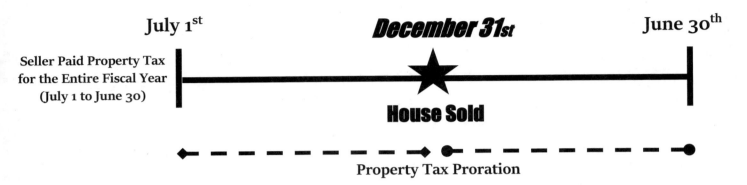

Figure 1.14 Property Tax Year Proration Example

(5) Title Insurance

Title insurance is used to insure the title to real property. When a buyer purchases a home, the buyer should be concerned with the condition of the property's title. Are there any clouds on the title that may surface after the buyer takes title to the property? Title insurance companies investigate a property's chain of recorded title and then insure the buyer against loss caused by breaks in the chain of title and other title defects that may affect the marketability of the property. Title insurance companies maintain title plants that continuously monitor recorded documents that may affect title to real property. If there is a cloud on the title that was caused by a recorded document not being discovered by the title insurance company, then the title insurance company may be required to pay for the buyer's loss.

In Northern California, title insurance is usually included with escrow services under one company. In Southern California, escrow and title insurance may come from separate companies.

Grant Deed: Document used in California to transfer legal title to real property.

F. Transaction Part 7

(1) Grant Deed Delivered by the Seller to the Buyer

At this point in the transaction, the grant deed will be signed by the seller and delivered to the buyer. A **grant deed** is a document used in California that transfers legal title to real property. The grant deed is normally delivered to the buyer through recordation of the grant deed at the county recorder's office in the county where the property is located.

G. Transaction Part 8
(1) Close of Escrow

Close of escrow occurs when all the terms and conditions of the escrow have been satisfied and the escrow is considered "perfected." However, before close of escrow the escrow agent is the agent for *both* the seller and buyer (together). After close of escrow, the escrow agent becomes the independent agent of the buyer and the independent agent of the seller.

3. After the Real Estate Transaction

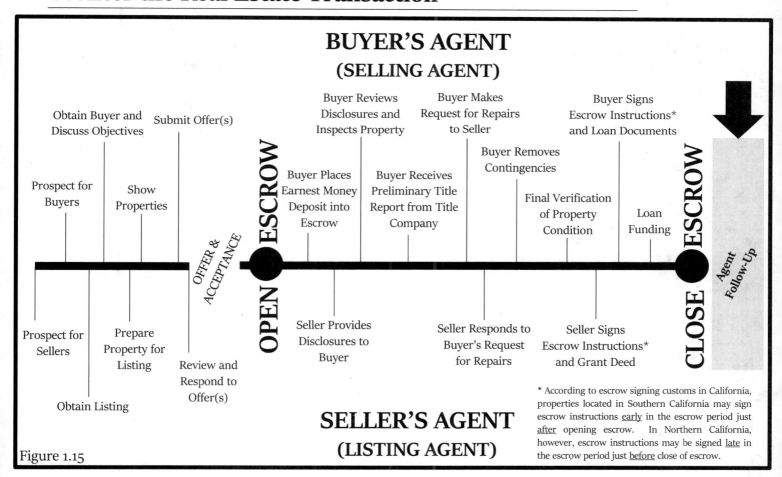

Figure 1.15

* According to escrow signing customs in California, properties located in Southern California may sign escrow instructions <u>early</u> in the escrow period just <u>after</u> opening escrow. In Northern California, however, escrow instructions may be signed <u>late</u> in the escrow period just <u>before</u> close of escrow.

A. Transaction Part 9

Some items may surface after close of escrow. These may include the seller occupying the property after close of escrow, home warranty policy issues, supplemental assessments, and a cloud on the title to the property.

(1) After Close of Escrow

If the seller occupied the property after close of escrow, a seller occupancy addendum may have been used to form a tenancy between the buyer and seller. This can have serious insurance ramifications because the seller is a tenant during the period from close of escrow to vacating the property, and the appropriate insurance policy may be an Owner, Landlord, and Tenant (OLT) policy instead of a homeowner's policy. After the seller vacates the property and the buyer moves in, a homeowner's insurance policy may be the best choice for the buyer.

The buyer may need to perform another walk-thru inspection after the seller vacates the property to verify it is in the same condition that it was at close of escrow. Some buyers may negotiate a security deposit from the seller prior to close of escrow and then return it to the seller if the property is left in good condition.

A home warranty policy may be used to protect the buyer against a home's major components becoming inoperable during the first year (or longer) of home ownership. If a home warranty policy was negotiated in the purchase agreement, the escrow agent will usually order the home warranty policy and it will be paid by the buyer and/or seller through escrow.

Furthermore, the buyer may need to be concerned about supplemental assessments surfacing six months or more down the road. If the seller had not sold the property for many years and had a very low property tax assessed value, then the buyer may not pay very much in property tax prorations at close of escrow–but will have to pay the remainder several months later. This is called a **supplemental assessment** and may also occur if the property is a new home and the builder had a very low property tax assessed value (i.e., cost) when the unimproved lot was subdivided.

Supplemental Assessment: When a buyer purchases a property with a low assessed value, and the new assessed value is significantly higher, a supplemental assessment may occur.

Lastly, title defects may surface after close of escrow. Depending on the type of title insurance policy and coverages involved, the title insurance company may be required to reimburse the buyer for their loss.

Of course, real estate agents should follow-up with their buyers and ask for referrals to their friends and relatives. Consistent follow-up with past clients can be a very good source of referrals and future commission income.

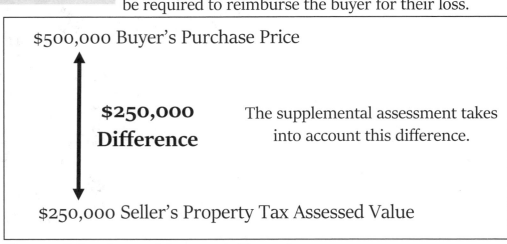

Figure 1.16 Supplemental Assessment Illustration

B. Transaction Part 9

(1) After Close of Escrow

After close of escrow, the seller will receive the proceeds from the sale. This is usually accomplished either through a wire transfer from the escrow company to the seller's bank account or a check from the escrow company.

If the seller moves out of the property after close of escrow, the real estate agent may use a seller in possession addendum that allows the seller to become a tenant for the buyer. This is common with large homes in which sellers have a significant amount of furniture and personal belongings that must be moved out of the house.

In addition, if there was a home warranty policy negotiated in the real estate purchase agreement, the seller may be insulated from items that stop working after close of escrow. Instead of the buyer wanting to sue the seller for non-disclosure of a material fact, the buyer will call the home warranty company and have the item repaired or replaced with the payment of a small deductible. It should be noted that home warranty policies also insulate both listing agents and selling agents from nondisclosure of items that stop working during the first year (or more) of homeownership.

A title insurance policy may insulate the seller from title defects that are discovered after close of escrow. Depending on the policy and coverages, the title insurance company may be required to pay for a buyer's loss resulting from a title defect.

Lastly, the agent should follow-up with the seller and ask for referrals to their friends and relatives. Real estate agents should continue to follow-up with past clients who are usually a fabulous source of referrals and future clients.

Chapter One Summary

The chapter provides an overview of the real estate brokerage business. It examines before, during, and after a real estate transaction. Real estate agents may prospect for new buyers and sellers by either finding them a home to purchase or selling their existing home for the highest possible price within the shortest possible marketing time. The real estate agent will be involved in writing offers and counter offers, helping to negotiate the terms of the transaction, and making sure the entire homebuying and home selling process is as painless as possible for the client. The structure of a real estate transaction is examined from the initial offer, to counter offer(s), opening of escrow, contingency removals, and finally to close of escrow. The few items that occur after close of escrow are considered with regard to their impact on the buyer and seller.

Chapter One Quiz

1. A listing agreement allows the agent to:
(A) place the property on the market
(B) find a suitable buyer
(C) receive a commission when the property sells
(D) all of the above are correct

2. Part of a real estate salesperson's license fees goes to the California Department of Real Estate's Recovery Account that is used to:
(A) help clients who have uncollectable judgments
(B) provide monetary assistance to real estate agents with health issues
(C) fund rehabilitation of real estate salespersons and brokers
(D) Both (B) and (C) are correct

3. When a buyer finds the right property to purchase, the real estate agent will write an offer to purchase the property. This is accomplished with a:
(A) real estate listing agreement
(B) real estate agency disclosure form
(C) real estate purchase agreement that will specify the price and terms of the property purchase
(D) real estate transfer disclosure statement

4. The escrow agent (also called escrow officer or escrow holder) is:
(A) the agent of both the buyer and seller during the escrow period
(B) only the independent agent of the buyer during the escrow
(C) only the independent agent of the seller during the escrow
(D) Both (B) and (C) are correct

5. The Real Estate Transfer Disclosure Statement (TDS):
(A) is used to disclose and elect agency relationships
(B) asks the seller to provide information regarding the condition of the property
(C) confirms agency relationships
(D) causes the agent to not be required to make a visual inspection of accessible areas

6. During the physical inspection contingency period (due diligence period), the buyer may:
(A) hire a home inspector to inspect the home
(B) have the home inspector provide information regarding any major items that may affect the usefulness, desirability, and value of the property
(C) decide to schedule one or more subsequent inspections resulting from the home inspector's findings
(D) all of the above are correct

7. In addition to a physical inspection contingency to the purchase contract, the buyer may have negotiated a(n):
(A) appraisal contingency
(B) financing contingency
(C) Both (A) and (B) are correct
(D) Neither (A) nor (B) are correct

8. A financing contingency that is in effect until the loan is funded tends to:
(A) benefit the buyer by allowing the buyer to not remove the contingency and not move forward with the transaction up until the loan is actually funded and escrow closes
(B) benefit the seller
(C) have no benefit whatsoever
(D) none of the above are correct

9. A _____ is a document that transfers title to real property.
(A) bill of sale
(B) grant deed
(C) purchase agreement
(D) listing agreement

10. A home warranty policy may be used to:
(A) insure the buyer against liability
(B) protect the buyer against a home's major components becoming inoperable during the first year (or longer) of home ownership
(C) insure the home against fire and liability
(D) pay for a pest inspection

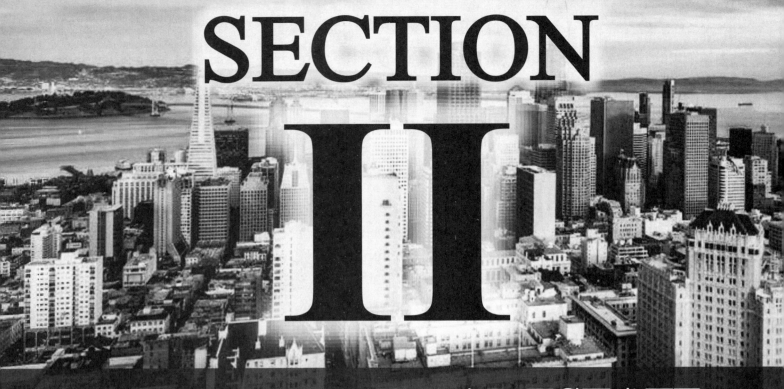

SECTION II

BEFORE THE REAL ESTATE TRANSACTION

Before the Real Estate Transaction

Real Estate Transaction Overview

BUYER'S AGENT
(SELLING AGENT)

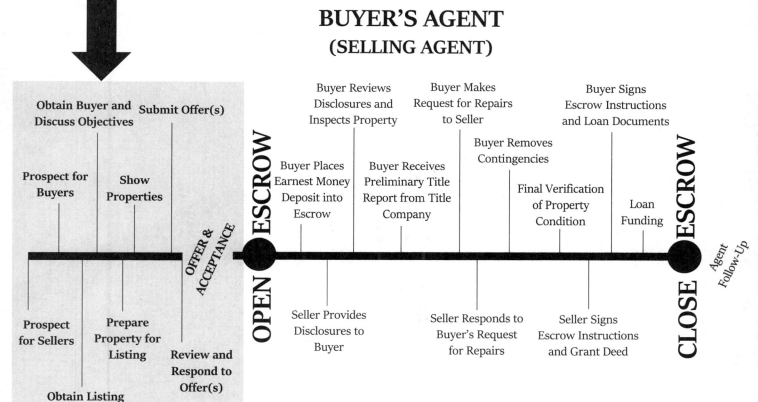

Obtain Buyer and Discuss Objectives

Submit Offer(s)

Prospect for Buyers

Show Properties

OFFER & ACCEPTANCE

OPEN ESCROW

Buyer Reviews Disclosures and Inspects Property

Buyer Makes Request for Repairs to Seller

Buyer Signs Escrow Instructions and Loan Documents

Buyer Removes Contingencies

Buyer Places Earnest Money Deposit into Escrow

Buyer Receives Preliminary Title Report from Title Company

Final Verification of Property Condition

Loan Funding

CLOSE ESCROW

Agent Follow-Up

Prospect for Sellers

Prepare Property for Listing

Review and Respond to Offer(s)

Obtain Listing

Seller Provides Disclosures to Buyer

Seller Responds to Buyer's Request for Repairs

Seller Signs Escrow Instructions and Grant Deed

SELLER'S AGENT
(LISTING AGENT)

Anthony Hitt

"To be successful in real estate, you must always and consistently put your clients' best interests first. When you do, your personal needs will be realized beyond your greatest expectations."

Chapter
TWO

Starting a Career in Real Estate

Real estate agents must be licensed by the California Department of Real Estate (DRE) to be involved in real estate transactions in California. Real estate agents are divided into two categories: **real estate brokers** and **real estate salespersons**. Most new real estate agents initially become a real estate salesperson and are required to place their real estate salesperson license under a real estate broker. Real estate brokers oversee and are responsible for all their salespersons' transactions. Some real estate salespersons may decide to remain salespersons during their entire careers, while others may obtain a real estate broker's license and start their own real estate brokerage company.

Principal (Seller or Buyer)

↑

Agency Relationship

↑

Agent (Real Estate Broker)

↑

Subagency Relationship

↑

Subagent (Real Estate Salesperson)

Figure 2.1 Subagency Diagram

Real Estate Broker: Person licensed to engage in the real estate brokerage business in California.

Real Estate Salesperson: Person licensed to engage in real estate brokerage in California but must place their real estate salesperson license under a licensed real estate broker.

Figure 2.2

1. Real Estate License Types and Requirements

A. California Real Estate Broker's License

According to Section 10131 of the California Business and Professions Code, a real estate broker's license is required for:

1. Collecting and offering to collect leases and rents

2. Negotiating the sale, purchase or exchange of real property, or business opportunities

3. Collecting payments for borrowers or lenders in connection with loans secured directly or collaterally by liens on real property

4. Any person who manages real property in California on behalf of another, such as an owner or other third party, for compensation, or with the expectation of compensation, must have a California real estate broker's license.

Someone who wants to obtain a California real estate broker's license will need to be at least eighteen (18) years old, complete eight California Department of Real Estate (DRE) required courses, have two years of full-time real estate experience within the preceding five years or a four-year degree in real estate (acceptable real estate experience and applicable real estate education varies, see the DRE for details), pass the California State Broker Licensing Examination, pass a background check performed by the California Department of Justice (DOJ) and Federal Bureau of Investigation (FBI), pay the required fees to DRE, and then start operating as a licensed California real estate broker.

B. California Real Estate Salesperson License

According to Section 10131 of the Business and Professions Code, real estate salespersons can only accept compensation (for licensed activities) from their real estate broker. The broker is normally paid by the seller, and then the broker pays the salesperson out of the funds collected. Salespersons *cannot* be compensated directly, they must be paid by their broker.

A person who wants to obtain a California real estate salesperson's license is required to be at least eighteen (18) years old, complete three DRE required courses, pass the California State Salesperson Licensing Examination, pass a background check performed by the DOJ and FBI, pay the required fees to the DRE, and then place their real estate salesperson license under a licensed real estate broker.

Licensing Requirements

	Salesperson	Broker
Education	3 Courses	8 Courses
Experience	None	Two years fulltime real estate experience within last five years **OR** four-year degree in real estate
Honesty	Conviction of a crime or failure to disclose all criminal history may result in the denial of a license	Conviction of a crime or failure to disclose all criminal history may result in the denial of a license
Minimum Age	18	18

Figure 2.3 California Real Estate Licensing Requirements

C. Real Estate License Renewal

Both real estate brokers and real estate salespersons must renew their real estate license every four years. Prior to paying the renewal fee to the DRE, the licensee must complete 45 hours of continuing education. Depending on the license type and whether it is the licensee's first or subsequent renewal, the course topics and corresponding hours may vary. However, the standard and required continuing education course topics are agency, ethics, trust fund handling, fair housing, risk management, and consumer protection. Other course topics licensees might complete include management and supervision and consumer service. Once the continuing education is completed, the licensee can submit course certificates, documentation, and fees to the DRE within 90 days of license expiration date.

If a broker or salesperson has not renewed their license by the end of the four-year license period, the broker or salesperson has a two-year grace period to renew their license. They cannot operate as a licensed real estate salesperson or broker during the two-year grace period. If the broker or salesperson has not renewed their license by the end of the two-year grace period, then their real estate broker or salesperson license will expire. The person will then be required to pass the California Department of Real Estate broker or salesperson state exam (again), go through another background check by the DOJ and FBI, and pay their fees to obtain either a real estate broker or real estate salesperson license.

2. Reasons People Get into the Real Estate Brokerage Business

People get into the real estate brokerage business because they: (1) want to run their own business, and (2) desire unlimited income potential. New real estate agents want to set their own schedule and have the freedom to choose the direction of their business.

Some people transition from the corporate world into the real estate brokerage business, while others go into the business with minimal prior experience. A former corporate employee is usually looking for a way to stay rooted in one community, while making a nice living for the family. The following story of Steve's life is a good example of this type of career change.

Tales from the Trade

The Story of Steve's Career Change

Steve graduated from high school and then went to a community college for two years. He then transferred to a four-year university and graduated with a degree in business. He was able to get a corporate sales job and worked in the corporate world for seven years. During this time period, he realized that the corporate world was not going to provide him with the income he needed to become independently wealthy. The corporation used several tactics to make sure he had enough money to live, but not enough to leave the corporation and start his own business ▼

The Story of Steve's Career Change

or invest enough money in passive investments (e.g., stock market, etc.) to be able to leave the corporation and live on income from his investments.

Some examples of corporate employee retention tactics included:

(1) A company car that Steve will have to replace by buying a car if he leaves the corporation.

(2) A hefty expense account that he would not have if he left and started his own business.

(3) A salary that is just high enough to allow Steve to buy a house in a modest neighborhood, and then if he gets married and has a family—the corporation will increase his salary, so he can support his family—but not much else. He will not be able to save enough money to start a business and go out on his own.

(4) A bonus structure that keeps a considerable amount of sales in a "slush fund" so corporate management could pay out more bonus income to the employees who stay with the company and do not leave at the end of the year (annual bonuses). Money from the slush fund is added or subtracted for the year and paid the following April, conveniently when federal and state income taxes are due.

(5) A plan to move the employee (to give him "well-rounded experience") every two to four years so he (and his family) will not get rooted down to one geographical location–the corporation wants to keep Steve and his family on-the-move so they will be bound to the corporation and not the local community for their disposable (survival) income.

(6) An excellent corporate benefits package that includes medical, dental, optical, and other benefits. It may cost the employee a large amount of money (e.g., $2,000/month or more) to replace this package as an independent business owner or passive investor. The corporation can obtain these benefits much cheaper (because of their size and resultant economies of scale) than the former employee—now turned business owner or investor.

(7) A corporate ladder structure to help long-term employee retention (through promotions) of the people the corporation wants to keep. This keeps the employees motivated.

(8) Peer recognition to keep employees motivated and trying to "outdo" their associates.

It was a risky move leaving the stability of a corporate job with its benefits and perks; however, Steve realized that corporate jobs are not as stable as they were in the past. Large corporations are having a difficult time surviving, and down-sizing of the labor force is a viable alternative to bankruptcy in a rapidly changing economic environment. Corporate pensions were being replaced with self-funded employee 401(k) and Roth IRAs.

Steve decided to leave the corporate world, where his income was capped off at an amount preventing him from achieving independent wealth, and enter the real estate brokerage business. Steve saw three avenues that may provide adequate income and a potential for independent wealth: (1) employee, (2) business owner, and (3) passive investor. He felt that being a business owner (real estate agent) and a passive investor (personally owning real estate) were the two best options to become independently wealthy.

The Story of Steve's Career Change

A. Employee

An employee works for a business owner or corporation. As mentioned above, there are a considerable number of amenities available when working for a business or corporation. The employee goes home each night and does not have to worry about the future survival of the business. However, the employee's income is capped.

B. Business Owner

As a business owner, the business owner is responsible for the survival of the business and is on-call 24 hours per day, 7 days per week. However, the business owner may reap the financial rewards resulting from talent, ability, and hard work over a long period of time.

Examples of local businesses include a florist, chiropractor, or a local real estate brokerage company. The interesting thing about real estate brokerage companies is that each real estate salesperson who works under the real estate broker's license is really running their own business. From a legal standpoint a real estate salesperson is considered an employee of the broker, but for tax purposes the real estate salesperson is considered an independent contractor.

The real estate salesperson's broker is paid the commissions from the real estate salesperson's sales and then pays the real estate salesperson an agreed upon split from those commissions. The amount of commissions the real estate salesperson earns is unlimited. Real estate salespersons keep track of their own expenses and pay federal and state income taxes quarterly–not at the end of the year like corporate employees— but during the year when they are earned. This provides the real estate salesperson with allowable tax deductions that a corporate employee cannot deduct from their corporate employee income.

C. Passive Investor

Passive investors derive their income from passive investments that are out of the investor's daily control. Examples of passive investments include stock purchases through the stock markets and real estate investments. Passive investors have an advantage over business owners because they are earning an income from their monetary investments—and not from their own labor or management abilities. Instead of using one's personal labor to earn income (employee) or using daily management abilities (business owner), passive investors are using their money to produce their income. One passive investor said, "I'm making money even when I'm asleep."

Another positive factor resulting from being in the real estate brokerage business is the ability to purchase real estate as an investment. Real estate agents learn the business by helping clients buy and sell properties. Then, as the real estate agent becomes more experienced, the agent may be able to use commission income to purchase properties and build up their own real estate investment portfolio.

3. Some Avenues to Pursue as a Real Estate Licensee

A new real estate agent may decide to become a real estate agent, an assistant working under an established real estate agent, or a property manager. Becoming a real estate agent has already been discussed, however, an assistant to an experienced agent can be a good place to begin a real estate career because the agent has existing business coming in, so an assistant to the agent should be able to immediately start earning commission income from the agent's existing business.

Becoming a property manager can be a good place to start as well, especially for someone who does not have many financial reserves. It usually provides an hourly wage or salary that can be beneficial to new licensees. As the agent becomes more experienced, the agent may want to consider getting a real estate broker's license and opening their own property management company. As property managers get to know their property owner clients, this can lead to additional income from real estate brokerage transactions in the future.

Some people who enter the real estate brokerage business may be looking for their first job. The next story is about a person who went into the real estate brokerage business right out of high school with no previous work experience.

Tales from the Trade

THE STORY OF MARY'S FIRST JOB THAT TURNED INTO A LIFELONG CAREER

Mary graduated from high school and did not want to go to college. She was looking for a profession in which she could make a lot of money without needing a college degree. Real estate seemed to be a good way to do this.

Mary had turned 18 years old, so she was eligible to take the California Department of Real Estate Salesperson Examination. She found out that she needed to complete three real estate courses prior to being able to take the State Exam. She completed all three real estate courses, which included Real Estate Principles, Real Estate Practice, and an elective course. For the elective course, Mary chose Property Management because she heard it provides a steady income for new real estate salespersons.

Mary studied exam preparation materials designed to help her pass the California Department of Real Estate's Salesperson's Examination. After spending many hours studying the exam preparation materials, Mary took the State Exam and passed it.

When she received her DRE salesperson license and number, she decided to meet with the sales managers of several real estate brokerage companies that had offices located near her ▼

THE STORY OF MARY'S FIRST JOB THAT TURNED INTO A LIFELONG CAREER

home. She selected one of the brokerage companies and started into a long-term career in real estate.

She found that the real estate brokerage business is a people business. She could find clients either through her sphere of influence (people she knows) or through client prospecting activities that brought in new clients. Mary found the real estate brokerage business provided her with the flexibility to work around her family activities, while providing a nice income and lifestyle during her real estate career.

Sales Manager: Real estate salesperson, with at least two years full-time experience within the last five years, who can approve other salespersons' transactions.

It is quite common for large real estate brokerage companies to delegate to a salesperson (usually called a **sales manager**) within an office the ability to review and initial documents completed by other salespersons within the office. The broker can delegate these reviews to a salesperson who has at least two (2) years full-time experience as a real estate salesperson within the past five (5) years.

4. Today's Employment Realities

Today's employees must have skills that can be immediately transferred into productivity and income by their employers. Examples include degrees in accounting, engineering, medical, and computer sciences that provide students with skills to immediately become effective in the corporate world.

Many traditional college and university curriculums, however, do not provide training in subjects that will get students jobs in the real world. Student loans are increasing the costs of tuition for training programs that do not provide students with the skills necessary to find a job after graduation. Due to easy-to-obtain government and private student loans, students may incur a huge amount of student debt and have no way to pay it back. Current federal laws do not allow students to use bankruptcy to eliminate student debt, so it may hang around their necks for the rest of their lives precluding them from buying a home or getting ahead in the future.

In contrast, a real estate salesperson license opens the door to a service-based business in which approximately 60% of the population owns their own home. The other 40% are renting and may be good prospects to buy a home in the future. Therefore, everyone a real estate salesperson knows is a potential client.

One of the best ways to learn about a profession is to ask current top professionals how they got started in the business and what makes them successful today. The real estate brokerage business is constantly changing; however, it remains a people business. Real estate professionals deal with people on a continuing basis, and generally the larger the sphere of influence the greater the commission income.

Top real estate professionals continually cultivate the people in their sphere of influence by following up and reminding them that they are in the real estate business. Social media and the internet with its connectivity has made this task more efficient and less expensive than any time in the past. Another key to their success is to constantly increase the size of their sphere of influence, thereby increasing the number of clients who may use their services, as well as the number of referrals received from past clients, friends, and relatives.

5. An Interview with a Top Producing Real Estate Agent

The following comments are from a top producer from a major national franchise in California:

Question (Q): **"What would you do if you parachuted into a strange town and had no money to get started in business?"**

Answer (A): "The first thing I would do is to get to know the market. I would become friends with as many successful Realtors as possible and listen and learn. I would meet the different escrow officers, lenders, termite companies, whole house inspectors, etc., and select the best ones that I think would make a good 'team' to back me up in my business. I would make sure that I knew the pricing and inventory of the product so when I did start taking listings, they would be priced competitively and sell.

Once I had zeroed in on the title/escrow company of my preference, I would ask for their help. They are more than happy to offer their 'free' services in hopes that you will become successful and use their escrow services. They will set up a 'farm' area for you (many times with telephone numbers) of a neighborhood. It would be a good selection to choose either the neighborhood you reside in or if agents are heavily working your neighborhood, pick an area not being worked as much.

When I started, I chose my neighborhood and selected 500 properties. Make up a brief introductory about yourself as the neighborhood specialist. If you do not have the money for the postage, then hand deliver them. The next step is crucial to your success. Follow-up, Follow-up, Follow-up! Set up a system for yourself. Make yourself call say 25 of those names or more per day (make sure they are <u>not</u> on the Do Not Call list!). The key is to contact as many people as possible. Make sure you are upbeat and tell them how excited you are about working in their great neighborhood and making new friends. Once you have contacted all 500, you start over.

You will be amazed to find that there will be very few people who will reject talking to you if you approach it as being the new neighborhood friend. Before you know it, listing appointments and referrals will come your way. Make sure you hand out your business card to as many people as possible. Let everyone know that you sell real estate. The more contacts you make, the more business you'll have. Keep track of all of the favorable contacts and befriending them, even though you have never sold them anything or sold anything for them, they will refer you. When they do refer you, make sure that you contact them again to thank them.

When you start making money, set some aside for your personal marketing. Personal marketing is making sure that your face is visible in whatever local websites/social media/paper/magazine your area reads. If you have no success personally to boast about yet, use your company's success.

A good personality and constant contacts in the real estate 'people' business is the formula for becoming a successful Realtor at little to no dollar outlay. When you have money to spend, personal promotion is the next and ongoing step."

Q: "Why are you a top producer?"
A: "There is a mix of things that I think contribute to my doing well. I love real estate and enjoy people. I have always had a leaning towards public relations and advertising since my beginnings working in the marketing field. A top producer needs to be organized and needs to set up a good team to assist them.

I have accomplished that. My Realtor Assistant and I have worked together over ten years. She and I have set systems and processing for every listing, sale, and follow-up. It is important to stay in touch and follow-up with your clients either by email, phone, mail, or all three.

I have a great family base. My husband, children, and mother are very supportive. You need to get your family involved enough so that they understand the demands of the job and will appreciate what you do.

I respect other Realtors. We are on the same team regardless of what company we work for. If other Realtors enjoy working with you, they will look forward to showing your listings and more will sell. I give the Realtor who sells my listing a little thank you gift which doesn't cost much, but is greatly appreciated.

You need to care for you clients and do the best job you can for them. If you do this, even if it does not culminate into a sale, you can feel that you did your best. Try to use every opportunity as a positive instead of a negative. I look for a way to utilize any time I've spent with someone to get business or a referral out of it.

I plan my time to suit my family and personality to try to avoid burnout. I take Sundays off to be with my family and attend church. I try to leave real estate out of my evenings at home. I think a top producer needs to know her/his limit and balance their lives. I have learned how to delegate responsibility to the escrow officer, my assistant, and our office escrow coordinator so that I can concentrate on generating sales.

I have a 'hot to do list' constantly in front of me to stay on focus. I avoid wasting time as much as possible. I have my clients meet me at the office as much as I can, and I have the title/escrow company's courier do a lot of my delivering. If I find myself not enjoying what I'm doing, it's time to take a break.

Most importantly, never assume that because you are a top producer you know more or are better than anyone else. If you stay open minded, you will continue to grow."

Q: "What skills/characteristics and aptitudes are needed to be a top producer?"
A:

"Determination"

"Organization"

"A willingness to learn."

"A willingness to care."

"A strong will to succeed and let the negative roll off and the positive stay in front."

"People skills."

"The fortitude to work an average of 60 hours per week."

"The desire to do well and then do it–set up plans on how to achieve your goals and to put them into action."

"To focus on what works and expand it and throw away what did not work as experience."

Q: "How do you presently operate?"
A: "I have my own office with my licensed assistant Realtor within our company's building. This helps me to concentrate without distractions. My listings are setup on a computer as well as my client base. I am constantly having email and mail out campaigns (sent). I spend a good portion of my advertising budget on advertising me, the Realtor. Most people in the community have seen my name or picture.

Every day I review my day timer for my appointments. If I am not at an appointment, I am working my list of possibilities. I keep a 'hot list' on my desk to focus on. Our company has an escrow coordinator who handles the escrow work. She does a very good job and it has freed up my time.

I have set up my clients so that I almost never work on Sundays. My assistant Realtor and I split checking email, voice-mail, and handling calls every other weekend. I have a separate home phone number that is connected directly to my voice mail, so that my evenings are less disturbed and I can check my voicemail and return calls when I want to. I have learned to gain control of my business, instead of it getting control of me and it has increased the sales I generate."

6. Success in the Real Estate Brokerage Business

A real estate agent must put their real estate transactions together. There is no one-size-fits-all template and each day is different; however, many tasks do remain the same. A few ingredients needed to succeed in the real estate brokerage business include: a good work ethic, expert product knowledge, ability to handle uneven income streams, and taking days off and planned vacations to avoid burnout.

A. Work Ethic

A good work ethic usually equates to good commission income. There is generally a direct correlation between hard work and greater commission income. There is no limit to a real estate salesperson's income and success, it all depends on a good work ethic. The real estate brokerage business is entrepreneurial in spirit and real estate salespersons oversee their own destiny. They pay all their own expenses and reap the benefits resulting from hard work and dedication to their clients on a long-term basis.

B. Expert Product Knowledge

Expert product knowledge is a key to success in any sales endeavor, and the real estate brokerage business is no exception. There is a difference between a real estate agent who is an order-taker, who merely facilitates the transaction, and a real estate agent who is a consultant to their clients and really knows real estate and the local real estate market.

Figure 2.4

For example, a real estate agent must understand types of financing that are available to buyers—including prevailing market interest rates for conventional, jumbo, Federal Housing Administration (FHA) insured, Department of Veterans Affairs (VA) guaranteed, and other types of real estate financing available to owner-occupied homebuyers and non-owner occupied real estate investors. Because of the internet, clients are now looking for value from their real estate agents and expert product knowledge provides that value.

The following story is about a new real estate agent who entered the real estate brokerage business, became a consultant to her clients, and has had a very successful career in real estate brokerage.

Tales from the Trade

THE STORY OF SUSAN

Susan graduated from college with a bachelor's degree in accounting. While she was attending college, she obtained her real estate salesperson's license and worked under a real estate broker doing property management and real estate brokerage activities. A few years later, she obtained a real estate broker's license and opened her own real estate company managing properties and helping clients buy and sell real estate.

She decided to purchase a new single-family home located in a high socio-economic area (i.e., affluent neighborhood). The home had not yet been built, so she selected a vacant lot and floorplan and signed a contract to purchase the new home after it had been completed.

She placed a picture of the home on her social media accounts, letting all her friends know about her new purchase. One of her friends was looking for a home in the area and contacted Susan to let her know that he and his family would like to buy one of the new houses in the same subdivision. Susan set up a time to show them the model homes, vacant lots that were available, pricing, and financing options.

The friends toured all the model homes and decided on one that would be perfect for their family. A new home salesperson, who was working for the homebuilder, scheduled a time to meet with the family to write the purchase agreement. Susan attended the meeting and was able to explain all the terms of the builder's contract to the buyers–because she had already gone over everything when she purchased her own home in the subdivision. Each builder uses their own purchase contract, so this is a more important contribution by Susan than if the buyer was purchasing an existing home and using the standard California Association of Realtors (CAR) contract.

After the purchase agreement was signed, the new home salesperson scheduled a meeting with the builder's construction superintendent to tour the model home and explain how everything worked. This was unusual. Most builders do not spend the time to go over a home until after close of escrow. This builder went the extra mile and performed a walk-thru before and after completion of the property.

The new home salesperson then scheduled a meeting with the design center to select color, styles, and upgrades of carpet and other items going into the home. Architectural and cosmetic upgrades are where home builders make most of their profit on a new tract home located in a subdivision. Home builders will typically quote a base price for homes under construction, including standard FHA-grade carpet and other lower-end features for the home. Buyers may then upgrade the lower-end features and finance them into the real estate loan being used to purchase the home. Most home builders make it very easy for new home buyers to add upgrades to their home by setting up a *design center* to help buyers decide on upgrades. The reality, however, is that the home buyer will usually receive approximately 50% of the price paid for the upgrades when the home is sold in the future. ▼

THE STORY OF SUSAN

Susan attended the buyer's design center meeting. Since she had already gone through this meeting for her own home, she was able to inform the buyers ahead of time regarding which of the upgrades would increase the value of the home and which ones would be a waste of money.

The buyers took Susan's advice on most of the upgrades and were able to keep the price within a reasonable range. Susan apprised them of which upgrades would have a positive effect on value when the property was resold in the future.

The costs for the upgrades were very reasonable when compared to some of the other builders who were building in the local market. Some upgrades that tend to increase the value of the home more than their costs include: kitchen upgrades (tile countertops upgraded to granite or other type of stone), adding a full bathroom or increasing a half bath to a full bath, adding a French door or sliding glass door to provide the master bedroom with access to the backyard, along with many others.

Upgrades are usually separated between architectural upgrades and cosmetic upgrades. The architectural upgrades change the architecture of the property. Examples include added bathrooms and French doors to a home. Frequently, builders try to collect deposits on these upgrades, so if the buyer does not buy the property, they may forfeit the deposit and the builder will be forced to find someone who is willing to accept these particular upgrades in the home. When the builder sells homes that are constructed, but not purchased by the buyer, they are called standing inventory homes by builders or quick move-in homes by consumers.

Cosmetic upgrades include carpet grade and color, carpet pad thickness, size of tiles and whether they are square or diamond cut. The builder may not collect as much of a deposit for cosmetic upgrades, because they are usually within the parameters of the builder's color scheme that was set forth in the design center.

The real estate agent met with the buyers and the designer in the design center and helped them to make the best long-term investments.

The home was completed, and the buyers did a walk-thru inspection prior to closing escrow and moving into their new home. Susan had already gone through the builder's walk-thru inspection just before she closed escrow on her new home, so she met with the buyers during their walk-thru inspection and provided some input into real estate industry norms for new homes.

Susan received a very nice real estate commission from the builder. Even though she had not personally written up the buyer's offer (like she would have done if it were an existing resale home), she was able to help the buyer during the new homebuying process. Some home builders pay real estate agents a 2.5% to 3% commission on the base price of the home—not including upgrades; while other homebuilders may pay nothing at all. It really depends on the builder and the real estate market at the time.

THE STORY OF SUSAN

Real estate agents should accompany their clients to the model homes on their first visit and register them with the builder. This assures that the real estate agent will be paid a commission after the property has been built and the buyer closes escrow. Thus, Susan had become a consultant to her buyers, rather than a mere order taker.

In areas of California where there is land available for development, new home sales may be a good career option. Sales licensees who work for new home builders receive many perks.

There is a great work environment in the model homes. Air-conditioned models with all the amenities of a working office and hours that are usually 10am to 6pm daily. New home sales agents usually work most weekends because of the amount of foot traffic that occurs during these days (single-family resale agents work weekends also because that is when clients are typically available).

Figure 2.5 Model Homes

New home sales agents normally have two days off during the week when there are fewer potential buyers entering the property.

New home salespeople need to have a retail mentality to stay in one place all day waiting for prospects to come to them. A person who needs to be "out and about" all the time may not enjoy new home sales and should consider existing single-family home sales.

Most new home salespeople start as a **relief sales agent** for the experienced **lead sales agent**. The lead sales agent will train the new relief sales agent and the relief sales agent may receive a salary at the beginning of their career. As the relief agent becomes more experienced, the builder may move the relief agent to an equal level with the lead sales agent and place them on a 100% commission basis. In time, the relief agent may become a lead sales agent in their own subdivision. This allows

Relief Sales Agent: Assistant to lead sales agent. Usually works during lead sales agent's days off. Paid a salary and/or percentage of each home sold in the subdivision.

Lead Sales Agent: Primary new home sales agent who is usually paid a percentage of each home sold in the subdivision.

them to make more money and average annual commission income can be into six figures in some subdivisions for top lead sales agents.

If getting a new home sales position has been difficult to attain, the agent may try going to work for a temporary agency that specializes in new home sales agents. A real estate salesperson license is required, and this can be a great way to get into this very desirable career field. In fact, new home sales do not have the pressure of having to continually prospect for new clients like existing home sales agents. However, the financial rewards for new home agents can be correspondingly less than resale agents too.

C. Understand and Anticipate Uneven Income Streams

Resale single-family home commission income is not steady and takes a person who can emotionally handle uneven income streams over a long period of time. The entire family must support the real estate agent throughout this demanding career. The agent will be gone during evenings and weekends–when their family is usually at home, yet this is when their clients are available. One way to cushion uneven income streams and increase family financial security is to save enough money to pay for several months of expenses to guard against months without any commission income.

Figure 2.6

D. Take Planned Vacations

There will never be a good time to take some time off, so do not cancel vacations because a "deal will fall apart." With today's inexpensive cellular telephone access and internet connectivity, many tasks can be accomplished with merely a laptop computer and internet access. The agent does not need to be physically present at the property. Take vacations when they are planned, or a real estate agent will experience burn out. A person needs to be at the top-of-their-game in the real estate brokerage business and burn out is not conducive to long-term success.

Figure 2.7

Tales from the Trade

the Story of the Forty-year old Self-made Millionaire

Advice from Porter Stansberry:

"First, I will tell them to work – hard, and for as long as possible. Second, I will tell them to save and save and save...

"Consider this. Let's say you begin working hard at age 15. That's when I got my first hard, regular job. I was the kennel boy at the local vet. I got up before school and hosed out dog feces every morning from 5 a.m. to 7 a.m. I repeated the routine every evening. I also mowed lawns and did other odd jobs as often as I could get them.

"Let's say you started working like this when you were 15. When you start out, you're making almost nothing – $9.50 an hour. Assuming you're able to work 40-hour weeks, you'll make $380 per week. Assuming you work 50 weeks a year, your gross take-home pay will be a paltry $19,000 a year. But that's OK... you're living at home. You can easily save half your gross pay. What about taxes? Well, you didn't build that. You gotta pay your taxes too, kid.

"In our example, the kid would turn 16 years old with $9,500 in the bank. True, that's a hardworking kid. But I've seen it done. It's not impossible. Now, let's assume he piles the money into a diversified portfolio of short-term, investment-grade corporate bonds. Nothing fancy. He earns 5% a year after taxes. Let's also assume our kid is a hustler. By looking for and taking better jobs and earning bonuses, he's able to grow his income by 10% a year. That's not very hard for good workers – especially when they're starting out at $9.50 per hour.

"If our kid keeps this up through when most of his peers have finished college, he'll have saved $157,000 by the time he turns 25.

"This approach doesn't require any special skills or degrees. It doesn't require any kind of miracle – other than hard work, discipline, and perseverance. Yes, those traits are very unusual, but they can all be learned. They don't require a gifted IQ.

"He simply has to do a good job. He has to learn skills that are valuable to businesses and other people. He has to be utterly reliable.

"By the way, the young people I meet today often have a very unfortunate characteristic: They tie their feelings about their self-worth to their spending, instead of to their net worth (their saving). They've badly confused the near-term experiences of living rich with the long-term goals of being rich.

"I can only chuckle at this sentiment. What breeds success is smarts, dedication, and a sustained effort to improve. I've never seen a man earn a raise or a commission because he was living better. I've seen lots of people forgo enjoying themselves today to be better-prepared for work tomorrow. ▼

the STORY OF the FORTY-YEAR OLD SELF-made MILLIONAIRE

"At some point... maybe 15 years after he starts working, our kid will need to start a side business to continue growing his income every year. That will require a bit more work. But it's not impossible. That's when his gross pay finally breaks well past average for a valuable employee (over $70,000 per year). But keep in mind... there's no windfall payday for our kid. He just keeps plodding along... earning a little bit more every year and faithfully saving like a squirrel in October.

"Just doing this... starting at just over minimum wage, working hard, saving, and growing income at a reasonable pace... will make you rich. By the time our boy is 40, he'll have a nest egg worth $976,000. He'll have an income over $187,000 per year. He will be rich by any standard.

"What variables really matter? Well, if you assume annual investment returns at 15% instead of 5%, his nest egg only goes up to $1 million at 40 – about $25,000 more net worth. Investment results make almost no difference to wealth building. (They make a huge difference to folks who are already wealthy.) What about saving? What if you drop our kid's savings rate back to a normal 15%? Even with a 15% annual investment return, the size of the nest egg collapses to only around $318,000.

"Saving is the single biggest variable.

"What about working? What if you assume our guy likes to take a lot of time off. Say he only works 40 weeks a year instead of 50. He goes to Europe or goes surfing... what happens then? Nest egg drops another $100,000 down to $254,000. In other words... even if our guy does well in his career... and does great with his investments... but he only saves like most people do... and he only works as hard as most people do... he'll end up like most people: without a pot to p– in.

"On the other hand, if he can learn to save like most people never will and work harder than just about anyone else... he's almost certain to be very, very rich by the time he's 40."

7. The Broker Interview

Broker-Salesperson Agreement: A written agreement between a real estate broker and real estate salesperson outlining the agency relationship and duties that exist between the parties.

Unlike most job interviews, when interviewing a real estate broker, the real estate salesperson should be the one asking the questions. Since the job is 100% commission, the real estate salesperson can usually place their license with almost any real estate broker they choose and move to another broker if the existing one is not fulfilling the obligations set forth in the **broker-salesperson agreement** (which must be in writing). A real estate salesperson should interview several real estate brokers and decide where to place their license.

A. Broker-Salesperson Agreement

California real estate brokers must have an employment contract (broker-salesperson agreement) with each of the licensed employees (real estate salespersons) in their office. This contract must be in writing; however, the form of the agreement is not regulated and can be any form the broker and salesperson choose. In other words, a written agreement between the broker and salesperson is required by the Real Estate Commissioner's Regulations; however, the agreement between a broker and salesperson is not required to be approved by the California Department of Real Estate. The broker must keep a copy of these agreements for three years after termination of the salesperson.

A real estate salesperson is legally an **employee** of the real estate broker, but is considered an **independent contractor** for income tax, unemployment insurance, and social security tax purposes. In fact, the real estate salesperson is considered an employee: (1) by law, (2) by the California Real Estate Commissioner, and (3) for worker's compensation purposes (although there are exceptions for real estate brokers and salespersons).

In contrast, for income tax, unemployment insurance, and social security tax purposes the real estate salesperson is considered an independent contractor. A real estate salesperson is required to pay their own federal and California state income taxes when they are due and pay for their own unemployment insurance if so desired. Most real estate salespersons will pay their income taxes quarterly in the year they are earned. This is in contrast to employees of other businesses who have their employers withhold income taxes from their earnings received during the year and then pay them when they come due.

Employee: A real estate salesperson is an employee by law, by the California Real Estate Commissioner, and possibly for worker's compensation purposes.

Independent Contractor: A real estate salesperson is considered an independent contractor for income tax, unemployment insurance, and social security tax purposes.

Chapter Two Summary

Many people who enter the real estate brokerage business are looking to run their own business and have some control over their lives. The big draw is the unlimited income potential that results from running a business that allows the business owner to receive the benefits of their own hard work and dedication to their clients.

Transitioning from the corporate world to the life of a real estate agent allows the new real estate professional to use some of the skills that were acquired in the corporate arena, along with new skills learned in the real estate brokerage business. A real estate agent is successful in the real estate brokerage business as a direct result of their own efforts and hard work. The harder one works, the more money one usually makes.

Employees work for business owners. Business owners work for stockholders. The board of directors for a corporation is comprised of major stockholders and other wealthy individuals who are working on behalf of the stockholders of the corporation. Thus, everyone has a boss. Whether it is an employee working for a business owner, a business owner working for the passive investors who capitalized the business (i.e., stockholders), the board of directors working for the stockholders, and ultimately *everyone* working for the customer. The *customer* determines who is successful and who is not.

Some barriers to entry into the real estate brokerage business in California are the applicant must be 18 years old or older, complete three required courses, pass the California State Salesperson Examination, pass a background check performed by the California Department of Justice and Federal Bureau of Investigation (FBI), pay required fees to the DRE, and place the real estate salesperson license under a licensed real estate broker.

Chapter Two Quiz

1. People get into the real estate brokerage business because they:
(A) want to run their own business
(B) desire unlimited income potential
(C) Both (A) and (C) are correct
(D) Neither (A) nor (C) are correct

2. Three avenues that may provide adequate income and a potential for independent wealth are:
(A) employee
(B) business owner
(C) passive investor
(D) all of the above are correct

3. The broker can delegate real estate salesperson reviews to a salesperson who:
(A) has at least two (2) years full-time experience as a real estate salesperson within the past five (5) years
(B) has a real estate broker's license pending with the DRE
(C) is a licensed attorney without a real estate broker's license
(D) has no experience as a real estate salesperson or broker

4. Real estate agents continually cultivate people who are:
(A) in their sphere of influence
(B) their relatives
(C) their friends
(D) all of the above are correct

5. Ingredients needed to succeed in the real estate brokerage business include:
(A) good work ethic
(B) expert product knowledge
(C) ability to handle uneven income streams
(D) all of the above are correct

6. Real estate agents should be:
(A) order takers
(B) consultants to their clients
(C) somewhat knowledgeable about real estate
(D) none of the above are correct

7. A real estate agent must understand types of financing that are available to buyers—including prevailing market interest rates for:
(A) conventional loans
(B) jumbo loans
(C) Federal Housing Administration (FHA) insured and Department of Veterans Affairs (VA) guaranteed loans
(D) all of the above are correct

8. Most new home salespeople start as a(n):
(A) lead sales agent
(B) relief sales agent
(C) sales manager
(D) unlicensed assistant

9. A written broker-salesperson agreement is:
(A) not required by law in California
(B) merely optional between a real estate broker and real estate salesperson
(C) required between all real estate brokers and salespersons in California
(D) only needed if the agent will be brokering real estate loans

10. A real estate salesperson is legally an _____ of the real estate broker, but is considered an _____ for income tax, unemployment insurance, and social security tax purposes.
(A) independent contractor, employee
(B) employee, independent contractor
(C) associate, employee
(D) attorney-in-fact, employee

Franklin D. Roosevelt

"Real estate cannot be lost or stolen, nor can it be carried away. Purchased with common sense, paid for in full, and managed with reasonable care. . .it is about the safest investment in the world."

Chapter
THREE

Working with Buyers and Sellers Prior to the Real Estate Transaction

A real estate salesperson represents either a buyer, a seller, or both buyer and seller in a real estate transaction. Most new real estate agents will usually work with a buyer as their first client because buyers are easier to find and easier to work with when a person is new to the real estate brokerage business.

As a real estate agent becomes more experienced, the agent will usually start listing properties for sellers. Listed properties tend to take longer to sell than working with buyers, however, listings are working 24 hours per day, 7 days per week to sell the property. Depending on the real estate agent's marketing program, listings can be an effective way to provide steady commission income over the agent's real estate career.

Figure 3.1

1. Working with Buyers Prior to the Real Estate Transaction

BUYER'S AGENT
(SELLING AGENT)

Obtain Buyer and Discuss Objectives

Submit Offer(s)

Buyer Reviews Disclosures and Inspects Property

Buyer Makes Request for Repairs to Seller

Buyer Signs Escrow Instructions and Loan Documents

Buyer Removes Contingencies

Prospect for Buyers

Show Properties

Buyer Places Earnest Money Deposit into Escrow

Buyer Receives Preliminary Title Report from Title Company

Final Verification of Property Condition

Loan Funding

OFFER & ACCEPTANCE

OPEN ESCROW

CLOSE ESCROW

Agent Follow-Up

Prospect for Sellers

Prepare Property for Listing

Review and Respond to Offer(s)

Seller Provides Disclosures to Buyer

Seller Responds to Buyer's Request for Repairs

Seller Signs Escrow Instructions and Grant Deed

Obtain Listing

SELLER'S AGENT
(LISTING AGENT)

Figure 3.2

A. Prospecting

(1) What is Prospecting in the Real Estate Brokerage Business?

Prospecting is the process of finding buyers and sellers and turning them into clients. The best prospectors are typically the highest grossing real estate agents. There is an old saying in the real estate brokerage business that is still true today, "If you stop prospecting for new clients, you die." The meaning, of course, is that real estate agents must continue prospecting for clients–even though they may have already sold several properties–because their pipeline of transactions will dry up and commission income will become very erratic. The best way to guard against this type of problem is to prospect, prospect, and prospect for new clients and repeat business.

Some new real estate agents close a few real estate deals and then stop prospecting, thinking that listings and buyers are going to appear out of the blue because they now have some real estate brokerage experience. This is not true, real estate agents must go after the business through consistent prospecting activities that fit their personality and comfort level.

Each real estate agent usually develops a prospecting technique that provides consistent real estate listings and qualified buyers. Before this can be accomplished, the real estate agent must develop a marketing plan and decide which market segments to pursue with their marketing efforts.

Real estate agents can divide the total real estate market into segments and direct their marketing efforts toward the most promising ones. A market segment is a group of potential clients who respond in similar ways to a marketing program.

Markets can be segmented through psychographics (lifestyles), geographical neighborhoods (farm areas), socio-economic/behavioral factors (social classes), and demographics (age, sex, marital status, etc.). The two most common market segmentation techniques used by real estate agents are psychographics and geographical neighborhoods.

a. Psychographics (Lifestyles)

A real estate agent's **sphere of influence** includes everyone the agent knows and usually consists of relatives, friends, and acquaintances. Since the advent of the internet, an agent's sphere of influence can be easily and consistently contacted through **social media**. The key is to continue reminding the agent's sphere of influence that the agent is "in the real estate business and loves referrals."

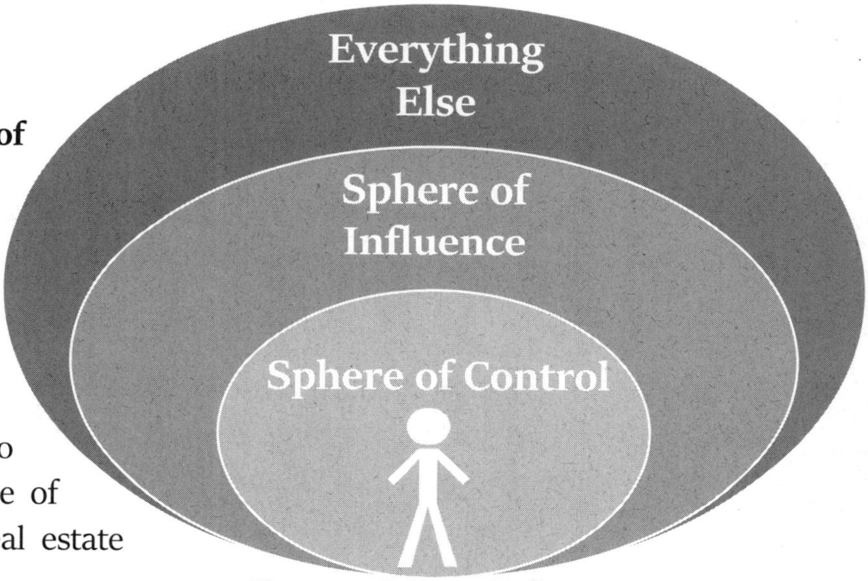

Figure 3.3 Sphere of Influence

In addition to social media, membership in local groups of like-minded people can be a good prospecting market segment as well. This is called **networking** and includes involvement in clubs and groups such as Rotary clubs, Moose clubs, etc. Another good prospecting method is to increase an agent's sphere of influence by involvement in volunteer organizations. Not only is this good for the local community, but it is also a great way to meet people. After all, the real estate brokerage business is a people business. The more people a real estate agent knows, the more potential referrals will come from their sphere of influence.

1. The Importance of Projecting a Successful Image

People tend to wear their success on their shirt sleeves and a successful image can be important to a real estate agent's success. Clients

Sphere of Influence: Everyone a person knows in their social group(s).

Social Media: Internet websites that connect social groups. Excellent way to keep in contact with a sphere of influence.

Networking: Increasing a real estate agent's prospecting base by tying spheres of influence together through referrals.

tend to make assumptions based on what they see, so a well-dressed real estate agent with a nice car, nice home, and affluent lifestyle indicates a successful agent whom a client will want to hire to sell their home. However, reality can be much different than the image being portrayed by the individual.

Tales from the Trade

the story of two medical doctors

A good analogy is a sick man, who has a life-threatening illness, consults with two medical doctors to decide which one to use for a delicate medical operation that is needed to save the man's life. The prospective patient calls up both medical doctors and arranges separate meetings with them at his home. Dr. #1 arrives in a late-model Mercedes, wearing a nice suit, an expensive Rolex watch, and says, "I can heal you." He then drives off in his expensive car.

Dr. #2 shows up in a 1962 Rambler automobile and is wearing Birkenstock sandals, comfortable jeans, an old polo shirt, and has a mullet (hair style, not fish) with a large orange colored and inexpensive watch. He says, "I can heal you," and putts off in his old rickety car.

Based on what the prospective patient can see, and with only this information, he will most likely pick Dr. #1 because he is obviously more successful than Dr. #2 and will, therefore be the best chance of survival for the patient.

However, there is more information of which the sick patient is unaware: Dr. #1 just recently graduated from medical school and owes hundreds of thousands of dollars in student loans that must be paid back before the doctor can start saving money for his own career and future retirement. He has one suit and the patient has seen it. He leased the car and can barely make the lease payments each month. His Rolex watch is actually a "Polex" which cost him $18 on Amazon–including shipping. Dr. #1 has seen the operation the patient must have to survive but has never successfully performed it himself.

Dr. #2, on the other hand, is the best surgeon in the world for the type of medical operation the sick patient needs to survive and continue with his life. Dr. #2 originated the medical procedure and is wealthy beyond his wildest dreams. He drives an old Rambler because he likes old cars. He wears Birkenstocks because they are comfortable, and he has a mullet because he thinks it "looks cool." His large orange watch is practical because it is easy to see. Based on this additional information, the patient would obviously pick Dr. #2 because he really wants to survive the operation. Real estate clients typically do not have this second bit of information and make their decisions based on what they "see," rather than what "is." Perception is reality in the real estate business, so image is very important to a successful real estate career.

Items such as a real estate agent's car, clothes, home where they live, and social groups with which they associate are called "*slicks*." They are the items used to portray a certain image the real estate agent believes will be effective when prospecting for clients while increasing real estate transactions and commission income. If a new real estate agent can initially afford some expensive slicks, they can be a good investment for their future career. However, most new real estate agents cannot afford many slicks when entering the real estate brokerage business because, after all that's why they are entering the business in the first place—to make money. For this reason, new real estate agents must use the slicks they already have in their possession when they begin a career in the real estate brokerage business.

b. Geographical Neighborhoods

The second most powerful prospecting method is targeting the **geographical neighborhood** (or "**farm area**") where a real estate agent lives. Marketing techniques include both **active prospecting methods** and **passive prospecting methods**. Active prospecting methods may include knocking on doors, telemarketing, and conducting open houses; while passive prospecting methods may include real estate for sale signs and newsletters.

Geographical Neighborhoods (Farm Area): The neighborhood where a real estate agent lives and prospects for clients.

Active Prospecting Methods: High-impact prospecting methods such as knocking on doors and open houses.

Passive Prospective Methods: Low-impact prospecting methods such as for sale signs and newsletters.

A neighborhood tends to be a somewhat self-contained community, frequently defined by physical boundaries such as hills, freeways, or major streets and usually with some sense of community. However, in urban areas, the neighborhood tends to become somewhat blurred due to modern transportation and area-wide cultural, educational, recreational, and commercial services.

When an appraiser is analyzing the "neighborhood" for a parcel that is being appraised, a good starting point is to ascertain the community identity and boundaries. After defining–even in vague terms–this community identity, an appraiser will look to common services and features, such as local shopping, street patterns, zoning boundaries, and cultural, religious, educational and recreational services. In short, an appraiser searches the local area by observation and through government and public utility investigation to find the factors most affecting use and value patterns in the area.

The appraisal principle of conformity states that a house will most likely appreciate (increase) in value if its size, age, condition, and style are similar and conform to other houses in the neighborhood. Thus, conformity to proper land use objectives contributes most to the maintenance of value in a well-planned residential community.

Factors that make up a neighborhood include types of people who live there, types of homes that are built there, and neighborhood trends.

1. Types of People Living in a Neighborhood

The types of people who live in a neighborhood usually have similar income levels, ages, family sizes, and reasons for owning a single-family home. Higher socio-economic neighborhoods tend to have more homeowners who live in a home with their families (owner-occupied) rather than real estate investors who purchase a home to be used as a rental property (non-owner occupied) that is rented to tenants.

Generally, the prices for higher-end homes is too high to provide a real estate investor with adequate cash flow (as a rental property) during the real estate investor's holding period. The desirability of homes located in higher socio-economic neighborhoods is so strong for owner-occupied homebuyers that they are willing to spend more money each month (i.e., accept a higher monthly loan payment) than tenants who are willing to rent the same property on a monthly basis.

2. Types of Homes that are Built in a Neighborhood

The types of properties located in and around a neighborhood can be a mix of single-family homes, condominiums, patio homes, townhouses, apartment buildings, and retail/office leased investments. The age and price range of typical homes built in an area are important considerations when projecting where a neighborhood will be ten or twenty years down the road.

Gentrification: Occurs when an old, lower socio-economic neighborhood is rejuvenated with young families who increase the value of the entire area.

3. Neighborhood Trends

The life cycle of a neighborhood moves from: (1) growth in desirability, to (2) peak desirability, to (3) stability for a time, and finally to (4) deterioration. The life cycle may then start over again as neighborhoods become more desirable through the rebuilding process called **gentrification**.

Neighborhood trends may indicate a depressed real estate market in the future caused by changes in geographical homebuyer preferences, demographics, psychographics, and socio-economics. For example, a neighborhood may change over time from newly married couples, to families

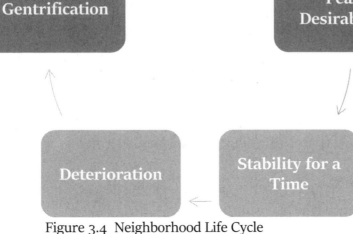

Figure 3.4 Neighborhood Life Cycle

with young children, to families with teenage children, and finally to empty nesters.

Buyers will continuously be faced with decisions among location, size, and age of a single-family property. For example, a buyer may be able to purchase a 1,200 square foot home located in a high socio-economic area for $400,000. At the same time, the buyer can purchase a 2,000 square foot home located in a lower socio-economic area for the same price. The buyer must decide whether neighborhood location or size of the home is the most critical factor when deciding to purchase a property. The age of the home comes into play with maintenance and styling issues that may devalue the property. Older homes generally have more maintenance issues (physical deterioration), smaller rooms, lesser number of bathrooms, and less closet space (functional obsolescence) than newer homes. Buyers must decide which factor is most important to them, as well as future homebuyers who will purchase the property in the future.

c. Socio-Economic Target Markets

Socio-economic target markets are defined by income and social class. Generally, a neighborhood where a prospect lives is an indicator of their social class. Social classes of like-minded people tend to flock together in specific neighborhoods and zip codes. Prices of properties tend to increase or decrease based on buyer and seller preconceived ideas of social class. Social class describes how people think and how they spend their money, not how much money they earn or their personal net worth.

> **Socio-Economic Target Markets:** A market segmentation tactic that divides target markets by social class.

d. Demographics

Demographics include age, sex, religion, and marital status. For example, real estate markets can be segmented by the age of homeowners in a neighborhood. As neighborhoods and residents become older, they move from newlyweds to parents, and finally to empty nesters. They may find a large four or five-bedroom home adequate when the children are young; however, by the time they become empty nesters they may only need a small house with two or three bedrooms. A real estate agent can help a homeowner sell their large home and buy a smaller one in a retirement community.

> **Demographics:** Age, sex, religion, etc. that describes a target market.

Real estate agents will discover it is easier to find clients through one's sphere of influence than any other prospecting method. It may not be necessary to impress a real estate agent's sphere of influence; however, a few slicks can be used to *remind* them of the real estate agent's success.

After the real estate agent has listed and sold a few properties, saved a lot of money, and decided to make the real estate brokerage business a career, then an investment in a nice car may be a good business decision for long-term success.

(2) Active Prospecting Methods
a. Knocking on Doors

Even though knocking on neighbors' doors can result in many "No, I'm not interested" responses, every "yes" response is a possible listing, sale, and commission. Another way to meet these same neighbors is to hold an open house in the neighborhood. This can be accomplished using one of the real estate agent's own listings or one of their broker's listings.

b. Open Houses

An open house allows a real estate agent to sell a listed property *and* prospect for buyers at the same time. The agent can contact houses located around each of their listings and inform the occupants (both owners and tenants) of the date and time of each upcoming **open house**. This can be accomplished by knocking on doors and talking to property owners and tenants, along with leaving behind a marketing piece that invites the person to the upcoming open house. The neighbors may have friends and relatives who are looking to buy a home, and who is better to sell a neighborhood than the local residents? The open house can be used to meet the neighbors and pick up listings of neighbors' properties as well. Neighborhood websites may be used to inform the neighbors of upcoming open houses.

Figure 3.5

c. Local Homeowner's Association

Becoming a member of the local neighborhood homeowner's association (HOA) where the real estate agent lives is a great way to meet the neighbors. Accordingly, becoming president of the homeowner's association is an even better way to meet all the neighbors and gain credibility at the same time.

(3) Passive Prospecting Methods
a. Real Estate For Sale Signs

One of the best ways to sell a home and pick up buyers and sellers at the same time is through a real estate sign located in the front yard of a property that is listed for sale. Calls or emails received from prospective buyers who see the sign while driving around the neighborhood may be used to either sell the listed home, pick up buyers who may be interested in buying a different home that is for sale in the same geographical area, or list their property for sale and then help them find a suitable home to purchase.

Figure 3.6

b. Newsletters and Mailers

Newsletters and mailers are very expensive and can be a huge waste of money if they are not targeted directly toward a market segment that will be receptive to this type of marketing effort.

For example, some real estate agents like to mail a newsletter once per month into a targeted geographical area that is close to their home or real estate brokerage office. The content in the newsletter must be interesting to the targeted segment of homeowners, such as what is going on in the local neighborhood where they live, real estate sales in the area, local, regional, and national economic factors that directly affect real estate and their own homes, and movement of interest rates.

Direct mail pieces are sometimes used by real estate agents to get their name out into the local geographical market area hoping to gain name recognition when they knock on doors or hold open houses in the future. However, generally the best use for direct mail pieces is to mail them to the real estate agent's sphere of influence. This tactic can be used in addition to normal social media and other electronic contacts with the sphere of influence.

c. Other Passive Prospecting Methods

Another passive prospecting methods that has been used in the past is to rent a kiosk in a local shopping mall. The kiosk can be used to prospect for new clients as they frequent the mall.

B. Factors Influencing Why People Buy Real Estate

Real estate agents should question prospective buyers to determine their motivations in buying a single-family home. Why do they want to buy a home? The agent must identify where the buyer wants to buy the home, number of bedrooms and bathrooms, age, style preferences, and what is the ideal home for the buyer.

Along with the financial stability and social prestige that come with owning a home, there are four other factors that influence why people buy real estate: price appreciation, leverage, taxation, and amortization.

(1) Price Appreciation

Price Appreciation: An increase in value of a parcel of real property.

Price appreciation is an increase in a property's value over a holding period (time the purchaser owns the property).

Price Appreciation Example	
Purchase Price	$100,000
x Price Appreciation Rate	20%
= Increase in Value	$20,000
Property's New Value	$120,000
	($100,000 + $20,000)

Figure 3.7

(2) Leverage

Leverage: A property owner increases return on investment by placing a small down payment and financing the balance of the purchase price.

When a buyer of real property pays 20% of the purchase price as down payment toward the purchase of a $100,000 property, the buyer is using **leverage** to acquire the property.

Leverage Example	
Sale Price	$100,000
• 20% Down Payment	$20,000
• 80% Loan	$80,000

If the buyer pays all cash for the property, and the property value increases to $150,000, then the buyer's return on investment is:

$$\frac{\$50,000 \text{ increase in value}}{\$100,000 \text{ original purchase price}} = 50\% \text{ return on investment}$$

However, since the buyer only paid $20,000 as down payment, the buyer is using leverage to increase the return on investment. Therefore,

$$\frac{\$50,000 \text{ increase in value}}{\$20,000 \text{ original investment}} = 250\% \text{ return on investment}$$

Figure 3.8

(3) Tax Shelter

Tax Shelter: Depreciation allows real estate to be considered a tax shelter.

One of the most important decision-influencing factors regarding the purchase of real estate is the tax implications and suitability as a **tax shelter**. Homeowners have a different tax situation than investors.

a. Homeowners

Homeowners may deduct mortgage interest from their real estate loans in the same year it is incurred. In addition, a homeowner who has lived in his home (primary dwelling) two years out the last five years may receive $250,000 (single person) or $500,000 (married couple) in net proceeds from the sale of their home without paying capital gains taxes. There are many variations and exceptions to this law, so an agent should always advise their clients to consult a tax expert and real estate attorney prior to any real estate endeavor.

b. Real Estate Investors

Real estate investors may be able to deduct mortgage interest paid on real estate loans, most property expenses, and some capital improvements made to a property in the year they occur. This gives an advantage to real estate investors because they can reduce active or passive income tax liability on a yearly basis. A real estate investor may also depreciate the building (improved) portion of a residential property over 27.5 years straight-line depreciation. All other non-residential investment properties use a 39 year straight-line depreciation schedule.

A real estate investor may be able to exchange the property for another property and defer the capital gains taxes on the relinquished property into the future. The real estate investor must sell the relinquished property and then purchase a new acquired property within 180 days of the sale of the original relinquished property (45 days to identify the new property). This is called a "1031 Exchange" and has derived its name from IRC 1031 of the Internal Revenue Code. It is also called a "Starker" and took this name from the court case T.J. Starker v. U.S. Government. This is the landmark court case that allowed delayed exchanges of real property. There are many restrictions to these exchanges. A real estate agent should always advise their clients to consult a tax expert (and an exchange expert in this case) prior to making any real estate investment decision.

> **Loan Amortization:** A loan is paid off with payments of principal and interest over the life of the loan.
>
> **Interest:** Rent on money.

(4) Loan Amortization

Loan amortization is the systematic liquidation of a debt obligation on an installment basis over a period of time. This means that each loan payment is part principal and part **interest**. As seen in Figure 3.9, the total monthly payment stays the same over the life of the loan, however the portion of the payment applied to principal increases and the portion that is paid in interest decreases with each payment. Accordingly, early in the loan

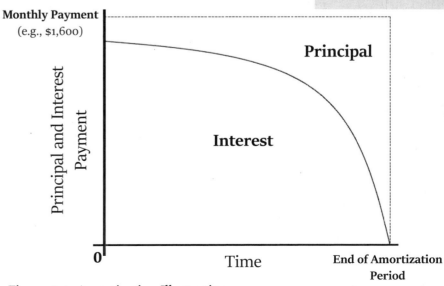

Figure 3.9 Amortization Illustration

amortization schedule most of the monthly payment is interest, while payments made later in the amortization schedule are mostly principal.

Lenders realize that most property owners sell or refinance their properties every five to seven years (or less). Consequently, most properties do not reach the point in time where a significant amount of the monthly payment is reducing the principal balance of the loan.

An astute real estate owner realizes that mostly interest is being paid early in the loan term, but as the loan moves through the amortization schedule more principal is being paid with each monthly payment. If the loan is fifteen years or more into a 30-year fully-amortized loan, the property owner may want to keep the loan until the loan is paid off at the end of the 30 year amortization schedule.

Most buyers have no idea how much they can qualify to purchase using a down payment and real estate loan. For this reason, every buyer should get preapproved with a lender prior to starting the search for their dream home.

C. Buyer Loan Preapproval

Real estate agents are paid to match ready, willing, and (most importantly) able buyers with sellers who are motivated to sell their home. The real estate agent must verify a buyer is able to purchase a home by having the buyer get preapproved for a loan with a lender. This usually requires the buyer to complete a loan application, have the lender run the buyer's credit report, and then submit this information to a loan underwriter who provides a "loan preapproval letter" verifying the buyer can qualify for a home purchase up to a certain maximum amount. A preapproval letter can be used to prove to the seller (and the seller's agent) that the buyer has the down payment in hand (money actually sitting in the bank) and has the income and credit score necessary to qualify for the loan.

D. Homebuyer is Fulfilling a Personal Need for Shelter

A real estate homebuyer is fulfilling a personal need for shelter. This may be a need to provide emotional and social stability for the family by owning their own home; or it may be a real estate investor looking to purchase a home, rent it to a tenant, and then sell it at the end of the holding period for (hopefully) a nice profit. Each type of buyer has different motivations. The owner-occupied homebuyer is looking for a home for the family, while the investor is looking for a good return on investment during the projected holding period. Owner-occupied single-family buyers are the most prevalent type of buyer in California and, for this reason, are covered extensively in the book.

2. Working with Sellers Prior to the Real Estate Transaction

Figure 3.10

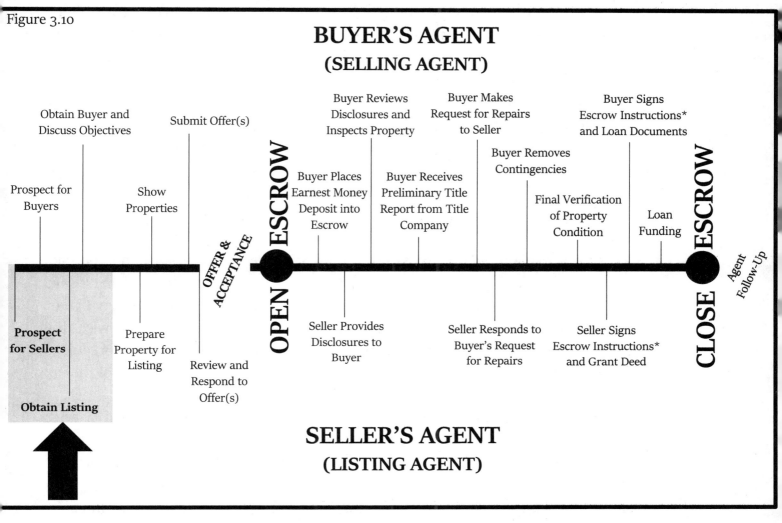

Most real estate property owners have little experience selling real estate. For this reason, property owners may hire a real estate agent to help them sell their home. In return, the property owner agrees to pay a commission (usually a percentage of the sale price) for the real estate agent's services. Most importantly, the sale of the home must be a win-win situation for the property owner and agent. The cost of a real estate agent's services must be *less* than the total benefits the agent provides to the seller in the sale of the home. The property owner wins by saving money when using an agent to sell the home. The real estate agent wins by collecting a commission with the sale of the property.

When a real estate agent lists a seller's home for sale, the real estate agent is asking the seller to pay a 5% to 6% commission (of the sale price of the home) as compensation for the real estate agent's services. However, what does a real estate agent do to earn this commission?

Some things real estate agents and brokers do behind the scenes include: constantly checking the MLS for new properties that come on the market; researching properties online, going out and looking at properties in person; spending their own money marketing their listings for sale; writing up offers, counter offers, addenda, and other contracts; attending home inspections and other inspections; putting out fires as problems arise; and keeping everyone calm during one of the largest financial transactions of their lifetimes.

A good analogy to this situation is a Certified Public Accountant (CPA) who is in the business of income tax consulting and filing services for clients who own real estate (both owner-occupied single-family homes and non-owner occupied rental properties). The CPA firm is paid $10,000 to file a client's current tax returns (federal and state) for one year. The property owner could personally file both income tax returns for zero cost and not pay the CPA $10,000 to do the same thing. However, tax returns have become so complex and convoluted over the years, that a CPA must spend several years learning the tax codes to be able to find and take every possible legal deduction provided by law. The key is that the CPA must save the property owner more money in legal tax deductions than the property owner pays for the CPA's services. This is called a value-added service. Otherwise, the property owner will find other less expensive ways to file their income tax returns (e.g., TurboTax) and thereby cut the CPA (and his hefty $10,000 bill) out of the tax filing arrangement altogether.

The real estate brokerage business has the same value-added service dynamic as CPA firms. The client must receive real estate brokerage services that are more valuable than the 5% to 6% commission paid for the agent's services. Some of the services that are provided by an agent present the buyer and seller with more benefits than the amount of commission paid to the agent and include: (1) agent provides a real estate listing agreement form, (2) agent provides an accurate listing price analysis, (3) agent provides a real estate purchase agreement and disclosure forms, and (4) agent places the property on-the-market to be sold.

A. Agent Provides a Real Estate Listing Agreement Form

A real estate listing agreement is a contract between the seller and real estate agent (called the seller's agent or listing agent) who is listing the property for sale. In contrast, the Real Estate Purchase Agreement and Joint Escrow Instructions (purchase agreement) is a contract between the seller and buyer for the purchase of real property.

According to the California Civil Code, "Listing agreement means a contract between an owner of real property and an agent, by which the agent has been authorized to sell the real property or to find or obtain a buyer." The authorization to sell the real property is a warranty of authority given by the seller to the agent. The agent has the authority to sell the property for the seller, find a buyer, and accept an earnest money deposit from the buyer and on behalf of the seller. In addition, by having a fully executed listing agreement, it usually allows the listing agent to receive a commission when the property sells (usually received after confirmation of recording of the grant deed at close of escrow).

One of the most efficient ways to sell a home is to list it with a real estate agent. The agent sells homes for a living and has the entire selling process set up in a systemized format that will sell the home for the highest possible price in the shortest possible marketing time. In return, real estate agents want to ensure they are not wasting their time with a seller who is not serious about selling their home, or a property that has deliverability issues caused by title defects or other situations that will cloud the title to the property (e.g., a spouse who is on title to the property and does not want to sell).

Even though real estate brokers normally try to use an exclusive authorization and right to sell listing agreement to list properties for sale, there are other types of listings that are used from time-to-time in the real estate brokerage

Figure 3.11

Types of Listing Agreements

TYPE	DESCRIPTION	LEVEL
Open Listing	Multiple brokers work simultaneously to sell the property. Commission only paid to the broker who is the *procuring cause* of the sale.	OK
Exclusive Authorization and Right to Sell Listing	Seller pays a commission to the agent—*no matter who sells the property.*	**BEST**
Exclusive Agency Listing	Seller pays a commission to the agent no matter who sells the property — *except if the seller sells the property him or herself.*	OK
Net Listing	Seller states: "I want $200,000 for my property and you can keep anything above that." If the agent can sell the property for $225,000, the agent will receive a $25,000 commission. Although legal in California, the agent may do everything correctly and not receive a commission.	OK
Option Listing	Agent lists a property for sale and, at the same time, the agent personally has an option to purchase the property for a specified purchase price and length of time to exercise the option.	OK
Oral Listing	Agency relationship created by oral agreement and is effective in establishing the relationship, but not enforceable.	WORST
Pocket Listing	When a listing agent "pockets a listing" and does not place it in the local multiple listing service (MLS). This is unethical, unless the seller instructs the listing agent to do so.	CAN BE UNETHICAL

business. Other listing types include an open listing, exclusive agency listing, net listing, option listing, oral listing, and pocket listing.

It should be noted that even though the real estate salesperson brings in a listing, the listing belongs to the real estate broker under which the salesperson has placed their real estate salesperson license.

(1) Open Listing/Open Agreement

Open Listing/Open Agreement: A listing agreement that provides for a real estate broker to be paid a commission if the broker brings in a buyer to purchase the property.

Procuring Cause: Broker who brings in the buyer under an open listing/open agreement.

An **open listing** or **open agreement** is a nonexclusive listing that is used when a seller states, "I'm not going to list the property with only one agent, I'm going to pay whoever brings in the buyer." This is a unilateral contract in which the seller promises to pay a commission upon the act of a real estate agent bringing in a buyer who purchases the property. Real estate agents must prove they are the **procuring cause** when an open listing is used. The agent who informs the buyer that the seller has accepted their offer is generally considered to be the procuring cause of the sale.

In other words, an open listing invites offers from many agents to find a buyer for a property. The agent who is the procuring cause of the transaction is the one who receives a commission for the sale of the property. If a real estate agent shows a property under an open listing, the agent should write a memorandum notifying the seller that the agent showed the property.

(2) Exclusive Authorization and Right to Sell Listing

Exclusive Authorization and Right to Sell Listing: A listing agreement that provides for the real estate broker to receive a commission no matter who sells the property.

In the past, real estate agents had difficulty getting paid for their work. In response, real estate agents began using an **exclusive authorization and right to sell listing agreement** that requires the seller to pay a commission to the agent—*no matter who sells the property.*

An exclusive authorization and right to sell listing agreement is a contract between the seller and real estate agent in which the seller agrees to compensate the agent who listed the property for sale (seller's agent/listing agent), along with compensating a cooperating real estate agent (buyer's agent/selling agent) who brings in the buyer and purchases the property. For example, if the seller has agreed to pay a 6% commission, the seller's agent/listing agent will usually receive 3% and the buyer's agent/selling agent will receive 3% of the sale price.

Requiring the seller to sign a contract to pay a commission if the property sells will assure deliverability of the property to the buyer. In other words, the seller has seriously considered selling the property and has contacted all the owners who are on title to the property and obtained their agreement before signing the exclusive authorization and right to sell listing agreement.

Agents must show they are the procuring cause under an open listing (non-exclusive listing), an exclusive agency listing (at least prove the seller did not personally sell the property), and a net listing. When using an exclusive authorization and right to sell listing agreement, the seller's agent/listing agent is not required to prove he or she is the procuring cause of the sale to earn a commission when the property sells. In other words, no matter who sells the property—the agent gets paid a commission.

An exclusive right to sell listing agreement is used to ensure the agent is paid a commission if the property sells during the listing period, or after the listing period if a **broker's protection clause** (also called safety clause or protection period clause) is contained in the listing agreement. If the property sells to a registered prospect who saw the property during the listing period and is on a list that was given to the seller by the listing agent by the end of the listing period, then the agent may be due a commission after the listing has expired.

Broker's Protection Clause: Clause in a listing agreement that allows the real estate broker to receive a commission after the listing agreement has expired.

Some broker's protection clauses/safety clauses/protection period clauses may give an agent up to five days after the end of the listing period to submit a list of buyers to the seller. However, the agent may have a difficult time collecting a commission after the listing expires (called an expired listing) if the seller lists the property with another agent and the agent lists the property under their own name with an exclusive authorization and right to sell listing agreement.

An exclusive authorization and right to sell listing agreement is a bilateral executory contract. It is a promise for a promise (bilateral) and is in the process of being completed (executory). In other words, the property owner/seller promises to pay the real estate agent a commission in return for the agent's promise to find a ready, willing, and able buyer to purchase the property. Thus, the agent is not required to prove that the agent is the procuring cause of the sale because no matter who sells the property, the real estate agent is paid a commission.

a. Proof of Procuring Cause Not Required

To reiterate, a real estate agent need not prove that he or she is the procuring cause when an exclusive right to sell listing is used. An exclusive right to sell listing is defined as a listing agreement in which the seller must pay the agent a commission no matter who sells the property, no exceptions. Since the agent gets paid no matter who sells the property when an exclusive right to sell listing is used, the agent is not required to prove that he or she is the procuring cause of the sale of the property. In contrast, an open listing (along with exclusive agency and net listings as well) requires the agent to prove he or she is the procuring cause of the sale to be paid a commission by the seller.

b. Owner Cancels Listing Agreement

If an owner signs an exclusive authorization and right to sell listing agreement but later cancels it, the owner can cancel the contract but may be liable for payment of damages under the agreement. Damages may include payment of all the broker's expenses during the listing period or possibly payment of a full commission, depending upon the agreement.

c. Maximum Time Period and Commission Amount for Exclusive Authorization and Right to Sell listing is Negotiable

An exclusive authorization and right to sell listing agreement must have a definite termination date that is negotiable between the seller and agent. Residential listings commonly have listing periods between ninety (90) and one-hundred and eighty (180) days, while commercial listings may be a year or longer.

d. Legal Description

An exclusive authorization and right to sell listing must contain a legal description of the property. Land description methods include the lots, blocks, and tracts method; government survey method; and metes and bounds method. Chapter 13 discusses each land description method.

(3) Exclusive Agency Listing

Exclusive Agency Listing: Provides for a real estate broker to receive a commission no matter who sells the property, except if the seller sells the property him or herself.

An **exclusive agency listing** is defined as a listing agreement in which the seller must pay the agent a commission no matter who sells the property, *except if the seller sells the property him or herself.* If the property is sold by the seller, under an exclusive agency listing agreement the seller does *not* owe the agent a commission.

In other words, an exclusive agency listing agreement is very similar to an exclusive authorization and right to sell listing agreement, with one important exception: no matter who sells the property the listing agent is paid a commission, *except if the property is sold by the seller.* When the seller sells the property, then the listing agent will not receive a commission.

Figure 3.12

For example, an agent has listed a seller's home using an exclusive agency listing agreement. The exclusive agreement is for four months. During this time period the agent expends considerable time, effort, and money marketing and advertising the property for sale. Ten days before the listing expires, the seller decides to sell his home to his next-door neighbor. The seller now owes the agent no commission.

a. Exclusive Authorization to Locate Property Agreement

Separate from exclusive agency listings is an **exclusive authorization to locate property agreement** that provides the agent who is representing the buyer will be paid a commission no matter which property the buyer purchases. This allows the agent to search for not only properties that are listed in the MLS, but for foreclosures owned by banks and for sale by owner (FSBO) properties. The agent is assured of being paid a commission, so the agent can expend time and effort finding potential properties for the buyer to purchase.

When a buyer signs an exclusive authorization to locate property agreement, there is usually a clause in the agreement that allows the agent to represent other buyers during the time limits of the agreement. In other words, the agent can represent other buyers during the term of the exclusive authorization to locate property agreement.

> **Exclusive Authorization to Locate Property Agreement:** Provides that the broker who is representing the buyer will be paid a commission no matter which property the buyer purchases.

b. Exclusive Listings Must Have a Definite Termination Date

Exclusive Authorization and Right to Sell, Exclusive Agency, and Exclusive Authorization to Locate Property Agreements each must have a definite termination date that states when the listing agreement will end.

When a real estate agent has an exclusive listing, the agent may be subject to disciplinary action by the Real Estate Commissioner for: (1) not giving a copy of the exclusive listing to the seller, and (2) not including a definite termination date in the agreement.

(4) Net Listing

When a **net listing** is used, the seller may state, "I want $200,000 for the property. Anything you can get over that amount you can keep." If the agent can sell the property for $225,000, then the agent will receive a $25,000 commission. Unfortunately, the property may be worth only $180,000 and the agent will receive no commission. Therefore, smart real estate agents use exclusive authorization and right to sell listings in which the agent gets paid a previously negotiated commission amount when the property sells. The agent gets paid no matter who sells the property. Conversely, with net listings the agent only gets paid if the sale price is over a certain specified amount agreed to by the agent and seller. A net listing is the only type of listing that a real estate agent can do everything correctly while selling a property, and not be paid a commission.

Net Listing Example

$225,000 Property Sale Price

$25,000 Difference

Listing agent will receive the $25,000 as a commission. However, if the property sells below $200,000, then the agent receives nothing.

$200,000 Amount Seller Wants for Property

Figure 3.13

> **Net Listing:** Broker is informed that the seller requires a certain amount from the sale of the property. Any amount above this price the broker can keep as a commission.

(5) Option Listing

Option Listing: A listing agreement that allows the broker to list the property for sale or personally purchase the property for a specific amount.

An **option listing** is used when a real estate agent lists a property for sale and, at the same time, the agent personally has an option to purchase the property for a specified purchase price and length of time. The real estate agent must use good faith when marketing the property for sale and make the seller aware of all offers made on the property. If the real estate agent exercises the option to purchase the property, the real estate agent must inform the seller of the amount of profit the real estate agent will realize during an immediate resale to another buyer. Option listings are sometimes used with large commercial properties in which the listing agent may also be a syndicator who bring investors together to buy attractive investment properties.

Tales from the Trade

THE STORY OF AN OPTION LISTING THAT TURNED INTO AN ILLEGAL SECRET PROFIT

The owner of a neighborhood shopping center decided to sell the property. A neighborhood shopping center usually consists of a supermarket and drug store either built separately or with both combined into one store. The owner listed the property with a real estate agent who also owned several retail properties in the same geographical area. The real estate agent was given an option listing that allowed the agent to sell the property for a negotiated commission or personally buy it for $11 million.

The real estate agent placed the neighborhood shopping center on the market for $12 million. At the end of the listing period the real estate agent informed the seller that there were no offers on the property, so the agent decided to move forward and exercise the option to buy the property for $11 million. The agent went ahead and exercised the option and closed escrow with a purchase price of $11 million. Two months after close of escrow, the seller discovered that the real estate agent indeed did have an offer for the property and it was for $12 million dollars. The real estate agent had purchased the property for $11 million and immediately resold it for $12 million to the buyer who was interested in the property. The seller immediately filed suit against the agent for breach of fiduciary duty and the real estate agent receiving a secret profit.

The real estate agent should have immediately presented the $12 million offer to the seller. By not doing so, the agent violated a fiduciary duty of utmost care, integrity, honesty, and loyalty to the seller. In addition, when the agent exercised the option to purchase the property, the agent was obligated to disclose the profit the agent made when it was resold to the buyer who had made the $12 million offer. The agent did not do any of these things, so the agent was ordered by the court to pay the seller the $1 million profit that was made on the sale of the property, plus the seller's attorney fees as the prevailing party in the lawsuit.

(6) Oral Listing

The real estate agency relationship between a principal and an agent can be made by written or oral agreement. An oral agreement to sell a person's property is effective in establishing the agency relationship; however, the agent does not have the ability to enforce collection of a commission that is included in the oral agreement. Therefore, most real estate agents do *not* use an **oral listing** but try to use an exclusive authorization and right to sell listing to help collect commissions that are due.

> **Oral Listing:** A verbal listing to sell a parcel of real property.

(7) Pocket Listing

When a listing agent "pockets a listing" and does not place it in the local multiple listing service (MLS), this is called a **pocket listing**. Real estate agents sometimes try to hold off placing a property into the MLS, so they can find a buyer themselves and collect both sides of the commission (dual agency).

> **Pocket Listing:** A listing that the broker does not place in the multiple listing service.

For example, a real estate agent lists a property for sale. The commission is 6% of the sale price, with 3% going to the listing agent (seller's agent) and 3% going to the selling agent (buyer's agent). The listing agent will normally place the listing into the MLS within a couple of days of listing the property. This immediately presents the property to many qualified buyers. If the listing agent does not place the property into the MLS and tries to find the buyer him or herself, then this is considered a pocket listing.

Pocket listings are considered unethical; however, if the seller instructs the listing agent not to place the property into the MLS, then the agent must follow the seller's instructions and not enter the listing into the MLS.

Tales from the Trade

The Story of a Resort Condominium

A client wanted to purchase a condominium near a Sierra Nevada ski resort. He enlisted the help of a real estate agent to find a suitable property. The real estate agent found a "for sale by owner" (FSBO) property that appeared to be a good deal. The agent showed the property to the buyer and the buyer decided to make an offer to purchase the property. The seller said verbally that he wanted $119,000 for the property. The buyer wrote up an offer for $119,000 and the agent presented it to the seller. The agent was representing only the buyer and not the seller in the transaction. The seller then stated that he had talked to his wife, and his wife would not take anything less than $125,000 for the property. The buyer said no way and revoked the $119,000 offer.

The Story of a Resort Condominium

Had the seller signed an exclusive authorization and right to sell listing agreement, the difference of opinions between the spouses would have been discovered *before* an offer was placed on the property. Unfortunately, the seller had not discussed the price of the property with his spouse and was mistaken regarding the price. This type of situation becomes a deliverability issue regarding whether the sellers are serious about selling the property.

B. Agent Provides an Accurate Listing Price Analysis

Another reason why a property owner should enlist the services of a real estate agent to sell their home is to correctly price the property for sale. For example, a husband and wife (or two spouses) inform a real estate agent of their desire to sell their home. The real estate agent performs a comparative market analysis (CMA) and provides several recent sales comparables (sales comps) of properties that have recently sold. The properties have comparable physical characteristics to the subject property in terms of location, age, size, style, and amenities.

For example, the sales comparables indicate the property is worth approximately $300,000. The reason this number is important is because a buyer, who will normally purchase a home using a down payment and obtaining a real estate loan, will be required by the lender to get a formal appraisal of the property to verify its value is sufficient collateral for the lender that is making the loan. If the owner stops making debt service payments in the future, the lender can foreclose the loan and have a reasonable chance of getting most of their money back.

If the property does not appraise for at least the purchase price, the lender will most likely not make the loan unless: the buyer increases the down payment, the purchase price is adjusted downward, or the buyer challenges the appraisal.

Owner-occupied real estate loans such as Federal Housing Administration (FHA) insured loans require a very small down payment (3.5%) and unfortunately, most buyers do not have enough cash on hand to increase the down payment and the deal will likely not go through (fall out of escrow). Accordingly, if the seller is not willing to reduce the sale price down to the market level that is indicated by the appraisal, then the deal will fall through as well. In either case, the buyer will lose the costs of a credit report, appraisal fee, and home inspection fee when the lender rejects the loan. Total costs can be more than $900, and the buyer may not have enough money left over to make a down payment on a more correctly priced property. If the appraisal is low compared to existing sales comparables, the buyer may challenge the appraiser's opinion of value and submit it to the lender for reconsideration.

When real estate agents initially price a home for sale, they tend to use the same appraisal approach that appraisers use to appraise a subject property (property being appraised). In this manner, there is a good chance the property will appraise for the sale price and the lender will be comfortable making the loan.

Property sales and listing data is obtained and compared with the property being valued. The real estate agent uses the Comparison Approach/Market Data Approach/Sales Comparison Approach (three different names for the same approach) to effectively price a single-family home as close as possible to its true market value.

Generally, sales comps that are in close proximity to the subject property are the best indicators of value. The data should be of comparable properties located in similar neighborhoods to the subject property. The data gathered should be from areas where the **purchasing power** or income levels of the surrounding population are the same as the subject property.

> **Purchasing Power:** The amount of money an area has to purchase items.

Sales comparables should be comprised of verified market transactions and be as recent as possible. As sales comparables become older, the real estate market may have moved upward, downward, or remained the same during the time between each sale date and the date of the subject property appraisal.

(1) Sources of Real Estate Sales Comparables

Sources of sales comparables include county tax assessor's records in the county where the property is located, title insurance company records, county recorder's office files, multiple listing service records, financial news, and other comparative market analyses completed by the agent on similar properties in the past.

(2) Appraisal, Comparative Market Analysis, Broker Price Opinion, and Automated Valuation Model

Differences among appraisals, comparative market analysis (CMA), broker price opinions (BPO), and automated valuation models are important for a real estate agent to understand while working in the real estate brokerage business.

a. Appraisal

A licensed or certified appraiser's professional training, experience, and ethics provide lenders with an objective third party opinion of value. An appraiser has significant personal and professional responsibility to be correct and accurate in their opinions of value. Value can be derived using the market data/comparison approach which uses sales comparables that are true indicators of market value–without pressures or prejudices from the seller and buyer. Appraised values can also be determined using the income/capitalization approach and cost approach.

b. Comparative Market Analysis

A real estate agent may use a comparative market analysis (CMA) to help the seller to determine an appropriate listing price for a subject property. The real estate agent applies the same techniques used by professional appraisers to appraise properties, so when there is a valid contract between the buyer and seller, the property will appraise for the agreed upon contract price, the loan will be funded, and escrow will close.

c. Broker Price Opinion (BPO)

Broker Price Opinion (BPO): An opinion of value provided by a real estate broker for a parcel of real property. Commonly used by lenders dealing with foreclosed properties.

Lenders may contact a real estate broker and ask for a broker's opinion of value called a **Broker Price Opinion (BPO)**. The broker uses recent sales comparables to help determine the subject property's value on the open market, and then provides the BPO amount to the lender for their review. The BPO amount may be used by the lender to select an opening bid price for a trustee's sale (foreclosure) auction.

d. Automated Valuation Model

Automated Valuation Model (AVM): Used by lenders to determine an estimated value for a parcel of real property.

An **automated valuation model (AVM)** uses sales comparables to come up with an estimated value for a subject property. The AVM is commonly used by lenders to determine a ballpark estimate of value for a subject property. Its major drawback is not being able to consider the condition of the subject property.

C. Provide a Real Estate Purchase Agreement and Disclosure Forms

California Association of Realtors (CAR): Industry group of real estate brokers, salespersons, and other affiliate entities.

Real estate agents provide sellers and buyers with real estate contracts and disclosure forms. The most common source of contracts and disclosures forms for real estate agents in California is the **California Association of Realtors** (CAR). Membership in this organization allows real estate agents to electronically access their highly-acclaimed forms that are continually updated in response to changes in the real estate law. This tends to be a very valuable membership benefit; however, there are other sources of real estate contracts and disclosures available in California as well.

CALIFORNIA ASSOCIATION OF REALTORS®

Figure 3.14

All of a real estate agent's services must add up to a *greater overall value* than the 5% or 6% commission being paid by the seller to have the real estate agent list and sell their home. Of course, most property owners have no idea how to sell their own home and tend to rely on the real estate agent to make the home selling process as easy and painless as possible. Therefore, one of the greatest services a real estate agent can provide to a home seller is *expertise in the home selling process.*

Owner-occupied single-family home sellers are paying a real estate agent to "hold their hands" all the way through the transaction. This type of power can cause less scrupulous real estate agents to try to manipulate their clients by pricing the property well under market value to sell it faster, and thus generate faster commission income for the real estate agent. Real estate agents must always remember their fiduciary duty of utmost care, integrity, honesty, and loyalty toward their clients. Thus, there can be a fine line between "consulting" and "manipulating."

Therefore, a real estate agent must provide more benefits (value) than costs to owner-occupied home owners by becoming a consultant and protecting their interests throughout one of the largest financial transaction of their lifetimes. As long as a real estate agent's value in the transaction is more than their cost, there will be a win-win situation for both parties, and this can lead to a successful long-term real estate brokerage career.

(1) Real Estate Investors have Different Needs than Owner-Occupied Homebuyers

Real estate investors are typically much more sophisticated than owner-occupied home owners. Sometimes real estate investors start out as real estate agents, learn the business helping clients buy and sell owner-occupied homes, and then move into property ownership using their commission income to buy real estate near the bottom of a downward-trending buyers' market. Some investors may come from the stock or securities market in which they are moving their capital into tangible real estate assets. Other real estate investors may be from inherited wealth, people with excess capital, and many other areas.

The value a real estate agent provides to real estate investors is *current market knowledge* and *convenience.* This includes research of sales comparables and prevailing capitalization rates for other similar income producing properties. Capitalization rate is the return an investor receives if the investor pays all cash (and no loan) to purchase the property. Capitalization rates are a good indication of current market values for income producing properties because they show what other investors have accepted as the return on similar properties they have purchased. The real estate agent makes it easy for a real estate investor to either sell and cash out (paying all capital gains taxes) or perform an Internal Revenue Code (IRS) 1031 tax-deferred exchange and defer the capital gains taxes into the future.

D. Place the Property on the Market

Once a single-family home has been placed on the market, the listing agent will implement their marketing plan to sell the property. This entails placing the property for sale in the MLS and then begin advertising the property for sale on other advertising mediums. There are three different levels of advertising normally seen in the real estate brokerage business:

Property Marketing: Advertising a property for sale.

Agent Marketing: Occurs when an agent advertises their name toward specific target markets.

Image Advertising: Advertising that promotes a real estate broker's business.

- Real estate salesperson advertising a property for sale. This is called **property marketing** and is advertising that brings in buyers to buy a listed property or may be used to pick up buyers and show them other properties to purchase.
- Real estate salesperson advertising their own name. Prospects call the agent directly to buy or sell a home. This is called **agent marketing** and is an important part of a real estate agent's prospecting activities.
- Real estate brokerage company advertising is for name recognition. This is called **image advertising**.

Advertising must first attract the audience's *attention*, garner *interest*, elicit *desire*, and generate *action* (remember: AIDA). An effective advertising strategy includes determining what has worked in the past and seeing if it is still working today. The best way to track advertising's effectiveness is to ask each prospect how they heard about the real estate agent and save this information in a database.

Misleading Advertising: Advertising that misleads a buyer into thinking a property is in better condition than its present state.

Risks associated with advertising include **misleading advertising**, blind advertisements/blind ads, and a real estate agent breaking a promise to advertise the property.

(1) Misleading Advertising

Advertising cannot mislead a prospective buyer regarding the condition or other facts about a subject property. A "fixer" property should be called a "fixer," and not a "move right in" dream home.

Prima Facie Evidence: Latin meaning first sight, a fact presumed to be true until disproved.

Prima facie evidence means the advertising is presumed either true or untrue (deceptive) unless there is substantial contradictory evidence against the prima facie evidence of deceptive advertising. An example of prima facie evidence of deceptive advertising is when a lender implies any specific yield on a note (promissory note) other than the rate specified in the note.

(2) Blind Advertising/Blind Ads

A **blind advertisement** or **blind ad** does not include the name of the real estate broker who has the property listed for sale. Blind ads are illegal because "agt.", "bro.", "bkr.", or the name of the broker must accompany each advertisement for the sale of real property that is listed for sale by a real estate broker. A real estate broker must disclose in their advertising that the broker is a licensed real estate broker. A blind ad makes the real estate broker appear to be the owner of the property and does not identify the real estate broker as the person who placed the advertising.

> **Blind Advertisement:** An advertisement that does not indicate that a real estate agent is selling the property.

When a real estate salesperson advertises a listed property for sale, it must include the name of the salesperson's real estate broker. The name of the salesperson by itself is not enough to fulfill this legal requirement.

a. DRE License Number

A real estate salesperson must include the broker's name and the salesperson's own DRE license number in most advertising.

According to the DRE, "all first point of contact solicitation materials must include: 1) the name and number of the licensee and 2) the responsible broker's 'identity,' meaning the name under which the broker is currently licensed by the DRE and conducts business in general or is a substantial division of the real estate firm. The broker's license number is optional. There is no longer an exception for advertisements in print or electronic media; or for newspapers and magazines. However, 'for sale,' 'open house,' rent, lease, and directional signs that contain no licensee information or only the broker's information are OK. The purpose of this law is to create uniform advertising standards across a variety of media and types. A licensee must disclose on all solicitation materials intended to be the first point of contact with consumers both their name and license number, and additionally, the solicitation must contain the responsible broker's 'identity,' meaning the name under which the broker is currently licensed by the DRE and conducts business in general or is a substantial division of the real estate firm. (The broker's license number is optional.)"

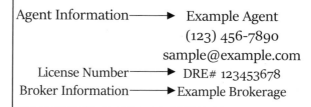

Real Estate Advertisement Example

123 Example Ct

Example, CA 12345

Beautifully updated 3 Bedroom, 2 Bathroom home in a quiet cul-de-sac. This spectacular 1,500 sqft home has a large yard and spacious layout. It is the perfect place to call home!

Agent Information → Example Agent
(123) 456-7890
sample@example.com
License Number → DRE# 123453678
Broker Information → Example Brokerage

Figure 3.15

b. Deceptive Advertising/Deceptive Ad

Broker Baker has a house listed for sale. It does not sell because the house is overpriced, has a leaky roof, and has structural defects. Baker places a newspaper ad that praises the property, does not state a price, and that it is ready to "move right in". This is a deceptive ad because of the work needed. Using the phrase "move right in" when the property is actually a "fixer" is deceptive advertising and may cause the agent (salesperson and broker) to be disciplined by the Real Estate Commissioner and possibly become the defendant in civil litigation brought forth by the buyer.

c. Real Estate Agent Breaks Promise to Advertise

It is illegal for a real estate agent to break a promise to advertise. If an agent promises to advertise a property and then does not do as promised, the agent may be liable for damages under actual fraud.

d. Puffing

Puffing: A statement of opinion that is not taken as a statement of fact.

Puffing is the use of words in advertising that are the broker's own opinion of the property and are not considered statements of fact about the property. For this reason, puffing is *not* illegal.

For example, a real estate agent states that a property is a "big and wonderful home." This is an opinion of the home and is considered puffing and is not illegal. In contrast, the statement, "the home will more than double in value in two years," is a statement of fact and will get the agent into trouble if the property does not double in value in the next two years.

Chapter Three Summary

Real estate prospecting includes psychographics (social media) and geographical farming. Active prospecting and passive prospecting methods are examined in light of what real estate agents may need to provide in today's real estate market. Factors influencing why people buy real estate include price appreciation, leverage, tax shelter, and amortization.

A real estate agent's services must provide more benefits to the seller than the costs of a commission. Agents do this by providing an accurate listing price analysis for a property, real estate contracts and disclosures, placing the property on the market, and advertising the property to fulfill commitments to the seller.

Types of listing agreements include an open listing, exclusive authorization and right to sell listing, exclusive agency listing, net listing, option listing, oral listing, and pocket listing.

Comparative market analyses are discussed along with sales comparables and where to find them. Contracts and disclosures are provided by real estate agents and the property is placed on the market using a marketing plan and different types of advertising.

Chapter Three Quiz

1. Active prospecting methods include:
(A) knocking on doors
(B) open houses
(C) Both (A) and (B) are correct
(D) Neither (A) nor (B) is correct

2. The types of people who live in a neighborhood usually have similar:
(A) income levels
(B) ages and family sizes
(C) reasons for owning a single-family home
(D) all of the above are correct

3. An exclusive right to sell listing agreement is used to ensure the agent is paid a commission if the property sells during the listing period, or after the listing period if a _____ is in effect.
(A) broker's protection clause
(B) safety clause
(C) protection period clause
(D) all of the above are correct

4. An exclusive authorization and right to sell listing agreement is a(n):
(A) unilateral contract
(B) bilateral executory contract
(C) unilateral executory contract
(D) open listing

5. When a real estate agent has an exclusive listing, the agent may be subject to disciplinary action from the Real Estate Commission by:
(A) not giving a copy of the exclusive listing to the seller
(B) not including a definite termination date in the agreement
(C) Both (A) and (B) are correct
(D) Neither (A) nor (B) are correct

6. An _____ is used when a real estate agent lists a property for sale and, at the same time, the agent personally has an option to purchase the property for a specified purchase price and length of time.
(A) oral listing
(B) option listing
(C) exclusive listing
(D) open listing

7. When the real estate agent performs a comparative market analysis (CMA) and provides several recent sales comparables of properties that have recently sold, the agent looks for properties with comparable physical characteristics to the subject property in terms of:
(A) location and age
(B) size and style
(C) amenities
(D) all of the above are correct

8. Lenders may contact a real estate agent and ask for a broker's opinion of value that is called a(n):
(A) broker price opinion
(B) formal appraisal
(C) narrative Appraisal
(D) desk appraisal

9. An automated valuation model is commonly used by lenders to:
(A) find property owners
(B) determine a ballpark estimate of value for a subject property
(C) determine property taxes
(D) pay property taxes

10. The value a real estate agent provides for real estate investors is:
(A) current market knowledge
(B) convenience
(C) Both (A) and (B) are correct
(D) Neither (A) nor (B) is correct

Answers: 1. C, 2. D, 3. D, 4. B, 5. C, 6. B, 7. D, 8. A, 9. B, 10. C

Please use this space for notes.

Alex Delgado

"Real estate practice is not about selling or buying a home. It's about representing your client's greatest asset to your client's greatest benefit."

Chapter
FOUR

Agency Relationships, Ethics, and Fair Housing

1. Agency Relationships

An agent is a person who is licensed as a real estate broker (or licensed real estate salesperson who is working under a licensed real estate broker) and under whose license a listing is executed or an offer to purchase is obtained.

For example, an agency relationship is created when Person A (the principal) gives Person B (the agent) the right to act on Person A's behalf. These acts are generally limited to a special agency of a broker (or, again a salesperson working under a broker) listing a property for sale, finding a buyer, and accepting an earnest money deposit on behalf of the seller. An earnest money deposit is money provided by the buyer to assure the seller that the buyer is in "earnest" and not wasting everyone's time. The agent is employed to find a ready, willing, and able buyer to purchase the property and cannot bind the principal to contracts for the sale of the property.

A buyer is a person who executes an offer to purchase real property from a seller. This may be accomplished through an agent with the object of entering into a real property transaction. Accordingly, a buyer is a person who seeks the services of an agent in more than a casual, transitory, or preliminary manner with the object of entering into a real property purchase transaction.

A. General Agent vs. Special Agent

General Agent: A person who can act for another person for many different tasks.

A **general agent** is a person who has been authorized by the principal to perform many different tasks for the principal. A real estate agent is generally not considered a general agent because the agent is only authorized to perform specific tasks for the benefit of the principal. For this reason, a real estate agent is considered a special agent of the principal.

Special Agent: A person who can act for another person for a specific task.

A **special agent** is a person who has been authorized by the principal to perform specific tasks for the principal (seller or buyer). These tasks may include listing a seller's home for sale, finding a buyer, and accepting an earnest money deposit from the buyer and on behalf of the seller.

B. Warranty of Authority

Warranty of Authority: The principal provides the agent with the authority to find a buyer and accept an earnest money deposit.

The usual listing contract authorizes an agent to find a purchaser and accept an earnest money deposit with an offer to purchase the property. This is called **warranty of authority** because the seller is giving authority to the listing agent (the real estate agent representing the seller, also called the seller's agent) to receive an offer to purchase the listed property from a potential buyer and accept an earnest money deposit from the buyer and on behalf of the seller.

The warranty of authority also provides a selling agent (the real estate agent representing the buyer, also called the buyer's agent) with the authority to find a suitable property for the buyer to purchase. After a contract has been formed between the buyer and seller, the buyer's earnest money deposit check will usually be deposited into escrow. Therefore, a real estate agent is a special agent who has been given a warranty of authority by the buyer to find a suitable property to purchase.

C. Agent Acting in Excess of their Authority

The seller is not liable for the agent's actions if the agent acts in excess of the agent's authority. An agent is a special agent of the principal and has specific authority to list the property for sale, find a buyer, and accept an earnest money deposit from the buyer and on behalf of the seller. If the agent performs actions not under the authority of a special agent, the agent is acting in excess of their authority.

D. Agency Relationships Created

An **agency relationship** can be created by express contract, which includes mutual agreement of the principal and agent, along with an implied agency which includes ostensible agency and agency by ratification. Both express agency and implied agency are considered actual authority.

Agency Relationship: Relationship of trust between a principal and their agent.

(1) Express Agency

The best way to establish an agency relationship and avoid litigation between a principal and an agent is to have an **express agency** that is evidenced by an express contract (oral or written agreement). A written agreement is usually better than an oral agreement because of enforceability under the statute of frauds.

Express Agency: An agency relationship that is expressed either orally or in writing.

(2) Implied Agency

An **implied agency** can be created by the conduct of the parties, oral agreement, or in some cases even a written agreement. When an agency relationship results from the conduct and actions of the parties, even though there is no express agency agreement between the agent and principal(s) in the transaction, this is called ostensible authority. For example, ostensible authority occurs when Seller Able lets Buyer Baker assume that Agent Charlie is Seller Able's agent.

Implied Agency: An agency relationship that is implied by the actions of the parties.

Agency by ratification occurs when a person acts as the agent for a principal without a written authorization to do so, and the principal accepts (ratifies) the agent's actions. This results in an implied agency and is considered ostensible authority given by the principal to the agent.

E. Agency Relationships Terminated

An agency relationship can be terminated by revocation, agreement, death of the agent or principal, destruction of the subject property, and close of escrow.

(1) Revocation

An agency relationship can be terminated by revocation by either the agent or the principal. For example, if an agent gives notice to the principal that the agency relationship is terminated, this will effectively end the agency relationship upon notice to the other party of the termination of the agency relationship.

When an agent has an exclusive authorization and right to sell listing agreement and the principle revokes the agency relationship before the end of the listing period, this will effectively revoke the agreement. However, the agent may be able to sue the

Figure 4.1

TERMINATED

principle for damages caused by termination of the exclusive authorization and right to sell listing agreement prior to its expiration date.

(2) Agreement

An agency relationship can be terminated by agreement of both the agent and principal. For example, the agent and principal both agree that terminating the agency relationship is in the best interests of both parties. They both agree to terminate the agency relationship at the same time.

(3) Death of the Agent

An agency relationship is terminated when the agent dies. All of a broker's listings will automatically terminate with the death of the broker. For example, a real estate broker dies and the broker's daughter (who is a licensed real estate broker) would like to list the properties under her own name. Thus, the daughter would have to list all the properties under her own name because the death of her father canceled all his real estate listing agreements.

(4) Death of the Principal

An agency relationship is terminated when the principal dies. The agent is required to have the heirs sign a new listing agreement to continue marketing the property and be paid a commission when it sells.

(5) Destruction of the Subject Matter

An agency relationship is terminated when a subject property burns to the ground. If there is no longer a house to sell, the subject of the agency relationship is destroyed along with the agency relationship between the agent and principal.

Figure 4.2

(6) Close of Escrow

An agency relationship is terminated at close of escrow. Close of escrow occurs when all the terms and conditions of the escrow have been satisfied.

F. Requirements of an Agency Relationship

An agency relationship requires a fiduciary, legality, and competence of the parties. An agency relationship does *not* require payment of consideration (i.e., bargained for exchange) to create an agency relationship. An agent who acts as an agent (with all the responsibilities and liabilities that go along with being an agent) and is not paid a commission is called a **gratuitous agent**.

(1) Fiduciary Duty

An agency gives rise to a **fiduciary duty** of utmost care, integrity, honesty, and loyalty in the agent's dealings with the principal. This is a higher standard of care than experienced in normal business relationships, and an agent must exercise due care when acting on behalf of the principal.

Fiduciary obligations include truth, confidentiality, competence, trust, and the broker's duty to keep a principal informed. A real estate agent must obey all lawful instructions provided by the principal. If the agent fails to do so, the agent could be liable for all damages or injuries caused by their actions.

For example, a listing agent informed the buyer that the seller will take less money for the property, this is a breach of fiduciary duty to the seller along with being unethical. The agent cannot reveal that the seller will take less money for the property because this knowledge will harm the seller in negotiations with the buyer. Accordingly, an agent may not reveal anything negative about the buyer to the seller. An agent is prohibited from sharing confidential information from one party to the other without the express permission of the client. Confidential information is defined as facts relating to the client's financial position, motivations, bargaining position, or other personal information that may impact price, explicitly including the existing law's restriction against sharing the seller's or buyer's flexibility on price. An agent is prohibited from sharing anything that could harm the buyer or seller in negotiations with the seller.

a. Disclosure of Material Facts

A **material fact** is a fact that if the buyer knew about it, the buyer would most likely not purchase the property. The duty to disclose material facts is a fiduciary obligation and a broker must reveal all material facts to their principal. Examples of material facts include a leaky roof and extensive plumbing repairs. In addition, if an agent has knowledge of a better offer coming in, this is a material fact that must be disclosed to the seller.

A material fact is a fact that may affect or reduce the value of a property. It is a fact that is so important to the buying decision that the buyer probably would not have purchased the property had this fact been known prior to close of escrow. If the seller does not disclose a material fact about a property, a **hold harmless clause** in the listing agreement will hold the listing broker harmless by keeping the liability for nondisclosure solely with the seller. In other words, if the seller misrepresents material facts about a property, the broker is indemnified (held harmless) by the seller and is entitled to receive a full commission.

Gratuitous Agent: Agent who acts as an agent (with all the responsibilities and liabilities that go along with being an agent) and is not paid a commission.

Fiduciary Duty: An agent has a duty of utmost care, integrity, honesty, and loyalty in dealings with the principal.

Material Fact: A fact that will affect the value of a parcel of real property.

Hold Harmless Clause: A clause in a real estate listing agreement that holds the real estate agent harmless for incorrect information provided by the seller.

Tales from the Trade

The Story of the Second Bathroom

A single-family home was being marketed as a 3 bedroom and 2 bathroom home. When the buyer decided to make an offer to purchase the property, the selling agent (agent representing the buyer) discovered that the county tax record database showed 3 bedrooms and only 1 bathroom in the home. This was a red flag for the agent because the second bathroom may not have been permitted when it was added to the home. When there is a discrepancy between the county tax records and the actual property, this is a strong indication of a non-permitted addition that has been built on the property. The agent did some investigating and confirmed that the second bathroom indeed was not permitted. The agent asked the seller if he would be willing to disclose this fact to a buyer. He refused to do so, therefore the agent immediately terminated the listing agreement and each party went their separate ways.

(2) Duty of Honest and Fair Dealing

Duty of Honest and Fair Dealing: An agent owes this duty to other parties in a transaction.

An agent owes a **duty of honest and fair dealing** to other parties in the transaction. This duty is not as high a standard of care as a fiduciary duty but does require the agent to disclose all material facts known about the property. For example, the seller's agent owes a duty of honest and fair dealing to the buyer. This is disclosure of all material facts about the property and may include a leaky roof or extensive plumbing repairs.

(3) Legal Purpose

An agency relationship must be for a legal purpose. For example, if a professional bank robber asks a person to help rob a bank, an agency relationship would not be formed between the parties because the agency relationship is for an illegal purpose.

(4) Competence

Both the principal and agent must *not* have been declared incompetent in a court of law. If either party has been declared incompetent, then an agency relationship will *not* be formed between the parties.

(5) Agency Relationship Does Not Require a Payment of Consideration

Consideration (bargained for exchange or something of value) is not required for a valid agency relationship. As mentioned earlier, when an agent represents a client for free, the agent is called a gratuitous agent.

Even though compensation is not essential to establish an agency relationship, an agent who acts without compensation remains under certain standards of care to the principal. In other words, a gratuitous agent assumes all the liability that comes with being an agent without being paid a commission in return for taking on this responsibility.

G. Subagency

As can be seen in the agency relationship diagram, the buyer and seller are the principals in the agency relationship. The real estate broker is the agent of the principal(s), and the real estate salesperson is the **subagent** of the real estate broker.

A real estate salesperson is required by the DRE to place their license under a real estate broker and the salesperson is *directly responsible* to the real estate broker. A real estate salesperson's listings are the property of the real estate broker who employs the real estate salesperson as a subagent under their real estate broker's license.

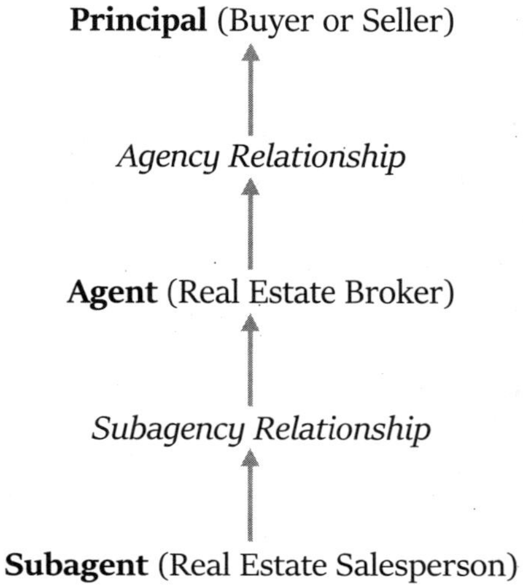

According to the California Civil Code, "subagent" means a person to whom an agent delegates agency power. In other words, a real estate salesperson who is working under a real estate broker is considered the subagent of the principal (buyer and/or seller). Thus, the real estate broker is the agent of the principal and the real estate salesperson is the subagent of the real estate broker.

Principal (Buyer or Seller)

↑

Agency Relationship

↑

Agent (Real Estate Broker)

↑

Subagency Relationship

↑

Subagent (Real Estate Salesperson)

Figure 4.3 Subagency Diagram

A listing broker, along with a listing broker who appoints a subagent (salesperson), owes a fiduciary duty to the seller. This means that a real estate salesperson who is working under a real estate broker has a fiduciary duty to the principal (buyer and/or seller) and to the broker as well.

However, "subagent" does *not* include an associate licensee who is acting under the supervision of an agent (another broker) in a real property transaction. In other words, a real estate broker who is working under another real estate broker is called a **broker associate** or **associate licensee** and is not considered a subagent of the principal. The broker who is working under a broker is considered an agent of the principal and is primarily responsible to the seller.

Subagency: A real estate broker is the agent of the principal. A real estate salesperson who is working under the real estate broker is the subagent of the principal.

Broker Associate/ Associate Licensee: A real estate broker who is working under another real estate broker.

Principal (Buyer or Seller)

↑

Agency Relationship

↑

Agent (Real Estate Broker)

↑

Agency Relationship

↑

Real Estate Broker

Associate Licensee of Real Estate Broker and an *Agent* of the Principal)

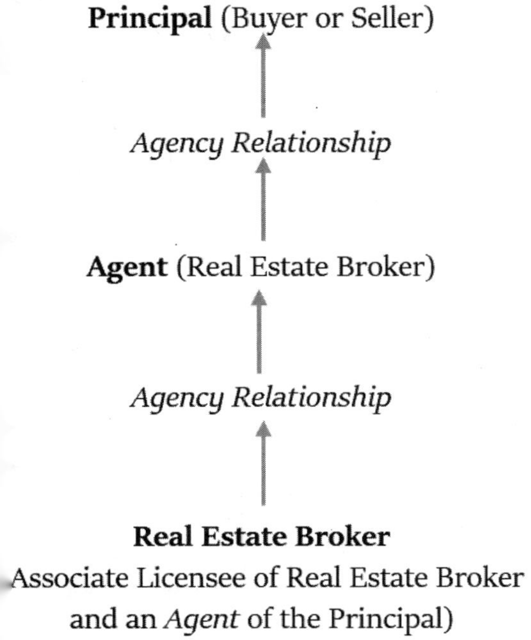

Figure 4.4 Associate Licensee Diagram

An associate licensee has more liability to a principle than a real estate salesperson who is working under a real estate broker. Since the associate licensee is a broker who is working under another broker, the associate licensee has the same duty to the principal (buyer and/or seller), that is *equivalent to the duty owed to that party by the broker for whom the associate licensee functions.* In other words, the associate licensee is a broker working under another broker, and since the associate licensee is a broker rather than a salesperson, the associate licensee has the same obligation to the principal (buyer or seller) as the broker (whom the associate licensee is working under).

(1) Vicarious Liability

Vicarious Liability: A real estate broker is liable for the actions of real estate salespersons who are working under his or her real estate broker's license.

If a real estate salesperson does something unethical, who is liable? The real estate salesperson and the real estate broker. If the real estate salesperson does something wrong, the real estate broker (under whom the real estate agent has placed their license) is also guilty of the infraction through the concept of **vicarious liability**.

When a real estate salesperson does something wrong, the real estate salesperson (who is working under the real estate broker's license) and the real estate broker are *both liable* for these actions under the legal concept of vicarious liability. For this reason, real estate brokers are required to manage and supervise real estate salesperson's who are working under their license.

In other words, anything the real estate salesperson does within the scope of their broker-salesperson agreement while working as a real estate salesperson under a real estate broker, causes the real estate broker to be liable for the real estate salesperson's actions under vicarious liability. For this reason, real estate brokers have the duty to supervise their real estate salespersons and avoid mistakes that will harm both clients and the general public.

Broker
- Liable
- Agent

Salesperson
- Liable
- Subagent

Vicarious Liability

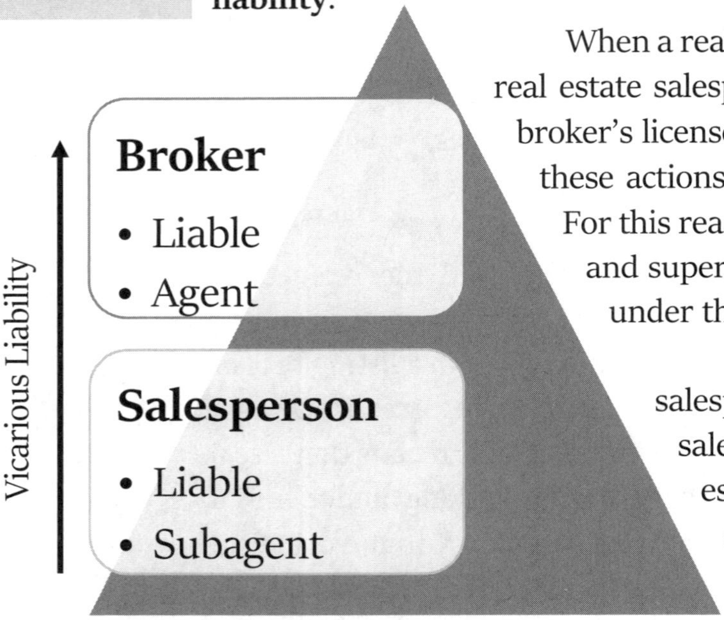

Figure 4.5 Vicarious Liability Diagram

H. Agent of the Seller

A listing agent is the exclusive agent of the seller only. The listing agent must not reveal that the seller will take less money for a property. For example, the listing agent cannot inform the buyer (or selling agent) that the seller is having financial problems, really needs to sell the property, and will accept an offer below list price. This is a breach of fiduciary duty to the seller.

When the agent is the agent of the seller, the agent owes the buyer a duty of honest and fair dealing. This is a lower standard of care than a fiduciary duty, yet it does require the agent to disclose all material facts known about the property to the buyer.

I. Agent of the Buyer

A selling agent is the exclusive agent of the buyer only. The selling agent cannot reveal anything negative about the buyer to the seller. For example, the selling agent cannot reveal to the seller that the buyer is having problems qualifying for a loan–without the express permission of the buyer.

When the agent is the agent of the buyer (selling agent), the agent owes the seller a duty of honest and fair dealing. This is a lower standard of care than a fiduciary duty, however, it does require the selling agent to disclose all material facts known about the property.

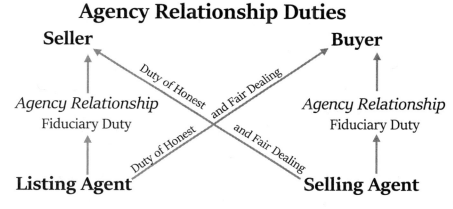

Figure 4.6 Agency Relationship Duties Diagram

J. Dual Agency

Dual agency occurs when an agent represents both the seller and buyer in a real estate transaction. Thus, the agent has fiduciary duties to *both* the seller and buyer and must act with extreme care. Loyalty and confidentiality can easily be compromised for each party under dual agency.

If an agent does not disclose dual agency to both parties in the transaction, the agent may be disciplined by the California Real Estate Commissioner, not receive a commission, and it may be grounds for either party to rescind the contract. Disclosure of dual agency can be accomplished using the Disclosure Regarding Agency Relationship form.

> **Dual Agency:** A real estate broker who represents both the buyer and seller.

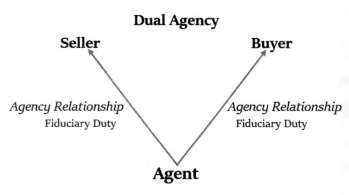

Figure 4.7 Dual Agency Diagram

Tales from the Trade

THE STORY OF DOUBLE DUAL AGENCY

Agent David listed Seller Able's Home (House #1) for sale. Agent David immediately scheduled an open house for the following Saturday afternoon between noon and 3pm. During the open house, Buyer Baker came into the open house, saw the inside of the property, and asked Agent David to represent him and write an offer to purchase House #1.

Agent David now represented both Seller Able and Buyer Baker in the same transaction, so Agent David became a dual agent representing both seller and buyer in the transaction. This is called *dual agency* because the real estate agent is the agent for both the seller and the buyer in the transaction. The agent owes a fiduciary duty of truth, competence, and confidentiality to both the seller and the buyer.

Consequently, Agent David owes a fiduciary duty to both Seller Able and Buyer Baker and will receive a commission for listing House #1 (representing the seller) and a commission for selling House #1 (representing the buyer).

Normally, Seller Able will sign a listing agreement with Agent David specifying the total commission amount to be paid upon the sale of the property (usually collected at close of escrow—with confirmation of recording of the grant deed transferring title from the seller to the buyer). Usually 50% of the commission is paid to the listing broker (seller's agent) and 50% is paid to the selling broker (buyer's agent) at close of escrow.

For example, if the seller agrees to a 5% total commission, then the listing broker will receive a 2.5% commission and the selling broker will receive a 2.5% commission of the sale price. In this instance, Agent David is both the listing agent and selling agent for the property owned by Seller Able. Thus, Agent David will receive a total commission of 5% of the sale price. The commission is 2.5% of the sale price paid to the listing agent (Agent David) and 2.5% of the sale price paid to the selling agent (Agent David) for a total commission of 5%.

Agent David wrote up an offer for Buyer Baker to purchase House #1 and presented it to Seller Able. Agent David had Buyer Baker get pre-approved with a lender to make sure Buyer Baker could qualify to purchase the property. The lender informed Buyer Baker of the need to sell his existing home to be able to qualify to purchase the new home. Buyer Baker then asked Agent David to list his home (House #2) for sale.

Therefore, Agent David listed Seller Baker's home (Buyer Baker is called Seller Baker when selling his existing home—which is House #2) for sale, placed it in the local multiple listing service (MLS), and placed a for sale sign in the front yard.

Buyer Charlie saw the "For Sale" sign at Seller Baker's House #2 and called Agent David to see the inside of the property. Buyer Charlie liked the inside of Seller Baker's property and asked Agent David to write an offer to purchase Seller Baker's House #2.

Agent David was concerned with "double dual agency" because he was representing

THE STORY OF DOUBLE DUAL AGENCY

both buyer and seller in two separate property transactions. A real estate agent is required to disclose dual agency to both the buyer and seller in a real estate transaction. Two separate agency disclosure forms were used with Agent David as dual agent for both transactions.

Time Line

House #1:   Seller Able lists the property for sale with Agent David.
Seller Able is the seller of House #1 and Agent David is the listing agent (broker representing the seller) for House #1.

Buyer Baker asks Agent David to write an offer to purchase House #1. Buyer Baker is the buyer of House #1 and Agent David is the selling agent (broker representing the buyer) for House #1.

House #2:   Seller Baker (who is now selling House #2 and still trying to buy House #1) asks Agent David to list his home for sale.
Seller Baker is the seller of House #2 and Agent David is the listing agent (broker representing the seller) for House #2.

Buyer Charlie (who wants to buy House #2) asks Agent David to write an offer to purchase House #2. Buyer Charlie is the buyer of House #2 and Agent David is the selling agent (broker representing the buyer) for House #2.

Making matters even more confusing for everyone in both transactions, without informing Agent David, the seller of House #1 (Seller Able) moved out of the house prior to close of escrow. In addition, the buyer of House #1 (Buyer Baker) moved out of House #2 and into House #1 prior to close of escrow and did not inform Agent David of their actions. When Agent David discovered what had happened, he informed all parties involved that this was not a smart thing to do. If Buyer Charlie does not close escrow for the purchase of House #2, then both transactions will not go through and the parties will be living in properties they do not own. Fortunately, Buyer Charlie's loan went through and both houses closed on time and on the same day.

(1) Non-Disclosed Dual Agency

An agent may legally represent all principals in the same transaction if it is disclosed that the agent is collecting a commission from each of the principals with the knowledge of the others, the agent obtains the consent of all parties in the agency relationship, and the agent informed all principals that the agent is the agent for each principal. Therefore, non-disclosed dual agency may result in contract rescission, loss of commission, and disciplinary action by the Real Estate Commissioner.

(2) Accidental Dual Agency

Accidental dual agency occurs when a real estate agent acts as an agent for both the buyer and seller in a transaction but does not specifically reveal this fact because the agent is unaware that both consider him their agent.

K. Conflicts of Interest

A real estate agent has a duty not to compete with their principal. This is called a conflict of interest. For example, if a property is offered for sale, the agent must not personally move forward and make an offer to purchase the property when their principal (i.e., buyer) is attempting to purchase the property as well.

L. Agency Disclosure

A real estate agent must disclose as soon as possible who is representing whom in a real estate transaction. This usually occurs when either the seller signs the listing agreement, or the buyer signs the purchase agreement.

The California State Legislature has attempted to codify the Easton v. Strassburger case that was the landmark case that defined agency relationships in California. Many brokers were having a difficult time obtaining errors and omissions (E&O) insurance because of the lack of clarity in the common law (case law) regarding agency relationships and disclosures. The California State Legislature was able to codify and clarify agency relationships in California, thus making E&O insurance easier to obtain for real estate brokers and salespersons in California.

DISCLOSE ASAP

Figure 4.8

Power of Attorney: Legal document that allows one person to act and execute documents for another person.

Attorney-in-Fact: The person who acts and executes documents for another person through a power of attorney.

M. Power of Attorney and Attorney-in-Fact

A **power of attorney** is a written instrument giving authority to a person to act on behalf of another person. The power of attorney allows another person to sign contracts and other duties that are well out of the realm of normal real estate agency relationships. An **attorney-in-fact** is the person who is authorized to act on behalf of another person through a power of attorney.

N. Secret Profit

A **secret profit** occurs when a real estate agent lists a property for sale at a below market price and either personally, or through a family member or friend, purchases the property at the below market list price and then immediately resells the property at the higher market price, thus keeping the profits. Since the real estate agent has a real estate license, the seller is relying on the agent to correctly price the property.

A real estate agent cannot receive a secret profit because it violates the laws of agency and the real estate law. If the real estate agent receives a secret profit, the agent may be subject to disciplinary action by the Real Estate Commissioner, along with a civil suit by the seller.

> **Secret Profit:** Occurs when a real estate broker buys a parcel of real property for less than market value by misrepresenting the value of the property to the seller.

O. Deposits

(1) Authorized to Accept an Earnest Money Deposit

A real estate agent is given the authority to accept an earnest money deposit in the listing agreement. This warranty of authority provides the agent with the authority to place the seller's property on the market and accept an earnest money deposit from a buyer.

The seller usually authorizes in the listing agreement that the agent can accept earnest money deposits on the seller's behalf. If there is no deposit with the offer, the agent must inform the seller of this fact.

(2) Earnest Money Deposit Check

A real estate agent is required to do as the principal instructs and must inform the seller of any earnest money deposit checks that are being held by the agent. This is considered a material fact and must be disclosed to the seller.

(3) Earnest Money Deposit in the Form of a Note

When a buyer uses an unsecured promissory note (similar to an "IOU") as an earnest money deposit in making an offer, the agent should inform the seller that the deposit is in the form of a note before the seller accepts the offer. Forms of earnest money deposits that are legal in California include a promissory note secured by a deed of trust, a postdated check, and an unsecured promissory note.

2. Real Estate Ethics

A. California Real Estate Commissioner

The **California Real Estate Commissioner (Real Estate Commissioner)** is appointed by the Governor of the State of California. The Real Estate Commissioner

> **California Real Estate Commissioner:** Head of the Department of Real Estate who uses an accusation to start a proceeding against a real estate licensee. The Commissioner issues citations and fines for licensed and unlicensed activity.

is head of the California Department of Real Estate and has primary regulatory authority over all real estate salespersons, real estate brokers, lenders, property managers, business opportunities, and subdivision law in the State of California.

The functions of the Real Estate Commissioner include suspending and revoking real estate licenses, issuing **desist and refrain orders** to licensees and subdividers who do not follow the law, and levying fines. The Real Estate Commissioner does not resolve commission disputes. Money disputes are usually decided through either mediation, arbitration, or litigation (civil courts).

Desist and Refrain Order: An order from the California Department of Real Estate directing a person to stop committing an act in violation of the Real Estate Law.

For example, when the Real Estate Commissioner discovers a developer has made certain misrepresentations in the marketing of parcels in a new subdivision, the Real Estate Commissioner can stop future sales by issuing a desist and refrain order. Moreover, a desist and refrain action can be taken by the Real Estate Commissioner to stop a real estate licensee from doing certain acts.

When an agent (licensee) has done something wrong, the Real Estate Commissioner will start an action against the licensee with an accusation. Agents can then plead their case and the Real Estate Commissioner may suspend their license for a certain period of time or revoke it entirely. The Real Estate Commissioner has three (3) years to act on a violation.

The Real Estate Commissioner's regulations require an agreement between a real estate broker and salesperson to be in writing. The broker-salesperson agreement must be kept by both the broker and salesperson for *three years* after cancellation of the agreement. However, the Real Estate Commissioner is *not* required to approve an agreement between a real estate broker and salesperson, it is only required to be in writing.

B. California Department of Real Estate May Dispense Citations and Levy Fines

The California Department of Real estate has wide latitude to address all violations of the real estate law committed by real estate licensees. It also allows action to be taken on the more serious issue of unlicensed activity conducted by persons not licensed by the DRE, yet acting as a real estate broker, salesperson, mortgage loan originator, or prepaid rental listing service. The authority to issue citations and assess fines helps in both obtaining a violator's attention and reinforcing compliance with the real estate law.

A citation or other formal action will be considered when a violation is found after an investigation, audit, or examination of a licensee's records by the DRE in response to a complaint, through random selection of a licensee for an office visit, or from completion of a routine audit.

Depending upon the nature (such as the level of seriousness and potential for harm) and type of violation, the appropriate action will be determined by the Real Estate Commissioner. For example, the maximum fine the Real Estate Commissioner can levy against a broker who, for example, pays an unlicensed person for soliciting borrowers or negotiating loans is $20,000. For relatively minor and technical violations, especially in those instances in which there has been no injury or loss to a consumer or there is little or no danger to the public, a citation is likely the appropriate action.

While the DRE may issue a citation for any violation of the real estate law, citations are particularly suited for minor violations that do not involve fraud, dishonesty, or loss or injury to a consumer.

Consumer protection remains paramount, but citations are especially intended for such minor violations as failure to notify the DRE of one's change in address, failure to disclose a real estate license identification number in their first point of contact advertising material, failure to notify the DRE of newly employed salespersons who were hired and added to office staff, or late or failure to submit required threshold or periodic business activity reports (lending).

Real estate professionals in California are constantly faced with decisions that require ethical and professional responses; and this is not an easy task. Every real estate transaction is unique, and real estate professionals must be "fast on their feet" in order to consummate real estate transactions and institute real estate loans. In so doing, real estate professionals must create transactions that are within an ethical framework.

The Real Estate Commissioner may investigate the actions of any person engaged in the real estate business. The Real Estate Commissioner can temporarily suspend or permanently revoke a real estate license at any time if the licensee is guilty of any of the following:

- Making any substantial misrepresentation. This can be either intentional misrepresentation (fraud or lying) or negligent misrepresentation (agent made an honest mistake and simply missed a material fact that should have been disclosed to the client).
- Making any false promises (i.e., lying).
- A continued and flagrant course of misrepresentation or making of false promises (e.g., a habitual liar).
- Acting for more than one party in a transaction without the knowledge or consent of all parties in the transaction (dual agency).
- **Commingling** clients' monies with the broker's own money, except for $200 the broker can keep in their trust account to cover expenses of the account.

Commingling: Mixing a broker's own funds with their trust account funds.

- Utilizing an exclusive agreement in which the agreement does not contain a definite termination date. In other words, all exclusive listings (exclusive authorization and right to sell listing, exclusive agency listing, and exclusive authorization to locate property agreement) must have a definite termination date. For example, an agent lists a home for sale on July 1st with an exclusive authorization and right to sell listing agreement. The listing ends on September 30th of that same year. This is a three month listing and is legal in California because it is an exclusive listing and has a definite termination date of September 30th.
- The claiming or taking by a licensee of any secret or undisclosed amount of compensation (secret profit).
- The use by a licensee of an option to purchase in an agreement as long as the licensee reveals in writing to the seller the full amount of the licensee's profit and obtains the written consent of the seller approving the amount of such profit.
- Obtaining the signature of a prospective purchaser to an agreement without the agent first having obtained the written authorization of the owner of the property concerned to offer such property for sale, lease, exchange or rent.
- Any other conduct which constitutes fraud or dishonest dealing.

The California Real Estate Commissioner may suspend or revoke the license of a real estate licensee who has done any of the following:

- Procured a real estate license by fraud, misrepresentation, or deceit, or by making any material misstatement of fact in an application for a real estate license.
- Entered a plea of guilty to a crime involving moral turpitude.
- Knowingly authorized the publication of any material false statement or representation concerning the licensee's business, business opportunity, land, or subdivision offered for sale.
- Willfully disregarded or violated the Real Estate Law or the rules and regulations of the California Real Estate Commissioner.
- Willfully used the term "Realtor" or any trade name or insignia of membership in any real estate organization of which the licensee is *not* a member.
- Demonstrated negligence or incompetence in performing any act for which a real estate license is required.
- A broker licensee failing to exercise reasonable supervision over the activities of the broker's agents.
- An agent used his or her employment by a governmental agency in a capacity giving access to records, other than public records, in a manner that violates the confidential nature of the records.

- Engaged in any other conduct which constitutes fraud or dishonest dealing.
- Induced property owners to sell their home because of a loss of value due to an increase in crime or decline of the quality of the schools due to the present or prospective entry into the neighborhood of a person or persons of another race, color, religion, ancestry, or national origin. This is called panic selling (also known as panic peddling) and is illegal.
- Failed to disclose to the buyer of real property the nature and extent of a licensee's direct or indirect ownership interest in that real property.
- Failed to disclose the direct or indirect ownership interest in the property by a person related to the licensee by blood or marriage or by any other person with whom the licensee has a special relationship.

The California Real Estate Commissioner may, without a hearing, suspend the license of any person who procured a real estate license by fraud, misrepresentation, or deceit.

C. Misrepresentation

Misrepresentation occurs when a principal or agent conceals or falsifies the condition and/or other material fact(s) about a property. A material fact is a fact that will affect the value of a property. In other words, had the buyer been aware of the nondisclosed material fact, the buyer would not have purchased the property. A leaky roof and extensive plumbing repairs are examples of material facts that are required by law to be disclosed to real estate buyers. There are two categories of misrepresentation: intentional misrepresentation and negligent misrepresentation.

> **Misrepresentation:** A false or misleading statement or assertion.

Figure 4.9

Misrepresentation

TYPE	DESCRIPTION
Intentional	Intentionally lying. • Actual Fraud: agent purposefully makes an untrue statement that detrimentally affects the principal • Negative Fraud: intentional nondisclosures of a material fact
Negligent	Honest mistake that causes a client harm.

> **Intentional Misrepresentation:** Occurs when a real estate agent (or principal) intentionally misrepresents information. It is also called fraud.

(1) Intentional Misrepresentation

Intentional misrepresentation of a property is considered fraud and illegal. Fraud is merely a nice word for lying. For example, if the seller and seller's agent are aware that the property being sold has a leaky roof and neither the seller nor the seller's agent disclose this fact to the buyer, this is concealment of a material fact. The intentional concealment of material facts is considered intentional misrepresentation (fraud).

There are two types of intentional misrepresentation: actual fraud and negative fraud.

a. Actual Fraud

Actual Fraud:
Intentional misrepresentation of a fact about a parcel of real property. As opposed to negligent misrepresentation which is an honest mistake.

Actual fraud occurs when the agent (or principal) purposefully makes a statement that is not true and this detrimentally affects the buyer or seller in a real estate transaction. For example, when an agent crosses out items in a contract without the approval of the buyer and seller, this is considered actual fraud. An agent may not cross out items in a contract without buyer and seller consent, thus the buyer and seller are the only parties who can change items in a contract and both must agree to do so.

Negative Fraud:
Intentional nondisclosure of a material fact.

b. Negative Fraud

Intentional nondisclosure of a material fact is called **negative fraud**. A broker cannot remain silent when a material fact is only known to the broker. Non-disclosure occurs when an agent and/or principal does not disclose material facts that are important to the purchase of real property. In other words, had the buyer been aware of the nondisclosed material fact(s), the buyer may not have gone forward with the property purchase.

(2) Negligent Misrepresentation

Negligent Misrepresentation:
Unintentionally misrepresents information (i.e., an honest mistake).

When a real estate agent (or principal) makes a mistake that causes someone harm, this is considered **negligent misrepresentation**. The difference between negligent misrepresentation and intentional misrepresentation is that negligent misrepresentation is an honest mistake, while intentional misrepresentation is intentionally lying.

Negligent Advice:
Incorrect information given when knowledge of the circumstances should have been within the agent's diligent observation.

a. Negligent Advice

Considering the normal education and training that goes into being a real estate agent, an agent must not give **negligent advice** to clients. If knowledge of the circumstances should have been within the agent's diligent observation, then the agent may be guilty of negligence.

False Promise: Agent makes a promise that influences a person to enter into a transaction, and then does not fulfill that promise.

D. False Promise

When an agent makes a promise that influences a person to enter into a transaction, and then does not fulfill that promise, this is called a **false promise**.

Examples of false promises include an agent's promise to advertise and does not do so, and an agent breaking a promise to find a person a home.

(1) Promise to Advertise

If an agent makes a promise to a seller to advertise their property for sale, the agent must follow through with the promise and advertise the seller's property for sale. Otherwise this is considered a false promise.

(2) Agent Breaks Promise to Find Home

If an agent breaks a promise to find a client a home, this is considered a false promise. Of course, there are many other real estate agents who are more than willing to take care of this problem for the client—and earn a nice commission in the process.

Figure 4.10

3. Fair Housing

A. Federal Fair Housing Laws

(1) Civil Rights Act of 1866

The **Civil Rights Act of 1866** was enacted just after the end of the American Civil War and gave all citizens in the United States the right to purchase, rent, sell, hold, and convey all (residential and commercial) real property and personal property without regard to race. In addition, all persons have the right to contract, sue, be sued, and enjoy the full benefits of the law.

> **Civil Rights Act of 1866:** A civil rights act that was passed in 1866 and largely ignored for over 100 years.

According to the Civil Rights Act of 1866, "All persons within the jurisdiction of the United States shall have the same right in every State and Territory to make and enforce contracts, to sue, be parties, give evidence, and to the full and equal benefit of all laws and proceedings for the security of persons and property as is enjoyed by white citizens, and shall be subject to like punishment, pains, penalties, taxes, licenses, and extraction's of every kind, and to no other."

The Civil Rights Act of 1866 gave all citizens in the United States the right to purchase real estate. It also gave everyone in the United States the right to enjoy the full benefits of the law. However, this act was largely ignored in the courts during the more than one hundred years from 1866 to 1968.

(2) Federal Fair Housing Act (Civil Rights Act of 1968)

The **Federal Fair Housing Act/Civil Rights Act of 1968** prohibits discrimination in the:

> **Federal Fair Housing Act/Civil Rights Act of 1968:** Landmark federal fair housing law that prevented discrimination in housing.

- sale
- rental
- advertising
- offer of brokerage services
- loans
- appraisal services

Discriminatory actions based on a person's:

- race
- color
- religion
- sex
- marital status
- national origin
- handicap

U.S. Department of Housing and Urban Development (HUD): Federal department over the Federal Housing Administration (FHA).

A person who has been a victim of discrimination may file a complaint with the **U.S. Department of Housing and Urban Development**. The statute of limitations (how long a person has to bring action) is one year from the time of the discriminatory act.

An agent may not discriminate in the sale or rental of a residential dwelling. Therefore, an agent may not:

- refuse to sell or rent for discriminatory reasons
- evict a tenant for discriminatory reasons
- use different qualification criteria for selling or purchasing a residential dwelling
- impose different sale or rental charges for discriminatory reasons
- use different terms, conditions, and privileges in the sale or rental of residential dwellings
- perform differing maintenance activities for certain persons
- limit use of common areas or facilities to certain persons
- refuse to provide service due to a person's refusal to provide sexual favors

Steering: The act of steering a buyer out of one neighborhood because of racial considerations.

Panic Selling: Occurs when an agent induces or attempts to induce a person to sell or rent their real property because of the entry of a certain class of people (e.g., race or religion) into the neighborhood.

Blockbusting: The result of panic selling is blockbusting. Both are illegal.

a. Steering, Panic Selling, and Blockbusting

An agent may not steer a person into or out of a residential neighborhood or community in an attempt to segregate housing patterns. This is called **steering** and is both discriminatory and illegal.

An agent may not induce or attempt a person to sell or rent their real property because of the entry of a certain class of people (e.g., race or religion) into the neighborhood. This is called **panic selling** and **blockbusting.** The act is called panic selling and the result is called blockbusting. Both panic selling and blockbusting are illegal.

(3) Americans with Disabilities Act of 1990, Title III

The **Americans with Disabilities Act of 1990, Title III (ADA)** was enacted to prohibit discrimination against people with disabilities. A disability is a physical or mental condition that limits a person's normal life activities. Public and private buildings must be built or altered to comply with ADA. A person who discriminates against a person with a disability may be liable for civil damages up to $50,000.

The Americans with Disabilities Act covers most commercial buildings and requires building owners to remove all architectural and communicative barriers that will impede reasonable access to any facility. However, the building may be exempted from this law if it can be shown that upgrading the building to ADA standards would be a disproportionate cost to the overall alteration.

Figure 4.11

Americans with Disabilities Act of 1990: A federal fair housing law that prohibits discrimination against people with disabilities.

Equal Credit Opportunity Act (ECOA): Federal law that prohibits discrimination in lending.

(4) Equal Credit Opportunity Act

The **Equal Credit Opportunity Act (ECOA)** is a federal law that prohibits discrimination in lending. Lenders (creditors) are prevented from doing the following:

- Discourage anyone from applying because of their sex, marital status, age, race, national origin, or because they receive public assistance income.
- Ask an applicant to reveal their sex, race, national origin, or religion. A lender may ask an applicant to voluntarily disclose this information (except for religion) if the person is applying for a real estate loan. This information helps federal agencies enforce anti-discrimination laws.
- Ask if a loan applicant is widowed or divorced. When permitted to ask marital status, a lender may only use the terms: married, unmarried, or separated.

- Ask about a loan applicant's marital status if they are applying for a separate, unsecured account. A creditor (lender) may ask the applicant to provide this information if they live in "community property" states such as California. A creditor in any state may ask for this information if the applicant applies for a joint account or one secured by property.
- Request information about a loan applicant's spouse, except when the spouse is applying for the loan with the applicant; the spouse will be allowed to use the account; the applicant is relying on the spouse's income or on alimony or child support income from a former spouse; or if the applicant resides in a community property state.
- Inquire about the loan applicant's plans for having or raising children.
- Ask if the loan applicant is receiving alimony, child support, or separate maintenance payments, unless the applicant is first informed that they do not have to provide this information if they are not relying on this information to get credit. However, a creditor (lender) may ask if the applicant is required to pay alimony, child support, or separate maintenance payments.

(5) Home Mortgage Disclosure Act

Home Mortgage Disclosure Act: An Act that requires lenders to disclose home loan information to the public.

The **Home Mortgage Disclosure Act** requires lenders to disclose home loan information to the public. Public data is important because it helps to show whether lenders are serving the housing needs of their communities; they give public officials information that helps them make decisions and policies; and they shed light on lending patterns that could be discriminatory.

Figure 4.12

The Home Mortgage Disclosure Act includes anyone making home loans, including state and federally regulated banks. Lenders must disclose:

1. Type and purpose of the loan
2. Whether it is an owner-occupied or investor loan
3. Income of the loan applicant
4. Amount of the loan
5. Sex and race of the loan applicant

a. Advertising Guidelines

An agent may not use advertising that discriminates in the sale or rental of real property. It is discriminatory to use words or phrases that request a particular buyer or tenant. Words such as "white", "black", "single", etc. are discriminatory. However, advertising that requests people who are 55 years of age or older is not discriminatory. This is many times used in adult housing communities.

Use of the U.S. Department of Housing and Urban Development's (HUD) Equal Housing Opportunity logo is a good way to advertise that the agent does not use discriminatory practices in their business. Next is a look at the California state fair housing laws.

B. California State Fair Housing Laws

There are several important fair housing laws that have been enacted in the State of California. They include the California Fair Employment and Housing Act (Rumford Act), Unruh Civil Rights Act, Ralph Civil Rights Act, California Housing and Financial Discrimination Act (Holden Act), and California Department of Real Estate regulations.

(1) California Fair Employment and Housing Act (Rumford Act)

The **California Fair Employment and Housing Act (Rumford Act)** prohibits harassment and discrimination in housing because of a person's race, color, religion, sex, gender, gender identity, gender expression, sexual orientation, marital status, national origin/ancestry, familial status (households with children under age 18), source of income, disability, genetic information and/or retaliation for protesting illegal discrimination.

> **California Fair Employment and Housing Act (Rumford Act):** State housing act that prohibits discrimination in housing in California.

a. Department of Fair Employment and Housing and the Fair Employment and Housing Commission

The Department of Fair Employment and Housing (DEFH) and the Fair Employment and Housing Commission receive complaints concerning fair housing laws in California. The mission of the Department of Fair Employment and Housing is to protect Californians from employment, housing and public accommodation discrimination, and hate violence. The DFEH is the largest state civil rights agency in the country and enforces the Rumford Act.

Other actions that are in violation of the California Fair Employment and Housing Act include a broker:
- Refusing to represent a minority person
- Asking about a prospective client's race, color, sex, religion, disability, national origin, or ancestry

- Placing advertising under discriminatory conditions

1. Boarders

An owner renting out a room in a single-family dwelling occupied by the owner is exempt from fair housing laws. Therefore, an owner who is renting out one room (where he or she lives) to a **boarder** is exempt from the act. A boarder is someone who lives in a property and pays for their room and board, hence the name "boarder."

Boarder: A person who is living inside someone's home.

(2) Unruh Civil Rights Act

Under the **Unruh Civil Rights Act**, all persons are entitled to full and equal

Figure 4.13

accommodations, advantages, facilities, privileges, or services in business establishments, including both private and public entities. The Unruh Civil Rights Act protects all persons against arbitrary and unreasonable discrimination by a business establishment and on the basis of race, color, religion, sex, gender, gender identity, gender expression, ancestry, national origin, physical or mental disability, medical condition, genetic information, marital status, or sexual orientation.

In cases alleging an Unruh Civil Rights Act violation, complaints must be filed with the Department of Fair Employment and Housing within one year from the date of the alleged discriminatory act. In cases alleging hate violence, complaints must be filed within one year of the day the victim becomes aware of the perpetrator's identity, but not more than three years from the date of injury.

Unruh Civil Rights Act: State housing act that prohibits discrimination in business establishments in California.

Ralph Civil Rights Act: California state law that prohibits violence or threats of violence based on an individual's race, color, religion, etc.

(3) Ralph Civil Rights Act

The **Ralph Civil Rights Act** (hate violence) prohibits violence or threats of violence based on an individual's race, color, religion, sex, gender, gender identity, gender expression, ancestry, national origin, physical or mental disability, medical condition, genetic information, marital status, or sexual orientation.

Specific violence or threats include: threats, both verbal and written; physical assault or attempted assault; hate-related graffiti, including offensive symbols; cross-burning; bomb threats; arson; disturbance of religious meetings; and vandalism or property damage.

(4) Housing Financial Discrimination Act (Holden Act)

The **Housing Financial Discrimination Act**, also known as the **Holden Act**, was an attempt by California to prevent discrimination in lending. The Holden Act states that a loan cannot be denied to an applicant based upon race, color, religion, marital status, sex, ancestry, and national origin. The Holden Act was enacted in response to discrimination in lending practices in California.

Lenders, realizing a higher foreclosure rate in urban areas where most minority owners reside, decided to curtail loans in these areas. They placed a red line (circle) around the areas the lender did not want to make loans to, thus coining the term "**redlining**." Redlining is illegal. The Holden Act placed restrictions on this practice by making it illegal to consider the racial, ethnic, religious, or national origin composition of trends in neighborhoods surrounding a housing accommodation.

Lenders cannot refuse a loan to a creditworthy borrower based upon the demographics of the neighborhood. They also cannot refuse a loan based upon a much lower appraisal of the property than in neighborhoods not composed predominantly of non-minority residents.

> **Housing Financial Discrimination Act (Holden Act):** State housing act that prohibits discrimination in lending in California.
>
> **Redlining:** Occurs when a lender uses a red pen or pencil and draws a circle around areas where the lender does not want to make loans.

(5) Disabled Persons have Full Use of Public Places

All disabled individuals are entitled to full and equal use of streets, highways, public places of accommodation (e.g., hotels, schools, medical facilities, telephone, etc.), and modes of transportation (e.g., buses, airplanes, trains, etc.). This law also protects a disabled person's right to be accompanied by a guide dog, signal dog, or service dog in any of these places.

(6) Death Disclosure

If a person died in a property, it must be disclosed to buyers and tenants for up to three years from the time of death. However, if the occupant died as a result of AIDS, the reason for the death (i.e., AIDS) does *not* need to be disclosed by the seller. In other words, the death must be disclosed, but the death caused by AIDS does not have to be disclosed to a buyer or tenant. If, however, the buyer or tenant asks the agent a direct question whether the person who died in the property died from AIDS, the agent must disclose the fact that the occupant died from AIDS.

(7) California Department of Real Estate (DRE)

The California Department of Real Estate (DRE) prohibits discrimination by real estate brokers. Discriminatory practices include:

- Discouraging a client from purchasing or renting a property because of the client's race, national origin, sex, etc.
- Discriminating in management of properties
- Limiting use of Multiple Listing Services
- Refusing to accept a listing, sale, or loan because of discriminatory reasons

The Real Estate Commissioner has enacted regulations prohibiting real estate brokers and their salespeople from any practice that discriminates against anyone based on race, color, sex, ancestry, religion, disability, marital status, or national origin.

Chapter Four Summary

Real estate agents represent principals under the authority of a special agency relationship. Agents are provided a warranty of authority that allows them to sell a property for the seller, find a buyer, and accept an earnest money deposit from the buyer. Agency relationships provide for a fiduciary duty between the principal and agent. The agent can represent the seller only, buyer only, or both buyer and seller at the same time, this is called dual agency. In addition, the agent has a duty of honest and fair dealing toward other parties in the transaction. An attorney-in-fact is established by a power of attorney that may allow the attorney-in-fact to convey the property. This is unlike an agency relationship that merely authorizes the agent to list the property for the seller, accept a deposit on behalf of the seller, or work with a buyer to find a suitable property to purchase.

The second part of the chapter discusses real estate ethics. The California Real Estate Commissioner has the authority to suspend and revoke real estate licenses when a real estate agent is guilty of making both intentional and negligent misrepresentations, including false promises, commingling trust funds, using exclusive listings without a definite termination date, making secret profits, fraud, misrepresentation, deceit, and crimes involving moral turpitude. In addition, real estate brokers must adequately supervise their salespersons.

The last part of the chapter discusses federal and state fair housing laws. Federal fair housing laws include the Civil Rights Act of 1866, Federal Fair Housing Act/Civil Rights Act of 1968, American's with Disabilities Act of 1990, Equal Credit Opportunity Act, Home Mortgage Disclosure Act, and advertising guidelines. The California state fair housing acts include the California Fair Employment and Housing Act (Rumford Act), Unruh Civil Rights Act, Ralph Civil Rights Act, Housing Financial Discrimination Act (Holden Act), the California Department of Real Estate's prohibition of discriminatory acts.

Chapter Four Quiz

1. An agency relationship can be terminated by:
(A) revocation
(B) agreement
(C) death of the agent or principal
(D) all of the above are correct

2. If the seller misrepresents material facts about a property, the broker is _____ by the seller and will receive a full commission.
(A) indemnified
(B) held harmless
(C) Both (A) and (B) are correct
(D) Neither (A) nor (B) are correct

3. Which of the following is correct?
(A) The real estate broker is the agent of the principal and the real estate salesperson is the subagent of the real estate broker
(B) The real estate salesperson is the agent of the principal and the real estate broker is the subagent of the real estate salesperson
(C) The real estate broker is the subagent of the real estate salesperson and the real estate salesperson is agent of the principal
(D) The principal is the agent of the broker

4. Non-disclosed dual agency may result in:
(A) contract rescission
(B) loss of commission
(C) disciplinary action by the Real Estate Commissioner
(D) all of the above are correct

5. _____ occurs when a real estate agent acts as an agent for both the buyer and seller in a transaction but does not specifically reveal this fact because the agent is unaware that both consider him their agent.
(A) Accidental dual agency
(B) Gratuitous agency
(C) Single agency
(D) Secret profit

6. The Commissioner can temporarily suspend or permanently revoke a real estate license at any time if the licensee is guilty of:
(A) making any substantial misrepresentation
(B) intentional misrepresentation (fraud or lying)
(C) negligent misrepresentation
(D) all of the above are correct

7. The California Real Estate Commissioner can suspend or revoke a real estate license if the licensee is guilty of:
(A) making false promises (i.e., lying)
(B) a continued and flagrant course of misrepresentation or making of false promises (e.g., a habitual liar)
(C) acting for more than one party in a transaction without the knowledge or consent of all parties in the transaction (dual agency)
(D) all of the above are correct

8. The Commissioner can revoke a real estate license if a licensee is guilty of:
(A) commingling clients' monies with the broker's own money
(B) utilizing an exclusive agreement in which the agreement does not contain a definite termination date
(C) claiming or taking by a licensee of any secret or undisclosed amount of compensation (secret profit)
(D) All of the above are correct

9. An owner renting out a room in a single-family dwelling occupied by the owner:
(A) is required to follow fair housing laws
(B) is exempt from fair housing laws
(C) must run a criminal background check
(D) must run a credit report

10. If a person died in a property, it must be disclosed to buyers and tenants for up to _____ years from the time of death.
(A) two
(B) three
(C) four
(D) five

Please use this space for notes.

Russell Sage

"Real estate is an imperishable asset, ever increasing in value. It is the most solid security that human ingenuity has devised. It is the basis of all security and about the only indestructible security."

Chapter
FIVE

Property and Estates in Land

After the real estate listing agreement has been signed by the seller and real estate agent, the agent will place the property on the market. The agent may help the seller prepare the property for sale by giving helpful suggestions regarding furniture, property staging, etc. In addition, the real estate agent will usually place a "For Sale" sign in the front yard of the property, place a Multiple Listing Service (MLS) lockbox (with a set of door keys inside the box) onto the outside of the house, and enter the listing into the Multiple Listing Service.

It is important to note that face-to-face time in front of the client is when a real estate agent is actually performing tasks that will directly produce commission income. Activities away from the client are support activities to help the agent perform during the face-to-face meetings.

Real estate is a large, complex, and emotional purchase that takes time and effort on the part of both principals and agents. Accordingly, showing properties to buyers is one of the critical tasks performed by real estate agents. Assisting buyers get inside a prospective property is where the agent becomes invaluable to the client. The seller must trust the buyer's agent to allow the agent to bring the buyer into their home. This trust is ensured by a real estate license (with background checks) and membership in the local multiple listing service (MLS) that allows agents to access lockboxes that contain the keys to sellers' homes.

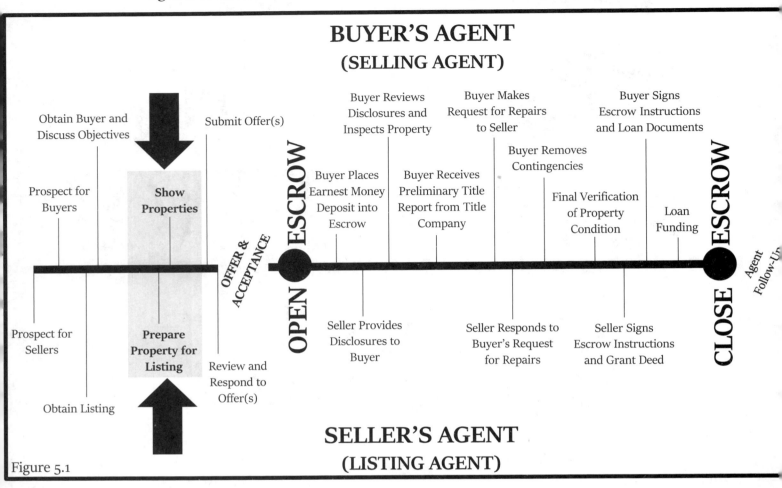

BUYER'S AGENT
(SELLING AGENT)

Obtain Buyer and Discuss Objectives

Submit Offer(s)

Buyer Reviews Disclosures and Inspects Property

Buyer Makes Request for Repairs to Seller

Buyer Signs Escrow Instructions and Loan Documents

Prospect for Buyers

Show Properties

Buyer Removes Contingencies

Buyer Places Earnest Money Deposit into Escrow

Buyer Receives Preliminary Title Report from Title Company

Final Verification of Property Condition

Loan Funding

OFFER & ACCEPTANCE

OPEN ESCROW

CLOSE ESCROW

Agent Follow-Up

Prospect for Sellers

Prepare Property for Listing

Seller Provides Disclosures to Buyer

Seller Responds to Buyer's Request for Repairs

Seller Signs Escrow Instructions and Grant Deed

Obtain Listing

Review and Respond to Offer(s)

SELLER'S AGENT
(LISTING AGENT)

Figure 5.1

Real Property: Land, anything attached to the land, and anything appurtenant to the land. It is immovable and usually transferred with a deed.

Personal Property: Anything not real property. It is movable and usually transferred with a bill of sale.

Understanding the differences between **real property** and **personal property** is extremely important for real estate agents who are in the real estate brokerage business. It is the real estate agent's duty to identify real and personal property in the home and address these items in both the listing agreement and purchase agreement. In other words, the agent must determine which items will stay with the home and which will go with the seller. By determining the items that are real property (immovable) and will stay with the home, the agent will avoid misunderstandings between the buyer and seller when the property closes escrow and title is transferred to the buyer. Items that usually go with the seller are movable and are considered personal property.

For example, a single-family home is attached to a concrete foundation and is considered real property. However, a portable microwave oven that is sitting on the kitchen counter is movable and considered personal property. In California, real property is usually conveyed with a grant deed and personal property is conveyed with a bill of sale. Thus, the single-family home will be conveyed with a grant deed, while the portable microwave oven can be conveyed with a bill of sale.

Estates in land are ownership interests in land and are important because the agent must understand what type of interest is being transferred. For example, a landlord who owns the real property has a freehold estate in land. This is the highest form of ownership in land. However, a tenant may own a less-than-freehold estate (also called leasehold estate) that is merely possession of the property for a short period of time. The landlord's freehold estate in land is considered real property and is transferred with a grant deed. In contrast, the tenant's less-than-freehold/leasehold estate is considered personal property and is evidenced by a lease or rental agreement.

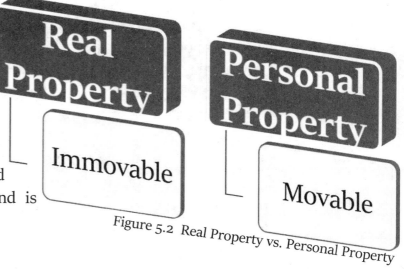

Figure 5.2 Real Property vs. Personal Property

1. Real Property

According to English common law, which is derived from court cases, the word property refers to an owner's rights and interests in the thing owned. Rights in real property are referred to as a "**bundle of rights**" and include the right to: use, possess, encumber, transfer, and exclude a thing. It infers the right to occupy and use; to transfer by contract for a specific period of time (lease); place a loan against the property; to sell in whole or in part; and, implies the right to not take any of these actions.

> **Bundle of Rights:** Rights in real property that include the right to: use, possess, encumber, transfer, and exclude a thing.

A property owner's bundle of rights is limited by the sovereign powers of the state, which include the government's power of taxation (taxes are always paid first, with property taxes paid before federal and state income tax), eminent domain (the government takes the owner's property, but must pay fair market value to the owner), police power (for safety, health and general welfare of the public, such as zoning and building codes), and the right of property to escheat (revert) to the State of California in the event the owner dies without a will and leaves no heirs.

Areas of concern regarding property ownership include the land, anything affixed to the land, and anything appurtenant or incidental to the land.

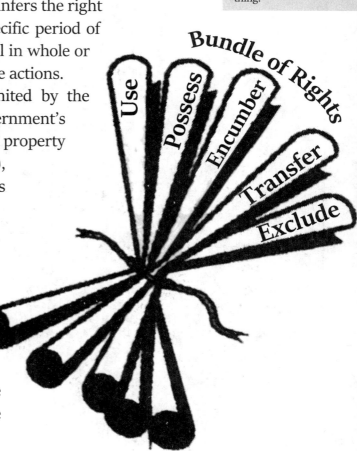

Figure 5.3 Bundle of Rights Illustration

A. Land

Land includes soil, rocks, and other substances that compose the earth. It also includes the space below the surface all the way to the center of the earth, as well as the airspace above the earth (at least as much as a property owner can reasonably use). However, the courts have recognized a public right to use the airspace above real property (e.g., aircraft flight paths) if the use does not unreasonably interfere with the landowner's enjoyment of the property.

In addition to air rights, the courts recognize the fluid nature of subsurface gas and oil and a property owner has the right to drill vertically to capture these substances. However, an adjoining landowner (i.e., next door neighbor) does not have the right to drill slantwise to capture a neighbor's subsurface gas or oil.

A real estate agent, buyers, and sellers should consider not only the surface area, but also the area underneath the surface, and the airspace above the surface of the land when considering real property.

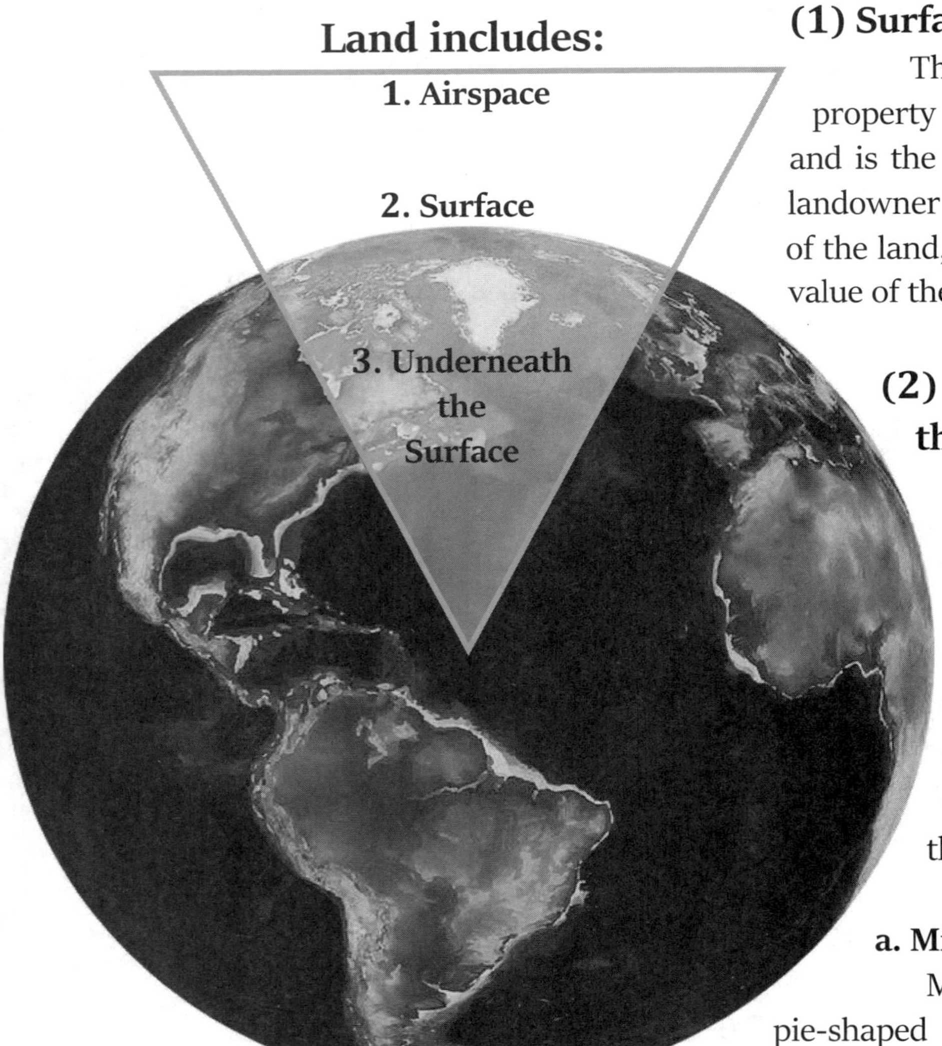

Land includes:

1. Airspace

2. Surface

3. Underneath the Surface

(1) Surface of the Land

The surface of the land between the property lines is considered real property and is the most useful for development. A landowner may build a home on the surface of the land, thus increasing the usability and value of the property.

(2) Area Below the Surface of the Land

A property owner owns the area below the surface of the land all the way down to the center of the earth. This is an inverted pie shape in which the point is at the center of the earth and the wide portion of the pie shape is at the top of the useable airspace above the earth.

a. Minerals

Minerals that occupy the inverted pie-shaped area between the surface and center of the earth are part of the land and are

Figure 5.4 Illustration of Land Components

considered real property. If this area contains minerals such as gold or silver, they are owned by the landowner. However, if a previous owner reserved the mineral rights for him or herself, then the present owner of the parcel would not own the mineral rights. They will continue to be owned by the previous property owner.

The fact that a property's mineral rights have been reserved in the past will usually be indicated in a preliminary title report that is normally received by the buyer (and buyer's agent) when there is a signed contract and escrow has been opened by the buyer and seller for the purchase of the property. The buyer's agent should read the preliminary title report and confirm the buyer is aware of any reserved mineral rights that are lying under the surface of the subject property.

Reserving mineral rights has been a fairly common occurrence in California subdivisions. Home buyers are usually interested in a home to live in and not in mining the minerals located under the surface of the land. For this reason, reservation of mineral rights typically has not had much of an impact on the desirability and value of real properties in California.

b. Oil and Gas Rights

Oil and natural gas rights are treated like minerals rights. Oil and natural gas lying under a person's property are considered real property and will normally be transferred to the buyer. However, if a previous owner reserved these rights in the past, the new owner may not own the rights to the oil and natural gas under the surface of the land. Oil and natural gas are fluid by nature and sometimes neighbors who own the parcel of land next to the property (adjoining lot), may be able to drill straight down into the oil and gas and remove it from the ground.

(3) Airspace Above the Surface of the Land

The airspace above the surface of the land is considered real property. However, this is restricted to the amount the property owner can reasonably use. For example, a property owner may be able to place a HAM radio antenna on the roof of the home to enhance reception. However, the owner may not be able to fly a drone up into the airspace above the property where airplanes take off and land at a local airport.

a. Drones

Drones can be used for personal and commercial use. One homeowner in Kentucky saw his neighbor's drone flying above his home looking at his garden and his daughter. The irate homeowner grabbed a shotgun and blasted the $1,800 drone out of the sky. The drone's owner filed suit in Federal Court arguing that the homeowner's actions were not justified since the drone was not trespassing on his land or invading anyone's privacy.

The drone owner stated that his drone was flying at about 200 feet above ground level for around two minutes when it was destroyed by a shotgun blast. The height at which the drone was flying is disputed as the shotgun toting homeowner insists it had to be much lower to be in "shotgun range." This is an integral part of the legal case because higher airspace used by commercial planes is clearly defined in the law and is not considered part of someone's property. Reasonable use of airspace above a person's home has been left to the courts to determine on a case-by-case basis.

Tales from the Trade

THE STORY OF A CHANGE IN FLIGHT PATHS

The flight paths for a local airport were changed and now fly across Homeowner Fred's land. The jet engines are extremely noisy and significantly reduce the value of Homeowner Fred's property.

When an appraiser appraises Homeowner Fred's property to determine an opinion of value, the appraiser will consider the value of the property before and after airplanes started flying over it and compare the two values to derive the amount of loss in value caused by the new flight path over Homeowner Fred's land. This loss of value is called economic obsolescence. Economic obsolescence is anything that is outside the property line that causes a loss in value. In this case, the flight path is above the area that Homeowner Fred could reasonably use, so it is not part of the land and is not considered real property. However, it is detrimentally affecting the value of Homeowner Fred's property.

In response, Homeowner Fred could institute an inverse condemnation action against the local government that changed the flight paths and devalued Fred's home. An inverse condemnation action forces the local government to buy Fred's home for its fair market value *before* the planes started flying over his property.

B. Anything Affixed to the Land

Buildings, trees, or anything permanently affixed to the land are all considered real property. Real property is *immovable* and includes houses and items permanently attached to a house, such as a built-in microwave oven, kitchen cabinets, and other items that are permanently affixed to the house. In contrast, personal property is defined as items that are *movable* and are not permanently attached to the house.

(1) House

The most important thing that is attached to the land is a house. It provides one of the basic necessities for human survival: shelter. Homeowners have a means to protect their family from the elements and external threats, along with the financial stability, social status, and prestige of owning a home. This makes the home buying process as much emotional as it is rational.

a. Traditional Architectural Styles in California

Some architectural styles commonly seen in California include small California Spanish, Monterey Spanish, and California bungalow or ranch house.

- **Small California Spanish:** stucco exterior, flat composition roof with mission tile trim in the front; suitable for small lots, no patio, and only one story.
- **Monterey Spanish:** two stories, stucco (generally white), red mission tiled roof, second story balconies, and decorative iron railings.
- **California Bungalow or Ranch House:** one story, stucco with wood trim, often on concrete slab, shingle or shake roof, low and rambling, generally attached garage, and indoor/outdoor living areas.

b. Architectural Styles of Newer California Homes

Some newer homes built in California may have a more modern contemporary style with many windows and an open floorplan.

- **Contemporary Architectural Style:** an architectural style with many windows and an open floor plan is called **contemporary**. Generally, a modern one story, usually flat or low-pitched roof, often on a concrete slab, large amount of glass, and indoor/outdoor living.

> **Contemporary Architectural Style:** Some newer homes built in California may have a more modern contemporary style with many windows and an open floorplan.

c. Other Architectural Styles

There are several other architectural styles that are less common in California, yet prevalent throughout the rest of the United States. These include: Colonial, including Cape Cod Colonial, Cape Ann Colonial, New England Colonial, Dutch Colonial, Georgian, and Southern Colonial; English Elizabethan, English Half-Timber; Regency; French Provincial; French Normandy; and True Spanish.

(2) Fixtures

A **fixture** is personal property that is incorporated into the land and becomes real property. Kitchen cabinets and a built-in microwave oven are generally considered fixtures and, therefore, real property because they are attached to the house. However, if a microwave oven is sitting on top of a kitchen counter (instead

> **Fixture:** Personal property that is incorporated into the land and becomes real property.

of being built into the cabinets) it will probably be considered personal property because it is movable.

The tests for a fixture include: **M**ethod of attachment, **A**daptability or annexation, **R**elationship of the parties, **I**ntent, and **A**greement. A good way to remember the tests for fixture is the acronym MARIA.

Tests for a Fixture	
M	Method of Attachment
A	Adaptability or Annexation
R	Relationship of the Parties
I	Intent
A	Agreement

Figure 5.5 Tests for a Fixture

a. Method of Attachment

Method of attachment is the method a property is incorporated into the land. The degree of permanence is important to its classification as a fixture. Therefore, an item of personal property that is attached by concrete is probably classified as a fixture, and thus real property.

For example, a property owner purchased a hot tub and used concrete to attach it to the backyard of his home. This shows a degree of permanence and will most likely make the hot tub a fixture and, therefore, real property. The reason this differentiation is important is because a hot tub that is attached to the land will be conveyed with the property by a grant deed. In contrast, a hot tub that is sitting on the ground in the backyard and is not attached to the land by concrete does not indicate permanence and will most likely be considered personal property. Personal property is transferred

Figure 5.6 Kitchen Cabinets

with a bill of sale.

This is important to real estate agents because items of personal property and real property should be classified at the time the property is listed for sale.

b. Adaptability or Annexation

Personal property that is attached to the land and is being used as an ordinary use in connection with the land is usually considered a fixture. A house key is a good example of annexation because it is an object used in connection with the home and is considered real property.

c. Relationship of the Parties

The relationship between the person who placed the item on the property and the person who disputes its classification is another important test in determining whether an item is a fixture. Since the buyer–seller relationship is adversarial in nature, the buyer's agent should specify in the purchase agreement whether possible disputed items are real or personal property.

For example, a buyer purchased a single-family home that had a very nice bookcase partially attached to the family room wall. The buyer and seller must agree whether the bookcase is considered a fixture and real property or is classified as personal property. However, their relationship is that of buyer and seller they may each have a different perception of whether an item normally will stay in the home and benefit the buyer (i.e., a fixture and considered real property) or go with the seller to their new home (i.e., not a fixture, and considered personal property).

d. Intent

Intent is the most important test for a fixture. If a seller's intent is that an item is considered personal property and will go with the seller to their new home when the property is sold, and the buyer's intent indicates that the item is considered real property and will stay with the property, then the buyer's and seller's intents are in conflict and the only answer is what is specified in the purchase agreement.

For example, a seller installed window coverings in the master bedroom of a home. The valances match the bedspread. However, because window coverings (e.g., drapes and blinds) are attached to the house by a curtain rod, they are considered fixtures and therefore, real property. They should stay with the house and benefit the buyer. Yet, in this case the valances match the bedspread (personal property) and the seller will most likely take the window valances (attached to the home) with the bedspread to their new home. The real estate agent should specify in the listing agreement whether the valances are going to stay with the property (i.e., a fixture and considered real property), or go with the seller (i.e., not a fixture and considered personal property).

e. Agreement

When there is a clear agreement between the buyer and seller as to whether an item is considered a fixture (and therefore, real property), there should not be a dispute whether an item is real or personal property.

Understanding fixtures is critical to the real estate brokerage business. For example, a real estate agent is listing a home for sale and the home has an heirloom chandelier hanging in the formal dining room. How should the real estate agent handle the conveyance of this item with the home?

The heirloom chandelier is attached to the home and is considered real property. However, the seller will most likely take the chandelier when he or she leaves the property after close of escrow. The seller may not understand that the heirloom chandelier is considered real property, so it will be disconnected from the ceiling and the only thing the buyer will see when moving into the home is three wires hanging down from the ceiling. The buyer may have believed the chandelier went with the property because it was attached to the ceiling when the property was sold. This can lead to misunderstandings and potential litigation after the sale between the buyer and seller, along with the real estate agent(s) who should have specified in the purchase agreement that the heirloom chandelier was personal property and will be going with the seller to their new property.

(3) Naturally Occurring Vegetation and Trees in Nature

Fructus Naturales: Naturally occurring vegetation and trees in nature.

Naturally occurring vegetation and trees in nature are called **fructus naturales**. They are considered real property because they are attached by a root system to the land. When vegetation and trees are severed (i.e., cut off from their root system) they become personal property because they are movable.

For example, a naturally occurring Ponderosa pine tree is considered a fructus naturales and real property because it is immovable and part of the land. However, when a timber crew cuts the tree down and loads it onto a logging truck, the logs on the logging truck are considered personal property because they are movable and are no longer attached to the land.

Figure 5.7 Vegetation

a. Vegetation

Natural vegetation that is attached to the land through a root system is considered real property.

b. Deciduous Trees vs. Coniferous Trees

Deciduous trees are trees and other plants that lose their leaves during the Fall (Autumn) of each year. An example of a deciduous tree is an oak tree because it loses its leaves in the Fall. In contrast, coniferous trees (such as Ponderosa pine trees) lose their leaves (pine needles) all year round.

(4) Fructus Industriales (Planted Trees and Crops)

Planted trees and crops are called **fructus industriales** and are considered real property because they are attached by a root system to the land.

For example, a seller of a parcel of real property would like to harvest an existing corn crop after the sale of the property but does not state this intention in the purchase agreement. In this case, the corn will transfer with the property as real property and will now be owned by the buyer.

a. Emblements

In another example, a growing crop is called an **emblement** and is considered real property because it is attached to the soil by a root system. Emblements are growing crops that grow from annual cultivation (e.g., wheat crop) rather than from fruit trees or timber that have permanent root systems. Once the crop is harvested (severed) from the land, it becomes personal property because it is movable. However, there is an exception to every rule.

When growing crops (both emblements and fruit attached to fruit trees) are sold, the **Doctrine of Constructive Severance** allows a landowner to sell growing crops (e.g., a wheat crop) while still attached to the land. When this occurs, the growing crops (wheat crop) are considered personal property even though they are still attached to the land. Accordingly, apples on an apple tree can be sold while they are still attached to the apple tree. When this happens, the growing crops (apples) are considered personal property, even though they are still attached to the tree.

C. Anything Appurtenant to the Land or Incidental to the Land

An **appurtenance** is anything that is used with the land and for its benefit. Hence the name, "runs with the land." Examples of appurtenances include easements, water company stock, riparian water rights, and covenants, conditions, and restrictions (CC&Rs).

(1) Easements

An **easement** is the right to use someone else's land. There are generally three major types of easements: appurtenant easements, prescriptive easements, and easements in gross. Appurtenant easements run with the land and are considered real property. All three easement types are discussed in Chapter 7.

Fructus Industriales: Planted trees and crops that are considered real property because they are attached by a root system to the land.

Emblements: Growing crops that grow from annual cultivation (e.g., wheat crop) rather than from fruit trees or timber that have permanent root systems.

Doctrine of Constructive Severance: Allows a landowner to sell growing crops as personal property while they remain attached to the land.

Appurtenance: Runs with the land and is considered real property.

Easements: The ability of a person or entity to use another person's land.

a. Appurtenant Easement

When one property owner has the right to use another property owner's property, this is called an **appurtenant easement**. For example, Owner Able owns Parcel A and Owner Baker owns Parcel B. Parcel A has an appurtenant easement over Parcel B. This easement benefits Parcel A because it allows the owner of Parcel A to use Parcel B's land. The easement is appurtenant to Parcel A and must stay with that parcel. If owner Able decides to sell Parcel A to a new owner, the easement will stay with the property (runs with the land). Owner Able cannot take the easement with him when he leaves the property. The new owner and any future owners of Parcel A will continue to enjoy the rights to use Parcel B.

In the above example, Owner Able owns Parcel A. Parcel A is the **dominant tenement** (as shown in the recorded title to Parcel A), so whoever owns Parcel A has the authority to drive over (use) Parcel B. Parcel B is called the **servient tenement** and the servient tenement must allow the dominant tenement to use their land and this fact is recorded in the title to Parcel B. So, whoever buys Parcel B in the future must allow the owner of Parcel A to drive over (use) their land. Appurtenant easements are commonly used to allow one property owner to drive over another property owner's property out to a public road.

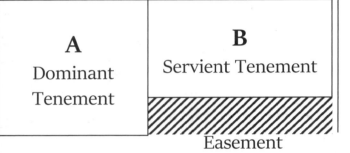

Figure 5.8 Appurtenant Easement Diagram

(2) Covenants, Conditions, and Restrictions

Covenants, conditions, and restrictions (CC&Rs) are used to restrict the use of real property. Violating a covenant is a minor breach of a promise. Violating a condition is a major breach that may result in loss of title to the property. Restrictions are private deed restrictions that limit the use of a property. CC&Rs are discussed in Chapter 7.

(3) Stock in a Mutual Water Company

Water users may organize a mutual water company to secure an ample water supply at a reasonable cost. In most cases, the stock is made appurtenant to the land; that is, each share of stock is attached to a specific parcel of land and cannot be sold separately. Therefore, when a seller sells a property that has water company stock appurtenant to it, the water company stock automatically transfers to the buyer because it runs with the land.

Moreover, a mutual water company is a corporation or nonprofit organization that is owned by the stockholders (homeowners) and used to obtain water for their own use. Each property owner owns stock in the mutual water company. The stock is appurtenant to the land (runs with the land) and is considered real property. If a property owner does not pay for water that is used, the mutual water company can place a lien against the property for the amount due. The major benefits of a mutual water company are reduced costs and a steady supply of water for the stockholders' properties.

a. Riparian Water Rights and Littoral Water Rights

Riparian water rights allow a parcel that is adjacent (abuts) to a river, stream, or watercourse to use as much water as can reasonably be used by the property owner. Riparian rights run with the land and are considered real property.

Littoral water rights allow a parcel that is adjacent to a pond, lake, or ocean to use as much water as can reasonably be used by the property owner. Littoral rights run with the land and are considered real property.

b. Doctrine of Appropriation

Riparian water rights allow the property owner to "appropriate" as much water as can reasonably be used from an adjacent river, stream, or watercourse; or littoral water rights allow the property owner to appropriate water from an adjacent pond, lake, or ocean. In contrast, the **Doctrine of Appropriation** allocates water to property owners who are *not* located adjacent to a river, stream, watercourse, pond, lake, or ocean and do not have the resulting riparian or littoral water rights.

The Doctrine of Appropriation allows non-riparian and non-littoral landowners (i.e., landowners who are not located adjacent to a stream or lake) to receive an allocation of water from the local watershed. For example, the State of California may give permission to a non-littoral owner of a farm to use a nearby lake to water the owner's crops. The property owner has received this right through the Doctrine of Appropriation that provides for a way to take water by appropriation.

Prior appropriation of water rights is ranked by priority of time of use and purpose for the use of the water. Therefore, when a property owner is not adjacent to a river, stream, or watercourse, the owner will obtain water through the Doctrine of Appropriation. This is accomplished by applying to the State Division of Water Resources.

(4) Other Water-Related Issues
a. Surface Waters, Percolating Waters, and Artesian Waters

Surface waters in California percolate back into the water table when they drain down into the soil on their way back to the Pacific Ocean. Percolating waters

Riparian Water Rights: Property owner can reasonably use water from a river, stream, or watercourse adjacent to a parcel of land.

Littoral Water Rights: Similar to riparian water rights, except it is for a pond, lake, or ocean.

Doctrine of Appropriation: The ability of a property owner who does not have riparian or littoral water rights to receive water that is appropriated (allocated) by the local water company.

drain down into the soil, but not through a defined channel. Separately, artesian waters are waters that seep from the ground from an unknown source.

b. Wells

Rural properties commonly use a **well** for their water supply. A well-driller drills down to below the water table and installs a system that pumps the water up to the surface for domestic use.

Figure 5.9 Well

Packa/Wikimedia Commons

1. Draw Down Test

It is usually a good idea for rural single-family homes with an existing well to have a draw down test performed during the due diligence period prior to close of escrow. A draw down test determines the number of gallons of water per minute the well can pump out of the ground. It is determined by pumping the well dry and then observing how long it takes for the water to replenish. If the well does not replenish itself fast enough, the homeowner may want to consider installing a pressurized holding tank on the well. The county where the property is located may require a pressurized holding tank installed on wells that produce less than a minimum number of gallons per minute. If there is a loan being used to purchase the property, a pressurized holding tank may be a loan condition that must be completed prior to loan funding and close of escrow.

2. Potability Test

A **potability test** is performed to verify well water is suitable for drinking. A lender may require the buyer to obtain a sample of the well's water and place it in a small plastic bag that is similar to a zip-lock sandwich bag. The owner sends it to a lab to look for harmful bacteria and other microorganisms existing in the water. A copy of the potability report is usually provided to the buyer and lender. If the well water contains any dangerous microorganisms, the lender will most likely not fund the loan until the water is made safe to drink. This type of due diligence on the lender's part may save the homebuyer from buying a home with a defective well.

In contrast, most urban properties use water supplied through a public utility or private utility with water lines running to the home from a main water line usually located under the street in front of the property.

c. Public Water System/Public Water Service

Builders like to build new homes on vacant lots that are serviced by a public water system. Even though there may be connection fees, which are costs the builder pays to connect to the public water supply, it is generally less risky than drilling a well. Wells have the uncertainty of depth, cost, finding water, water quality, and the need of a pressurized holding tank.

1. Water Meters

Water meters measure a property's water usage from public or private utilities and bill the owner accordingly. Water meters are a normal occurrence in California and nonpayment of water bills will result in a lien being placed on the property. Of course, as soon as a homeowner receives the water (meter) bill from watering a luxurious front yard during the month of August, this may trigger a decision to change the landscaping to a more "low maintenance desert-style motif."

d. Waste Disposal

Many rural properties use a septic system to hold and dispose of liquid and solid waste products. In contrast, urban properties commonly utilize a sewer system that carries the liquid and solid waste products from the home to a sewer line (normally located under the road in front of the property), then to a sewage treatment plant, and then out to the watershed that flows back to the ocean.

Septic System/Septic Tank: Installed in rural areas to trap solid wastes and allow gray water to percolate back into the watershed.

Leach Field/Leach Lines: Horizontal lines buried underneath the ground that allow gray water to percolate back into the water table.

1. Septic System/Septic Tank

A **septic system** is used for sewage disposal in rural areas where there are no sewer lines. The system usually consists of a **septic tank** that holds solid waste materials that must be pumped out on a periodic basis. Liquid waste materials, on the other hand, move through the septic tank into the leach field beyond.

The leach field is comprised of either **leach lines** or dry wells that allow the liquid waste materials to percolate back into the soil and make their way through streams and rivers back to the

Figure 5.10 Septic System

129

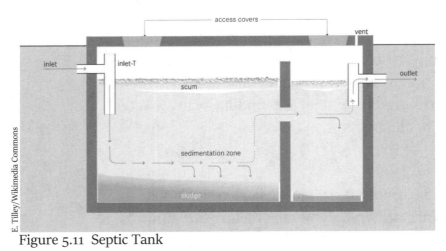

E. Tilley/Wikimedia Commons

Figure 5.11 Septic Tank

ocean.   Leach lines are usually approximately 100 feet in length and run horizontally about six feet beneath the surface of the ground. In contrast, dry wells usually run straight downward perpendicular to the earth's surface. Most houses that use a septic system have at least two leach lines or dry wells to dispose of liquid waste products.

2. Percolation/Percolation Test

Percolation:
Determines how fast water percolates back into the soil and whether a parcel of real property can be used for a septic tank and leach field.

Percolation occurs when surface water is absorbed back into the soil. Hydraulic engineers perform a percolation test (also called "perc" test) to determine the ability of the ground to absorb and drain water.   This is especially important when trying to determine whether a site is suitable for a septic tank. Therefore, a percolation test is a test used to determine whether a property is suitable for the construction of a septic tank. Percolation relates to the water table, while a percolation test relates to septic tanks.

For example, when a person owns a vacant parcel of land and would like to build a single-family home on it, the person may decide to obtain a perc test prior to purchasing the property. A perc test is performed by a professional perc tester who digs a hole where the septic tank will be located on the vacant parcel of land, fills it up with water, and then tries to determine how long it will take for the water to "percolate" back into the soil. If the water does not percolate back into the soil at a fast-enough rate, the property owner will not be able to get a building permit to build a single-family home on the vacant parcel. If the water does percolate back into the soil within a reasonable length of time, then the property owner may be able to get a building permit and build a single-family home on the property.

Existing homes may already have a septic tank installed on the property, so a septic tank inspector is used to perform either a visual inspection or a full inspection of the septic system. The visual inspection is less expensive than a full inspection and does not inspect areas of the septic tank that cannot be easily observed.   In contrast, a full inspection is performed at the time the septic tank is pumped out. The inspector can see the entire inside of the tank and determine its overall condition. After pumping out the septic tank, the owner will usually place yeast in the tank to help the deterioration of solid waste materials in the future.

One problem that may arise when a septic tank needs to be pumped out is to determine where the septic tank lid or lids are located. Septic tanks usually have one or two lids that can be accessed from the surface of the ground. If the homeowner is not aware of a lid's location, the septic inspector may be able to research the county records in the county where the property is located and find a schematic that will reveal the location of the lid(s).

3. Sewer

Most urban properties have a sewer system that carries both solid and liquid waste products through a high-pressure line from the property to a waste disposal facility. The liquid waste is then treated and released back into the local watershed system.

For example, Seller Able accepted an offer from Buyer Baker to purchase a single-family home. Before the contract was formally accepted, Buyer Baker made inquiries and was assured the property was connected to a sewer line. The contract was accepted, but escrow had not yet closed when Buyer Baker discovered that there was not a sewer connection, but that a new septic tank had been recently installed on the parcel. Buyer Baker could rescind the contract/back out of the contract before close of escrow. Since the septic tank was discovered *before* close of escrow, the buyer may rescind the contract. However, if it had been discovered *after* close of escrow the buyer would be required to use the civil courts to obtain restitution for the loss.

Furthermore, it is important to know that a **soil pipe** runs from the bathroom(s) in a home out to the septic tank or sewer line. It is commonly called a sewer lateral in the building trades.

Soil Pipe: Sewer line between the house and main sewer line (usually in the street).

Chattel Real: Personal property located on a parcel of real property.

2. Personal Property

An item that is *immovable* is considered real property. In contrast, if the item is *movable* it is considered personal property. For example, a portable microwave oven that sits on the kitchen counter and is movable is considered personal property. However, a built-in microwave oven that is installed into the kitchen cabinetry is immovable and is considered real property.

Personal property that goes with a parcel of real property is called a chattel. **Chattel real** is all personal property that goes with an estate in land. Everything that is not real property is considered a chattel and is, therefore, personal property.

Figure 5.12 Movable Microwave

Some items of personal property that may be conveyed with the real property include a(n): refrigerator, washer, dryer, and unattached (freestanding) microwave oven. These items can be conveyed separately with a bill of sale; or if they are being conveyed with "no value," they may possibly be included in a provision of the real estate purchase agreement.

A. Bill of Sale

Bill of Sale: Used to transfer personal property.

A **bill of sale** is used to transfer personal property. A bill of sale can be witnessed or acknowledged (notarized) to prove its validity. The required elements for a valid bill of sale include:

- Names and addresses of both buyer and seller
- Description of the property being sold
- Price paid (i.e., consideration given or received)
- Date of the sale
- Seller's signature

Tales from the Trade

The Story of the Potted Plants

One seller had many potted plants sitting on her patio. After close of escrow the buyer wanted to know why the plants were gone. He was informed that the potted plants were movable and were considered personal property. The seller was able to take the potted plants to her new home and there was nothing contractually the buyer could do about it.

Additionally, the same seller covered up and did not disclose a large hole in the door between the kitchen and garage. This was a serious safety issue because the door is a fire door and is designed to keep fire from moving from the garage into the living space of the home. The agent was concerned with the safety of the buyer and immediately filled in the hole. The agent made sure the nondisclosure of the hole in the door by the seller would not cause harm to the buyer.

The same seller unscrewed an attached bookcase and took it with her to her new property. The bookcase was attached to the wall and therefore considered real property. It should have stayed with the property. The seller was in breach of contract when she took the bookcase to her new home.

B. Mobile Homes and Manufactured Homes

Mobile Home: Portable home on wheels that was built *before* July 15, 1976.

Both mobile homes and manufactured homes are built at a factory and transported to a location where they are hooked up to utility services such as electricity, water, and a sewer line or septic system. Mobile structures of this nature that were built before July 15, 1976 are called **mobile homes**. In contrast, mobile structures that were built on or after July 15, 1976 are called **manufactured homes**.

Manufactured Homes: Portable home on wheels that was built *on or after* July 15, 1976.

Mobile homes and manufactured homes that are placed in a mobile home park or manufactured home park and are sitting on the ground (not attached to the ground), are considered personal property. A real estate agent can list and sell personal property mobile homes and manufactured homes that have been registered with the California Department of Housing and Community Development.

Mobile homes and manufactured homes that are *not* registered with the California Department of Housing and Community Development cannot be sold by a real estate agent but must be sold by a person who has a mobile home dealer's license (the mobile home dealer's license is good for manufactured homes as well). The mobile home dealer's license can be used to sell either new or registered mobile homes and manufactured homes.

A real estate agent can list and sell a new or used mobile home or manufactured home that is attached to the land because it is considered real property (immovable). If the mobile home or manufactured home is sitting on wheels on the parcel of land, a real estate

Figure 5.13 Mobile Home

agent can sell the personal property mobile home or manufactured home (whether new or used) along with the vacant land because the land is being conveyed with a deed for real property. A deed is used to transfer real property and is used when purchasing a parcel of land. In other words, a real estate agent can sell a new or used mobile home or manufactured home that is sold with a deed.

C. Trade Fixtures

Trade Fixtures: Items used in the course of trade that are attached to real property and are considered personal property.

As mentioned earlier, fixtures are personal property that is incorporated into the land and become real property. **Trade fixtures** are an exception to this rule. Trade fixtures are items that are attached to the real estate but are used in the course of trade (by a business) and are therefore considered personal property.

For example, metal shelves are used in retail stores to display merchandise and are bolted to the walls of the store. When the tenant moves their business to another location, the tenant can remove these shelves from the wall and take them to their

Figure 5.14 Retail Shelves as Trade Fixtures

new location. Even though they are attached to the wall, they are considered trade fixtures and are personal property.

Moreover, if the tenant sells the business, the trade fixtures (that are attached to the wall of the retail space) are considered personal property and are conveyed with a bill of sale.

3. Ownership Interests in Land: Estates in Land

Freehold Estates: Highest form of ownership in land and is comprised of fee simple and life estates.

Less-than-Freehold (Leasehold) Estate: A tenant's right to occupy real estate during the term of the lease.

Freehold estates originally came from England many years ago. When the King of England wanted outlying lands protected from conquest, he appointed someone of good fighting ability to pledge his allegiance to the King in return for ownership of the lands. The new landowner was called a "freeman" and, therefore, held title as a freehold estate in land. All the other people living on the new landowner's property were called tenant farmers and held **less-than-freehold estates**, also called leasehold estates, that were merely possession of real property for a very short period of time.

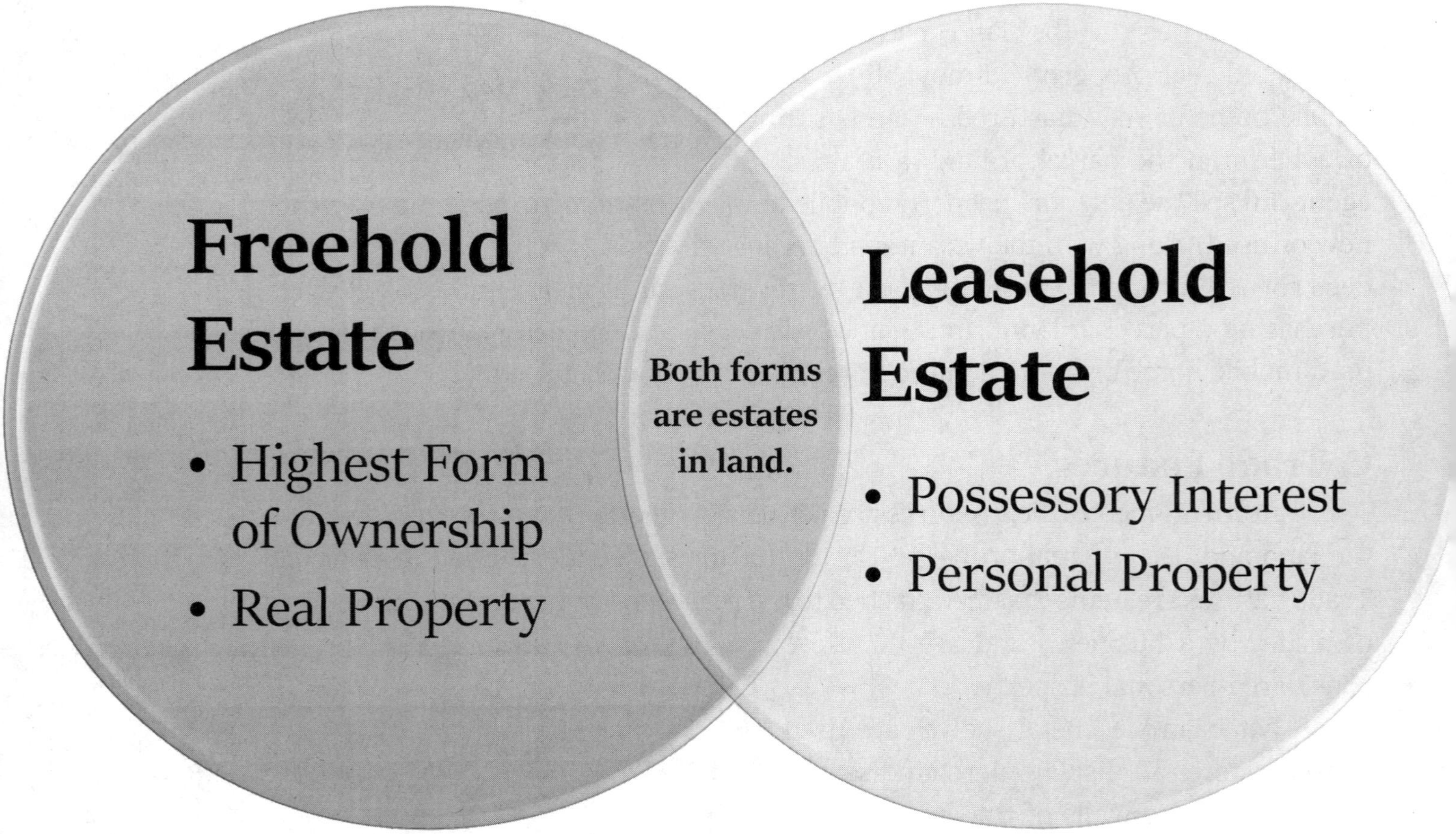

Freehold Estate

- Highest Form of Ownership
- Real Property

Both forms are estates in land.

Leasehold Estate

- Possessory Interest
- Personal Property

Figure 5.15 Freehold vs. Leasehold Estate Venn Diagram

FREEHOLD	LEASEHOLD

• Fee Simple
  • Fee Simple Absolute
  • Fee Simple Defeasible
• Life Estate
	• Estate for Years
	• Estate from Period-to-Period/Periodic Tenancy
	• Estate at Will
	• Estate at Sufferance/Tenancy at Sufferance

Figure 5.16 Freehold vs. Leasehold Estate

A. Freehold Estates

There are two major types of freehold estates: fee simple estates and life estates. **Fee simple estates** are the highest form of ownership, of indefinite duration, can be willed (estate of inheritance), and are the greatest interest a person can own in land. In contrast, while **life estates** are considered freehold estates, they are only for the duration of a person's life.

> **Fee Simple Estate:** Highest form of ownership of real property.
>
> **Life Estate:** Freehold estate for the life of the owner or a designated person.

(1) Fee Simple Estates

With fee simple estates there are several rights that come into existence:

- **Of indefinite duration**. The ownership interest continues for an indefinite period of time. Therefore, the period of ownership is not a set amount of time but continues indefinitely.
- **Can be willed (estate of inheritance)**. The ownership interest can be willed to the owners' heirs and to their heirs, on down through the generations. The fee simple estate can be willed to heirs, or to any devisee (person who receives real property by will) the freehold owner would like to receive it.
- **Greatest interest a person can own in land**. Fee simple estates are the highest form of ownership a person can have in land.

There are two types of fee simple estates: *fee simple absolute* and *fee simple defeasible*.

a. Fee Simple Absolute

A **fee simple absolute estate** is the highest form of ownership recognized by law. The owner has the entire *bundle of ownership rights* (the right to use, possess, encumber, transfer, and exclude a thing) without any restrictions. The

> **Fee Simple Absolute:** No conditions on the title to the real property.

term "fee" denotes the highest form of ownership and is commonly seen in preliminary title reports and policies of title insurance. Since a fee simple estate is an estate of indefinite duration and can be willed, it is also called an estate of inheritance. Other names used to describe fee simple absolute title to real property include estate in fee and fee estate.

b. Fee Simple Defeasible

Fee Simple Defeasible: An estate in fee subject to the occurrence of a condition subsequent whereby the estate may be terminated.

If a fee simple absolute owner places a restriction on the use of a property and then disposes of the property by sale, will, or gift; the new owner has taken **fee simple defeasible** title to the property. Fee simple defeasible title is also called fee simple qualified or a condition subsequent. The name "fee simple defeasible" came about because the title to the property can be "defeated." Accordingly, a condition subsequent is a condition placed on the title to real property so that if a specific thing occurs in the future, this will cause the property owner to lose the title to the property.

For example, an oil company owns two parcels of land located on two diagonal corners of a major road intersection. Parcel A and Parcel B. The oil company would like to sell Parcel B and keep Parcel A to sell gasoline and operate a convenience store. The oil company does not want a competitor to come in and either buy or lease Parcel B. The oil company sells Parcel B to Buyer Baker and includes a condition subsequent that prohibits Buyer Baker (and/or any tenant renting the property from Buyer Baker or any subsequent owners) from ever using Parcel B to sell gasoline and/or operate a convenience store.

Buyer Baker has taken fee simple defeasible title to Parcel B. If Buyer Baker (or a tenant or future owner) uses the property to sell gasoline and/or operate a convenience store, they will have breached a condition in the title to Parcel B and could be forced to either stop using the property to sell gasoline and/or operate a convenience store or sell the property back to the oil company.

A condition must be contained in the deed that transfers title to real property. Thus, the grant deed (the most common type of deed used to transfer real property in California) will most likely contain a condition on the title that prevents the owner from using the property to sell gasoline and/or operate a convenience store.

(2) Life Estate

The second type of freehold estate is a life estate. This type of freehold estate allows a person to enjoy all the benefits of freehold ownership, but only for their lifetime or the lifetime of another person. The holder of a life estate can rent, sell, or encumber a property. However, the holder of a life estate cannot will (devise) it to their heirs. To devise is to leave real property by will.

a. Example #1: Estate in Reversion vs. Estate in Remainder

Aunt Alice owns a property and gives a life estate to her son Charles for his lifetime. When Charles dies, title to the property will either revert to Aunt Alice (**estate in reversion**) if she is still alive or, if Aunt Alice has already died, then it will pass to Cousin Carl (**estate in remainder**). Cousin Carl is called the remainder person. A life estate is a way for a person to direct who gets their property both during their lifetime and long after they have passed.

> **Estate in Reversion:** A life estate is a type of freehold estate and its duration is for the life of someone. When that person dies, the property may revert to the previous owner (estate in reversion).

b. Example #2: Rent the Property to a Tenant

Able gave a life estate to Baker for Baker's lifetime. Baker can rent the property to a tenant, but when Baker dies the property will revert to either Able (estate in reversion) or to someone Able designates to receive the property (estate in remainder called a "remainder person"). The tenant will lose possession of the property and will be forced to relocate to another property.

> **Estate in Remainder:** A life estate is a type of freehold estate and its duration is for the life a someone. When that person dies, the property may go to another designated person (estate in remainder). The other person is called the remainder person.

c. Example #3: Sell the Property to a Buyer

Able gave a life estate to Baker for Baker's lifetime. Baker can sell the property to a buyer, but when Baker dies the property will revert to either Able (estate in reversion) or to someone Able designates to receive the property (estate in remainder called a "remainder person"). The buyer will lose both legal title and possession of the property and will be forced to relocate to another property.

d. Example #4: Encumber the Property with a Loan

In the last example, Able gives a life estate to Baker for Baker's lifetime. Baker can encumber (place a loan against) the property, but when Baker dies the property will revert to either Able (estate in reversion) or to someone Able designates to receive the property (estate in remainder called a "remainder person"). The death of Baker could cause the loan on the property to become due and payable or possibly even cancel out the loan. For this reason, lenders are careful making loans on properties held in a life estate.

B. Less-than-Freehold Estates (also called Leasehold Estates)

The owner of the fee simple (freehold) estate is called the **lessor** and is also called the landlord. The owner of the leasehold estate (less-than-freehold estate) is called the **lessee** and is also called the tenant. There are four types of leasehold estates: estate for years, estate from period-to-period/periodic tenancy, estate at will, and estate at sufferance/tenancy at sufferance.

> **Lessor:** Landlord
>
> **Lessee:** Tenant

(1) Types of Leasehold Estates
a. Estate for Years

Estate for Years: Leasehold estate for a specific period of time.

A lease of a definite duration is called an **estate for years**. An estate for years leasehold estate starts and ends without being renewed. Even though an estate for years has the word "years" contained in it, it can be for *any* length of time–including seven years, two years, six months, two months, or even 34 days. It is commonly seen in permanent rentals, short-term rentals (e.g., vacation rentals), and commercial leases (retail, office, and industrial properties).

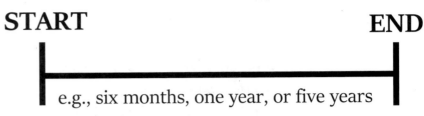

Figure 5.17 Estate for Years Diagram

b. Estate from Period-to-Period/Periodic Tenancy

Estate from Period-to-Period/Periodic Tenancy: Leasehold estate that renews each month or other period of time.

An **estate from period-to-period** is also called a **periodic tenancy**. The best example of this type of leasehold estate is a month-to-month rental agreement commonly seen with apartment rental units.

An estate from period-to-period/periodic tenancy may be renewed every month by the lessor/landlord or lessee/tenant. The period for the estate from period-to-period/periodic tenancy can be weekly, monthly, yearly or any other period specified in the rental agreement.

For example, a tenant pays the rent on June 1st for the month of June (June 1st to June 30th). The estate from period-to-period/periodic tenancy then renews on July 1st, the tenant pays the rent for July (July 1st to July 31st) on July 1st and the process continues each month thereafter.

If the tenant has been renting the property for one year or more, the landlord must by law give the tenant a minimum of a 60 day notice to vacate the property. If the tenant has been renting the property for less than one year, then the landlord by law must give the tenant a minimum of a 30 day notice to vacate the property. The tenant is required to give the landlord only a 30 day notice of vacating the property for any length of time the tenant has occupied it.

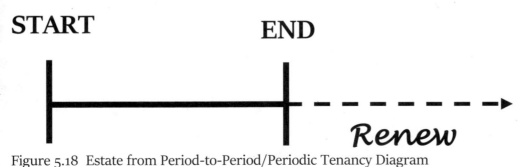

Figure 5.18 Estate from Period-to-Period/Periodic Tenancy Diagram

c. Estate at Will

An **estate at will** is a leasehold estate that can be ended by either the lessor (landlord) or lessee (tenant). It is commonly seen when an estate for years lease has ended and converts to an estate from period-to-period/periodic tenancy.

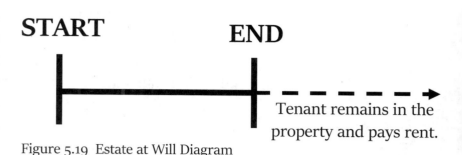

Figure 5.19 Estate at Will Diagram

d. Estate at Sufferance/Tenancy at Sufferance

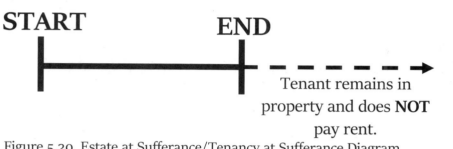

Figure 5.20 Estate at Sufferance/Tenancy at Sufferance Diagram

An **estate at sufferance** or **tenancy at sufferance** is a leasehold estate in which the tenant has stopped paying rent but continues to occupy the property. The landlord must start **eviction** proceedings to evict the non-paying tenant. This is usually accomplished by: (1) a 3 day notice to pay rent or quit (eviction notice), (2) an unlawful detainer action (court action to evict a nonpaying tenant), and (3) a writ of possession (gives possession of the property back to the lessor/landlord).

> **Estate at Will:** Leasehold estate that can be ended either by the lessor (landlord) or lessee (tenant).
>
> **Estate/Tenancy at Sufferance:** Leasehold estate in which the tenant is not paying rent.

(2) Eviction Process

When a tenant does not pay the rent that is due each month, the lessor/landlord must use legally-prescribed procedures to remove the non-paying three tenant from the premises. In California, this entails a 3 day notice to pay rent or quit, an unlawful detainer action, and a writ of possession.

- **a. 3 Day Notice to Pay Rent or Quit** (eviction notice)
  A **3 day notice to pay rent or quit** is the actual eviction notice. This notice lets the lessee/tenant know they are about to be evicted from the property. The lessee/tenant has three (3) court days to pay the rent or the lessor/landlord will start eviction proceedings through an unlawful detainer action in court. A court day is a day the courts are open.
- **b. Unlawful Detainer Action** (filed in court to evict a non-paying tenant)
  An **unlawful detainer action** is a court action to legally evict a non-paying tenant. It is usually filed with the small claims court, or other

> **3 Day Notice to Pay Rent or Quit:** Eviction notice that lets a tenant know they are being evicted from the premises. The tenant has three court days to respond to a three day notice.
>
> **Unlawful Detainer Action:** A lawsuit filed to evict a non-paying tenant.

lower court in California that is specifically designed to hear evictions and other minor civil disputes.

c. **Writ of Possession** (issued by the court to return possession to the lessor/landlord)

When the court has ruled in favor of the lessor/landlord for the unlawful detainer action, the court will provide a **writ of possession** that provides a legal means for the lessor/landlord to recover possession of the property. A law enforcement officer is normally used to serve the writ of possession to the lessee/tenant. If the tenant has not already vacated the premises by the eviction date, the law enforcement officer has the authority to physically remove the lessee/tenant from the property and give possession back to the lessor/landlord.

Unlike an eviction, **abandonment** occurs when the tenant relinquishes the right to possession with intent to terminate the lease before the end of the lease term.

Writ of Possession: Used by courts to give possession of real property back to the property owner after the tenant has been evicted from the property.

Abandonment: Occurs when a tenant leaves a property without prior notice to the landlord (lessor).

(3) Covenant of Quiet Enjoyment

The essence of a tenant's leasehold interest is possession of a leased premises. In every lease, the law implies a covenant (promise) on the part of the lessor/landlord to provide the lessee/tenant with possession and quiet enjoyment of the property.

The promise of quiet enjoyment for a tenant who rents a property from the landlord is called a **covenant of quiet enjoyment**. The landlord cannot interfere with the tenant's quiet enjoyment of the property, even when the tenant is not paying rent.

Covenant of Quiet Enjoyment: The landlord cannot disrupt the tenant's quiet enjoyment of a property.

For example, a tenant stops paying rent to the landlord, yet continues to live in the property. This is an example of an estate at sufferance or tenancy at sufferance. The landlord must use proper eviction procedures to evict the non-paying tenant. This usually requires a 3 day notice to pay rent or quit (eviction notice), an unlawful detainer action (court action to evict a non-paying tenant), and a writ of possession (the court gives possession back to the landlord).

The landlord cannot turn off the heat, hot water, electricity, lights, water service, or refrigeration to the property because this will breach the tenant's covenant of quiet enjoyment. Accordingly, the landlord cannot harass the tenant with on-going construction work in the inside or outside of the property.

Examples of actions that breach a tenant's covenant of quiet enjoyment may include: deliberately defacing the tenant's property, creating loud noises to create a nuisance for the tenant, physical and financial intimidation or threats, and repeatedly entering the property without a proper 24-hour notice to the tenant.

(4) Types of Leases

a. Gross Lease/Full Service Lease

A **gross lease** or full-service lease is commonly used with office building leases. The tenant generally pays a set amount each month as rent and the property owner pays all the property's expenses, including water, sewer, garbage, electricity, heating, ventilating, and air conditioning (HVAC), and all common area maintenance costs.

As negotiated in the lease agreement, landlords may shut off the electricity to a space during non-business hours or they may place expense stops in the lease agreement, thereby limiting electrical usage to prevent tenants from running up exorbitant electrical bills and other expenses during non-business hours.

> **Gross Lease:** Lease in which the rent includes all expenses such as electricity, gas, water, etc.

b. Industrial Lease

Industrial leases usually consider different amenities and tenant improvements than office and retail properties. Industrial properties tend to have ceiling heights of between 18 feet to 22 feet, so the walls that divide the space (called tenant improvements) into smaller spaces can be quite expensive.

Additionally, industrial properties may have 110v, 220v, and even 440v electrical lines running into the property to supply manufacturing equipment. The space may have an office built into the front with an open warehouse or manufacturing area in the back. The building can be accessed by a rail line and usually has good proximity to major transportation thoroughfares. Multiple loading docks and roller doors are amenities that will usually increase lease amounts and subsequent value of the property.

Lastly, industrial spaces are measured and leased by the *square foot*; however, real estate appraisers may appraise them by the *cubic foot* due to varying ceiling heights.

> **Industrial Lease:** A lease for an industrial property that usually comprises an office in the front of the space and warehouse in the back.

c. Net Lease/Triple Net Lease

The most common type of retail lease is a **net lease**. A net lease requires the tenants in the building to pay their pro-rata (fair) share of the property owner's total operating expenses, including property taxes, property insurance, janitorial supplies, and other services.

Consequently, the major benefit of a net lease is the lessor (landlord) receives net income. A triple net lease is a net lease in which the tenants agree to pay their pro-rata fair share of the property owner's property taxes, property insurance, and common area maintenance (CAM) charges. CAM charges are defined as the property owner's expenses to operate the

> **Net Lease:** Lease that requires the tenants in the building to pay their pro-rata (fair) share of the property owner's total operating expenses.

Base Rent
Pro-Rata Share of
+ Operating Expenses

Total Rent Due

Figure 5.21 Net Lease Rent Calculation

property and are divided among the tenants based on the percentage of the building space they are leasing. Pro-rata shares of a property's CAM charges are usually calculated by dividing a tenant's gross leasable square footage of space they are occupying into the total gross leasable area of the entire property.

d. Modified Gross Lease

Modified Gross Lease:
A lease that is between a gross/full-service lease and net lease.

A **modified gross lease** combines the attributes of a gross lease with those of a net lease. In other words, the property owner may pay some of the expenses related to the property and the tenant may pay others. This type of lease is usually the result of negotiations between the property owner and tenant.

e. Percentage Lease

Percentage Lease:
Lease that is paid as a percentage of the gross sales of the business.

Rent on a **percentage lease** is computed on the gross sales of the business. The greater the gross sales, the greater amount of rent paid by the tenant. Percentage leases are frequently used in retail shopping centers where the landlord would like to participate in any increases to a tenant's business. Mall promotions are commonly used to help increase foot traffic for retailers and thus increase tenant sales. This in turn, increases rental income to the landlord through the percentage leases.

Percentage leases are generally set up as a base rental amount plus overages (gross sales over a predetermined amount) or a base rental amount versus a percentage of sales, whichever is greater. A percentage lease is the most favorable type of lease a property owner can enter into for an improved business property in which the surrounding population is increasing over time. Under these circumstances, rent could become a major expense for the tenant in the operation of their business.

Graduated Lease: A lease that increases every year.

Consumer Price Index (CPI): Index that measures inflation.

Inflation: An increase in the price of consumer goods caused by too much money chasing too few goods.

Discount stores generally pay the highest percentage profit in a percentage lease. However, a parking lot or storage unit will have the highest percentage of gross receipts because it does not do the volume like discount stores and mass merchandisers. For example, a parking garage may have $100,000 in gross annual sales and the rent may be $25,000 per year, so it is 25% of the gross receipts. In contrast, discount stores and mass merchandisers (such as Walmart and Target) may have $30,000,000 or more in gross sales each year and their annual lease amount will be only 1% to 3% of their gross annual sales.

f. Graduated Lease and Consumer Price Index (CPI)

Graduated leases are used with many commercial real estate properties (shopping centers, office buildings, industrial properties, etc.) and may be tied into the **Consumer Price Index (CPI)** that measures **inflation** (increases in consumer prices). Each year the lease amount paid by the tenant will increase through an **escalator clause** that adjusts the amount of rent paid by the tenant.

Escalator Clause: When a lease includes a provision that increases the rental amount each year to adjust for inflation.

If inflation is increasing (prices are going up), then the tenant's rent will increase as well. The landlord will then receive more rental income each month; however, due to inflation it will be worth the same amount (have the same value) as the monthly income received prior to the increase in the CPI that tracks increases in inflation. In other words, it keeps the property owner even on the rents, so the property owner does not lose money if the value of the U.S. dollar declines over the length of the lease.

Therefore, the Consumer Price Index (CPI) is most often used when a graduated lease contains an escalator clause to adjust the rental amount periodically (usually annually) for inflation. The CPI measures changes in the prices paid by urban consumers for a representative basket of goods and services. CPI adjustments allow the property owner to maintain the future value of rental income by adjusting for excessive price inflation. Additionally, an escalator clause may provide for an upward adjustment for property taxes and maintenance costs over time.

When the economy is experiencing **deflation** (reduction in consumer prices), property owners and property managers may decide not to tie leases into the CPI, but instead negotiate set rental increases during each year of the lease.

Deflation: When the prices of consumer goods decrease.

g. Sublease vs. Assignment

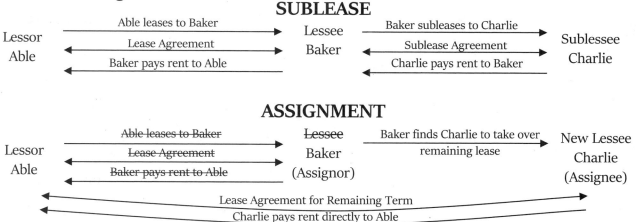

Figure 5.22 Sublease vs. Assignment Diagram

1. Sublease

When a lessor/landlord leases a property to a lessee/tenant, the lessee/tenant owns the less-than-freehold estate (called leasehold estate) that is merely possession of the property for a short period of time. If the lessee/tenant (who will now be called the sublessor) subleases the property to another lessee/tenant (called the sublessee) this is called a **sublease**. The sublessee (new tenant) will pay rent to the sublessor (old tenant), who in

Sublease: Lessee (tenant) becomes the sublessor and subleases a property to the sublessee. Lessee/sublessor remains liable for the lease.

turn pays rent to the lessor/landlord. Since the lessee/sublessor is sandwiched between the lessor and sublessee, this is called a sandwich lease.

If the lease agreement does not specify whether a tenant can sublease a property to a sublessee, then the tenant may be able to go ahead and sublease the property without the lessor/landlord's approval. For this reason, most lease agreements prevent subleasing without the lessor/landlord's approval.

2. Assignment

An **assignment** is the transfer of rights, interests, or title to property of a person (assignor) to another person (assignee). In an assignment, the assignee (person receiving the rights, interest, or title) becomes primarily liable for obligations occurring from the assignment.

In the Figure 5.22 Sublease vs. Assignment diagram, Lessee Baker is the assignor who assigns his rights to possess the space for the term of the lease to New Lessee Charlie who is the assignee. New lessee Charlie then pays rent directly to Lessor Able and Lessee Baker is no longer the lessee nor liable to pay rent in the future.

h. Agricultural Leases/Rural Leases

Even if the landlord and tenant specify a lease term, the following restrictions will limit the length of the lease term:

- A lease for **agricultural** or horticultural purposes cannot have a term exceeding 51 years.
- A lease for any town or city lot (**urban**) cannot have a term exceeding 99 years.
- A lease of land used to produce minerals, oil, gas, or other hydrocarbon substances cannot have a term exceeding 99 years.
- A lease of property owned by an emancipated minor or an incompetent person cannot have a term longer than the probate court may authorize.

i. Lease-Options

A person who has a **lease-option** for a property is making payments each month to lease the property, but also has an option to purchase the property for a specified amount during a certain period of time. The down payment for the future purchase is usually collected by the owner during the lease period and applied to the future down payment when the tenant exercises the option to purchase the property.

Assignment: Existing lessee (tenant) assigns the lease to a new lessee/tenant. Existing lessee is no longer liable for the lease.

Agricultural Lease: Maximum 51 years

Urban Lease: Maximum 99 years

Lease-Option: Leasehold estate in which the tenant has an option to purchase the property from the landlord.

j. Sale-Leaseback/Sale-and-Leaseback

A **sale-leaseback** or **sale-and-leaseback** occurs when an owner of a commercial property sells the property to an investor and leases it back from the investor. This is a financing technique used by companies to convert equity in real property to operating capital. It also allows a company to expand locations faster than they could with their existing cost of capital.

For example, a property owner owns a business, as well as the real estate (land, building, and appurtenances) where the business is located. The property owner sells the real estate (i.e., freehold estate) to a real estate investor for a negotiated purchase price. The former property owner (who is now the tenant) receives the amount of the property purchase price and transfers the freehold estate to the real estate investor. The former property owner is now the tenant and merely owns the less-than-freehold estate (also called leasehold estate) which is possession of the property for a very short period of time. Rent paid by the tenant to the real estate investor is now 100% deductible by the tenant for tax purposes. The process of selling a property and leasing it back is called "sale-leaseback" or "sale-and-leaseback."

> **Sale-Leaseback/Sale-and-Leaseback:** Business owns the land and building and sells it to an investor. Business becomes the tenant that pays rent to the investor.

Tales from the Trade

THE STORY OF WALGREENS

Walgreens has been able to use sale-leaseback arrangements to expand their stores on a national scale. Walgreens buys land that is located on a busy intersection, builds a Walgreens store on the land, and then sells the land and building to an investor (sale-leaseback) while occupying the property on a long-term lease. This results in Walgreens receiving most of their money back—so they can find another vacant parcel of land in a good location, build another Walgreens building on the lot, and then do another sale-leaseback...and the process continues.

4. Condominiums

A. Condominium Defined

A **condominium** owner owns the airspace of the condominium separately as a freehold (fee simple) estate and the common areas (owned fee simple as well) in common with all the other condominium owners in the complex. Common areas include pools, clubhouses, and sidewalks.

B. Apartment Building vs. Condominium

An **apartment** building is owned by the property owner (fee simple), while the tenant owns the leasehold estate (also called less-than-freehold estate) which is

> **Condominium:** Condominium owner owns the airspace of their unit separately as fee simple, along with the common areas in common with the other condominium owners.

> **Apartments:** One owner owns the property fee simple and rents out the units to tenants. Each tenant has a leasehold estate which is possession of the unit for a very short period of time.

merely possession of the unit's airspace (along with the use of the apartment building's amenities specified in the lease agreement between the property owner and tenant) for very short period of time.

The property owner's fee simple estate is considered real property because it represents the land, building, and all the appurtenances to go with it and is the highest form of ownership a person can own in land.

APARTMENTS

The owner of an apartment building owns the entire building (all units and their air space) and land (including all the appurtenances that run with the land) as a freehold estate.

OWNER

Owner owns the entire building (all 4 units) and the land.
Tenants #1 through #4 merely have possession of each of
their units for a very short period of time.

Figure 5.23 Apartment Diagram

Conversely, the leasehold estate (an estate owned by the tenant) is merely possession of the property for a short period of time. The leasehold estate is considered personal property.

When a tenant's lease ends, the leasehold estate will terminate and possession of the unit's airspace (and all the amenities in the lease agreement) will revert back to the fee simple owner (property owner who already owns the land, building, and appurtenances). The fee simple owner will then rent the property to another tenant who will receive a leasehold estate representing possession of the property (and the apartment amenities) for a short period of time. . .and the process repeats.

CONDOMINIUMS

A condominium owner owns the airspace of his or her individual unit as a freehold estate.

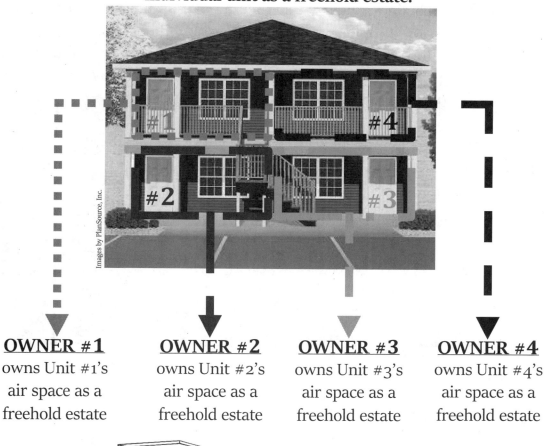

Images by PlanSource, Inc.

OWNER #1	**OWNER #2**	**OWNER #3**	**OWNER #4**
owns Unit #1's air space as a freehold estate	owns Unit #2's air space as a freehold estate	owns Unit #3's air space as a freehold estate	owns Unit #4's air space as a freehold estate

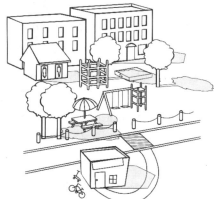

Figure 5.24 Condominium Diagram

+ Common Areas

Common areas are freehold estates owned in common (joint ownership) by all the condominium owners.

Common areas (e.g., clubhouses, pools, sidewalks) are located within the condominium project.

Therefore, both apartment tenants and condominium owners each have an estate in real property. The apartment tenant owns the leasehold estate which is merely possession of the unit for a short period of time. In contrast, the condominium owner owns a fee simple estate (highest form of ownership in land) in the airspace (owned separately by the condominium owner) and a fee simple estate in the common areas (owned fee simple in common with all the other condominium owners in the condominium complex).

C. Residential Condominium

Residential condominiums are located all over California and are used to provide housing for people who live in areas where land is expensive. Condominiums allow residents who have normal incomes to be able to purchase fee simple title to real property in expensive areas—and actually own their own condominium unit. A **homeowner's association (HOA)** is usually elected to meet, interpret, and enforce the rules for the residential condominium owners.

Homeowner's Association (HOA): Condominium complexes and planned unit developments usually have a homeowner's association that is tasked with following and enforcing the bylaws of the association.

Figure 5.25 Residential Condominiums

(1) Townhomes (Townhouses)

Townhomes are usually two or three stories high and are attached to other townhomes in a similar fashion to condominiums. In a similar manner to condominiums, townhome owners own the airspace inside the townhome separately as fee simple ownership. In addition, the townhome owner owns the fee simple ownership of the common areas around the townhome in common with all the other townhome owners in the complex or development.

(2) Planned Unit Development

Planned Unit Development (PUD): A group of single-family homes that usually have common areas such as a community swimming pool.

A **planned unit development** is a subdivision that utilizes separate units (usually single-family homes, patio homes, and other free-standing high density properties) along with common areas such as a clubhouse and/or swimming pool. Each owner owns their property separately, along with the common areas in common with the other owners.

D. Commercial Condominium

Developers tend to build commercial condominiums in areas of high commercial real estate land costs. Urban areas near a city's central business district (CBD) tend to be located where office building condominiums can perform well. Some business owners (e.g., dentists, medical doctors, etc.) like to own their own space so they have long-term control over it. A building owner's association is usually elected to meet, interpret, and enforce the rules for commercial condominium owners.

5. Sovereign Powers of the State that Affect Property

There are four **sovereign powers of the state**: eminent domain, taxation, escheat, and police power. The first three sovereign powers (eminent domain, taxation, and escheat) allow the state (government) under certain circumstances to take real property from private owners. The last sovereign power is police power and it allows the state to use zoning to implement its general plan or master plan and limit the uses for real property.

> **Sovereign Powers of the State:** Include eminent domain, taxation, escheat, and police power.

A. Eminent Domain

Eminent domain is one of the sovereign powers of the state and allows the government (e.g., public agencies) to take private property for public use. The government must, however, compensate the landowner at full market value for the loss. Thus, eminent domain is associated with severance damages.

> **Eminent Domain:** Sovereign power of the State to take a person's property for the public good.

(1) Condemnation Action

A city or county may take a piece of property for public use through a **condemnation action** (under the power of eminent domain). This action is called an involuntary conversion. However, if the government condemns a property due to health and safety reasons, the owner may possibly not be compensated for the loss.

> **Condemnation Action:** Government action to take a private person's real property. Must be for the public good and the government must pay the owner fair market value.

(2) Inverse Condemnation Action

An **inverse condemnation action** occurs when an owner sues to recover damages caused by the State. For example, an airport changes the flight path so airplanes now fly over a person's home. The homeowner files an inverse condemnation action against the local government (that owns the airport) and forces them to buy the property at its previous value before the flight path was changed.

> **Inverse Condemnation Action:** Government is forced to buy a person's property because of something they did to reduce its value.

B. Taxation

A tax lien sale is used to sell a property that is behind in paying its property taxes. **Taxation** is covered in Chapter 15.

C. Escheat

The State of California may acquire property by **escheat**. When a person dies and does not have any heirs, the property will escheat to the State of California if no heirs are found within five (5) years.

D. Police Power

The last sovereign power of the state is **police power**, which provides for the safety, health, and general welfare of society. In addition, it includes zoning and building codes.

(1) Zoning

Zoning is a public restriction that limits the use of a property to specific uses that will best implement a county's master plan or general plan.

(2) Building Codes

Local, state, and federal governments enact building codes to ensure properties are built to the highest level of safety. Local governments institute building codes, along with the national Uniform Building Code. Accordingly, local building inspectors enforce building codes.

Chapter Five Summary

Real property is compared to personal property. Real property includes the land, anything affixed to the land, and anything appurtenant to the land. Riparian and littoral water rights, along with wells, septic systems, and sewers are discussed. Personal property is anything that moves and includes mobile homes and manufactured homes.

Estates in land include freehold and less-than-freehold estates. Freehold estates include fee simple and life estates. Less-than-freehold estates (called leasehold estates) include estate for years, estate from period-to-period/periodic tenancy, estate at will, and estate at sufferance/tenancy at sufferance. Types of leases include gross/full service lease, industrial lease, net lease/triple net lease, modified gross lease, percentage lease, graduated lease and consumer price index (CPI), subleases vs. assignment, and rural leases. Sale-leasebacks are a financing tool used companies to convert equity in real property to operating capital. In addition, apartment buildings are compared to condominiums.

The sovereign powers of the State of California are discussed through eminent domain, condemnation action, inverse condemnation action, taxation, escheat, and police power.

Chapter Five Quiz

1. _____ that occupy the inverted pie-shaped area between the surface and center of the earth are part of the land and are considered real property.
(A) Airplane flight paths
(B) Fixtures
(C) Minerals
(D) Trade fixtures

2. Personal property that is attached to the land and is being used as an ordinary use in connection with the land is usually considered a:
(A) freehold estate
(B) fixture
(C) appurtenance
(D) life estate

3. Water users may organize a _____ to secure an ample water supply at a reasonable cost.
(A) mutual water company
(B) protest
(C) political action committee
(D) none of the above are correct

4. It is usually a good idea for rural single-family homes with an existing well to have a _____ performed during the due diligence period prior to close of escrow.
(A) draw down
(B) potability test
(C) Both (A) and (B) are correct
(D) Neither (A) nor (B) are correct

5. The holder of a life estate cannot _____ a property.
(A) rent
(B) sell
(C) encumber
(D) devise

6. A lease of a definite duration is called an:
(A) estate for years
(B) life estate
(C) fee simple defeasible estate
(D) unlawful detainer action

7. The correct order of the eviction process is:
(A) unlawful detainer action, three day notice to pay or quit, writ of possession
(B) three day notice to pay or quit, writ of possession, unlawful detainer action
(C) three day notice to pay or quit, unlawful detainer action, writ of possession
(D) writ of possession, unlawful detainer action, three day notice to pay or quit

8. A _____ combines the attributes of a gross lease with those of a net lease.
(A) gross lease
(B) full service lease
(C) modified gross lease
(D) percentage lease

9. A lease for agricultural or horticultural purposes cannot have a term exceeding:
(A) 27.5 years
(B) 51 years
(C) 99 years
(D) unlimited

10. A condominium owner owns the airspace of the condominium separately as a:
(A) leasehold estate
(B) less-than-freehold estate
(C) fee simple estate
(D) estate for years

Please use this space for notes.

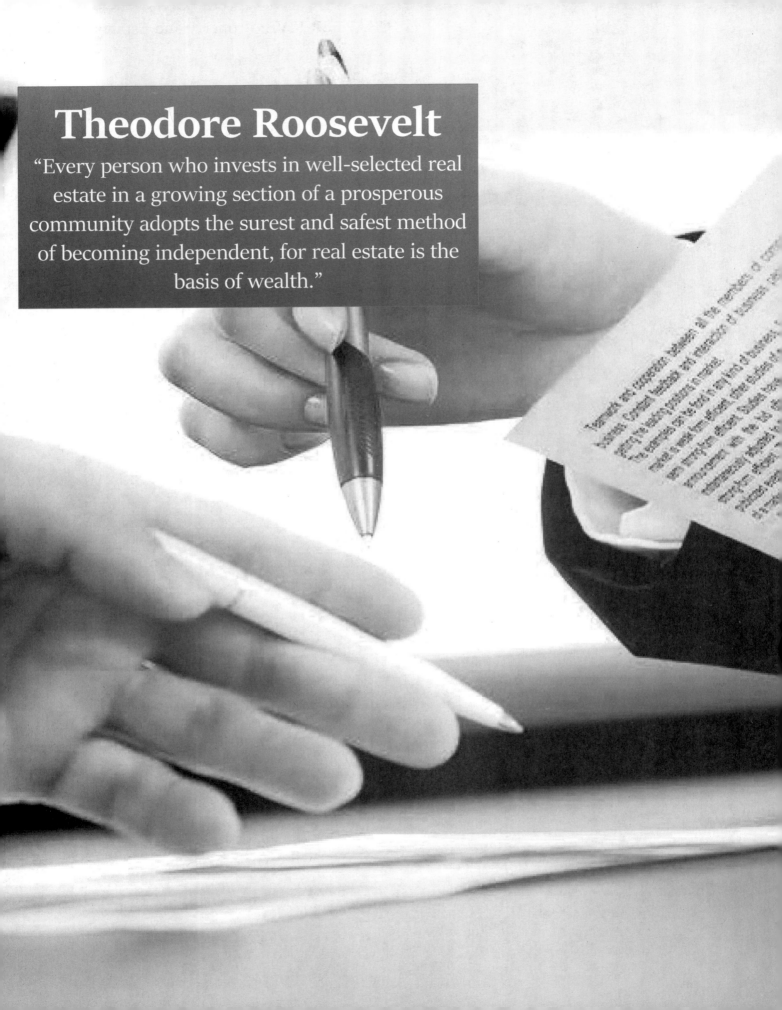

Theodore Roosevelt

"Every person who invests in well-selected real estate in a growing section of a prosperous community adopts the surest and safest method of becoming independent, for real estate is the basis of wealth."

6

Chapter
SIX

Real Estate Contracts: Offer and Acceptance

Two of the most common types of contracts used in the real estate brokerage business are the real estate listing agreement and real estate purchase agreement. Real estate agents must understand contract law to be able to effectively create valid contracts for their clients.

From a legal standpoint, a **contract** is a legally enforceable agreement between competent parties who have agreed to perform certain acts for consideration or refrain from performing certain acts. In other words, a contract is an agreement to do or not to do something.

Contract: A contract is an agreement to do or not to do something.

Figure 6.1

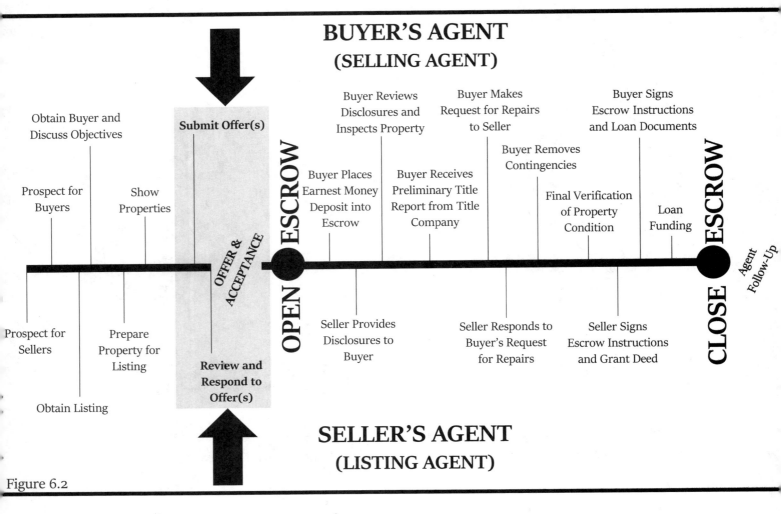

Figure 6.2

1. Contract Requirements

There are four essential elements of any valid contract (all contracts):

1. **Competent Parties/Capacity to Contract** – The parties to the contract must not have been declared incompetent in a court of law. In addition, the parties to the contract must have the capacity to contract—specifically, minors (under 18 years of age) may not contract for real property. The exceptions to this rule are minors who are married, divorced, in the military, or emancipated by a court of law.

2. **Mutual Assent** – This is mutuality of agreement. In other words, what the buyer thinks they have agreed to in the contract is the same as the seller thinks they have agreed to in the contract. There is a meeting of the minds. Genuine offer and genuine acceptance is used to facilitate a meeting of the minds.

3. **Lawful Objective** – The purpose of the contract must be for a legal purpose. For example, a contract to smuggle illegal drugs into the U.S. would not be a valid contract because it has an unlawful objective.

4. **Sufficient Consideration** – Consideration is the bargained for exchange that occurs when two people contract to do or not to do something. For example, if

Able pays Baker $100,000 for Baker's real property and Baker signs a grant deed conveying the real property to Able, there is sufficient consideration to become a valid contract. Able's $100,000 is consideration on Able's part, and Baker conveying the property to Able is Baker's consideration.

5. Real estate contracts have a fifth element: ***in writing***. Not all contracts are required to be in writing, however, all *real estate contracts* are required to be in writing (except leases of a year or less are not required to be in writing). It is important to note that *any* contract (real estate or anything else) that cannot be performed within one year of its making (takes over one year to complete) must be in writing.

2. Elements of a Valid Contract

A. Competent Parties/Capacity to Contract

Incompetents, minors, and convicts are all restricted from contracting. Non-resident aliens, however, do have the capacity to contract.

(1) Competent Parties

Either of the parties to a contract must not have been declared **incompetent** in a court of law. If this is the case, then the contract will be void and have no legal effect.

> **Competent:** Legally qualified.
>
> **Incompetent:** One who is mentally incompetent or incapable.

(2) Capacity to Contract

Some members of society may not have the capacity to sign a valid contract. Minors who are under 18 years of age cannot contract in California, except if the minor is married, divorced, in the military, or emancipated by the courts (courts declare the minor an adult). Accordingly, a minor can receive title to real property by gift or inheritance without court approval; however, the minor cannot convey real property without court approval.

Figure 6.3 Minors

(3) Convicts

According to the DRE, "Persons sentenced to imprisonment in state prisons are deprived of such of their civil rights as may be necessary for the security of the institution in which they are confined and for the reasonable protection of the public. Convicts do not forfeit their property. They may acquire property by gift, inheritance or by will, under certain conditions, and they may convey their property or acquire property through conveyance."

(4) Non-Resident Aliens

Non-resident aliens are not citizens of the United States of America, however, they do have the capacity to contract. For example, a Canadian citizen could sign a contract to purchase real estate in the U.S. The Canadian citizen is considered a non-resident alien and has the capacity to contract in the U.S.

B. Mutual Assent – Offer and Acceptance

(Remember: with a counter offer, the offer<u>ee</u> becomes the offer<u>or</u>.)

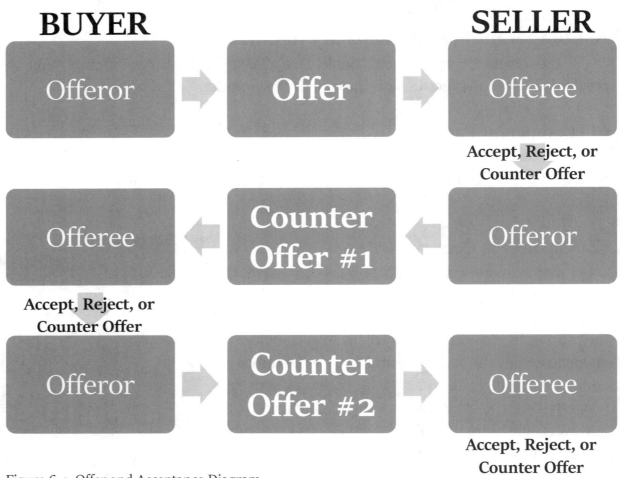

Figure 6.4 Offer and Acceptance Diagram

(1) Offers

An **offeror** makes an offer to an **offeree**. Remember: The "or" is always doing something to the "ee" (offer<u>or</u> makes an offer to the offer<u>ee</u>). The offeror may revoke the offer anytime up until acceptance by the offeree is communicated back to the offeror.

Offeror: Person making an offer.

Offeree: Person receiving an offer.

The buyer uses a purchase agreement to make an offer to purchase a parcel of real property. It specifies how much the buyer is offering and the terms of the purchase. The purchase agreement is then signed by the buyer and presented to the seller. The seller reviews it and then accepts the buyer's offer in its present form, rejects it entirely, or produces a counter offer back to the buyer. The counter offer is an offer from the seller to the buyer that makes changes to the buyer's original offer. The buyer then reviews the counter offer from the seller and either accepts it in its present form, rejects it entirely, or makes a counter offer to the seller. The counter offer process may go back and forth several times until there is agreement between the buyer and seller regarding the price and terms of the real property purchase.

The reason the purchase agreement is so important to the real estate brokerage business is because it provides buyers with a formal written way of describing the price and terms that are acceptable for the purchase of a specific parcel of real property. The purchase agreement is presented to the seller in a written form, so the seller can understand the buyer's requirements without any misunderstandings between the parties.

The offeree (seller) can accept the buyer's offer, reject the offer, or make a counter offer back to the offeror (buyer). If the seller (offeree) decides to accept the buyer's (offeror) offer, then acceptance must be communicated back to the buyer (offeror). Once this has occurred, there is a valid contract between the buyer and seller.

If the seller (offeree) decides to reject the buyer's (offeror) offer, the rejection by the seller (offeree) will terminate the offer when the rejection has been communicated back to the buyer (offeror). Therefore, if the seller (offeree) rejects the buyer's (offeror) offer, then the offer is terminated.

(2) Counter Offers

A buyer (offeror) usually makes an offer to the seller (offeree). If the seller (offeree) does not like the buyer's offer, the seller may make a counter offer (the seller now becomes the offeror) to the buyer (who now becomes the offeree). When the seller (who is now the offeror) communicates the counter offer to the buyer (now the offeree), the original offer from the buyer (offeror) is now terminated. The seller could not change his or her mind and accept the original offer from the buyer.

For example, Buyer Able makes an offer to Seller Baker for the purchase of a parcel of real property. Seller Baker thinks the offer is too low and submits a counter offer to Buyer Able. When Buyer Able receives the communication of the counter offer, the original offer made by Buyer Able to Seller Baker is terminated.

Seller Baker cannot change his or her mind and go ahead and accept the original offer because it is effectively terminated when the counter offer was made by Seller Baker and communicated to Buyer Able.

(3) More than One Counter Offer

The buyer's agent writes the offer to purchase the property, having the buyer sign the offer, and then submits it to the seller's agent. The seller's agent presents the buyer's offer to the seller. The seller can either accept the offer, reject the offer, or submit a counter offer back to the buyer.

If the seller accepts the buyer's original offer, a contract is formed between the buyer and seller (with communication of acceptance back to the buyer). If the seller rejects the buyer's original offer, there is no contract formed between the buyer and seller (with communication of the rejection back to the buyer). If the seller decides to make a counter offer to the buyer's offer, then the seller's agent will write counter offer #1, have the seller sign it, and then submit it to the buyer's agent.

The buyer's agent will present counter offer #1 to the buyer. The buyer can either accept counter offer #1 (and there is a contract formed after acceptance by the buyer has been communicated back to the seller), reject counter offer #1 (a contract is not formed with communication of the rejection back to the seller), or decide to submit a counter offer to counter offer #1. This new counter offer from the buyer to the seller is called counter offer #2. Counter offer #2 is written by the buyer's agent, the buyer signs it, and it is submitted to the seller's agent.

The seller's agent presents counter offer #2 to the seller. The seller can either accept counter offer #2 (and there is a contract formed after acceptance is communicated back the buyer), reject counter offer #2 (a contract is not formed with communication of the rejection back to the buyer), or decide to counter counter offer #2 with counter offer #3. The process continues back and forth until the buyer and seller have found mutual assent (both agree to the price and terms of the transaction).

(4) Offer Terminated
a. Offer Terminated by Revocation (Revoked)

If a buyer (offeror) communicates a notice of revocation causing the offer to be revoked before the seller (offeree) communicates acceptance back to the buyer, then the buyer's offer will be revoked and this will terminate the offer to purchase the parcel of real property. In contrast, if a buyer (offeror) communicates a notice of revocation after the seller (offeree) properly communicates acceptance back to the buyer, this will not terminate the buyer's offer to purchase real property and there will be a contract formed between the buyer and seller.

b. Offer Terminated by Death

If a buyer (offeror) makes an offer to a seller (offeree) and then dies before the offer is presented to the seller (offeree), the offer is terminated, and a contract is not formed. Accordingly, if a seller (offeror) makes a counter offer to a buyer (offeree) and the seller (offeror) dies before the counter offer is presented to the buyer (offeree), the counter offer is terminated, and a contract is not formed.

c. Offer Terminated by Rejection

An offer may be terminated with rejection by the offeree. Rejection of the offer by the offeree will terminate an offer to purchase real property. For example, a buyer (offeror) makes an offer to the seller (offeree). If the seller (offeree) rejects the buyer's offer, then the offer is terminated. Therefore, an offer can be terminated by a seller rejecting a buyer's offer. In other words, rejection of the offer by the offeree (seller in this case) will terminate an offer to purchase real property. Of course, the rejection of the offer by the offeree must be communicated back to the offeror.

d. Counter Offer

An offer may be terminated by an offeree making a counter offer to the offeror. For example, Buyer Edward (offeror) makes an offer to purchase a property owned by Seller Francis (offeree). When Seller Francis (who now becomes the offeror) makes a counter offer to Buyer Edward (who now becomes the offeree) and once this counter offer is communicated to Buyer Edward (offeree), this terminates Buyer Edward's (offeror) original offer to Seller Francis (offeree).

In other words, the buyer makes an offer to the seller. The seller does not like the offer and makes a counter offer to the buyer. After the buyer receives the counter offer, this terminates the buyer's original offer to the seller. Therefore, the seller could not change his or her mind and go back and accept the buyer's original offer once the seller's counter offer has been communicated to the buyer.

(5) Acceptance Must Be Communicated Back to the Offeror: Death of Offeror or Offeree

If an offer is made, acceptance is not communicated back to the offeror, and then the offeror dies, a contract is not formed. Accordingly, if a seller dies *before* receiving an offer that has been made on his property, this is a void contract (no contract).

For example, an offer is made by the buyer and accepted by the seller. The seller dies a day after the acceptance. Since the buyer was not notified of the seller's acceptance of the offer, the offer is terminated with the death of the seller. To have a valid contract, the buyer must be notified of the seller accepting the buyer's offer, otherwise there is no contract formed and the offer is terminated with the death of the seller. Death will terminate an offer; therefore, a contract has not been formed. If a buyer dies after mailing an offer to a seller, the offer is terminated as well.

(6) Patently Frivolous Offer

Patently Frivolous Offer: An offer that is not to be taken seriously. For example, an offer of $1 to purchase a $1 million home.

An agent is relieved of the obligation to present an offer to purchase real property to the principal when the offer is **patently frivolous**. For example, if a buyer makes an offer of $1.00 to purchase a listed property valued at $1,000,000, the agent is not required to present the offer to the seller because is it patently frivolous and the buyer is not serious about the offer.

(7) Surviving Contract

If a buyer and seller enter into a valid binding contract and one of the parties dies or becomes incompetent, the contract is valid, if it was signed before the party died or became incompetent. Therefore, if a buyer and seller sign a contract and then die there is a valid contract.

An existing contract will not terminate with the deaths of the buyer, seller, or broker. A contract will survive the parties to the contract. If a person dies or becomes incompetent (declared legally incompetent in a court of law) after entering into a valid and binding contract, then the contract will survive the person and be valid if it was signed before the party died or became incompetent. However, if the person had merely made an offer and there was not a valid binding contract, then a contract had not been formed and the offer would terminate with the person's death.

C. Lawful Objective

A contract must be for a lawful objective. For example, a contract to commit a crime is a void contract (has no legal effect) because it is not for a legal purpose.

D. Sufficient Consideration

Consideration: Bargained for exchange used in a contract.

Consideration is bargained for exchange and is required for a valid contract. Anything of value can be used as consideration including services rendered, a promise to perform an act, or an exchange of money. However, consideration is not required to be money because money is only one form of consideration.

(1) Illegal Consideration

Coast Guard News/Flickr

Figure 6.5 Illegal Drugs

A contract based on illegal consideration is void (has no legal effect). An example of illegal consideration is a contract to purchase illegal drugs from a drug cartel. The illegal drugs are consideration and are illegal to possess, so the contract is void.

E. In Writing (Statute of Frauds)

The **statute of frauds** requires all real estate contracts (except leases of one year or less) to be in writing. This is an attempt to prevent parol (oral) evidence from changing the meaning of a written agreement.

Statute of Frauds: Federal law that requires all real estate contracts to be in writing, except leases of one year or less. Also requires all contracts that cannot be performed within one year to be in writing.

Listing agreements and purchase agreements generally have priority over all prior discussions, negotiations, and agreements. It is usually the entire contract and may not be contradicted by prior or simultaneous oral agreements. Any changes to a real estate contract must be in writing and signed by both buyer and seller. Today's real estate contracts normally use electronic signatures sent via email and other electronic methods to handle the negotiations and resulting contracts between the parties.

(1) Preprinted Clauses vs. Handwritten Information

Many real estate contracts contain preprinted clauses and spaces for information to be handwritten into the contract. In a legal dispute, when there is a conflict between the preprinted clauses and the handwritten information, the handwritten information takes precedence (priority) over the preprinted clauses. In other words, handwritten changes to a contract that are initialed or signed by both the buyer and seller will take precedence over the preprinted clauses in the contract.

a. Agent Crosses Out Items in the Contract

If an agent crosses out items in a contract without the knowledge of the buyer or seller, this is called intentional or fraudulent misrepresentation. Fraudulent misrepresentation by a real estate broker is misrepresentation of a material fact with the full knowledge and intent of the broker. A real estate agent is permitted to make changes to a contract if the changes are directed by the buyer and seller. Normally, the buyer and seller will initial the changes that have been made to the contract.

3. Types of Contracts

Contract Classification Chart
Express / Implied
Bilateral / Unilateral
Executory / Executed
Enforceable / Unenforceable
Valid / Void / Voidable

A contract can be classified as express, implied, bilateral, unilateral, executory, executed, enforceable, unenforceable, valid, voidable, or void.

A. Express Contract

Figure 6.6

An **express contract** is a contract in which the parties put their intentions and the terms of the agreement into words, either verbal or written. Most real estate contracts in California are express contracts because of the statute of frauds that requires all real estate contracts to be in writing, except leases of one year or less. Therefore, a contract to purchase real estate in California is considered an express contract.

Express Contract: A contract expressed orally or in writing.

Implied Contract: A contract that is formed by the actions of the parties.

B. Implied Contract

An **implied contract** is a contract in which the agreement between the parties is shown by acts or conduct, rather than words. The statute of frauds requires that all real estate contracts must be in writing except leases of one year or less, therefore, implied contracts are more commonly seen in everyday life and not in the real estate brokerage business.

For example, a person takes her cat to a veterinarian for a checkup. The veterinarian is expected to provide services of examining the cat, and the cat owner is expected to pay for these services. Even though there is not a written contract between the cat owner and veterinarian, there is an implied contract between the parties. An implied contract (actions of the parties) has the same force and effect as an express contract (words, both verbal and written).

C. Bilateral Contract

A **bilateral contract** is a promise for a promise. The promise of one party is given in exchange for the promise of the other party. For example, when a seller promises to pay the agent a commission when the home is sold, and the agent promises to use diligence in marketing the property, this is called a bilateral contract. A listing agreement is usually considered a bilateral contract.

Bilateral Contract: A promise for a promise.

D. Unilateral Contract

A **unilateral contract** is a promise for an act. A promise is given by one party to induce an act by the other party. For example, Person A promises to pay Person B $10 if Person B will walk across the Golden Gate Bridge. Person B walks across the Golden Gate Bridge, therefore, Person A owes Person B $10. Person B performs her requirements under the contract with an act rather than a promise.

Unilateral Contract: A promise for an act.

An example of a unilateral contract in the real estate brokerage business is an open listing agreement. An open listing agreement specifies that the seller agrees to pay a commission (promise) to any real estate agent who brings in a buyer who purchases the seller's property (act). So, the promise of a payment of a commission results in the act by a real estate agent of bringing in a buyer to purchase the property.

E. Executory Contract

An **executory contract** is a contract that is in the process of being performed and has not yet been completed. *Executory* is present tense and denotes a contract in the process of being completed. In contrast, *executed* is past tense and denotes a contract that has already been completed.

Executory Contract: A contract that is in the process of being performed and has not yet been completed.

For example, a bilateral executory contract is a contract in which the seller agrees to pay the agent a commission, if the agent agrees to use diligence in finding a buyer.

Executed Contract: A contract that has been completed.

F. Executed Contract

An **executed contract** is a contract that has been completed. If a contract has been executed, both parties have performed completely their obligations as provided by the contract.

Figure 6.7

G. Unenforceable Contract

An **unenforceable contract** is a contract that is valid; however, for some reason cannot be proved or sued upon. An example of an unenforceable contract is an oral contract to purchase real estate. Because of the statute of frauds, real estate contracts (except leases of one year or less) must be in writing, therefore an oral contract to purchase real estate will be unenforceable in a court of law.

However, an oral agreement for real estate may be enforced if the purchaser has gone into possession, paid part of the purchase price, and made improvements to the property.

(1) Statute of Frauds

The statute of frauds is an old concept that came from England (where it was abandoned several years ago); however, it is still in use in California today. The statute of frauds states that all real estate contracts must be in writing except leases of one year or less. The statute of frauds includes all agreements that are not to be performed within one year of their making. Thus, if the contract takes over one year to complete (i.e., long-term contract), then it must be in writing. This applies to all contracts, including real estate contracts and all other contracts that do not include real estate.

H. Voidable Contract

A **voidable contract** is a contract that appears valid and enforceable but is subject to rescission by one of the parties who acted under duress or a disability. In other words, one of the parties can void the contract or not void the contract at their sole discretion.

(1) Duress

An example of a voidable contract is one that is signed under **duress**. Duress occurs when one party forces the other party through threat of violence to do something against their will or better judgment. The person who was held under duress while signing the contract can void the contract (rescind it so it has no legal effect) or enforce it at their sole discretion (make it a valid contract). To rescind is to terminate and a voidable contract is good until it is rescinded. Prior to close of escrow a contract can be rescinded, however, after close of escrow the aggrieved (harmed) party must file a lawsuit in civil court.

(2) Community Property

Community property is property held by both husband and wife (or two spouses). California is a community property state and all property acquired by husband and wife (or two spouses) during marriage is considered community property and is owned 50% husband and 50% wife (or 50% for each spouse).

A contract for the sale of community property signed only by the husband (spouse) is voidable by the wife (spouse). It is voidable at the discretion of the wife (spouse). Both husband and wife (both spouses) must sign the contract for the sale of community property.

Figure 6.8

I. Void Contract

A **void contract** has no legally binding effect. It is unenforceable from the very beginning and is not a contract at all. Examples of void contracts include contracts to commit a crime (illegal contracts), real estate contracts with minors, contracts with someone who has been formally committed to a mental institution, and contracts with someone who has been declared incompetent by a court of law. Another type of void contract is an **illusory contract**. An illusory contract is not a contract at all because it does not bind the parties to a legal agreement. There is no mutuality of obligation between the buyer and seller. An example of an illusory contract is an agreement that states, "Buyer will pay $100,000 to purchase a property and the seller will sign the grant deed if the seller decides to do so." There is not obligation on the seller's part to sign the grant deed and convey the property to the buyer.

> **Void Contract:** A contract that has no force or effect. An example of a void contract is a contract to commit an illegal act.
>
> **Illusory Contract:** Occurs when one of the parties is not bound by the agreement.

4. Breach of Contract

When a person fails to perform a duty specified in a contract or a party to a contract does not complete their portion of the contract, this is called a **breach of contract**. The damaged party may seek relief through compensatory damages and possibly punitive damages in a court of law.

Compensatory damages are the actual losses sustained by the plaintiff (person who was harmed and brought the lawsuit) and are paid by the defendant (person who harmed the plaintiff). **Punitive damages** are designed to punish the defendant by taking money away from the defendant and giving it to the plaintiff who was harmed by the defendant's actions.

> **Breach of Contract:** When a party to a contract breaks the contract.
>
> **Compensatory Damages:** Actual losses sustained by the plaintiff and are paid by the defendant.
>
> **Punitive Damages:** Designed to punish the defendant by taking money away from the defendant and giving it to the plaintiff.
>
> **Liquidated Damages:** Damages that are set ahead of time in the event of a breach of contract.

A. Liquidated Damages

Liquidated damages are the predetermined amount of damages the parties to a contract agree to pay as the total amount of compensation an injured party will receive if the other party breaches the contract. For example, if a buyer of an owner-occupied one-to-four (1-4) unit residential property defaults on a real estate transaction, and all contingencies have been removed, the seller may retain up to 3% of the purchase price or the amount of the earnest money deposit, whichever is less. This is called liquidated damages and both the buyer and seller must initial the liquidated damages clause in the contract for it to become effective.

An agent's commission is usually limited to negotiations unless a liquidated damages clause is included in the agreement. If a liquidated damages clause is initialed by the buyer and seller, then the damages paid to the seller (and possibly the listing broker) if the buyer defaults are specified at the time of signing the contract. Again, the maximum liquidated damages for an owner-occupied one-to-four unit residential property is 3% of the purchase price, not to exceed the amount of the earnest money deposit.

For example, a buyer and seller initial the liquidated damages clause in a real estate purchase agreement. The buyer removes all contingencies to the contract and then defaults on the purchase of the property (changes his or her mind and does not go through with the contract). The maximum amount of damages the seller can receive from the defaulting buyer has already been predetermined by the liquidated damages clause in the contract. The amount is usually 3% of the purchase price or the earnest money deposit, whichever is lower for all one-to-four unit dwellings in California. Some liquidated damages clauses allow the seller and real estate agent to each keep 50% of the liquidated damages paid by the buyer.

5. Contract Rescission

To rescind is to terminate. If a buyer would like to terminate a contract before close of escrow, the buyer can rescind the contract. However, if it is after close of escrow, the buyer must file a civil lawsuit against the seller.

For example, the buyer and seller have mutually decided to terminate a contract. There is no mention of escrow or money being placed in a broker's trust account. Therefore, the real estate agent should return the buyer's earnest money deposit. However, the agent does have the option of filing suit in civil court to collect a commission.

It is important to note that if the buyer's earnest money deposit had been deposited into escrow, the escrow agent would need both the buyer and seller to sign an escrow rescission form and then the escrow agent could return the buyer's earnest money deposit. If there is a dispute between the buyer and seller, then the escrow agent will need to have their attorneys file an interpleader action with the civil courts and let the courts decide what to do with the buyer's earnest money deposit. The escrow agent's attorneys will be paid out of the buyer's earnest money deposit to file the interpleader action, and the amount left over (if any) may be disbursed to the buyer or seller.

6. Partition Action

A co-owner of property may sue the other co-owners, requesting a severance of their respective interests. This proceeding is called a partition action. If the property cannot be physically divided, as is usually the case, the court may order a sale of the property, transfer of title to a buyer, and divide the proceeds among the former owners.

7. Contract Contingencies/Contingency Clause

A **contingency clause** defines specific conditions or actions that must take place before a real estate contract becomes binding. The most common contingencies that appear in residential real estate contracts are physical inspection contingencies, appraisal contingencies, and financing contingencies.

A. Physical Inspection Contingency

A **physical inspection contingency** provides the buyer with a certain amount of time to inspect a single-family home and then decide whether to move forward with the purchase. A home inspection is usually performed by a professional home inspector during this time-period and the buyer must decide whether to remove the contingency to the contract and move forward with the purchase of the property. Both residential and commercial real estate contracts normally utilize an active contingency removal method.

Figure 6.9

> **Contingency Clause:** Specific conditions or actions that must occur before the buyer moves forward with the purchase of the property.
>
> **Physical Inspection Contingency:** Allows a buyer adequate time to thoroughly inspect a single-family home and have experts inspect it prior to moving forward with the purchase.

(1) Active Contingency Removal

The **active contingency removal** method requires the buyer to physically remove the contingency by signing a contingency removal form and presenting it to the seller. The seller signs the contingency removal form and delivers a copy to the buyer and the contingency is removed. Active contingency removals are commonly used with single-family homes, apartment buildings, and leased investments (retail shopping centers, office buildings, and industrial properties).

> **Active Contingency Removal:** The buyer signs a contingency removal form that removes a contingency to the contract.

(2) Passive Contingency Removal

Passive Contingency Removal: Buyer is not required to sign contingency removal to remove a contingency. As time passes and the buyer does nothing, this removes the contingency.

The **passive contingency removal** method allows inaction by the buyer to automatically remove the contingency and obligate the buyer to move forward with the purchase. This was the predominant contingency removal method used in California Association of Realtor (CAR) provided purchase agreements until a few years ago. Today, the passive contingency removal method has been replaced by the active contingency removal method in CAR-provided real estate purchase agreements. Commercial properties have always used the active contingency removal method to remove contingencies for these types of sophisticated properties.

B. Appraisal Contingency

Appraisal Contingency: Contingency to the contract that allows the buyer to not remove the contingency if the property does not appraise for the purchase price.

A second contingency commonly seen in residential single-family purchase contracts is an **appraisal contingency**. If the property does not appraise for the purchase price, the buyer can decide not to remove this contingency to the contract and not go forward with the purchase. When a contingency is not removed, and the buyer does not move forward with the purchase, escrow will be cancelled, and the buyer's earnest money deposit will usually be returned to the buyer. However, both buyer and seller must sign an escrow rescission (cancellation) form before the escrow officer can give the earnest money deposit back to the buyer.

Financing Contingency: Contingency to the contract that allows the buyer to not remove the contingency if the buyer is not able to obtain financing to purchase the property.

If the seller does not sign the escrow rescission form, then the escrow officer cannot return the buyer's earnest money deposit and the escrow officer must file an interpleader action in court and let the courts decide what to do with the buyer's earnest money deposit. The escrow officer usually uses the buyer's earnest money deposit to pay their attorneys to file the interpleader action; thus, a few motions by the escrow company's attorneys and the earnest money will be used up in attorney fees and court costs. Therefore, the buyer is usually motivated to rectify the situation as soon as possible.

C. Financing Contingency

Figure 6.10

A third contingency commonly used in residential single-family purchase contracts is a **financing contingency**. If the buyer is not able to obtain financing to purchase a property, this contingency will not be removed by the buyer and the escrow officer will release the earnest money back to the buyer. This, of course, is with the seller's approval by signing the escrow rescission form.

(1) Auctions

When real estate is sold using an auction, the auctioneer is the seller and the bidders are the buyers. Auctions can be with reserve or without reserve. An auction with reserve allows the auctioneer (seller) to remove the property from the auction anytime up until the gavel is dropped and a sale is consummated. In contrast, an auction without reserve does not allow the auctioneer to remove the property from the auction. If a bid is over the minimum bid amount set for the property, the auctioneer must sell the property to the successful bidder.

For example, Tom Crown is in Europe bidding on some paintings when he hears about an auction for a wonderful chateau in the Napa Wine Country of California. He thinks this may be a nice place to store some of his art work and decides to fly to California to bid on the luxury property. He asks the auction company if the auction is, "with or without reserve." The auction company informs him that it is without reserve and the minimum bid is $1,000,000. He exclaims, "Great!" and flies to California in his private jet. He knows that if he bids at least $1,000,000, the auctioneer will be required to sell the property to him. When the auction starts, Tom bids $1,000,000 for the property. A young lady bids $1,100,000 million. Tom decides to not increase his bid amount and lets her have the property for her bid price. Tom knows although he was not the successful bidder, the trip was not a waste of time as the auction was without reserve. If the auction had been with reserve, the property could have been pulled off the market just prior to the auction causing Tom to have no chance at acquiring the property. An auction with reserve would allow the property to be pulled out of the auction anytime up until the fall of the auctioneers gavel, making the trip a much riskier option.

In an auction without reserve, the auctioneer is required to accept bids. An auctioneer is not required to accept a bid unless the auction is without reserve. For example, an auctioneer sets a minimum bid to begin an auction. Someone offers to buy at 10% more than the opening bid. The auctioneer must accept this bid in an auction without reserve.

Figure 6.11

D. Contingency Sale

A buyer who must sell an existing home before being able to qualify for a loan to purchase a new one may use a 72 hour contingency in the purchase contract. The normal period of time used for this type of contingency is seventy-two (72) hours, hence the name "72 hour contingency."

The seller continues marketing the home after accepting an offer with a 72 hour contingency in the purchase agreement. If the seller obtains another buyer who wants to buy the property and the buyer does *not* need a 72 hour contingency in the purchase agreement to be able to buy the home, then the existing 72 hour contingency buyer is given 72 hours to remove the 72 hour contingency and move forward with the purchase. If the existing 72 hour contingency buyer cannot remove the 72 hour contingency to the purchase agreement and move forward with the purchase, then the 72 hour contingency buyer will not be able to remove the 72 hour contingency and the purchase agreement will be terminated. The escrow agent will return the buyer's earnest money deposit after the escrow rescission has been signed by the buyer and seller. The new buyer then can move forward and purchase the property from the seller.

8. Other Important Contract Terms

A. Novation

Novation: A substitution of a new contract for an old one. An example is a loan assumption to replace one borrower for another.

A **novation** is the substitution of a new contract for an old one (existing contract). For example, if a lender releases a seller from the obligation to pay a loan during a loan assumption and substitutes the buyer as the one responsible to repay the debt, this is called a novation.

B. Statute of Limitations

Statute of Limitations: The length of time a person has to take action in a court of law.

The **statute of limitations** is the amount of time a person has to bring action in a court of law. A purchaser of real property generally has two (2) years to bring a claim in court if the claim is related to physical defects in the property (i.e., non-disclosure of a material fact on the Real Estate Transfer Disclosure Statement). In contrast, the statute of limitations for a breach of fiduciary duty is generally four (4) years from the close of escrow or when the defect is discovered by the plaintiff in the lawsuit. If these time periods are exceeded, then the statute of limitations takes effect and the person who was harmed is prevented from bringing an action in court.

C. Options

Option: A person pays consideration to another person for the option of purchasing a property for a specific amount and within a certain length of time.

An **option** is an agreement to keep an offer open for a specified period of time. In other words, if a person enters into a contract and agrees not to terminate the contract for a certain period of time, this is called an option.

For example, a developer pays $50,000 as consideration for the option to purchase a farmer's property for $2 million over the next two years. The developer pays the farmer the $50,000 and then contacts the local government entities near the subject property to determine the density of housing that can be built in the area. Up until the option ends in two years, the developer can pay the additional $1,950,000 and move forward with the purchase of the property. The farmer is contractually obligated to convey the property to the developer for the amount specified in the option. If the real estate market turns downward and prices decline, the developer may decide not to exercise the option to purchase the property. At the end of the two-year option period the option will expire. The farmer will keep the $50,000 consideration for the option and can sell the property to anyone he wants to since the option has expired. The farmer is the **optionor** who gives an option to the developer who is the **optionee**.

> **Optionor and Optionee:** Optionor (landowner) gives an option to the optionee (developer). Optionee can exercise an option to purchase real property.

An option is a unilateral contract (promise for an act). The optionor/farmer gives an option to an optionee/developer. If the optionee/developer elects to exercise the option and pay the purchase price specified in the option agreement (promise), then the optionor/farmer must perform by conveying the property to the optionee/developer (act).

Options are commonly used in the purchase of raw land, allowing the buyer to resolve zoning, entitlement, and feasibility questions prior to committing the necessary funds to purchase the property. An option must be accompanied by consideration (bargained for exchange) and options are usually assignable to other parties.

D. Specific Performance

Specific performance is a court action brought to force a party to carry out the terms of a contract. Specific performance is usually used to force the seller to convey real property as stated in the purchase agreement. Each piece of real estate is considered unique and legal damages are many times not adequate to compensate a buyer for a seller's breach of contract. Therefore, the courts may force the seller to convey the property to the buyer under the terms of the contract. Consideration for the contract, however, must be reasonable or sufficient relative to value for the courts to require specific performance. In other words, the price the seller is accepting for the property must be close to the value of the property. If consideration for the contract is significantly less than the actual value of the property, then the buyer may have difficulty prevailing in a specific performance suit.

> **Specific Performance:** If seller refuses to convey property, buyer can sue seller for specific performance and ask the courts to force the seller to sell the property to the buyer.

9. Dispute Resolution

When there is a civil (i.e., money-related) dispute between a buyer and seller, dispute resolution can be in the form of litigation in the civil courts or through alternative dispute resolution procedures such as mediation or arbitration.

Civil courts deal with money disputes such as real estate commissions and buyer/seller disputes. In contrast, **criminal courts** are used by the **district attorney** to prosecute a non-licensee who performs acts required by a real estate license. For example: Jones, who does not have a real estate license, is the owner and president of an investment firm. He advertises and sells properties for his clients. Since these transactions involve real estate, the district attorney will prosecute him for violating the real estate law.

If alternative dispute resolution (i.e., mediation and arbitration) are not effective in resolving a civil dispute, the parties may pursue litigation in the courts. With litigation, a judge or jury hears the case, they reach a verdict, and there is an appeal process. Generally, the trial courts hear the case, and one of the appellate courts in California can review the case on appeal. The three appellate court justices check the rules of law that relate to the trial court's decision and either affirm the judgment, reverse the decision, or remand the case back to the trial court for further review.

A. California Real Estate Consumer Recovery Account Fund

Real estate agents are custodians of the public's interest when conducting licensed activities. For this reason, the DRE takes its regulatory duties very seriously.

When an agent harms a member of the general public and then skips town and does not pay the judgment(s) against him, the DRE has a real estate recovery fund to help the harmed person obtain some measure of damages. The Recovery Fund is paid through real estate license fees.

The primary purpose of the **California Real Estate Consumer Recovery Account Fund** is for members of the general public, who hold uncollectable judgments against a licensee, to collect limited damages.

It is also called the Consumer Recovery Fund or Consumer Recovery Account and is a fund of last resort for a member of the general public who has obtained a final judgment against a real estate licensee and who has been unable to satisfy the judgment through normal post-trial proceedings. The judgment must be based upon fraud (lying), misrepresentation (honest mistake), deceit (lying), or conversion (theft) of **trust funds**. If payment from the Consumer Recovery Account is made, the license of the judgment debtor is automatically suspended until the licensee has repaid the total amount of the judgment plus interest.

Maximum recovery limits are $50,000 per occurrence and $250,000 per licensee. Therefore, the maximum the court can levy against the Consumer Recovery Account for one licensee is $250,000.

Tales from the Trade

THE STORY OF A CLAIM FROM THE CONSUMER RECOVERY ACCOUNT

The following excerpt is from the California Department of Real Estate:

"The following is an example of one of the many ways one can be victimized by a dishonest licensee. This is a true story taken from an application filed with the Consumer Recovery Account that resulted in payment to the victims.

The owners of property located in Southern California entered into an exclusive listing agreement with the Broker. The property was advertised as a large five bedroom and three bath home with a garage that had been converted to guest quarters. The advertisement stated that the property was in good condition and excellent for a large family.

When Mr. and Mrs. Buyer, who were looking for a property to accommodate their family of five children, saw the advertisement, they contacted the Broker. The buyers were introduced to the real estate agent (Agent)—who is a licensed real estate salesperson in this story. Upon inspecting the property, the buyers were assured by the Agent that the roof was new and had no leaks, that all additions had been built to code and with the proper permits, that the heating, plumbing and electrical systems were in good working condition, and that only one master release bar was needed to operate security bars on all the windows. Based upon these representations, the buyers purchased the property for $155,000.

Throughout negotiations, the buyers had requested a copy of what is known as the transfer disclosure statement from the Agent. The buyers were not provided with a copy until one day after the close of escrow. Upon reviewing the disclosure statement, the buyers discovered that the roof was actually ten years old, that the garage conversion had been done without the proper permits, and that the third bathroom was not properly constructed.

After moving into the house, the buyers further discovered that the roof had been leaking to such an extent that it had caused severe damage to the interior of the property including the collapse of one of the ceilings. Because the plumbing, heating and electrical systems had not been installed according to the building codes, the buyers received "red tag" notices from the utility companies preventing them from operating the heaters. Finally, the buyers were told by building inspectors that the security bars could not remain on the windows without a separate release bar for each window.

The property was inspected by several contractors who verified the unlivable condition of the property. The contractors' estimates were all in excess of $40,000 to repair the property. The buyers executed a Notice of Rescission requesting the purchase of the property be rescinded. After failing to receive any satisfaction, the buyers filed a lawsuit against the sellers, the broker and the salesperson in superior court alleging fraud, negligence and breach of fiduciary duty. The buyers settled with the Broker. Judgments were entered against the sellers and the Agent ▼

THE STORY OF A CLAIM FROM THE CONSUMER RECOVERY ACCOUNT

in the amount of $50,000. The court found that the defendants defrauded the buyers by intentionally misrepresenting the condition of the property, concealing known defects, and failing to provide a disclosure statement.

The buyers tried unsuccessfully to enforce their judgment against the sellers and the Agent. They then filed an application for payment from the Consumer Recovery Account. Payment of the application was granted in the amount of $20,000, the statutory maximum allowable for one transaction at the time the application was filed (it is now $50,000 today). The Agent's real estate agent's license was indefinitely suspended as a result of the payment from the Consumer Recovery Account. The suspension of the Agent's license cannot be lifted until the Consumer Recovery Account is reimbursed the amount paid in full plus 10% interest. In addition, the Agent's real estate license has been revoked as a result of a disciplinary enforcement action filed by DRE."

10. Alternative Dispute Resolution

Plaintiff: Person bringing a lawsuit in court.

Defendant: Person being sued in court.

In lieu of civil litigation in the courts, both **plaintiff** (the person bringing the lawsuit) and **defendant** (the person being sued) may agree to alternative dispute resolution which involves mediation and/or arbitration of the dispute. This is generally a less expensive and easier way to decide a matter of contention.

A. Mediation of Disputes

Mediation: A non-binding process outside the courts to decide a dispute.

Mediation is a mutually agreeable attempt by a third party to resolve a civil dispute between a buyer and seller in a real estate transaction. If an agreeable solution cannot be reached, then the parties may resort to binding arbitration. Mediation is not binding upon the parties; however, arbitration usually is binding upon both parties.

B. Arbitration of Disputes

Arbitration: A binding process outside the courts to decide a dispute.

Arbitration is a private and informal means to resolve a civil dispute. It refers a dispute to an impartial intermediary for a final and binding decision, however, there is an appeal process. A seller who signs an arbitration of disputes clause in a listing agreement gives up their right to the judicial court system. Both parties, however, may be represented by legal counsel in the arbitration proceeding.

The parties to the dispute usually take depositions and utilize the discovery phase of the arbitration with the same "rights, remedies, and procedures" as a civil action in the Superior Court of California.

An arbitrator hears the case and makes a determination. The determination is an award that is binding between both parties. For example, if both the buyer and seller agree to the type of dispute resolution used by initialing the arbitration clause in the purchase agreement and/or listing agreement, then a binding arbitrator (usually a former judge or real estate attorney with at least five years of experience) will hear the case and make a determination. There is an appeal process through the courts.

There have been instances in which arbitration of a dispute has cost as much or more than a civil court proceeding. Generally, however, arbitration reduces the costs of dispute resolution and expedites final verdicts and remedies.

C. Exclusions from Mediation and Arbitration

Excluded from mediation and arbitration are:
- judicial and non-judicial foreclosure of trust deeds, mortgages, and land contracts
- unlawful detainer actions to evict a non-paying tenant
- mechanics lien filing and enforcement
- probate
- small claims court disputes
- wrongful death tort actions

Chapter Six Summary

A contract is an agreement to do or not to do something. There are four elements required for all contracts: competent parties/capacity to contract, mutual assent, lawful objective, and sufficient consideration. Real estate contracts have a fifth element: in writing because of the statute of frauds.

Offer and acceptance is important with offers and counter offers. Types of contracts include an express, implied, bilateral, unilateral, executory, executed, unenforceable, voidable, and void contracts. Breach of contract is examined in light of liquidated damages, along with contract rescission. Physical inspection, appraisal, and financing contingencies are discussed, along with 72 hour contingencies. Other important contract terms include novation, statute of limitations, options, and specific performance. Dispute resolution is considered through civil and criminal courts, dispute resolution, mediation, arbitration, DRE citations and fines, and the Consumer Recovery Account.

Chapter Six Quiz

1. Who of the following are restricted from contracting?
(A) Incompetents
(B) Minors
(C) Convicts
(D) All of the above are restricted from contracting

2. A minor who is under 18 years of age cannot contract unless he or she is:
(A) married or divorced
(B) in the military
(C) emancipated by the courts
(D) all of the above are correct

3. An offer can be terminated through:
(A) revocation
(B) death of the offeror
(C) rejection
(D) all of the above are correct

4. A contract to commit a crime is a:
(A) valid contract
(B) void contract
(C) voidable contract
(D) incomplete contract

5. A(n) _____ is a contract in which the agreement between the parties is shown by acts or conduct, rather than words.
(A) implied contract
(B) express contract
(C) void contract
(D) voidable contract

6. A unilateral contract is a(n):
(A) promise for a promise
(B) promise for money
(C) promise for an act
(D) illusory contract

7. A verbal contract to purchase real estate is:
(A) void
(B) unenforceable
(C) valid
(D) ilusory

8. _____ deal with money disputes such as real estate commissions and buyer/seller disputes.
(A) Criminal courts
(B) Civil courts
(C) City ordinances
(D) None of the above are correct

9. _____ is a mutually agreeable (non-binding) attempt by a third party to resolve a dispute between a buyer and seller.
(A) Arbitration
(B) Mediation
(C) Litigation
(D) All of the above are correct

10. _____ is a private and informal (yet binding) means to resolve a dispute.
(A) Arbitration
(B) Mediation
(C) Litigation
(D) None of the above are correct

SECTION III

DURING THE REAL ESTATE TRANSACTION

During the Real Estate Transaction

Real Estate Transaction Overview

BUYER'S AGENT
(SELLING AGENT)

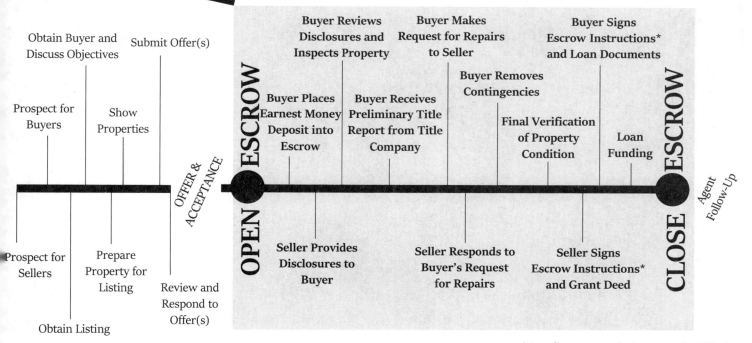

Obtain Buyer and Discuss Objectives

Submit Offer(s)

Prospect for Buyers

Show Properties

OFFER & ACCEPTANCE

OPEN ESCROW

Buyer Reviews Disclosures and Inspects Property

Buyer Makes Request for Repairs to Seller

Buyer Signs Escrow Instructions* and Loan Documents

Buyer Places Earnest Money Deposit into Escrow

Buyer Receives Preliminary Title Report from Title Company

Buyer Removes Contingencies

Final Verification of Property Condition

Loan Funding

CLOSE ESCROW

Agent Follow-Up

Prospect for Sellers

Prepare Property for Listing

Review and Respond to Offer(s)

Obtain Listing

Seller Provides Disclosures to Buyer

Seller Responds to Buyer's Request for Repairs

Seller Signs Escrow Instructions* and Grant Deed

SELLER'S AGENT
(LISTING AGENT)

* According to escrow signing customs in California, properties located in Southern California may sign escrow instructions <u>early</u> in the escrow period just <u>after</u> opening escrow. In Northern California, however, escrow instructions may be signed <u>late</u> in the escrow period just <u>before</u> close of escrow.

Robert Kiyosaki

"If I have cash and I can't figure a way to put it into real estate or my business, I hold it in gold and silver."

Chapter
SEVEN

Opening Escrow and the Escrow Process

Real estate agents are involved with **escrows** on a continual basis and need to understand the entire escrow process to be successful in the real estate brokerage business. Understanding earnest money deposits and escrow signing requirements will help a real estate agent correctly advise their clients regarding the best ways to buy and sell a home.

> **Escrow:** The deposit of instruments and/or funds with instructions with a third neutral party to carry out the provisions of an agreement or contract.

1. Escrow Process

When one party wants to sell an item and another party wants to buy the item, the buyer pays the seller, takes the item, and the transaction is concluded. For example, when a buyer purchases a computer, cash is placed in the seller's hand and the buyer walks away with the computer.

What happens, however, when the item being purchased is complex and expensive like a single-family home? The buyer may want to spend time and money investigating the home to verify it is in good condition before moving forward with the purchase. The buyer is usually concerned with inspecting the property for physical defects, examining the title, and obtaining financing (including the property appraising for the purchase price). For this reason, the buyer and seller may hire an escrow agent (also called escrow holder or escrow officer) to handle the transaction.

BUYER'S AGENT (SELLING AGENT)

Obtain Buyer and Discuss Objectives

Submit Offer(s)

Buyer Reviews Disclosures and Inspects Property

Buyer Makes Request for Repairs to Seller

Buyer Signs Escrow Instructions* and Loan Documents

Prospect for Buyers

Show Properties

Buyer Places Earnest Money Deposit into Escrow

Buyer Receives Preliminary Title Report from Title Company

Buyer Removes Contingencies

Final Verification of Property Condition

Loan Funding

OFFER & ACCEPTANCE

OPEN ESCROW

CLOSE ESCROW

Agent Follow-Up

Prospect for Sellers

Prepare Property for Listing

Review and Respond to Offer(s)

Seller Provides Disclosures to Buyer

Seller Responds to Buyer's Request for Repairs

Seller Signs Escrow Instructions* and Grant Deed

Obtain Listing

* According to escrow signing customs in California, properties located in Southern California may sign escrow instructions <u>early</u> in the escrow period just <u>after</u> opening escrow. In Northern California, however, escrow instructions may be signed <u>late</u> in the escrow period just <u>before</u> close of escrow.

SELLER'S AGENT (LISTING AGENT)

Figure 7.1

A. Escrow Agent

Escrow Agent: A disinterested third-party intermediary who holds all funds and facilitates the escrow process.

An **escrow agent** is a disinterested third-party intermediary who holds all funds and facilitates the escrow process. Escrow allows the buyer to investigate the property without being obligated to move forward with the purchase if the property turns out to be in poor physical condition or has other problems.

After escrow is opened, the escrow agent becomes the agent of the buyer and seller (together) during the escrow process. After close of escrow (all the terms and conditions are met, and the escrow is considered "perfected"), the escrow agent becomes the independent agent of the buyer and the independent agent of the seller.

In other words, during the escrow period both the buyer and seller must agree with all instructions made to the escrow agent. If the buyer wants to do something, the seller must agree. If the seller wants to do something, the buyer must agree. However, after close of escrow the escrow agent is the independent agent of the seller and independent agent of the buyer. The escrow agent can then follow the instructions of the buyer or seller without the other party's agreement.

For example, if the seller would like the escrow agent to wire proceeds from the sale to three different bank accounts, the buyer would not have to agree with this request. Since escrow has closed, the escrow agent is no longer the agent of both parties. However, before escrow had closed both buyer and seller must agree with everything the escrow agent is instructed to do during the escrow period.

B. Earnest Money Deposits

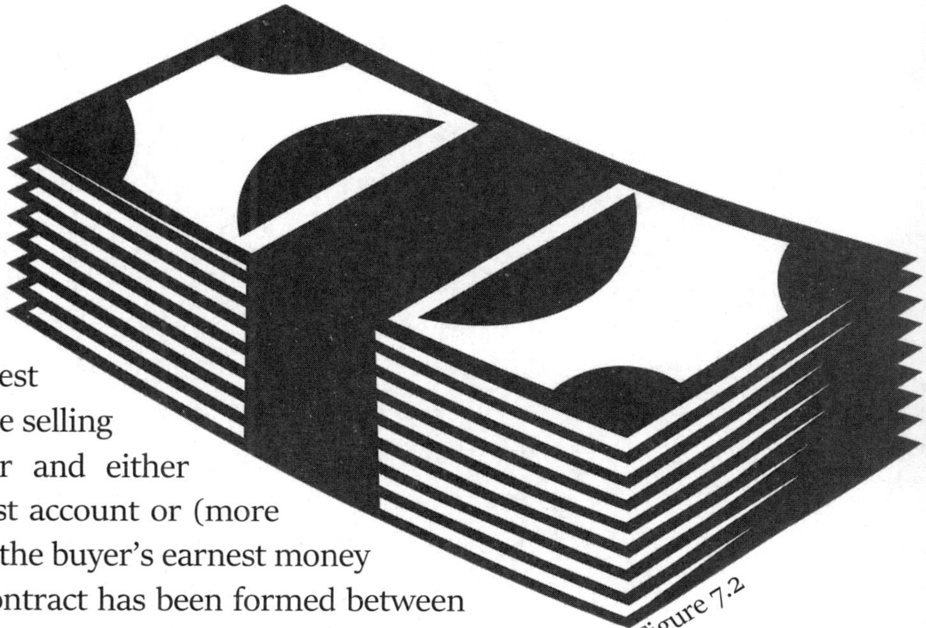

In the purchase agreement the buyer may be required to provide an earnest money deposit (usually $1,000 to $5,000 for single-family resale homes) to ensure the buyer is in "earnest" and serious about purchasing the property. The earnest money deposit is normally given to the selling agent (buyer's agent) by the buyer and either deposited into the selling agent's trust account or (more commonly) the selling agent deposits the buyer's earnest money deposit directly into escrow after a contract has been formed between the buyer and seller.

Figure 7.2

If the buyer's earnest money check is deposited into the selling agent's trust account, the selling agent will usually transfer the deposit to the escrow agent after there is a signed contract and an escrow agent has been selected by the buyer and seller. If the earnest money is deposited directly into escrow (buyer and seller have already agreed which escrow agent to use), then the escrow agent holds the buyer's earnest money deposit during the entire escrow period. Even though the selling agent does not touch the earnest money check in this case, the selling agent must log the check as undeposited funds in their real estate broker's trust account ledger.

At this point, one of three things will happen: 1. Buyer moves forward and purchases the property, or 2. Buyer does not move forward with the purchase, buyer and seller sign escrow rescission forms, and the buyer is reimbursed for the earnest money deposit, or 3. Buyer does not move forward with the purchase, buyer signs the escrow rescission form but the seller does not sign the escrow rescission form, and the escrow agent directs their attorneys to file an interpleader action in court and let the court decide what to do with the buyer's earnest money deposit.

1. **Buyer moves forward and purchases the property.**

   The buyer investigates the property, decides it is in good physical condition, and moves forward to close escrow. At this time the earnest money deposit is included in the sale of the property and is commonly used by the buyer as part of the down payment when the buyer obtains a loan to purchase the property.

2. **Buyer does not move forward with the purchase, buyer and seller sign escrow rescission form, and the buyer is reimbursed for the earnest money deposit.**

   The buyer investigates the property, decides it is not in good physical condition, does not remove the physical inspection contingency to the purchase agreement, and does not move forward to close escrow. When this occurs, the escrow agent will be directed by the buyer to return the buyer's earnest money deposit. The buyer will sign an escrow rescission form directing the escrow officer to return the deposit. However, before the escrow agent can return the buyer's earnest money deposit, the seller must agree to return the buyer's earnest money deposit as well. The seller will sign the escrow rescission form and the escrow agent will then return the buyer's earnest money deposit.

3. **Buyer does not move forward with the purchase, buyer signs the escrow rescission form, but the seller does not sign the escrow rescission form and the escrow agent directs their attorneys to file an interpleader action in court and let the court decide what to do with the buyer's earnest money deposit.**

   If the seller thinks the buyer has been wasting their time, the seller may decide not to sign the escrow rescission form and the escrow officer will not be able to return the buyer's earnest money deposit. At this point, the escrow officer will direct the escrow company's attorneys to file an interpleader action asking the courts to determine what to do with the buyer's earnest money deposit. The escrow agent will usually use the buyer's earnest money deposit to pay their attorneys to file the interpleader action. When this happens, the earnest money deposit is quickly reduced to zero and the buyer may not get any money back.

(1) Liquidated Damages and Escrow

Due to the above problems, most one-to-four unit residential real estate purchase agreements have a liquidated damages clause that sets the damages ahead of time if the buyer removes all contingencies to the contract (all the ways for the buyer to get out of the contract have been removed) and then does not go forward with the purchase.

Liquidated damages are a maximum of 3% of the purchase price, not to exceed the amount of the earnest money deposit for owner-occupied one-to-four unit residential properties in California. If the liquidated damages clause has been initialed by the buyer and seller in the purchase agreement, this clause becomes effective and the seller may be able to collect liquidated damages of 3% of the purchase price, not to exceed the amount of the earnest money deposit.

Earnest money deposits normally range between $1,000 and $5,000 for most resale single-family home transactions in California. However, this amount can be $10,000 or more for higher-end resale homes and new construction from a homebuilder. Earnest money deposits for large commercial properties can be $50,000 or more.

For example, a $400,000 single-family home will have liquidated damages of $12,0000 ($400,000 x 3% = $12,000). However, if the earnest money deposit is only $1,000, the maximum the seller could collect as liquidated damages is $1,000.

In addition, some real estate contracts provide for the seller to split the liquidated damages with the listing agent on a 50%/50% basis. Thus, the seller may collect $500 and the listing agent may collect $500. However, if the buyer is not willing to sign a release of the earnest money deposit (being held in escrow) to the seller, then the escrow agent cannot release the funds to the seller and the escrow agent will be required to file an interpleader action and let the courts decide what to do with the $1,000 earnest money deposit.

As mentioned earlier, the escrow agent will use the $1,000 earnest money deposit to pay their attorneys to file the interpleader action, so the entire amount will most likely be consumed with filing motions in court and the seller and listing agent will probably not end up with any compensation for their efforts.

The escrow period usually correlates with the financing contingency period in the purchase agreement and is usually the most limiting factor in the buyer and seller being able to close escrow. Conventional loans usually average 15-30 days from the effective date of the contract (when the purchase agreement was signed by both parties) to loan funding and close of escrow. Government-insured (FHA) and government-guaranteed (VA) loans average 15-45 days to fund and close escrow.

C. Buyer and Seller Select Escrow Agent

An escrow agent is selected by the buyer and seller. Even though a seller cannot legally insist on a specific escrow agent, the selection of an escrow agent is many times a point of negotiation between the parties. Agents many times make recommendations of potential escrow officers; however, the buyer and seller must decide which escrow officer to use in the transaction.

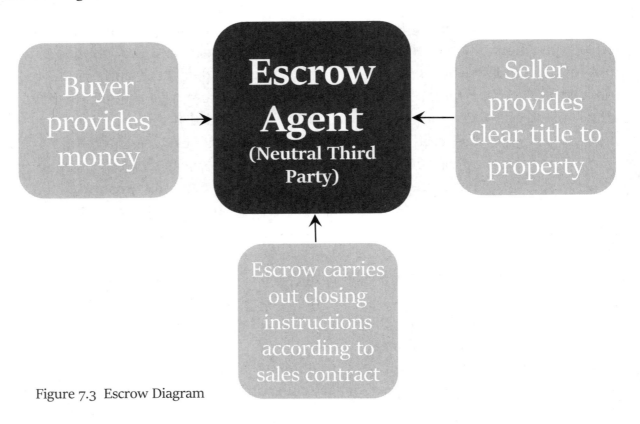

Figure 7.3 Escrow Diagram

D. Northern California and Southern California Differences

In California there are regional differences in escrow procedures. Southern California uses separate escrow companies and title insurance companies. In addition, escrow instructions are normally signed at the beginning of the escrow period usually a few days after escrow is opened. The signed escrow instructions take precedence over the purchase agreement during the escrow period.

In contrast, Northern California uses escrow and title insurance companies that are combined under one company. In addition, escrow instructions are signed near the end of the escrow period, usually a few days prior to close of escrow. By signing late in the escrow period, the purchase agreement remains the controlling document through the escrow period. This is convenient when there are repairs being negotiated during escrow.

For example, the buyer pays for a home inspection during the physical inspection contingency period prior to close of escrow. The home inspector notices that the water heater is not strapped to the wall and notes this in the inspector's findings. The selling agent (buyer's agent), per buyer request, uses a request for repairs addendum to ask for the water heater strapping to be installed before close of escrow. The seller signs the request for repairs addendum and agrees to install the two required straps.

During the **walk-thru inspection** just prior to close of escrow, the selling agent should advise the buyer to verify whether the two straps have been installed

Walk-thru Inspection: Buyer's inspection prior to close of escrow to verify the property is in the same condition and any requested repairs have been completed.

prior to close of escrow. If they have not been installed, the buyer will submit a request to have them installed before moving forward to close escrow.

In Southern California, where escrow instructions may have been signed early in the escrow period, the buyer and seller may be required to sign updated escrow instructions in addition to signing the request for repairs addendum. This will require coming back into the escrow officer's office to sign in front of the escrow officer who is a notary public or incurring the added expense of a mobile notary meeting the buyer and seller at their homes and having the updated escrow instructions signed there.

Both methods used in Northern California and Southern California work well in practice, but the Northern California method seems to be more convenient. For this reason, signing escrow instructions later in the transaction is becoming more prevalent throughout California.

E. Joint Escrow Instructions to Escrow Agent

A purchase agreement may also act as **joint escrow instructions**. Historically, an escrow officer has taken contractual information from the purchase agreement and transferred the information to the escrow instructions that are then signed by the buyer and seller. These are instructions in narrative form that specify the conditions of the escrow, including price, terms, and conditions of the sale.

> **Joint Escrow Instructions:** The purchase agreement is part of the escrow instructions.

Escrow officers have traditionally drawn up escrow instructions without "seeing" the purchase agreement and incurring any liability for the purchase agreement. Some contracts attempt to make the escrow officer liable for mistakes made in transferring important provisions and information within the purchase agreement to the escrow instructions. Today, however, purchase agreements are commonly *combined* with joint escrow instructions making purchase agreements part of the escrow instructions. Therefore, all the items in the purchase agreement will be correctly transferred to the escrow instructions because the escrow officer can look at the purchase agreement itself when drawing up the escrow instructions.

When a buyer and seller sign the escrow instructions, the escrow instructions take precedence over the previously signed Real Estate Purchase Agreement and Joint Escrow Instructions. This is especially important in Southern California where the escrow companies are very strong and tend to sign escrow instructions early in the transaction. Once the escrow instructions have been signed by the buyer and seller, they are the *controlling document* and are used to direct the escrow.

In contrast, in Northern California escrow instructions are signed late in the transaction, so the controlling document is the purchase agreement throughout the escrow period until the escrow instructions are signed a few days prior to close of escrow.

F. Escrow Terminated

Escrow is terminated at close of escrow or if both the buyer and seller agree to terminate the escrow. If this occurs, the buyer and seller must sign an escrow rescission form thereby cancelling the escrow.

G. Escrow Prorations

Items that will benefit the buyer may have been paid ahead of time by the seller and prior to close of escrow. Thus, to make things fair to both parties, the prepaid items are credited back to the seller on a prorated basis. This is called a **proration**.

Proration: Seller may have paid items ahead of time prior to close of escrow. To make things fair, the prepaid items are credited back to the seller from the buyer.

For example, the seller paid the property taxes for the entire fiscal tax year of July 1st to June 30th. The seller then closes escrow on December 31st causing the seller to have overpaid his property taxes by six months (January 1st to June 30th). To make things fair, the seller will receive a credit (money back to the seller) in escrow for the property taxes that have been over-paid. Since the seller will not own the property from January 1st to June 30th, the seller should not be required to pay the property taxes for this period of time, so the escrow officer will debit (take from) the buyer the amount of money necessary to credit (pay to) the seller for the six-month overpayment of property taxes.

Property Tax Year Proration Example

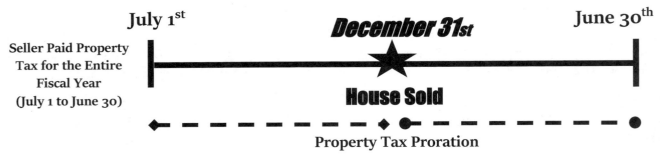

Figure 7.4 Property Tax Year Proration Example

Another common proration is property insurance. Insurance is usually paid at one time for the entire year. Since the seller will not receive the benefit of property insurance for the part of the year after the property has been sold, the seller may receive a credit in escrow for property insurance that was overpaid.

Insurance does the following three things: (1) it protects the insured for the amount and time agreed in the policy, (2) it transfers risk of loss from the insured to the insurance company, and (3) it substitutes uncertainty for certainty.

When a lender collects property tax and homeowner's insurance payments on a monthly basis and then pays them for the homeowner, these are called **impounds**. Impounds are a very common proration item. In an **escrow closing statement**, recurring costs such as property taxes and homeowner's insurance commonly include impounds.

With loans that are greater than 80% loan-to-value ratio, lenders are not comfortable with a homeowner's ability to pay the property taxes and homeowner's insurance on time. For this reason, lenders may require impounds for loans that are greater than 80% loan-to-value because the buyer does not have enough money invested to keep from going into default at the first sign of financial trouble.

Impounds are collected at the same time as the principal and interest payments are collected, hence the acronym "PITI" that denotes principal, interest, taxes, and insurance. The lender usually collects 1/12th the property taxes and 1/12th the homeowner's insurance along with each monthly principal and interest loan payment. The lender then pays the homeowner's property tax bill (twice per year) and the homeowner's insurance (once per year) on behalf of the borrower when they become due.

A **recurring cost** is a cost that continues to occur after close of escrow. Property taxes and homeowner's insurance payments that are being impounded by a lender are common recurring costs. Non-recurring costs are costs that are a one-time charge during escrow. Escrow fees and title insurance costs are examples of non-recurring costs.

To reiterate, during the escrow closing process, the escrow officer may discover that the seller has paid for certain items (pre-paid property taxes) ahead of time. To make things fair to the seller, prepaid items are credited back to the seller on a prorated basis and are called prorations. Prorations are many times impounds of property taxes and homeowner's insurance and are considered a recurring cost (because the buyer continues paying them each month after close of escrow).

If the seller had already paid the second property tax installment (January 1st to June 30th) and then closed escrow in the middle of this time-period, the seller will receive a credit (money back to the seller) for property taxes the seller has paid ahead of time. This is because the seller will not own the property for the other portion of the second property tax installment period. However, when property taxes are pending during escrow, the seller is responsible for them until close of escrow.

> **Impounds:** A lender collects property tax and homeowner's insurance payments on a monthly basis and then pays them for the homeowner.

> **Escrow Closing Statement:** Shows amounts paid to and from buyer and seller during escrow, including property taxes and property insurance.

> **Recurring Cost:** Costs that continue to occur after close of escrow. Examples include property taxes and homeowner's insurance.

Prorations may include: property taxes, assessments, interest, rents, homeowner association dues and assessments, homeowner's insurance, bonds and assessments assumed by a buyer, Mello-Roos bonds, and special assessment district bonds.

H. Escrow Funds

Funds usually include the buyer's down payment and loan funds used to purchase the property, as well as funds from all cash buyers.

(1) Loan Documents: Promissory Note and Deed of Trust

Loan Documents: Sent by the lender to escrow for buyers' signatures.

If a loan is being used to purchase a property, the escrow officer will receive the **loan documents** (promissory note, deed of trust, and a myriad of other loan documents and disclosures) from the lender. The escrow officer will have the buyer sign the loan documents and then call for funding of the buyer's loan. Funding is usually accomplished by wire transfer from the lender to the escrow company's bank. Escrow companies have been very careful with wire transfers due to the amount of wire fraud seen in California.

(2) Payment of Commissions Through Escrow

Broker Demand: Sent from broker into escrow directing the escrow agent to pay the broker's commission at close of escrow.

Brokers usually become a party to the escrow only for the sole purpose of compensation. Brokers usually send a **broker demand** to escrow and are paid their commission out of the escrow proceeds at close of escrow. Confirmation of recording of the grant deed is generally required prior to the escrow officer disbursing commission funds. Commission funds are paid to the real estate broker and the broker pays the real estate salesperson or associate broker from these funds.

I. Additional Escrow Information
(1) Real Estate Brokers Can Perform Escrows

Real estate brokers can perform escrows for their own properties and for their clients' properties. However, they cannot perform escrows for anyone else without a license from the California Department of Business Oversight (DBO) that regulates escrow companies in California.

Figure 7.5

Affiliated Business Arrangements/Broker Controlled Escrows: A controlled escrow could be owned and operated by, but is not limited to, an attorney, a real estate broker, a title insurance company, among others.

(2) Affiliated Business Arrangements/Broker Controlled Escrows

According to the DBO, "In the terminology of the escrow industry, all escrow agents performing escrow services in California are either 'licensed' or 'controlled' escrow companies. A 'licensed' escrow company, which is also known as an 'independent' escrow company, is licensed by the Department of Business Oversight. This license can only be obtained after the escrow company has met and satisfied all of the licensing requirements set forth by the Escrow Law, which are enforced by the Department of Business Oversight. A 'controlled' escrow, which may be known as a 'non-independent' escrow, is not licensed by the Department of Business Oversight. A controlled escrow could be owned and operated by, but is not limited to, an attorney, a real estate broker, a title insurance company, among others. The licensing and regulation of controlled escrows depends on the jurisdiction of the licensing and regulatory authority; therefore, the licensing requirements, laws, and regulations that they are subject to vary widely."

2. Preliminary Title Report

A **preliminary title report** ("prelim") is an offer by a title insurance company to issue a policy of title insurance. The prelim is usually provided by the title insurance company after escrow is opened, but before a title insurance policy is issued. A prelim reports those items affecting title such as encumbrances and how the seller holds title to the property. It is a type of "laundry list" for the real estate agent to ensure there are no title issues that may cause problems (i.e., red flags) for the buyer now or in the future.

Preliminary Title Report: An offer by a title insurance company to issue a policy of title insurance.

Examples of red flags in a preliminary title report are restrictions on the title to the property, the seller not having complete title to convey to the buyer, unpaid and delinquent property taxes, judgment liens, and other specific types of liens–such as "mosquito abatement liens" in which the county places mosquito fish, that eat the mosquito larvae in the seller's scummy green-colored swimming pool, to reduce the reproduction of mosquitos. The seller usually must completely pay off all liens affecting the property by the close of escrow, because the lender will normally not make a loan without clear title to the property. Thus, clouds on the title to real property may cause the buyer to not be able to purchase it.

3. Title Insurance

A title insurance company insures the title to real property. So, when the title insurance company issues a policy of title insurance, the buyer can be confident there are no clouds on the title to the property. If clouds on the title appear after close of escrow, the title insurance company may be required to pay for the buyer's loss.

Title insurance is one of the few types of insurance in which the insurance company can reduce or eliminate claims by doing a thorough title search prior to issuing a policy of title insurance. For this reason, title insurance companies operate title plants that provide thorough title searches and reduce title defects that may harm the deliverability of the property in the future. Buyers benefit from thorough title searches because they are assured marketable title to the property at close of escrow.

There are two types of title insurance policies commonly used in California: California Land Title Association (CLTA) policy and American Land Title (ALTA) policy.

CLTA	ALTA
Standard Coverage Policy (Owner's Policy)	**Extended Coverage Policy** (Lender's Policy)
• all recorded items in the chain of title to the property • forgery (someone is NOT who they say they are) • incompetence (declared incompetent in a court of law) • lack of capacity (a minor under the age of 18) • improper delivery of a recorded deed	• All CLTA coverage + • physical survey • boundary lines • unrecorded encumbrances • encroachments

Figure 7.6 CLTA vs. ALTA

A. California Land Title Association (CLTA) Standard Coverage Policy of Title Insurance

California Land Title Association (CLTA) Standard Coverage Policy of Title Insurance: Insures a property's title against all recorded documents, forgery, incompetence, capacity, and improper delivery of a recorded deed.

A **California Land Title Association (CLTA) Standard Coverage Policy of Title Insurance** insures primarily against defects in title which are discoverable through an examination of the public records (usually recorded items). This includes defects in title, recorded liens, encumbrances–such as unpaid taxes or assessments, and defects due to lack of access to an open street.

A CLTA policy also covers a limited number of risks that are not discoverable through a search of the public records. These include forgery, incompetence, capacity, and improper delivery of a recorded deed. The CLTA is commonly called the "owner's policy" and fees are calculated on the purchase price of the property.

B. American Land Title Association (ALTA) Extended Coverage Policy of Title Insurance

An **American Land Title Association (ATLA) Extended Coverage Policy of Title Insurance** is commonly called a "lender's policy," and fees are usually calculated based on the loan amount. Lenders usually require the use of this policy because it affords greater protection than a CLTA policy. An ALTA policy usually covers all the CLTA coverage plus the following:

- Physical survey
- Boundary lines
- Unrecorded encumbrances
- Encroachments

An ALTA policy is usually issued concurrently with the CLTA policy. In other words, the CLTA owner's policy is usually purchased with the ALTA lender's policy at the same time. The buyer may pay for the ALTA lender's policy and the seller may pay for the CLTA owner's policy for single-family homes in California; however, this varies depending upon county custom, and whether it is an upward-trending sellers' market or downward-trending buyers' market. The ALTA lender's policy covers the loan amount and the CLTA owner's policy covers the entire purchase price of the property. If a property has been insured for title insurance within the previous five years, it may be eligible for a short-term fee schedule that will reduce the title insurance costs.

Neither a CLTA standard coverage policy of title insurance, nor an ALTA extended coverage policy of title insurance will cover new laws that are enacted, nor government regulations such as zoning laws. Of course, no title insurance policy covers everything.

> **American Land Title Association (ALTA) Extended Coverage Policy of Title Insurance:** Insures a property's title against all CLTA coverage plus physical survey, boundary lines, unrecorded encumbrances, and encroachments.

4. Items that Limit Title to Real Property (Encumbrances)

Encumbrances appear in a preliminary title report and limit the title to real property. They may include money encumbrances (liens) that limit the title to real property based on money, or non-money encumbrances that limit the use of real property.

An **encumbrance** limits title to real property. There are two types of encumbrances: money encumbrances (**liens**) and non-money encumbrances based on use.

> **Encumbrances:** Items that limit title to real property.

> **Liens:** Money encumbrances.

Money Encumbrances (Liens)	Non-Money Encumbrances (Based on Use)

• Deeds of Trust and Mortgages
• Mechanic's Liens
• Attachments
• Judgments
• Federal and State Income Taxes
• Property Taxes
• Special Assessments
• Mello-Roos Bonds
	• Easements
	  • Appurtenant Easement
	  • Prescriptive Easement
	  • Easement in Gross
	• CC&Rs
	• Public Restrictions (Zoning)
	• Encroachments
	• Leases
	• Setback Requirements

Figure 7.7 Money vs. Non-Money Encumbrances

A. Money Encumbrances (Liens)

There are several types of money encumbrances (called liens) that limit the title to real property. They include deeds of trust and mortgages, mechanic's liens, attachments, judgments, federal and state income taxes, property taxes, special assessments, and Mello-Roos completion bonds.

(1) Deeds of Trust and Mortgages

A deed of trust (also called a trust deed) is used to secure real property as collateral for a loan. It is a money encumbrance (lien) because it limits a property and is based on money. A loan may have been used to buy the property and it must be paid off (or assumed by the buyer) before title can be passed to a new owner when the property is sold in the future

A mortgage is similar to a deed of trust and is used to secure a real estate loan (the borrower places the property as collateral for repayment of the loan). If the borrower does not repay the loan on time, the lender can foreclose and take over the property, sell it, and get their money back. Deeds of trust and mortgages are discussed in Chapter 12. Most real estate loans in California are deeds of trust. Mortgages are typically *not* used in California.

(2) Mechanic's Liens

When a property owner does not pay for work that has been completed on a property, the contractor or subcontractor who does not get paid can file a **mechanic's lien** against the property. This lien will either force the property owner to pay the amount owed, sell the property and pay the amount owed, or wait until the property is sold in the future and then pay the amount owed out of escrow. A mechanic's lien is usually recorded and appears in the chain of recorded title to a parcel of real property.

For example, Person Able has Contractor Baker do some work on Person Able's property. Person Able does not pay Contractor Baker for the work that is completed, so Contractor Baker files (records) a mechanic's lien

Figure 7.8

Mechanic's Lien: When a property owner does not pay for a contractor's work that was completed on the property, the contractor can file a mechanic's lien.

against the property. The mechanic's lien will now be in the chain of recorded title to the property and must be paid off whenever the property is sold in the future. In other words, sometime in the future the contractor will likely be paid for the work that was performed on the property.

Real estate agents should review the preliminary title report issued by the title company after escrow is opened and verify there are no mechanic's liens existing on the title to the property. There is a rule in real estate that states: "First to record is the first in right." This means that the first person to record a document is the first in right to collect their money if the property is sold in the future. This rule holds true most of the time, however there are three important exceptions to the rule: mechanic's liens, subordinated loans, and taxes.

a. Mechanic's Lien Exception

Mechanic's liens take precedence (priority) when materials are delivered or work is started on the property, and *not* when the contractor files (records) a mechanic's lien. For this reason, real estate lenders who are making a construction loan on a property may drive by the property before funding the loan to verify materials have not been delivered or work started on the property. Otherwise, the construction loan may be "impaired" and the contractor will collect his money before the lender (even though he recorded his mechanic's lien after the lender recorded the deed of trust) in the event of a sale of the property. In other words, the lender will receive whatever is left over after the contractor has been paid.

In upward-trending sellers' markets that are increasing in value, this is usually not a problem because there is plenty of equity in the property to pay for the mechanic's lien and loan amount. However, in downward-trending buyers' markets that are decreasing in value, this can be a big problem for the construction lender. If the sale of the property does not produce enough money to pay off the mechanic's lien and construction loan, the lender may not get all of their money back.

b. Subordinated Loan Exception

Subordinated loans are another exception to the "first to record is the first in right" rule. When a lender signs a subordination clause, the lender is allowing the borrower/property owner to switch the position of loans securing the property.

c. Tax Exception

Property taxes are always paid first. Real estate lenders know this, so they are careful to ensure borrowers always pay their property taxes on time. Lenders will usually require borrowers who obtain loans that are greater than an 80% loan-to-value ratio to pay impounds of property taxes. The borrower pays $1/12^{th}$ the property taxes each month to the lender and the lender pays the borrower's property taxes that become due on the home. Lenders additionally collect $1/12^{th}$ of the property insurance that is due each month and then pay the borrower's property insurance bill.

If a property is sold to pay for delinquent property taxes (tax sale), any money that is left over goes to the lender who recorded their loan (deed of trust) first. If there is any money left over after that, the lender(s) of junior loan(s) (loans that were recorded after the first loan was recorded and are called second deeds of trust or second trust deeds) will be paid. Lastly, if there is any money left over after all these entities have been paid, then the borrower/property owner will receive the balance of the money. It should also be noted that property taxes are paid before federal and state income taxes.

(3) Attachments and Judgments

If a person has been harmed by another person, the person who was harmed may file a lawsuit against the person who harmed them.

For example, Person A injures Person B. Person B (called the plaintiff) files a lawsuit against Person A (called the defendant) in a civil court of law (not criminal court). Person B may file an **attachment** against the assets (i.e., real estate) of Person A. The attachment freezes Person A's assets so they cannot be sold prior to the judgment being rendered by the court. When the judge makes a ruling regarding who wins the lawsuit, this is called a **judgment**. Lastly, the plaintiff (winner of the lawsuit in this particular case) will file a **writ of execution** that will move the defendant's (Person A) frozen assets to the plaintiff (Person B) to satisfy the judgment. Assets may include things of value that can be used to satisfy a judgment such as real estate, bank accounts, etc.

> **Attachment:** Court freezes a person's assets prior to a judgment being rendered.
>
> **Judgment:** When a court makes a ruling.
>
> **Writ of Execution:** Moves the defendant's attached assets to the plaintiff.

Since attachments and judgments are both considered general liens (over all of a person's properties) a plaintiff can go after all of a person's assets to satisfy a judgment.

(4) Federal and State Income Tax

The U.S. federal government and the State of California both collect income tax from their citizens. For businesses such as real estate brokers and salespersons, income tax is usually paid quarterly in the year the income is earned.

In contrast, normal employees, who use employer withholdings to pay their income tax, pay their income tax by April 15th of the following year after the income was earned. New real estate salespersons and brokers should see a tax planning professional as soon as there is commission income on the horizon, so estimated quarterly tax payments can be made to the IRS and State of California in the quarter they are earned. This will prevent the new real estate agent from being penalized for earning too much money during the year and then trying to pay income taxes on or before April 15th of the following year.

Since real estate salespersons and brokers are independent contractors (for tax and unemployment insurance purposes), they pay their income tax themselves and usually on a quarterly basis. In contrast, normal employees' have their income taxes withheld by their employer who pays the amount due to the IRS (federal income taxes) and the State Franchise Tax Board (California state income taxes). Brokers do not withhold anything (this includes social security taxes) from their salesperson's commission income, so salespersons must pay their own taxes when they are due. This is usually quarterly in the year they are earned.

Figure 7.9

Therefore, real estate brokers are not required to withhold social security taxes, federal income tax, California state income tax, and unemployment insurance from the commission income paid to their salespeople.

According to the Special California State Rule, the requirement to withhold tax from compensation paid does not apply to a licensed real estate salesperson who is compensated only on a commission-for-sales basis and not based on hours worked, and the services are performed pursuant to a written agreement with the employing broker that provides that the salesperson will not be treated as an employee for state tax purposes (refer to Unemployment Insurance Code 13002, 13004.1.)

(5) Property Taxes

Property Taxes: Taxes paid by a property owner.

County Tax Assessor: Entity that collects property taxes for the county.

Property taxes are assessed by the county where the property is located. The **county tax assessor** determines an assessed value for the land and another assessed value for the improvements (buildings) that are located on the land. The assessed value of the land is multiplied by the property tax rate (usually 1.15% to 1.25% of the assessed value and is determined by the county board of supervisors or other county entity) to determine the amount of property taxes that must be paid by the property owner for the land during the property tax year (July 1st to June 30th). The assessed value of the building(s) is/are then multiplied by the property tax rate with the result being the amount of taxes due for the building(s) during the tax year. The two property tax amounts are added together to determine the total amount of property taxes that are due for the tax year.

Property Tax Year: Property tax year is July 1st to June 30th. First installment is due November 1st and delinquent December 10th. Second installment is due February 1st and delinquent April 10th.

The **property tax year** is a fiscal year (not a calendar year) that starts on July 1st and ends on June 30th of the following year. The property tax year is divided into two portions: the first half of the property tax year starts on July 1st and runs through December 31st. The second half of the property tax year starts on January 1st and runs through June 30th.

The first installment of property taxes (1/2 of the total property tax bill) is due November 1st and delinquent December 10th for the first half of the property tax year (July 1st to December 31st). The second installment of property taxes (1/2 of the total property tax bill) is due February 1st and delinquent April 10th for the second half of the property tax year (January 1st to June 30th).

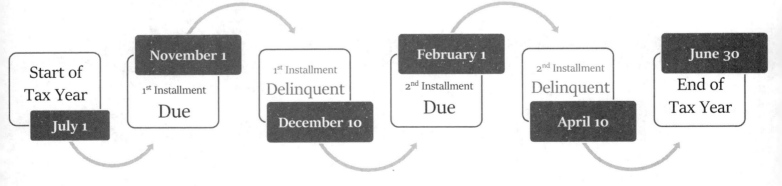

Figure 7.10 Due and Delinquent Property Tax Diagram

Each property tax installment must be paid during the due and delinquent dates; however, both installments can be paid during the first installment period from November 1st to December 10th if the property owner so desires. An easy way to remember property tax due and delinquent dates is "**No Darn Fooling Around**" which stands for **N**ovember 1st and **D**ecember 10th; along with **F**ebruary 1st and **A**pril 10th.

1st Installment		2nd Installment	
November 1st Due	**D**ecember 10th Delinquent	**F**ebruary 1st Due	**A**pril 10th Delinquent
No	**D**arn	**F**ooling	**A**round

Figure 7.11 No Darn Fooling Around Diagram

a. Delinquent Property Taxes

Property taxes become a lien on real property on January 1st of each tax year. For example, the property taxes for the tax year from July 1st, 2020 to June 30th, 2021 become a lien on the property back on January 1st, 2020 (not in 2021). Non-payment of property taxes will result in a tax lien being placed on the property and the property will eventually be sold at a tax sale.

b. Assessor's Parcel Number (APN Number)

Each property in a county is given an assessor's parcel number (APN). It identifies the property in relation to subdivision maps that were approved by local government officials under the Subdivision Map Act. APN numbers are commonly used in the lots, blocks, and tracts land description method to identify individual parcels of real property.

c. Tax Base

The **tax base** is the amount of property taxes the county tax assessor collects for the entire county. Each property owner owes a portion of the overall tax assessment (tax base) and is calculated by dividing the property's combined annual tax assessment (for the land and building) by the tax assessment for the entire county (tax base). The result is the proportion of property taxes the property owner is paying in relation to the overall tax assessment (tax base) for the entire county.

> **Tax Base:** Amount of property taxes paid for the entire county.

d. Ad Valorem, Reassessment, and Over-Assessed

Ad valorem means "according to value." Real properties located in California are assessed at 100% of the sale price when they are sold or reassessed. In other words, a property can be reassessed when the property is sold or when the property owner adds an improvement (e.g., a structure, pool, etc.) to the property.

> **Ad Valorem:** Property taxes are taxed according to value.

As properties increase in value during an upward-trending sellers' market, they are sold at increased prices as they near the top-of-the-market. This causes an increase in assessed values and an increase in property tax revenues.

Later, real property prices will decrease as the real estate market moves from an upward-trending sellers' market to a downward-trending buyers' market. Unfortunately, the county tax assessor may be a little slow adjusting assessed values downward to the lower market levels, thereby causing many properties to be over-assessed. This results in property owners paying more property taxes than they should be paying based on current real estate market values.

When this happens, property owners can appeal to the **assessment appeals board** and ask them to reduce the assessed value down to the present real estate market level. To do this, the owner normally completes an assessment appeals form and provides three sales comparables of similar properties that have recently sold in the same geographic area as the owner's property. The assessment appeals board will consider the property owner's request and either reduce the property's assessed value down to the true market value provided by the owner, partially reduce the assessed value, or deny the request altogether. A reduced assessed value will reduce the owner's property taxes, so it is generally advantageous for the property owner to keep an eye on their property's assessed value and ensure they do not pay too much in property taxes.

> **Assessment Appeals Board:** Homeowners can ask the assessment appeals board to reduce their assessed value and therefore, the amount of property taxes paid.

e. Supplemental Assessment

When an older property that has been held by the seller for many years is finally sold, the existing property taxes being paid on the property may be rather low due to Proposition 13. Property tax increases are limited under Proposition 13 to no more than 2% per year as long as the property was not sold. Once sold, the property is reassessed at 1% of the sale price (plus local assessments that usually total .15% to .25% above the 1% Prop. 13 level), and the 2% yearly cap becomes applicable to future years. Therefore, when the property is sold many years later, the property tax bill may increase to several times more than the existing property tax bill.

The escrow officer must prorate property taxes based on the seller's existing assessed property value and not on the buyer's new assessed property value. Therefore, a large amount of property taxes that should have been collected in escrow is not collected and paid by the escrow officer. The additional taxes not collected in escrow will be collected by the County Tax Assessor through a supplemental assessment. Therefore, a supplemental tax bill will be mailed to the buyer several months down the road. Real estate agents should prepare their buyers for this situation at close of escrow.

For example, Aunt Martha is an eighty-three year old lady living alone in her home. She would like to sell the home and move in with her daughter to make it easier to care for herself. She places her home on the market and quickly finds a suitable buyer. She has lived in the property since 1963 when she paid $20,000 for the property and presently pays $212 in real estate property taxes each year ($106 in each installment, remember No Darn Fooling Around, the first installment is paid between November 1st and December 10th and the second installment is paid between February 1st and April 10th, but she could pay both installments during the first installment period).

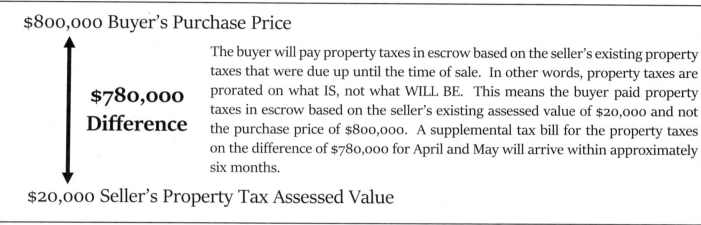

Figure 7.11 Supplemental Tax Assessment Example

Aunt Martha sells the property for $800,000. The buyer's new property taxes will be approximately $9,200 per year ($800,000 x 1.15% = $9,200). The escrow officer who is handling the escrow must prorate the existing taxes based on the $212 Aunt Martha is presently paying in property taxes (not the new property taxes the buyer will be paying, because the escrow officer cannot estimate the new property tax amounts the county tax assessor will assess the new buyer).

Close of escrow occurs at the end of April and Aunt Martha had already paid her property taxes (paid on April 10th) for the second half of the tax year (January-June). Since she will not own the property in May or June, yet has paid property taxes for these two months, Aunt Martha will receive a credit (credits go in and debits go out) in escrow for two months of property taxes she has already paid . . .this will amount to $35.33 ($212 divided by 12 x 2 months = $35.33). The escrow officer will then debit the buyer (buyer will pay out) for two months property taxes amounting to $35.33. However, the new property owner's tax bill will be $1,533.33 for the two months that were prorated at only $35.33 in escrow ($9,200/year new property tax bill divided by 12 x 2 months = $1,533.33). The difference between the actual proration of $35.33 and the taxes that will be paid by the buyer ($1,533.33) is $1,498.00 and will be collected by the County Tax Assessor in a *supplemental tax bill* that will arrive one to six months or more after close of escrow. It is many times wise to inform buyers of this supplemental tax bill, so they do not have a big surprise when it arrives several months after close of escrow.

f. Property Tax Liens

Property taxes in California are considered a specific lien, so nonpayment of property taxes will result in a lien against the property. Since property taxes are not a general lien, the county where the property is located could *not* go after an owner's other properties to satisfy the lien.

g. Businesses Opportunities in California

When a business is sold in California, the buyer must obtain a **clearance certificate** from the **California State Board of Equalization (BOE)** that assures the buyer there are no outstanding sales tax payments due from the business to the BOE. The reason this is important to buyers of a business is because sales taxes are paid quarterly to BOE and if the business purchase occurs in the middle of one of these quarters, the buyer is responsible for sales tax collected from the first day of the present quarter until the date of close of escrow (a period of time when the buyer did *not* own the business). The buyer should hold back enough money to pay these sales taxes, otherwise, the buyer will be required to pay this money at the end of the quarter. Thus, the buyer could be obligated to pay collected sales tax to the BOE when the buyer did not even own the property!

Clearance Certificate: Certificate obtained from the California State Board of Equalization verifying that the seller has paid all sales taxes that are due.

California State Board of Equalization (BOE): California state entity that collects sales taxes.

(6) Special Assessment

Special assessments provide for specific local improvements. Local governments may levy special assessments on homeowners who benefit from local improvements, which may include water districts, sewage treatment facilities, street lights, and other local improvements.

Special Assessment: Collected from homeowners who benefit from specific local improvements.

Mello-Roos Community Facilities Act: A seller of any one-to-four unit residential property must make a good faith effort to obtain a disclosure notice concerning the special tax from each local agency.

(7) Mello-Roos Community Facilities Act

The **Mello-Roos Community Facilities Act** is a bond issue that pays for offsite improvements to local neighborhoods. A Mello-Roos bond usually runs from twenty (20) to twenty-five (25) years in duration and normally does not renew.

A Mello-Roos District is a special property tax that is paid in

The Tax You Choose

Figure 7.12

addition to regular property taxes. The tax pays for the principal and interest payments on the Mello-Roos bonds that were issued to pay for public improvements and public services that include streets, schools, parks, police protection, water, sewage/drainage, electricity, and other infrastructure.

B. Non-Money Encumbrances (Based on Use)

Non-money encumbrances are based on the use of a property. Common non-money encumbrances include easements; covenants, conditions, and restrictions (CC&Rs); public restrictions (zoning); encroachments; leases; and setback requirements.

Non-Money Encumbrance: Encumbrance based on the use of a property.

(1) Easements

There are three types of easements that affect real property in California. They include appurtenant easements, easements by prescription/prescriptive easements, and easements in gross.

a. Appurtenant Easements

An appurtenant easement runs with the land and allows one property owner to drive over (use) another property owner's property out to the road.

For example, Mr. Smith owned a rectangular-shaped lot with a home located at one end of the lot and a roadway abutting the other end. Mr. Smith subdivided the parcel into two parcels: Parcel A and Parcel B. Mr. Smith's home was located on Parcel A and Parcel B was vacant and is adjacent to (abuts) the street.

Mr. Smith built a home on Parcel B and then sold it to Buyer Baker. Mr. Smith wanted to be able to drive from Parcel A (from his home) across Parcel B (owned by Buyer Baker) out to the road. So, Mr. Smith gave himself (and any future owners of Parcel A) an *appurtenant easement* that allows the owner of Parcel A to drive across Parcel B out to the road. Thus, whoever owns Parcel A can use the easement to drive over Buyer Baker's property out to the road. Whoever owns Parcel B must allow the owner of Parcel A to drive over their property out to the road.

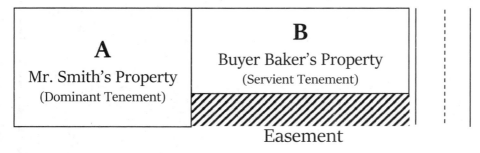

Figure 7.13 Appurtenant Easement Example

The appurtenant easement was recorded in the deed to Parcel A (called the *dominant tenement*), as well as recorded in the deed to Parcel B (called the *servient tenement*). The dominant tenement can drive over the servient tenement out to the road. The servient tenement must allow the dominant tenement to drive across their property to access the road.

Separately, road agreements are frequently seen in rural areas of California. Several farmers may use the same road to enter and exit their properties. Each farmer who uses the road usually agrees to maintain and repair the road as needed for their mutual benefit. The costs may be split among all the farmers, so each farmer pays for their fair share of the costs to maintain the road.

Prescriptive Easement/ Easement by Prescription: Easement gained by use and lost by nonuse.

b. Easement by Prescription/Prescriptive Easement

An **easement by prescription** or **prescriptive easement** is gained by use and lost by nonuse. For example, a surfer has been crossing a person's yard for many years on his way to his favorite surfing spot. The property owner places a fence across his yard stopping the surfer from using his property to access the great surf break on the other side of the property. The surfer files suit to remove the fence claiming he has an easement by prescription/prescriptive easement to walk across the property to get to his choice surf spot. The court will find that the surfer

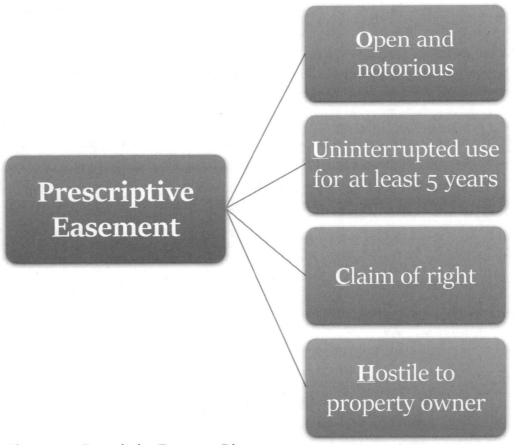

Figure 7.14 Prescriptive Easement Diagram

does indeed have an easement by prescription/prescriptive easement over the person's property and the property owner will be required to remove the fence to allow the surfer access to his favorite surfing spot.

The surfer's use of the property was open and notorious (everyone knew he was doing it), uninterrupted (continuous) use for at least five (5) years, the surfer had a claim of right because it was the only way to access the surf spot, and it was Hostile to the property owner's intent. The property owner knew about the surfer using the path across his property, but he let it happen anyway. The acronym "OUCH" can be used to help remember the four required elements in an easement by prescription/prescriptive easement: **o**pen and notorious, **u**ninterrupted for at least five years, there is a **c**laim of right, and it is **h**ostile to the owner's intent (OUCH).

An easement by prescription/prescriptive easement can be lost by nonuse for five (5) years or a reasonable length of time. Since this type of easement is gained by use and lost by nonuse, it is *not* recorded in the chain of recorded title. The only indication a real estate agent will have of the existence of this easement is a worn pathway across the property.

c. Easement in Gross

An **easement in gross** is an easement for a person or utility company to be able to use a parcel of land for a specific use. If a person is allowed access to a property through an easement in gross, the person is called a dominant tenement because he or she is legally allowed to enter the property.

> **Easement in Gross:** Easement for a person or utility company to be able to use a parcel of land for a specific use.

Accordingly, a utility company (dominant tenement) will have an easement in gross (called a utility easement) to allow the utility company to enter a person's property to repair disconnected power lines and complete any other maintenance issues.

(2) Covenants, Conditions, and Restrictions (CC&Rs)

Even though covenants, conditions, and restrictions (CC&Rs) are very common in today's urban and suburban new home subdivisions, some rural homes, in-fill locations (vacant lots located in existing subdivisions), and older homes may not have CC&Rs–or if they do exist–they will be short, simple, and have minimal effect on the subject property.

CC&R's is an abbreviation for Covenants, Conditions, and Restrictions. CC&R's usually run with the land and are thus appurtenant to the land and automatically transfer to the new owner.

CC&R's can be created by deed, agreement, or recorded declaration of restrictions. A breach of a covenant (promise) is a minor breach and is remedied by monetary damages. In contrast, a breach of a condition is a major breach and is remedied by loss of title to the property. Because of loss of title, a condition must be contained in the deed.

Private Deed Restrictions: Private restrictions restrict the use of real property. An example is CC&Rs.

A **private deed restriction** is the "R" in CC&Rs and restricts the use of a property. A private deed restriction is a limitation placed on the use of a property and is usually placed by an owner or developer through private deed restrictions. An injunction (issued by the court) can be used to enforce private deed restrictions.

(3) Public Restrictions

Public Restrictions: Public restrictions for the use of real property. An example is zoning.

A county's master plan or general plan indicates specific planned land uses for vacant parcels of land in the path of progress. Zoning is used to implement a county's general plan or master plan. Accordingly, **public restrictions** relate to zoning, which is under police power, and local governments can pass zoning ordinances to limit properties to specific uses.

(4) Encroachments

Encroachment: When one parcel of real property crosses over onto another parcel of real property.

An **encroachment** occurs when one parcel of real property crosses over onto another parcel of real property. For example, a homeowner's tree limbs have grown over their fence and reach into the adjacent neighbor's airspace. This is considered an encroachment and the adjoining neighbor will usually have the right to trim the tree limbs that are on the adjoining neighbor's side of the fence. Other types of encroachments include leaning fences, buildings, stairways, bushes, and other fixtures that encroach on another person's property.

Tales from the Trade

The Story of an Encroachment

A buyer purchased a parcel of real property. After the sale, the buyer discovered that an adjoining neighbor had erected a fence that was eight inches onto the buyer's property (called an *encroachment*). The seller was not aware that the fence was eight inches onto her property. The buyer could file a civil suit against the seller and request that the courts award the buyer damages. The damages will most likely be *compensatory damages* because they will place the buyer into a position as if the neighbor's fence encroachment had not occurred. The buyer will most likely not be able to collect *punitive damages* from the seller because the seller was not aware of the encroachment at the time of the sale. Punitive damages are usually awarded when there is *intentional misrepresentation (fraud)* on the part of the seller. However, because the seller was not aware of the encroachment, the seller may have been guilty of *negligent misrepresentation* (innocent mistake) and not intentional misrepresentation (fraud).

Within some older neighborhoods, property lines may not be as well-defined as they are in newer neighborhoods. The use of Global Positioning Satellite (GPS) units for surveying today's properties is much more accurate than older methods that used benchmarks as known starting points. Most lot line disputes today usually come from older properties that were surveyed prior to the use of GPS coordinates.

(5) Leases

Leases are a non-money encumbrance that limit the use of a property by giving a tenant possession for a short period of time. The owner of the freehold estate will be the legal owner of the property but will not have possession until the lease expires and the tenant returns the less-than-freehold/leasehold estate back to the owner of the freehold estate.

(6) Setback Requirements

Setback requirements restrict a parcel of land by requiring a building to be built a certain minimum distance from the property lines. For example, setback requirements for the county where the property is located require a home to be built at least twenty (20) feet distance from the front of the parcel, and ten (10) feet distance from each of the other three property lines (both sides and rear). Setback requirements will affect the size of the footprint that can be built on a property and can be limited by a city, county, or CC&Rs for the property.

Chapter Seven Summary

The chapter discusses escrow and the escrow process. It includes the purpose of an escrow, obligations of the escrow agent, earnest money deposits, liquidated damages, selecting an escrow agent, Northern California vs. Southern California differences, joint escrow instructions, escrow termination, escrow prorations, private mortgage insurance, loan documents, payment of commission through escrow, and real estate brokers can perform escrows for their clients and their own properties.

Title insurance is examined including a preliminary title report and encumbrances. Encumbrances include money encumbrances (liens) and non-money encumbrances (based on use). Liens include deeds of trust, mortgages, mechanic's liens, attachments, judgments, federal income tax, state income tax, property taxes, special assessments, and Mello-Roos bonds. Non-money encumbrances include easements, CC&Rs, encroachments, zoning, leases, and setback requirements.

Chapter Seven Quiz

1. A(n) _____ is a disinterested third-party intermediary who holds all funds during the escrow process.
(A) real estate salesperson
(B) escrow agent
(C) principal
(D) unlicensed assistant

2. A purchase agreement may also act as:
(A) joint escrow instructions
(B) a listing agreement
(C) a transfer disclosure statement
(D) an agency disclosure

3. _____ is one of the few types of insurance in which the insurance company can reduce or eliminate claims by doing a thorough title search prior to issuing a policy of title insurance.
(A) Homeowner's insurance
(B) Owner, Landlord, and Tenants insurance
(C) Title insurance
(D) Earthquake insurance

4. An exception to "First to record is the first in right" is:
(A) mechanic's liens
(B) subordinated loans
(C) taxes
(D) all of the above are correct

5. Which of the following are considered general liens?
(A) Attachment
(B) Judgment
(C) Both (A) and (B) are correct
(D) Neither (A) nor (B) is correct

6. The _____ sets an assessed value for the land and another assessed value for the building(s) that are located on the land.
(A) county tax assessor
(B) county board of supervisors
(C) city council
(D) state of California

7. Ad valorem means:
(A) according to value
(B) payment is due
(C) Both (A) and (B) are correct
(D) Neither (A) nor (B) is correct

8. Which of the following is a type of easement?
(A) Appurtenant easement
(B) Easement by prescription
(C) Easement in gross
(D) All of the above are correct

9. What is used to enforce a private deed restriction?
(A) Writ of execution
(B) Write of possession
(C) Injunction
(D) None of the above are correct

10. _____ restrict a parcel of land by allowing a building to be built a certain distance from the property lines.
(A) Downzoning
(B) Setback requirements
(C) Liens
(D) Specific liens

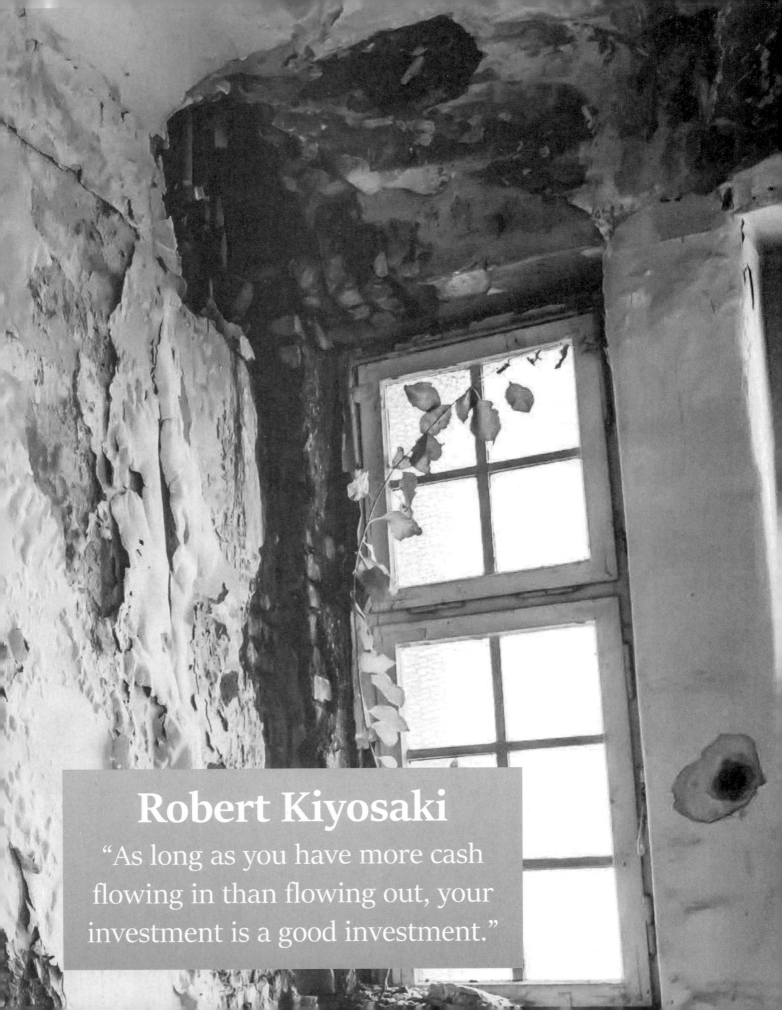

Robert Kiyosaki

"As long as you have more cash flowing in than flowing out, your investment is a good investment."

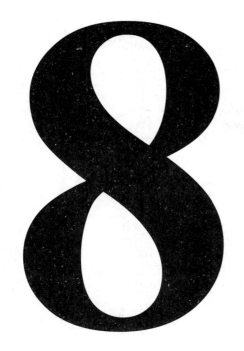

Chapter
EIGHT

Real Estate
Disclosures Part I

Buying a car, boat, RV, or other moderately expensive item is different than buying a home. Homes can cost into the millions of dollars, while cars and other items may only be in the tens of thousands of dollars. This cost difference makes buying a home one of the largest purchases a person will make during their lifetime.

For this reason, the term "caveat emptor" or buyer beware does not apply to a person's home purchase. There are many disclosures that are required for one-to-four unit residential properties in California. They provide the buyer with a good idea of the condition of the home because sellers and agents are required to disclose all material facts about a property. A material fact is a fact that may affect the value of the property and if the buyer knew about it, the buyer may not have purchased the property.

In contrast, properties with five (5) or more residential units and commercial leased investment properties, such as retail, office, and industrial buildings, have less disclosures and less safeguards for buyers than owner-occupied one-to-four unit residential properties. This is because real estate investors, who buy these types of investment properties, are sophisticated enough to make their own decisions regarding suitability for investment. For this reason, there are very few disclosures for 5+ unit apartment buildings and commercial leased investments.

The following is a list of disclosures used in California:

1. Disclosure Regarding Real Estate Agency Relationship
2. Real Estate Transfer Disclosure Statement
3. Seller Property Questionnaire
4. Death Disclosure
5. AIDS Disclosure
6. Homeowner's Guide to Earthquake Safety
7. Commercial Property Owner's Guide to Earthquake Safety
8. Natural Hazards Disclosure (including mold and airport proximity)
9. Environmental Hazards and Earthquake Safety Booklets
10. Energy Rating Program and Booklet
11. Lead-Based Paint Disclosure/Lead Hazard Pamphlet
12. Smoke Detector Compliance
13. Alquist-Priolo Special Studies Zones
14. Subdivision Map Act and Subdivided Lands Law
15. Common Interest Subdivision Conversion
16. Mello-Roos Disclosure
17. Military Ordnance Disclosure
18. Seller Financing Disclosure
19. Loan Broker Disclosure
20. Appraisal - Disclosure of Fair Market Value in Loan Transactions
21. Advertising of Loan - License Disclosure
22. Advertising Disclosure
23. Disclosure of Compensation for Obtaining Financing
24. Disclosure of Intent to Make Sales Presentation
25. Notice of No Policy of Title Insurance
26. Blanket Encumbrance on Subdivisions
27. Possible Representation of More than One Buyer or Seller
28. Wire Fraud Advisory
29. Mobile Home Park Conversion - Disclosure Regarding Prices
30. Water Heater Bracing Statement of Compliance
31. Carbon Monoxide (CO) Detector & Compliance
32. Gas and Hazardous Pipeline Notice
33. Megan's Law (Registered Sex Offender Database)
34. Rent Control
35. Private Transfer Fees
36. Supplemental Assessment/Supplemental Property Tax Notice
37. Water Conserving Fixture Compliance/Water Conserving Fixture Disclosure
38. Window Security Bars and Safety Release Mechanism
39. Acrylonitrile Butadiene Styrene (ABS) Pipe Disclosure
40. Commercial Industrial Disclosure

Next is a look at *when* and *how* each disclosure is used during a real estate transaction in California.

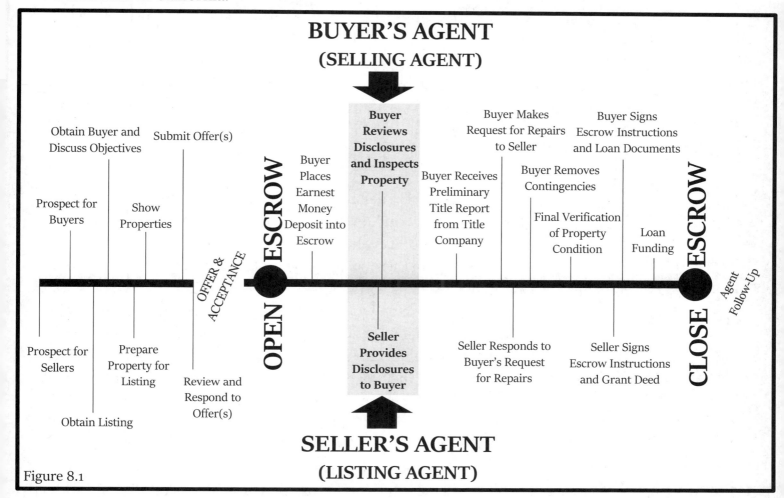

Figure 8.1

1. Disclosure Regarding Real Estate Agency Relationship (Agency Disclosure)

Since January 1988 an agent must disclose who is representing whom in the sale of a one-to-four unit residential property when a real estate agent is involved in the transaction. This includes who is representing the seller, who is representing the buyer, or whether a dual agency exists (agent represents both buyer and sell in the transaction).

The agency disclosure must be in writing and disclosed as soon as practicable (possible). For this reason, the **Disclosure Regarding Real Estate Agency Relationship** form (agency disclosure form) is usually completed and signed by the seller (and the seller's agent/listing agent) when the listing agreement is signed. In addition, a separate agency disclosure form is completed and signed by the buyer (and the buyer's agent/selling agent) when the buyer signs the purchase agreement. The buyer then signs the agency disclosure form that was already completed and

Disclosure Regarding Real Estate Agency Relationship: Form used to disclose, elect, and confirm agency relationships between principals and agents.

signed by the seller and the seller signs the agency disclosure form that was already completed and signed by the buyer. All the signatures assure that everyone understands who is representing whom in the transaction. The buyer or seller cannot say, "I didn't know who was representing me in the deal." The agency disclosure clearly spells it out to both buyer and seller.

The California Civil Code requires all real estate transactions comprising one-to-four unit residential properties (including mobile homes and manufactured homes), in which an agent is involved in the transaction, must provide an agency disclosure form to both the buyer and seller. Again, this must be provided as soon as practicable (possible).

Principal (Buyer or Seller)

Agency Relationship

Agent (Real Estate Broker)

Subagency Relationship

Subagent (Real Estate Salesperson)

Figure 8.2 Subagency Diagram

Agency is best defined as the relationship between a principal (seller or buyer) and another person who can act on their behalf–called an agent. A real estate broker is the agent of the principal and is acting on their behalf. The broker may employ salespersons who are subagents of the broker.

A salesperson who obtains a listing from a seller is really the seller's subagent. The broker is the seller's agent. Moreover, according to California Real Estate Law a salesperson is considered an employee of the broker for legal purposes, and a broker thus has vicarious liability for the actions of the salesperson. This means the broker is liable for all misrepresentations regarding the agency relationship or other material misrepresentations made by the salesperson in the performance of their real estate brokerage duties.

Errors and Omissions Insurance (E&O): Insurance used by real estate brokers to cover errors and omissions made by the real estate broker and salespersons who are working under their license.

Real estate brokers generally carry **errors and omissions (E&O) insurance** to cover real estate brokers and salespersons for negligent misrepresentation caused by missing a material fact that should have been brought to the buyer or seller's attention. In contrast, intentional misrepresentation (fraud) occurs when a salesperson purposefully does not disclose a material fact about a property. Thus, E&O insurance will help the broker and salesperson with negligent misrepresentation, but not with intentional misrepresentation.

A. Professional Liability Insurance (Errors and Omissions Insurance/E&O)

Professional liability insurance (E&O) is used to insure against liability for damages caused by any act or omission of a real estate licensee in rendering professional services in California. An insurer may exclude coverage against liability arising out of a dishonest, fraudulent, criminal, or malicious act, error, or omission committed by, at the direction of, or with the knowledge of the insured.

B. Disclosure of Single Agency

For example, Broker Able represents Seller Echo and Broker Baker represents Buyer Frank. Salesperson Charlie is a subagent of Broker Able, and Salesperson David is a subagent of Broker Baker.

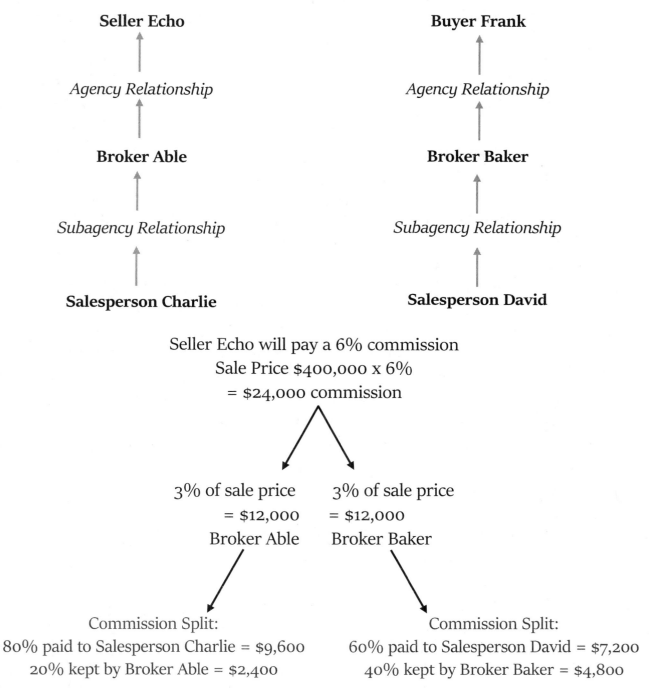

Figure 8.3 Single Agency Diagram

Using Figure 8.3 as an example, Salesperson Charlie lists a property for sale for $400,000. Broker Able is the agent of Seller Echo and Salesperson Charlie is the subagent of Broker Able. Seller Echo agrees in the listing agreement to pay a 6% commission for the sale of the property ($400,000 x 6% = $24,000). If Salesperson Charlie lists Seller Echo's property for sale and Salesperson David brings in the buyer, the commission will usually be split 3% to Broker Able who is the seller's agent ($12,000) and 3% to Broker Baker who is the buyer's agent ($12,000).

Broker Able will then split the $12,000 commission received (3% of the sale price) with Salesperson Charlie (who is his subagent). A written employment agreement between Broker Able and Salesperson Charlie indicates that Broker Able will keep 20% ($2,400) of the commission paid to Broker Able and Salesperson Charlie will receive the other 80% ($9,600) of the commission that was paid to Broker Able. Broker Baker and Salesperson David have a different commission split arrangement through their written employment agreement. In their agreement, Broker Baker keeps 40% ($4,800) of the commission paid to Broker Baker and Salesperson David receives 60% ($7,200) of the commission paid to Broker Baker.

(1) Seller's Agent

A seller's agent (also called listing agent) is the broker who represents only the seller in the transaction. A seller's agent owes a fiduciary duty of utmost care, integrity, honesty, and loyalty in all dealings with the seller. However, to all third parties in a transaction (including the buyer), the seller's agent owes diligent and reasonable skill and care in the performance of the agent's duties, a duty of honest and fair dealing, and a duty to disclose all known material facts affecting the value of a property and are not known by the third parties.

In other words, the broker (agent) and salesperson (subagent) have a fiduciary duty to their principal (seller) and a duty of honest and fair dealing to other parties in the transaction (i.e., the buyer). However, the agent is not under a duty to disclose confidential information provided by one's principal. Examples of confidential information is the amount a seller is willing to accept for a property and buyer loan qualification information.

(2) Buyer's Agent

The buyer's agent (also called selling agent) is the agent who represents only the buyer in the transaction. To the buyer, the agent owes a fiduciary duty of utmost care, integrity, honesty, and loyalty in all dealings with the buyer. The buyer's agent owes a duty of honest and fair dealing to the seller and other third parties to the transaction.

For example, a property is not listed for sale. A buyer who wants to buy the property executes an offer to purchase it through a real estate broker. In doing so, the buyer gives the broker a $5,000 check as an earnest money deposit. The broker can accept the check as the exclusive agent of the buyer.

C. Disclosure of Dual Agency

A dual agent is an agent who is representing both the seller and the buyer in a real estate transaction. This type of agency relationship must be agreed to by both the seller and the buyer in the transaction and it must be with their knowledge and consent.

During dual agency, the agent has a fiduciary duty to both the seller and the buyer, as well as all the other duties of diligent and reasonable skill, and honest and fair dealing. The agent may not inform either party regarding how much money the other will accept for the property, nor can the agent reveal anything negative regarding the buyer to the seller (e.g., the buyer not being able to qualify for a loan).

(1) Two Salespersons Working Under the Same Broker

Dual agency occurs when the broker acts as the agent for both the seller and the buyer in a real property transaction. However, what happens when Broker Able is the broker for both Salesperson Charlie and Salesperson David in the same transaction? The answer is that Broker Able is a dual agent in the transaction even though each salesperson represents different principals in the same transaction.

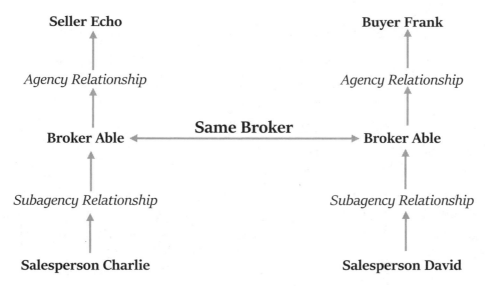

Figure 8.4 Dual Agency with Two Salespersons Under the Same Broker

An agency relationship exists between Broker Able and Seller Echo in the transaction and an agency relationship exists between Broker Able and Buyer Frank in the same transaction. Since Broker Able is representing both Seller Echo and Buyer Frank in the transaction, Broker Able is the dual agent of both parties.

Therefore, even though Salesperson Charlie and Salesperson David are two separate salespersons in the same transaction, they both work under Broker Able who is representing both Seller Echo and Buyer Frank and will be considered a dual agent.

D. Disclosure of Relationship with Principal or Licensed Principal

When a real estate agent is related to the principal by blood, marriage, an entity in which the agent has an ownership interest, or any other person with whom the agent has a special relationship, this is a material fact and the agent must disclose this relationship to the other principal in the transaction. In addition, if a principal who has a real estate license personally buys or sells real property, the agent must disclose this fact to the other principal in the transaction.

E. Acknowledgement of Receipt of Agency Disclosure Form

The seller and buyer are required to sign an acknowledgment indicating they have received a copy of the agency disclosure form. The agent(s) representing each party will have their principal(s) sign the form and then the agent(s) will sign below them and date the document. Both principals sign, date, and record the time when receipt of the document is acknowledged.

F. Disclose, Elect, and Confirm Agency Relationships

The agent must disclose to both the buyer and seller the nature of agency relationships (i.e., agency laws). After explaining agency relationships, the buyer and seller are then asked to elect who is representing each of them in the transaction. Both tasks are completed on the agency disclosure form. Lastly, the buyer and seller are asked to confirm their agency relationship (i.e., who is representing each of them in the transaction). This is usually accomplished in the agency confirmation section of the real estate purchase agreement.

Agency Relationships	
Disclose	Disclosure *explains* agency relationships to buyer
	Disclosure *explains* agency relationships to seller
Elect	Buyer *elects* who is representing them in the transaction
	Seller *elects* who is representing them in the transaction
Confirm	Buyer *confirms* who is representing them in the transaction
	Seller *confirms* who is representing them in the transaction

Figure 8.5 Disclose, Elect, and Confirm Agency Relationships

G. Disclosure Regarding Real Estate Agency Relationship Form

Figure 8.6 Disclosure Regarding Real Estate Agency Relationship

DISCLOSURE REGARDING
REAL ESTATE AGENCY RELATIONSHIP
(As required by the Civil Code)

When you enter into a discussion with a real estate agent regarding a real estate transaction, you should from the outset understand what type of agency relationship or representation you wish to have with the agent in the transaction.

SELLER'S AGENT

A Seller's agent under a listing agreement with the Seller acts as the agent for the Seller only. A Seller's agent or a subagent of that agent has the following affirmative obligations:
To the Seller:
A fiduciary duty of utmost care, integrity, honesty, and loyalty in dealings with the Seller.
To the Buyer and the Seller:
(a) Diligent exercise of reasonable skill and care in performance of the agent's duties.
(b) A duty of honest and fair dealing and good faith.
(c) A duty to disclose all facts known to the agent materially affecting the value or desirability of the property that are not known to, or within the diligent attention and observation of, the parties.
An agent is not obligated to reveal to either party any confidential information obtained from the other party that does not involve the affirmative duties set forth above.

BUYER'S AGENT

A Buyer's agent can, with a Buyer's consent, agree to act as agent for the Buyer only. In these situations, the agent is not the Seller's agent, even if by agreement the agent may receive compensation for services rendered, either in full or in part from the Seller. An agent acting only for a Buyer has the following affirmative obligations:
To the Buyer:
A fiduciary duty of utmost care, integrity, honesty, and loyalty in dealings with the Buyer.
To the Buyer and the Seller:
(a) Diligent exercise of reasonable skill and care in performance of the agent's duties.
(b) A duty of honest and fair dealing and good faith.
(c) A duty to disclose all facts known to the agent materially affecting the value or desirability of the property that are not known to, or within the diligent attention and observation of, the parties. An agent is not obligated to reveal to either party any confidential information obtained from the other party that does not involve the affirmative duties set forth above.

AGENT REPRESENTING BOTH SELLER AND BUYER

A real estate agent, either acting directly or through one or more associate licensees, can legally be the agent of both the Seller and the Buyer in a transaction, but only with the knowledge and consent of both the Seller and the Buyer.

In a dual agency situation, the agent has the following affirmative obligations to both the Seller and the Buyer:

(a) A fiduciary duty of utmost care, integrity, honesty and loyalty in the dealings with either the Seller or the Buyer.

(b) Other duties to the Seller and the Buyer as stated above in their respective sections.

In representing both Seller and Buyer, the agent may not, without the express permission of the respective party, disclose to the other party that the Seller will accept a price less than the listing price or that the Buyer will pay a price greater than the price offered.

The above duties of the agent in a real estate transaction do not relieve a Seller or Buyer from the responsibility to protect his or her own interests. You should carefully read all agreements to assure that they adequately express your understanding of the transaction. A real estate agent is a person qualified to advise about real estate. If legal or tax advice is desired, consult a competent professional.

Throughout your real property transaction you may receive more than one disclosure form, depending upon the number of agents assisting in the transaction. The law requires each agent with whom you have more than a casual relationship to present you with this disclosure form. You should read its contents each time it is presented to you, considering the relationship between you and the real estate agent in your specific transaction.

This disclosure form includes the provisions of Sections 2079.13 to 2079.24, inclusive, of the Civil Code set forth on the reverse hereof. Read it carefully.

Agent	Date	Buyer/Seller	Date
Salesperson or Broker Associate	Date	Buyer/Seller	Date

H. Seller or Buyer Refuses to Sign Acknowledgment of Receipt of Agency Disclosure Form

If a principal (seller or buyer) refuses to acknowledge receipt of the agency disclosure form, the agent must sign and date a written declaration of the facts of the refusal.

I. Confirmation of Agency Relationship

As soon as practicable, the seller's agent shall disclose to the seller whether the seller's agent is acting in the real property transaction exclusively as the seller's agent, or as a dual agent representing both the seller and the buyer. This relationship must be confirmed in the purchase agreement.

In addition, as soon as practicable the buyer's agent must disclose to the buyer whether the buyer's agent is acting in the real property transaction exclusively as the buyer's agent, exclusively as the seller's agent, or as a dual agent representing both the buyer and the seller. Again, this relationship is confirmed in the purchase agreement. It should be noted that the agency disclosure form uses "seller's agent" and "buyer's agent," while the agency confirmation paragraph in the real estate purchase agreement used "listing agent" and "selling agent." Thus, the listing agent is the seller's agent and the selling agent is the buyer's agent.

AGENCY CONFIRMATION:

The following agency relationships are hereby confirmed for this transaction:

Listing Agent _____ (Print Firm Name) is the agent of (check one): [ ] the Seller exclusively; or [ ] both the Buyer and Seller.

Selling Agent _____ (Print Firm Name) (if not the same as the Listing Agent) is the agent of (check one): [ ] the Buyer exclusively; or [ ] the Seller exclusively; or [ ] both the Buyer and Seller.

Figure 8.7 Confirmation of Agency Relationships contained in the Real Estate Purchase Agreement

2. Real Estate Transfer Disclosure Statement (TDS)

Transferors (sellers) are required to disclose all material facts that relate to a one-to-four unit residential property that is being sold in California. Sold refers to a normal purchase transaction with the buyer purchasing a property from the seller, a 1031 tax-deferred exchange, real property sales contract (also called a land contract), and a lease that is over one year in length.

The disclosure of material facts is normally accomplished with the Real Estate Transfer Disclosure Statement (TDS). The TDS is required for both owner-occupied one-to-four unit residential properties and non-owner occupied one-to-four unit residential properties (rented to tenant(s)). The TDS also applies to personal property mobile homes and manufactured homes.

A. Transfers Exempt from TDS Requirement

A Real Estate Transfer Disclosure Statement (TDS) must be completed by the seller prior to the sale of most one-to-four unit residential properties in California.

However, there are several transfers that are exempt from the TDS disclosure requirement:

1. The sale of new homes as part of a subdivision project in which a public report must be delivered to the purchaser. However, when such new homes are sold through a real estate broker, the broker owes the buyer a duty to disclose all material facts which affect the value, desirability and intended use of the property. An Agent's Visual Inspection Disclosure (AVID) form can be used to provide this disclosure.

2. Foreclosure sales

3. Court ordered transfers

4. Transfers by a fiduciary in the administration of a decedent's estate, a guardianship, conservatorship, or trust except where the trustee is a former owner of the property

5. Transfers to a spouse or to a person or persons in the lineal line of consanguinity (heirs)

6. Transfers resulting from a judgment of dissolution of marriage, or of legal separation, or from a property settlement agreement incidental to such a judgment

7. Transfers from one co-owner to another

8. Transfers by the State Controller for unclaimed property

9. Transfers resulting from failure to pay taxes

10. Transfers to or from any governmental entity

The TDS asks, "Mr. and Mrs. Transferor (seller), are you aware of any structural defects, material facts, or any other items that the buyer should be made aware of in the purchase of your home?" It is the seller's duty to disclose all material facts about the property on the TDS form.

The TDS requires the seller to disclose all material facts known about the property. As mentioned earlier, a material fact is a fact that, if known to the buyer, may cause the buyer to not purchase the property. The buyer must sign they have received the disclosure, plus both brokers (listing broker and selling broker) must complete their portion of the form disclosing any material facts they are aware of in the property.

B. Disclosure of Material Facts

The owner of a single-family residence lists the property for sale with a real estate broker. The owner informed the broker of a roof leak, but the broker did not inform the buyer. The buyer could recover damages from both the seller and the broker. The seller could then recover damages from the broker. The listing broker should have disclosed the leaky roof (material fact) to the buyer. The listing broker can do this through the Real Estate Transfer Disclosure Statement. The seller should also disclose the leaky roof through this same form. In this manner, there are no misunderstandings in the future.

C. Amendment to Real Estate Transfer Disclosure Statement

If the seller gave the buyer an amendment (change) to the Real Estate Transfer Disclosure Statement (TDS), then the buyer will have up to five (5) days from receipt of the TDS amendment to decide whether to move forward with the purchase or cancel the contract and rescind the escrow.

D. Agent Must Make a Visual Inspection of Accessible Areas

A real estate agent must visually inspect the property and reveal pertinent information on the TDS form. For example, during an inspection of a seller's residence, the agent noticed cracks in the walls and slab floor. In addition, the windows and doors were jammed and would not open and close properly. The agent should disclose these material facts and recommend a soils report.

According to the California Association of Realtors (CAR), "California law requires, with limited exceptions, that a real estate broker or salesperson (collectively, "Agent") conduct a reasonably competent and diligent visual inspection of reasonably and normally accessible areas of certain properties offered for sale and then disclose to the prospective purchaser material facts affecting the value or desirability of that property that the inspection reveals."

CAR also stated, "The duty applies regardless of whom the Agent represents. The duty applies to residential real properties containing one-to-four units, and manufactured homes (mobile homes). The duty applies to a stand-alone detached house (whether or not it is located in a subdivision or a planned development) or to an attached home such as a condominium. The duty also applies to a lease with an option to purchase, ground lease, and a real property sales contract."

CAR continues with, "California law does not require the Agent to inspect areas that are not reasonably and normally accessible, areas off site of the property, public records or permits, and common areas of planned developments, condominiums, stock cooperatives and the like."

There is an area in the TDS form for both the listing agent and selling agent to make a visual inspection of accessible areas and note their findings on the form. The visual inspection is an observation by the real estate agent and not a diagnosis regarding why it is occurring. Therefore, a real estate agent may observe a "crack in the ceiling" and write this on the TDS form–rather than stating, "crack in the ceiling caused by settling of the foundation." Real estate agents are not licensed contractors nor home inspectors and are not qualified to diagnose problems occurring in a property.

According to the California Civil Code, an **Agent Visual Inspection Disclosure (AVID)** can be used when a real estate transfer disclosure statement is not required for the transaction. For example, a bank foreclosure is exempt from providing the TDS; however, the agent(s) must make a visual inspection of the property. The Agent Visual Inspection Disclosure form (AVID) can be used to accomplish this task.

Agency Visual Inspection Disclosure (AVID): Both the listing and selling agent of a 1-4-unit residential property have the duty to conduct a reasonably competent and diligent visual inspection of the property and to disclose to a prospective buyer all material facts affecting value, desirability, and implicitly intended use.

E. Seller Refuses to Complete and/or Sign the TDS

If a seller refuses to complete the seller's section of the real estate transfer disclosure statement, the listing agent should complete the listing agent's portion and deliver it to the buyer. The listing agent should also notify the buyer of their rights to receive the real estate transfer disclosure statement.

F. Seller Lists Home "As Is"

A person who lists a home for sale "as is," is obligated to provide a real estate transfer disclosure statement to prospective buyers. The term "as is" merely indicates the seller is not willing to repair anything; however, the seller must disclose all material facts that will affect the value of the property.

For Sale by Owner (FSBO): A property being sold by the owner without the help of a real estate agent.

G. For Sale by Owner Properties

The real estate transfer disclosure statement required by the Civil Code must be provided if a single-family residence is offered **for sale by owner (FSBO)**. One of the advantages of using a real estate agent to list and sell a home is their access to the most up-to-date contracts and disclosures available in California.

Figure 8.8

H. Additional Condominium Disclosures: Sale of a Condominium

California condominiums that are being sold require most, if not all, of the disclosures required for single-family homes plus several other disclosures that are specific to condominiums. Condominium disclosures can usually be obtained through the condominium's homeowner's association and may include:

1. Articles and Bylaws of the condo association
2. Homeowners Association (HOA) operating expenses
3. Covenants, Conditions, and Restrictions (CC&Rs)
4. Minutes to the last twelve months HOA meetings

Furthermore, there are many California condo associations in litigation against the builder who built the property. Most of these lawsuits have resulted from inferior construction and other construction defects. For example, one condo HOA sued their builder due to faulty underlying foundations in all the buildings. The court ruled in favor of the condo HOA against the builder and required the builder to repair all the foundations located in the complex. Needless to say, all the condo owners may have a very difficult time selling their properties during the litigation period. In California, there is a legal requirement to disclose any existing or pending litigation that is or will be occurring against the seller's property. This, of course, will probably scare potential buyers away from buying defective condos. It will also probably scare lenders away from making loans, at least until the defects are repaired.

3. Seller Property Questionnaire (SPQ)

Real estate agents in California commonly use the seller property questionnaire form that asks the seller to disclose additional items that are not included in the real estate transfer disclosure statement. This is a second layer of disclosures that helps protect the buyer, selling agent, and listing agent from lapses in a seller's memory regarding material facts about a property.

4. Death Disclosure

If a death occurred in a home within the last three years (three years or less), the seller and agent(s) must disclose this fact to a prospective buyer or tenant. If a death occurred in a home more than three years ago, the seller and agent(s) are not required to disclose this fact to a prospective buyer or tenant.

Death Disclosure: If a person dies in a home, this must be disclosed for three years.

Tales from the Trade

The Story of a Death Disclosure

An agent showed a buyer a townhouse that was also his own listing. After spending a while at the property, they went to the agent's office to discuss a possible offer. The buyer asked the agent if there was anything else to know about the property, since the agent was acting as a dual agent and had information about the seller. The agent said, "Well there is one thing. The owner died in the master bedroom." "Oh, in his sleep?" they inquired. "No. His wife murdered him. But don't worry, she's now institutionalized." They decided to look for another property to buy.

5. AIDS Death Disclosure

The seller and seller's agent are not required to disclose whether an occupant was afflicted or died from AIDS. No cause of action arises against an owner of real property or the owner's agent for failure to disclose to the buyer the occurrence of an occupant's AIDS-related death upon the real property.

However, if the buyer asks a direct question concerning deaths occurring on the real property, this statute will not protect the owner or agent(s) from misrepresentations. In other words, if the owner or agents are asked a direct question from the buyer regarding how a person died in the property, they must be truthful and disclose the AIDS-related death in the property. If the death occurred more than 3 years ago, neither the death nor AIDS-related death disclosure are required to be disclosed to the buyer.

6. Homeowner's Guide to Earthquake Safety Booklet and Residential Earthquake Hazards Report

The Seismic Safety Commission has developed a Homeowner's Guide to Earthquake Safety booklet for residential property owners. The Seismic Safety Commission consulted with the Office of Emergency Services, Division of Mines and Geology of the Department of Conservation, and the California Department of Real Estate to determine appropriate material for the guide. This disclosure relates to residential dwellings built prior to January 1, 1960 with one-to-four living units of conventional light-frame construction.

The Homeowner's Guide to Earthquake Safety booklet contains:
- Maps and information on geologic and seismic hazard conditions in California
- Explanations of typical structural and nonstructural earthquake hazards
- Recommendations for mitigating or reducing the hazards of an earthquake

- That there are no guarantees of safety or damage prevention that can be made with respect to a major earthquake and that only precautions, such as retrofitting (improving existing properties to withstand earthquakes), can be taken to reduce the risk of various types of earthquake damage

7. Commercial Property Owner's Guide to Earthquake Safety

The Seismic Safety Commission has developed a Commercial Property Owner's Guide to Earthquake Safety. The Seismic Safety Commission consulted with the Office of Emergency Services, Division of Mines and Geology of the Department of Conservation, and the California Department of Real Estate to determined appropriate material for the guide. Any purchaser of an unreinforced masonry (e.g., old brick or concrete block) building with wood frame floors or roofs and constructed before January 1, 1975 must receive a copy of the "Commercial Property Owner's Guide to Earthquake Safety."

The Commercial Property Owner's Guide to Earthquake Safety contains:

- Maps and information on geologic and seismic hazard conditions in California
- Explanations of typical structural and nonstructural earthquake hazards
- A definition of "adequate wall anchorage"
- That there are no guarantees of safety or damage prevention that can be made with respect to a major earthquake and that only precautions, such as retrofitting, can be taken to reduce the risk of various types of earthquake damage
- Notice of the obligation to post a sign as required by Section 8875.8 of the Government Code

Next is a return to residential disclosures.

> **Natural Hazards Disclosure:** Includes special flood hazard area, potential flooding, very high fire hazard severity zone, wildland area, earthquake fault zone, and seismic hazard zone.

8. Natural Hazards Disclosure

There are six statutorily (laws enacted by the California State Legislature) required disclosures that are made within the **Natural Hazards Disclosure Statement.** These disclosures include: special flood hazard area, an area of potential flooding shown on a dam failure inundation map, a very high fire hazard severity zone, wildland area that may contain substantial forest fire risk and hazards, an earthquake fault zone, and a seismic hazard zone.

K, STREET, FROM THE LEVEE.

INUNDATION OF THE STATE CAPITOL,
City of Sacramento, 1862.

Published by A ROSENFIELD; San Francisco

Figure 8.9 The Great Sacramento Flood of 1862

A. Special Flood Hazard Area Disclosure and Responsibilities of Federal Emergency Management Agency (FEMA) and Dam or Reservoir Inundation Area

Flood Hazard Boundary Maps identify the general flood hazards within a community. They are also used in flood plain management and for flood insurance purposes. Flood Hazard Boundary Maps developed by the Federal Emergency Management Agency (FEMA) in conjunction with communities participating in the National Flood Insurance Program (NFIP) identify areas within the 100-year flood boundary termed "special flood zone areas." Also identified are areas between 100 and 500-year levels termed "areas of moderate flood hazards" and the remaining areas above the 500-year level termed "areas of minimal risk."

A seller of property located in a special flood hazard area, or the seller's agent and any cooperating agent, must disclose this fact to the buyer and that federal law requires flood insurance as a condition of obtaining financing on most structures located in a special flood hazard area. Since the cost and extent of flood insurance coverage may vary, the buyer should contact an insurance carrier or the intended lender for further information.

B. Potential Flooding (Inundation Areas)

If a home is located within a 100-year flood zone, there is the possibility of becoming a flood victim. When potential homebuyers or investors are made aware of this fact, they may decide to purchase a home that is not located within a flood zone.

Flooding is considered frequent in a flood hazard area if flooding occurs on an average of once every 10 years. When a flood hazard is found to exist, the flood hazard report will describe the degree and the frequency of flood hazard using the following terminology:

1. Degree of Hazard Inundation:

Ponded water, or water in motion, of sufficient depth to damage property due to the mere presence of water or the depositing of silt refers to the degree of hazard inundation.

Figure 8.10 Inundation

- **Inundation (Flood):** Flowing water having sufficient velocity to transport or deposit debris, to scour the surface soil, or to dislodge or damage buildings. It also indicates erosion of the banks of watercourses. Possible flood hazard of uncertain degree.
- **Sheet Overflow**: Overflow of water in minor depths, either quiescent or flowing, at velocities less than those necessary to produce serious scour. This type of overflow is a nuisance rather than a menace to the property affected.
- **Ponding** of local storm water is standing water in local depressions. It originates on or in the vicinity of the property and due to the condition of the ground is unable to reach a street or drainage course.

2. Frequency

- **Frequent**: Flooding which may occur, on average, more than once in 10 years.
- **Infrequent**: Flooding which may occur once in 10 years or more.
- **Remote**: Flooding which is dependent on conditions which do not lend themselves to frequency analysis, such as break of levee, obstruction of a channel, etc. For example, on July 17, 1995, Folsom Dam failed. Over 40,000 cubic feet of water per second spilled over Folsom Dam and the National Weather Service issued a flash flood warning for areas below the dam. On September 21, 1998, 5 million gallons of water poured out of the City of Westminster's water storage tanks due to a rupture. A six-foot wall of water tore through the adjacent neighborhood. Thirty homes were red tagged (unlivable) and ten homes had to be demolished.

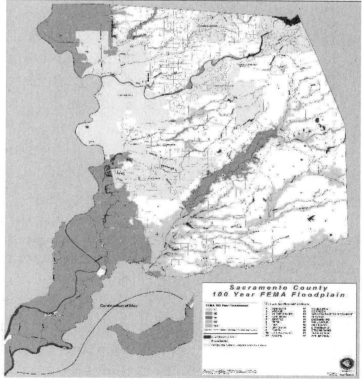

Therefore, a flood hazard report considers it "frequent" if flooding occurs, on average more than once in a ten-year period.

Under FEMA, areas designated on Flood Hazard maps include a Special Food Zone within the 100-year flood boundary, Moderate Flood Hazard between 100 and 500 year flood boundaries, and Minimal Risk above 500 year flood boundary. Many lenders require flood insurance if a home is located within a designated flood area. Flood insurance will usually cover the house when it becomes flooded; however, it may

Figure 8.11 Sacramento County 100 Year FEMA Floodplain

not cover a homeowner's personal belongings or those of a tenant. Homeowner's insurance or renter's insurance may be needed to take care of this problem.

If the entire city is located within a flood zone, anyone who wants to live in that particular city will probably be required, usually by their lender, to obtain flood insurance. If all the houses located in the city require flood insurance, then "everyone is in the same boat." A home buyer will not have to worry about tenants or future buyers buying another property within that city because it is not located within a flood zone. All the homes in the city are located in a flood zone.

A prospective buyer may decide to buy a home located in an outlying suburban area that is not within a flood zone. If this is the case, the suburb is usually located a greater distance from work sources that usually lie within the city. For this reason, suburban homeowners generally have longer commute times to work sources than urban city dwellers. In other words, if a tenant or homeowner wants to avoid a flood zone that is located in a city, they will most likely have to pay for it through longer commute times. Rents and property prices will usually reflect these issues because tenants and homebuyers are usually well informed when it comes to the trade-off between location and commuting time.

Tales from the Trade

The Story of the Flood Zone in Sacramento, CA

Most of the city of Sacramento is located within a 100-year flood zone, so literally everyone who purchases a home located in the city will probably need flood insurance. Property prices of homes located in the higher socio-economic neighborhoods within the city tend to be some of the highest per square foot costs in the area. Homes located in higher socio-economic suburban neighborhoods tend to cost less per square foot than those located in urban areas. This is generally because of the smaller sized homes and close proximity to job sources in the downtown area.

Property sizes tend to be larger in the outlying suburbs and do not require flood insurance, yet the commute time to and from Sacramento can range from thirty minutes to one hour or more. Homeowners must decide whether a larger house located outside the flood zone is worth the extra time needed each day to commute to and from their work source. Property values and rents tend to reflect this disparity as well.

An insurance agent can help determine whether a home is located within a flood zone, and if so, what the annual premium will be to insure it. The insurance agent can also help determine whether the home has had previous insurance claims against it. If this is the case, it may preclude a new homeowner from obtaining insurance for the property or the insurance premiums may be extremely expensive. Insurance agencies usually get very nervous if there has been a water-related claim in the home during the previous five-year period. The insurance agent can consult the CLUE report and determine if there will be a problem obtaining insurance for the home. It is a good idea for a buyer to do this during the normal physical inspection contingency period prior to close of escrow.

C. Disclosures Regarding State (Fire) Responsibility Areas

The Department of Forestry and Fire Protection has produced maps identifying rural lands classified as state (fire) responsibility areas. In a state (fire) responsibility area, the state (as opposed to a local or federal agency) has the primary financial responsibility for the prevention and extinguishing of fires. Maps of these state responsibility areas and any changes (including new maps to be produced every five years) are to be provided to county tax assessors in the affected counties. If a seller knows that the property is in a state (fire) responsibility area or the property is included on a map given by the Department of Forestry and Fire Protection to the county tax assessor, the seller must disclose the possibility of substantial fire risk and that the land is subject to certain preventative requirements.

With the agreement of the Director of Forestry and Fire Protection, a county may, by ordinance, assume responsibility for all fires, including those occurring in state (fire) responsibility areas. Absent such an ordinance, the seller of a property located in a state (fire) responsibility area must disclose to the buyer that the state is not obligated to provide fire protection services for any buildings or structures unless such protection is required by a cooperative agreement with a county, city, or district.

D. Wildland Areas That May Contain Substantial Forest Fire Risk and Hazards

The broad objective of the Wildland-Urban Interface Fire Area Building Standards is to establish minimum standards for materials and material assemblies and provide a reasonable level of exterior wildfire exposure protection for buildings in Wildland-Urban Interface Fire Areas. The use of ignition resistant materials and design to resist the intrusion of flame or burning embers projected by a vegetation fire (wildfire exposure) will prove to be the most prudent effort California has made to try and mitigate the losses resulting from a repeating cycle of interface fire disasters.

E. Disclosure of Geological Hazards and Earthquake Fault Zones

According to the Alquist-Priolo Earthquake Fault Zoning Act, the State Geologist is in the process of identifying areas of the state susceptible to "fault creep" and delineating these areas on maps prepared by the State Division of Mines and Geology. Fault creep is the slow and constant slippage that occurs within active earthquake faults that causes fault lines to move without there being an earthquake.

A seller of real property situated in an earthquake fault zone, or the agent of the seller (listing agent) and any agent acting in cooperation with such agent (selling agent), must disclose to the buyer that the property is or may be situated in an earthquake fault zone. This disclosure must be made on the Natural Hazard Zone Disclosure Statement.

Sellers and real estate licensees must disclose that a property is in an earthquake fault zone and the existence of known hazards affecting the real property being transferred in the Homeowner's Guide booklet during the following transactions:

- Transfer of any real property improved with a residential dwelling built prior to January 1, 1960 and consisting of one-to-four units any of which are of conventional light-frame construction; and,
- Transfer of any masonry building with wood-frame floors or roofs built before January 1, 1975.

F. Seismic Hazard Zone

Seismic hazard zone includes landslides in earthquake-induced landslide hazard zones and liquefaction in liquefaction hazard zones. Liquefaction is the conversion of soil into a fluidlike mass during an earthquake or other seismic event.

Figure 8.12 Landslide

G. California State-Wide Disclosures

In addition to statutory disclosure requirements from the California State Legislature, other local government entities pass ordinances for properties located under their jurisdiction. Most of the third-party vendors that provide the natural hazards disclosure for real estate transactions in California try to include these disclosures through state-wide and local disclosures. Real estate agents must also be aware of common law (case law) appellate court decisions on a local, state-wide, and national level.

California state-wide disclosures include:

1. Fire hazard rating in area with low fire hazard severity rating
2. Earthquake Faults – U.S. Geological Survey (USGS) indicates whether a property is within 1/4 mile of an active earthquake fault
3. Ground shaking: property in areas subject to strong ground shaking and moderate damage to property.
4. Landslides and Landslide Deposits
5. Liquefaction
6. Naturally occurring asbestos in areas surrounding property
7. Groundwater management in California
8. Radon gas
9. Protected species and habitats with protected species, habitats, or conservation plan areas. Habitats in area where sightings of rare species and/or natural communities
10. Duct sealing requirement in zone subject to California energy commission duct sealing requirements
11. Airport influence area
12. Airport vicinity within two miles of a Federal Aviation Administration (FAA) approved landing facility
13. Military facilities
14. Within 1 mile of a presently or formerly used defense site
15. Mining operations within 1 mile of the property
16. Abandoned mining operations within 1 mile
17. Property located within 500ft of active or abandoned oil or gas well
18. Right to farm agricultural activity within one mile of property
19. Property under the California Land Conservation Act (Williamson Act)
20. Property located in a special tax assessment district
21. Property tax rate based on ad valorem (according to value)
22. Property has a Mello-Roos tax levied against it. The Mello-Roos Community Facilities Act authorizes the formation of community facilities districts, the issuance of bonds, and the levying of special taxes thereunder to finance designated public facilities and services. A seller of a property consisting of one-to-four dwelling units, subject to the lien of a Mello-Roos community facilities district, must make a good faith effort to obtain from the district a disclosure notice concerning the special tax and give the notice to a prospective buyer. The same exemptions apply as for delivery of a Real Property Transfer Disclosure Statement.

H. Local Disclosures

Some areas of California may have disclosure issues that are not common throughout the State. In response, local disclosure forms have been developed to allow sellers to disclose these issues to buyers. They include:

1. Local area is subject to very strong ground shaking and moderate damage to the property during potential earthquake scenarios
2. Property located in an area of potential liquefaction
3. Local area within ¼ mile of light industrial, office, retail, mixed use, and unspecified commercial uses
4. Salt water flooding: property located in an area with high potential for salt water flooding from failure of dikes
5. Earthquake faults: located ¼ mile from an active earthquake fault, fault rupture zones, landslides, or liquefaction
6. Compressible soil: in an area with high potential for compressible soils and differential settlement
7. Perchlorate: property located in perchlorate study area
8. Property in viewshed protection area
9. Geotechnical: property in a special geologic hazard study area with soil hazards

I. Disclosure Notices

1. Methamphetamine contamination
2. Megan's law - sex offender database
3. Abandoned wells
4. Carbon monoxide devices
5. Natural gas and hazardous liquid pipelines
6. Water conserving plumbing fixtures

If a seller and seller's agent do not provide a buyer with a Natural Hazards Disclosure Statement, when in fact the property is located in one of the designated earthquake, fire, or flood areas, and since maps are available to identify these areas, the seller and listing agent are both considered to have knowledge that a property is located within a hazardous area, the seller and listing agent will be liable to the buyer for not disclosing the areas covered in the Natural Hazards Disclosure. For this reason, listing agents tend to advise the seller to hire a third-party company that specializes in Natural Hazard Disclosures and can provide the buyer with more accurate information whether the subject property is located in one of the hazard zones.

9. Environmental Hazards and Earthquake Safety Booklets

The California Business and Professions Code requires the California Department of Real Estate to appropriate funds from the Education and Research Account in the Real Estate Fund and develop a booklet to educate and inform consumers regarding common environmental hazards that are located on, and affect, real property. The Office of Environmental Health Hazard Assessment has been used to assist in the development of the Environmental Hazards Booklet.

> **Environmental Hazards and Earthquake Safety Booklets:** A booklet that is used to educate and inform consumers regarding common environmental hazards that are located on, and affect, real property.

Types of common environmental hazards include: asbestos, radon, lead-based paint (discussed in Chapter 9), formaldehyde, fuel and chemical storage tanks, water and soil contamination, geotechnical hazards (discussed in Chapter 10), methane gas, electromagnetic fields, nuclear sources, mold, and fungus.

A. Asbestos

Until 1978, many homes with blown "popcorn" type ceilings contained asbestos. Asbestos was a common insulator and its potential carcinogenic (cancer causing) qualities were mostly unknown to the general public before 1978. When a ceiling becomes old and starts to flake, asbestos can become airborne and may be inhaled by a tenant or homeowner. Of course, it is always best to consult with an environmental expert whenever asbestos or any other hazardous material is involved.

In older homes built before 1978, the popcorn ceiling can be removed by an asbestos abatement contractor wearing a "moon suit." This protects the contractor against airborne asbestos particles that result from scraping off the hazardous asbestos ceiling materials. Some property owners have tried to seal up their popcorn ceilings with paint or other spray-on materials designed specifically for this purpose. This is an attempt to seal-up the hazardous materials, so they do not become exposed to the air.

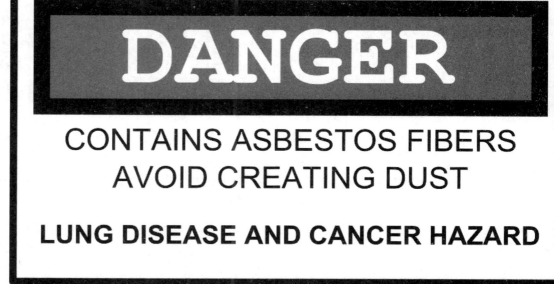

Figure 8.13

B. Radon/Radon Gas

Radon may exist in soil located in certain areas of the U.S. As radon gas, it may become airborne and accumulate in single-family homes that have crawl spaces or basements. Due to a possible pressure gradient between the crawl space or basement and the rest of the house, radon gas may move into the home and become a potential carcinogenic problem for both homeowners and tenants.

A radon inspector captures air within a crawl space or basement, and then uses a spectrometer to measure the amount of radon in the air. If the resulting test indicates more radon gas than is legally allowed, the homeowner will need to hire a radon abatement contractor to mitigate the problem. This may cost $1,500 or more and usually consists of the abatement contractor drilling holes into the concrete slab of the basement or drilling no holes at all if the home has a crawlspace, and venting (with a fan) the radon gas out of the basement or crawl space and into the outside air. The vent usually looks like a down spout from a water drain, with a big bulge that contains the fan near the surface of the ground. It vents the radon gas out above the roof line and into the outside air.

Figure 8.14

C. Formaldehyde

Formaldehyde is a colorless, flammable, strong-smelling chemical that is used in building materials and to produce many household products. It is used in pressed-wood products, such as particleboard, plywood, and fiberboard; glues and adhesives; permanent-press fabrics; paper product coatings; and certain insulation materials.

The EPA recommends the use of "exterior-grade" pressed-wood products to limit formaldehyde exposure in the home. These products emit less formaldehyde because they contain phenol resins, not urea resins. Pressed-wood products include plywood, paneling, particleboard, and fiberboard and are not the same as pressure-treated wood products, which contain chemical preservatives and are intended for outdoor use. Before purchasing pressed-wood products, including building materials, cabinetry, and furniture, buyers should ask about the formaldehyde content of these products. Formaldehyde levels in homes can also be reduced by ensuring adequate ventilation, moderate temperatures, and reduced humidity levels through the use of air conditioners and dehumidifiers.

D. Fuel and Chemical Storage Tanks

An underground storage tank (UST) system is a tank (or a combination of tanks) and connected underground piping having at least 10 percent of their combined volume underground. The tank system includes the tank, underground connected piping, underground ancillary equipment, and any containment system. The federal UST regulations apply only to UST systems storing either petroleum or certain hazardous substances. Old gas stations can be particularly troublesome because underground gasoline storage tanks may leak into the surrounding soil and become a hazardous substance issue.

E. Water and Soil Contamination

Ground water contamination is nearly always the result of human activity. In areas where population density is high and human use of the land is intensive, ground water is especially vulnerable. Virtually any activity whereby chemicals or wastes may be released into the environment, either intentionally or accidentally, has the potential to pollute ground water. When ground water becomes contaminated, it is difficult and expensive to clean up.

(1) Brownfields

According to the Federal Environmental Protection Agency (EPA), "A brownfield is a property, the expansion, redevelopment, or reuse of which may be complicated by the presence or potential presence of a hazardous substance, pollutant, or contaminant. It is estimated that there are more than 450,000 brownfields in the U.S. Cleaning up and reinvesting in these properties increases local tax bases, facilitates job growth, utilizes existing infrastructure, takes development pressures off undeveloped, open land, and both improves and protects the environment."

Beginning in the mid-1990s, the EPA provided small amounts of seed money to local governments that launched hundreds of two-year Brownfields "pilot" projects and developed guidance and tools to help states, communities and other stakeholders in the cleanup and redevelopment of Brownfields sites. The 2002 Small Business Liability Relief and Brownfields Revitalization Act (the "Brownfields Law") codified many of EPA's practices, policies and guidance. The Brownfields Law expanded EPA's assistance by providing new tools for the public and private sectors to promote sustainable Brownfields cleanup and reuse.

Brownfields grants continue to serve as the foundation of EPA's Brownfields Program. These grants support revitalization efforts by funding environmental assessment, cleanup, and job training activities.

F. Methane Gas

Methane gas is commonly produced in wetlands and can be very dangerous to homeowners and tenants. It is extremely flammable and if breathed into the lungs can cause shortness of breath and, when combined with oxygen, can cause asphyxiation and usually results in death.

Carbon Monoxide (CO): Odorless, colorless, and tasteless poisonous gas produced by the combustion of natural gas.

Natural gas is approximately 97% methane. **Carbon monoxide (CO)** is a byproduct of methane gas (when it is burned) and is very dangerous to homeowners and tenants because it is odorless, colorless, and tasteless. This is especially true with natural gas furnaces.

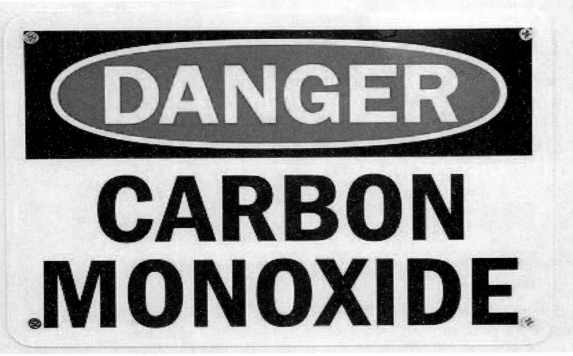

Figure 8.15

If a homeowner or tenant breathes in carbon monoxide, symptoms may include headache, dizziness, nausea, rapid heartbeat, unconsciousness, and immediate death. A carbon monoxide detector is required to be installed in single-family homes to detect carbon monoxide problems.

Methane detectors are available to detect the existence of methane gas in the air of a home. Carbon monoxide and methane detectors can be installed, along with smoke detectors, to ensure homeowners and tenants are safe living in the home.

A natural gas leak may be detected by the odor of the natural gas. Methane does not have an odor, however, for safety reasons natural gas has had an odor (rotten eggs) added to it—so homeowners and tenants can detect it if there is a leak. When natural gas permeates throughout a single-family home, it can be devastating. An explosion is generally extremely violent and may bring the entire house and surrounding houses in the neighborhood to the ground.

G. Electromagnetic Fields

There has been an on-going debate whether very low frequency electromagnetic fields (EMF) surrounding power lines and electrical devices have potential health risks. It appears to depend upon the frequency and intensity that a homeowner or tenant is subjected to an EMF. Some studies have shown an increased likelihood of childhood leukemia when children live near high power lines. However, the studies were inconclusive and scientists are hesitant to declare high power lines a definite health risk. The studies relate to the extremely tall high power lines that reach two hundred feet or more above the ground, not the small power poles that are approximately thirty feet in the air and are located in many older neighborhoods in California.

H. Nuclear Sources

Proximity to nuclear sources, such as a nuclear power plant, can be a definite disclosure issue during the sale of a single-family home. Being downwind of one of these plants can be especially unnerving, especially since the Chernobyl Disaster of 1986. A reactor vessel ruptured at the Chernobyl Nuclear Power Plant in the Ukraine and a series of explosions sent a plume of radioactive fallout into the atmosphere. Over 336,000 people were evacuated from the immediate area. The long-term effects are unknown from exposure to the fallout. Another example is the earthquake, tsunami, and nuclear melt-down in Northern Japan in 2011.

I. Mold

When mold spores become airborne, they can cause serious health problems. A homeowner or tenant may experience an allergic reaction, asthma flare-up, eye irritations, nose and throat problems, sinus congestion, infections, and other health problems. Some molds excrete toxic compounds called mycotoxins. If there is high enough exposure, some of these mycotoxins can be lethal to humans.

A water leak in a single-family home may have mold

Figure 8.16 Mold

growing in it. A mold inspector looks at over one hundred different varieties of mold, with only a few strains that are toxic to humans. A mold inspector can be used to determine if there is mold in the home and if it is one of the toxic varieties.

J. Fungus

One type of airborne fungus is called Cryptococcus Gattii. It is usually found in tropical regions, however, since 2006 it was discovered on Vancouver Island in Canada and has steadily worked its way south through Washington, Oregon, and Northern California. The new strain affects healthy people and, at last report, has a 25% mortality rate. The fungus ties itself to certain trees and releases into the air. Symptoms may occur two weeks to several months or more after exposure, and may include a cough that lasts for weeks, sharp chest pain, shortness of breath, headache, fever, nighttime sweats, and weight loss.

Real estate disclosures are divided into chapters eight and nine. The next chapter discusses the remaining disclosures that are important to the real estate brokerage business.

Chapter Eight Summary

There are many disclosures that are required with the sale of real property in California. Part I of these disclosures include: Disclosure Regarding Real Estate Agency Relationship, Real Estate Transfer Disclosure Statement, Seller Property Questionnaire, Death Disclosure, AIDS Disclosure, Homeowner's Guide to Earthquake Safety, Commercial Property Owner's Guide to Earthquake Safety, Natural Hazards Disclosure (including mold and airport proximity), and the Environmental Hazards and Earthquake Safety Booklets.

Chapter Eight Quiz

1. The California Civil Code requires all real estate transactions comprising one-to-four unit residential properties (including mobile homes and manufactured homes), in which an agent is involved in the transaction, must provide an:
(A) agency relationship disclosure to both the buyer and seller
(B) agency relationship disclosure to only the seller
(C) agency relationship disclosure to only the buyer
(D) none of the above are correct

2. A seller's agent owes a _____ in all dealings with the seller.
(A) fiduciary duty
(B) duty of utmost care, integrity, honesty, and loyalty
(C) Both (A) and (B) are correct
(D) Neither (A) nor (B) are correct

3. _____ are required to disclose all material facts that relate to a one-to-four unit residential property that is being sold.
(A) Transferors
(B) Sellers
(C) Both (A) and (B) are correct
(D) Neither (A) nor (B) are correct

4. A person who lists a home for sale "as is" is:
(A) not obligated to provide a real estate transfer disclosure statement to prospective buyers
(B) obligated to provide a real estate transfer disclosure statement to prospective buyers
(C) not required to disclose material facts
(D) required to complete requested repairs

5. Which form is commonly used in California by real estate agents that asks the seller to disclose additional items that are not included in the real estate transfer disclosure statement?
(A) Disclosure Regarding Real Estate Agency Relationship form
(B) Seller Property Report form
(C) Seller Property Questionnaire form
(D) Additional Property Information form

6. Which of the following are part of the Natural Hazards Disclosure?
(A) Special flood hazard area
(B) An area of potential flooding
(C) A very high fire hazards severity zone
(D) All of the above are part of the Natural Hazards Disclosure

7. _____ is a colorless, flammable, strong-smelling chemical that is used in building materials and to produce many household products.
(A) Formaldehyde
(B) Radon
(C) Asbestos
(D) Mold

8. _____ is commonly produced in wetlands and can be very dangerous to homeowners and tenants.
(A) Radon gas
(B) Methane gas
(C) Carbon monoxide gas
(D) Carbon dioxide gas

9. When _____ become(s) airborne, they/it can cause serious health problems.
(A) carbon dioxide
(B) water
(C) mold spores
(D) none of the above are correct

10. One type of airborne fungus is called:
(A) Cryptococcus Gattii
(B) radon
(C) carbon monoxide
(D) carbon dioxide

Answers: 1. A, 2. C, 3. C, 4. B, 5. C, 6. D, 7. A, 8. A, 9. C, 10. A

Please use this space for notes.

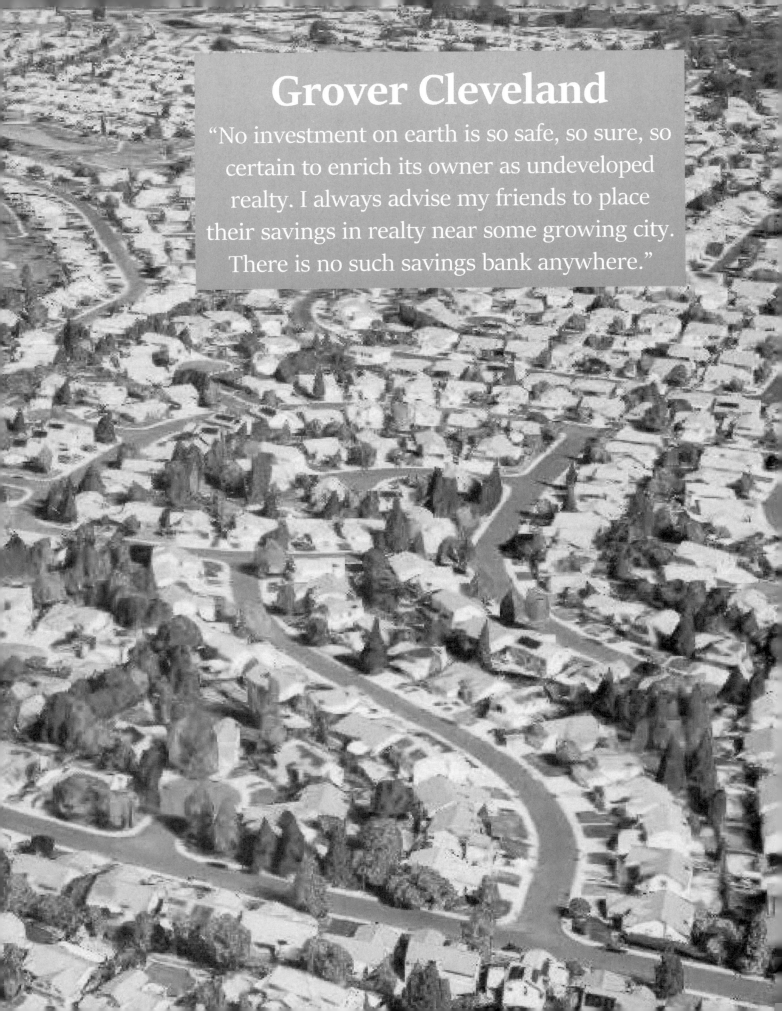

Grover Cleveland

"No investment on earth is so safe, so sure, so certain to enrich its owner as undeveloped realty. I always advise my friends to place their savings in realty near some growing city. There is no such savings bank anywhere."

Chapter NINE

Real Estate Disclosures Part II

Real Estate Disclosures Part I in Chapter Eight discussed the first nine required disclosures. Real Estate Disclosures Part II in Chapter Nine examines the remaining required disclosures that are used in California.

10. Energy Rating Program and Booklet

On July 1, 1995 the California Energy Commission adopted a statewide home energy-rating program for residential dwellings. Some local areas have adopted residential energy audit and conservation regulations for energy efficiency. These regulations vary among cities, counties, and states. Eight possible areas of compliance include:

- Minimum R-19 attic insulation. This indicates 19 inches of insulation in the attic between the ceiling and roof. R-19 insulation is also used between the 2" x 6" exterior walls of a single-family home and is generally considered standard wall insulation for homes located in colder climates. Homes located in both cold and warm climates may use R-38 or higher insulation in the attic. This prevents warm air loss in cold areas and cool air loss in warm areas. A whole house fan can be used to blow warm air out of the house and attic.

- Weather stripped no-flow type doors reduce airflow into and out of a home. Sometimes outside doors are difficult to open and close; however, the difficulties experienced are probably minor compared to the savings in energy costs.

- Minimum R-6 insulated water heater(s) that reduces natural gas, propane, or electricity costs. A tank-less water heater may be an alternative to a traditional water heater and may initially cost more; however, the energy savings over time may ultimately save money. Of course, having unlimited hot water is nice too.

- Minimum R-5 HVAC duct insulation. This can be a problem for older homes because ducts tend to wear out and replacing them can be expensive. If a property owner replaces a heating, ventilating, and air conditioning (HVAC) unit for a home located in California, a duct test may be required to obtain a building permit for the new unit. If the ducts leak

Figure 9.1 HVAC Condensing Unit

more air than is allowable by law, the owner will be forced to pay thousands of dollars to repair or replace the ducts.

- Minimum R-4 insulation for the first five feet of a water heater tank line. This saves energy by preventing heat loss.

- No broken windows or holes in the outside walls.

- Maximum three gallon per minute shower heads. Saves water and energy costs; however, it may take a long time to take a shower.

- Home Energy Rating System (HERS) Booklet. This is part of the combined Environmental and Earthquake Hazards booklet and applies to the transfer or exchange of all real property, including personal property manufactured homes and mobile homes. If an energy ratings booklet is delivered to the transferee (buyer), then a seller or agent is not required to provide additional information concerning the existence of a statewide energy rating program.

CONTINUED FROM CHAPTER 8

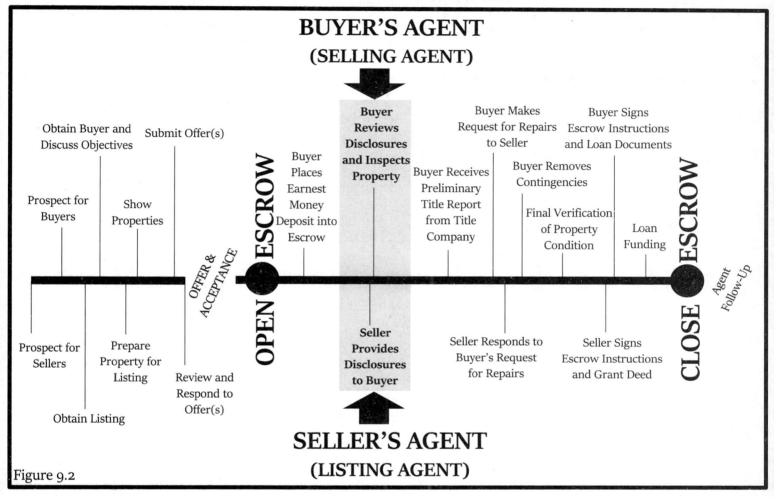

Figure 9.2

11. Lead-Based Paint Disclosure/Lead Hazard Pamphlet

A large percentage of all housing units in California still contain **lead-based paint**, which was banned for residential use in 1978. Homes that were built prior to 1978 and are regulated by the lead-based paint regulations are called target housing.

Lead-based paint can peel, chip, and deteriorate into contaminated dust, thus becoming a lead-based paint hazard. Each year, thousands of children in California ingest lead-laced chips or dust. The resulting high blood levels of lead can cause learning disabilities, delayed development, behavioral disorders, and hyperactivity.

Lead-Based Paint: Paint that can peel, chip, and deteriorate into contaminated dust, thus becoming a lead-based paint hazard.

More than 1.7 million children nationwide are known to have suffered lead poisoning.

In September 1996 the Federal Real Estate Disclosure and Notification Rule (the Rule) required that owners of residential buildings with more than four units,

Figure 9.3

built before 1978, disclose to their agents and to prospective buyers or lessees/renters the presence of lead-based paint and/or lead-based paint hazards and any known information and reports about lead-based paint and lead-based hazards (for example, location and condition of painted surfaces). Owners of single-family homes and residential buildings with four or fewer units (built before 1978) must comply with these disclosure requirements also.

A. Environmental Protection Agency (EPA)

The EPA pamphlet "Protect Your Family from Lead in Your Home" must be given to the buyer or lessee/renter, as well as the Lead-Based Paint Disclosure form.

The disclosure form answers the following questions:

1. What is lead poisoning?
2. Who gets lead poisoning?
3. Where does it come from?
4. How do I know if my child is affected?
5. What can I do about it?
6. How do I know if my home has lead-based paint?
7. What do I do if my home does have lead?
8. Will HUD insure a mortgage loan on a home with lead-based paint?

Until 1978 many paint manufacturers used lead in their manufacturing process. If window sills in a single-family home have been painted with "lead-based paint," and a child bites the window sill, lead may be ingested into the body. Ingesting lead has been known to cause learning disabilities and other illnesses in children and adults.

There may be several layers of paint on the inside walls of older homes located in California, making it difficult to determine whether a single-family home contains lead-based paint. To compound this problem, home inspectors do not usually investigate potential lead-based paint hazards during a home inspection, so the homeowner will need to have the home tested specifically for lead-based paint. Lead-based paint is usually mitigated by scraping off all the lead-based paint and repainting with modern non-toxic paint.

In addition to the federal requirements, California has its own requirements. Within the Real Estate Transfer Disclosure Statement, the seller must include any lead-based paint hazards which he or she is aware. Lead-based paint comes under the heading "Environmental Hazards." The agent(s) in the transaction are also required to inspect the property and disclose any material facts (such as lead-based paint) to the buyer.

A seller or the seller's agent(s) can give the buyer a pamphlet entitled, "Environmental Hazards: A Guide for Homeowners, Buyers, Landlords, and Tenants." If the buyer receives this pamphlet, neither the seller nor the agent is required to say more about general environmental hazards (assuming no awareness to any specific problems).

12. Smoke Detector/Alarms Compliance

State law requires, per the DRE Reference Book, "dwelling units be equipped with smoke detectors approved by the State Fire Marshall. In an existing dwelling, there must be a battery operated smoke detector outside each sleeping area. As of August 14, 1992, new construction (or an addition, alteration or repair that exceeds $1,000 and requires a permit or includes addition of a sleeping room) must include smoke detectors in each bedroom and at a point centrally located outside the bedroom(s). In new construction, the smoke detector(s) must be hard-wired, with battery backup. The seller must give the buyer written certification of smoke detector compliance, as required by Health and Safety Code Section 13113.8."

13. Alquist-Priolo Special Studies Zones

California has enacted the **Alquist-Priolo Special Studies Earthquake Zones Act** to control development of homes located near hazardous earthquake faults and may experience surface fault rupture. Earthquake insurance can be purchased to protect against the possibility of an earthquake destroying a home.

Alquist-Priolo Special Studies Zones Act: Act to control development of homes located near hazardous earthquake faults and may experience surface fault rupture.

14. Subdivision Map Act and Subdivided Lands Law

Figure 9.4

Subdivision Map Act vs. Subdivided Lands Law		
Subdivision Map Act	2 or more	Subdivides a parcel of real property into two or more parcels
Subdivided Lands Law	5 or more	Applies if a parcel of real property is subdivided into five or more parcels

A. Subdivision Map Act

The **Subdivision Map Act** relates to anyone who subdivides a parcel of real property into two or more parcels. The subdivider must go to the local government officials in the area where the property is located and get approval to subdivide the property. A planning commission is considered a local government official and is usually tasked with providing a general plan or master plan for the county where the property is located. Zoning is used to implement the general or master plan. It specifies the types of uses that are permitted by the local government to fulfill the intent of the master plan.

The Subdivision Map Act requires the subdivider to prepare a tentative map and file it with the city or county where the subdivision is located. It also authorizes cities and counties to enact subdivision regulations. In a city, local government officials govern setback requirements, vacant lots, and buildings according to the master plan (i.e., who decides when it is permitted to build on certain lots and who determines the size and placement of buildings).

(1) Infill

An infill location is a vacant lot among already developed lots with structures on them. Residential and commercial infill locations are common throughout California.

B. Subdivided Lands Law

The **Subdivided Lands Law** relates to subdividers who are subdividing a parcel of real property into *five (5) or more parcels* and is called a **subdivision**. Under these circumstances, the subdivider must go to the California Real Estate Commissioner to obtain approval to sell the subdivided parcels of land. The California Real Estate Commissioner issues a **public report** thus allowing the subdivider to commence selling the parcels covered under the report.

Once a preliminary public report has been issued, a real estate agent may take a listing on the property. The California Real Estate Commissioner issues a preliminary public report and then a final public report for a subdivision. Both reports are designed to disclose material facts to home buyers who purchase properties in the subdivision.

No subdivision lots can be legally sold until a copy of the Commissioner's Final Public Report is provided to the customer, a signature from the buyer is obtained verifying that the buyer has received a copy of the Commissioner's Final Public Report, and the customer has been given a chance and the time to read the Commissioner's Final Public Report. A copy of the California Real Estate Commissioner's Final Report must be provided to all customers who intend to buy

Subdivision Map Act: Relates to anyone who subdivides a parcel of real property into two or more parcels.

Subdivided Lands Law: Relates to subdividers who are subdividing a parcel of real property into five or more parcels.

Subdivision: When a parcel of land is subdivided into five or more parcels.

Public Report: Allows the subdivider to commence selling the parcels covered under the report.

lots in the subdivision. In fact, the subdivider must provide a copy of the report to anyone requesting it verbally or in writing. The subdivider must have the intended buyer sign a document verifying receipt of the report.

A Real Estate Commissioner's Final Public Report discloses all pertinent material facts that relate to the subdivision. For example, the report may disclose to the buyer that halfplexes (one side of a duplex) will be built next to a high-end single-family home subdivision where the buyer is contemplating buying a home. This could cause a loss in value to the single-family home in the future and is disclosed to the buyer through the Real Estate Commissioner's Final Public Report.

If the subdivider tries to sell the parcels before the Commissioner's Final Public Report is issued, the California Real Estate Commissioner may issue a desist and refrain order to stop the sale of the parcels.

(1) California Environmental Quality Act

The **California Environmental Quality Act (CEQA)** was enacted in 1970 with the purpose of disclosing to the public the significant environmental effects of a proposed discretionary project, through the preparation of an Initial Study (IS), **Negative Declaration (ND)** – no visible impact on the environment, so it is okay to build on the property; or **Environmental Impact Report (EIR)**. A "Negative Declaration," as discussed in an Environmental Impact Report, is a statement by an expert affirming that a new subdivision will have no significant negative impact on the environment.

(2) Land Project

A **land project** is a rural subdivision in which the subdivider uses a substantial amount of direct mail or internet advertising to find prospective buyers. In addition, subdividers sell the lots to individual owners and not to other subdividers and builders. The Real Estate Commissioner requires that any advertisement of a land project must be approved by the Real Estate Commissioner prior to issuance of a final public report. Sales of lots have a fourteen (14) day rescission period.

(4) Interstate Land Sales Full Disclosure Act

A federal law that regulates subdivisions of 25 or more parcels across state borders. The Department of Housing and Urban Development (HUD) issues a public report.

California Environmental Quality Act (CEQA): Purpose of disclosing to the public the significant environmental effects of a proposed discretionary project.

Negative Declaration (ND): There is no visible impact on the environment, so it is permitted to build on the property.

Environmental Impact Report (EIR): It discloses to the public the significant environmental effects of a proposed discretionary project.

Land Project: Rural subdivision in which the subdivider uses a substantial amount of direct mail or internet advertising to find prospective buyers.

15. Common Interest Subdivision Conversion

When a developer converts five or more apartments to a form of common ownership resulting in the separate ownership of the individual units and shared ownership of the common areas (condominiums), this is called a subdivision.

The minimum time required for an owner to give notice to the tenants in an apartment building (when that building is being converted by the owner to a condominium form of ownership) is 180 days. Existing tenants must also receive the first right of refusal to purchase the condominium unit where they live. In other words, the tenant has the first right to purchase the property. If they do not purchase the property, they will be required to vacate the property at the condo conversion date.

Figure 9.5 Water-Front Residential Condominiums

As soon as practicable before transfer of title for the first sale of a unit, the owner or subdivider (or agent of the owner or subdivider) must deliver to the prospective buyer a written statement listing all substantial defects or malfunctions in the major systems in the unit and common areas of the premises, or a written statement disclaiming knowledge of any such substantial defects or malfunctions, in a residential condominium, community apartment project, or stock cooperative which was converted from an existing dwelling to a condominium project, community apartment project, or stock cooperative.

16. Mello-Roos Disclosure

A seller of any one-to-four unit residential property must make a good faith effort to obtain a disclosure notice concerning the special tax from each local agency under the Mello-Roos Community Facilities Act for the property being transferred. *Good faith* means honest in fact in the conduct of the transaction. This disclosure notice must be provided by the seller and delivered to a prospective purchaser. It is generally included with the Natural Hazards Disclosure.

17. Military Ordnance Disclosure

On December 10, 1983 lives were lost at Tierra Santa because of live munitions exploding in a residential area that was formerly a military ordnance location. For this reason, the California State Legislature requires sellers and landlords to disclose former military ordnance locations that are within one mile of the subject property. The disclosure must be made in writing as soon as practicable and before transfer of title or execution of a rental agreement.

18. Seller Financing Disclosure

A Seller Financing Disclosure Statement must be prepared by the arranger of credit and provided to BOTH the purchaser and the seller in a residential

transaction involving one-to-four units whenever a seller has agreed to extend credit to a buyer as part of the purchase price.

Figure 9.6

19. Loan Broker Disclosure

Lenders are required to provide a loan estimate and a closing disclosure to borrowers. They are discussed in Chapter 12.

20. Appraisal - Disclosure of Fair Market Value in Loan Transactions

A real estate agent must disclose fair market value in all loan transactions. The delivery of a certified appraisal (performed by an appraiser who is licensed by the Office of Real Estate Appraisers) to the lender and purchaser, as well as full and complete disclosure of all material facts affecting the value of a property are sufficient to not require a broker to provide a separate estimate of value.

In any loan transaction in which a fee is charged to a borrower for an appraisal of real property that will serve as security for a loan, a copy of the appraisal report must be given to both the borrower and the lender at of before the closing of the loan transaction.

21. Advertising of Loan - License Disclosure

A real estate licensee cannot place an advertisement (disseminated primarily in California) for a loan unless their license is disclosed within the printed text or oral text of that advertisement.

22. Advertising Disclosure

Advertising by a licensee must not be under the name of an agent unless the name of the employing broker is also included. Use of the terms broker, agent, realty, or loan correspondent, or other abbreviations such as bro., bkr., or agt. are generally considered sufficient. The agent's DRE license number is required on all first point-of-contact advertising. The broker's identity is required, but the broker's DRE license number is optional.

In addition, to reiterate the DRE's requirements for all first point of contact solicitation materials, "The definition of first point of contact solicitation material now includes all of the following: business cards, stationery, advertising flyers, advertisements on television, advertisements in print, advertisements in electronic media, 'for sale' signs*, rent signs, lease signs*, 'open house' signs*, directional signs*, and any other materials designed to solicit the creation of a professional relationship between the licensee and a consumer. The minimum information that needs to be in these first point of contact solicitation materials includes:

- Your name
- Your license ID number (the type size shall be no smaller than the smallest size type used in the solicitation material)
- NMLS unique identifier number (if you are a mortgage loan originator)
- Your responsible broker's identity

*Note: If the 'for sale,' rent, lease, 'open house,' and directional signs display the responsible broker's identity, then their name, license ID number, and NMLS unique identifier are not required to be placed on the solicitation materials.

In summary, many advertisements and solicitations now fall under 'First Point of Contact' rules, which require the licensee to list on the advertisement their name, license ID number, responsible broker's ID number, and NMLS unique identifier if applicable."

23. Disclosure of Compensation for Obtaining Financing

It is a substantial misrepresentation for a real estate licensee who acts as the agent for either party in a transaction for the sale, lease, or exchange of real property (or business opportunity or mobile home) and who receives compensation (or anticipates receiving compensation) from a lender in connection with the securing of financing for the transaction, to fail to disclose to both parties, prior to the closing of the transaction, the form, amount, and source of compensation received or expected.

In other words, if a licensee involved in the sale, lease, or exchange of real property procures a loan for a buyer and receives compensation from a lender, he or she must disclose this fact to both the buyer and seller.

24. Disclosure of Intent to Make Sales Presentation

It is unlawful to by email, electronic device, mail, telephone, billboard, or in person offer a prize or gift without disclosing at the time of the offer that the intent is to offer a sales presentation. It is also unlawful to charge a shipping and handling charge for prizes or gifts.

25. Notice of No Policy of Title Insurance

In any escrow transaction for the purchase (or simultaneous exchange) of real property, in which a policy of title insurance will *not* be issued to the buyer, the following notice must be provided in a separate document to the buyer. It must also be signed and acknowledged by the buyer.

The notice reads:

> "IMPORTANT: IN A PURCHASE OR EXCHANGE OF REAL PROPERTY, IT MAY BE ADVISABLE TO OBTAIN TITLE INSURANCE IN CONNECTION WITH THE CLOSE OF ESCROW SINCE THERE MAY BE PRIOR RECORDED LIENS AND ENCUMBRANCES WHICH AFFECT YOUR INTEREST IN THE PROPERTY BEING ACQUIRED. A NEW POLICY OF TITLE INSURANCE SHOULD BE OBTAINED IN ORDER TO ENSURE YOUR INTEREST IN THE PROPERTY THAT YOU ARE ACQUIRING."

Figure 9.7 Notice of No Policy of Title Insurance

26. Blanket Encumbrance in Subdivisions

A blanket encumbrance is a loan that blankets several lots in a subdivision. When the developer sells one of the lots, a release clause or partial release clause is used to remove the lot from under the blanket encumbrance.

27. Possible Representation of More than One Buyer or Seller

Real estate agents must disclose to buyers that they may be representing other buyers or sellers at the same time.

28. Wire Fraud Advisory

According to the California Association of Realtors, clients are advised to:

1. Obtain telephone numbers and account numbers only from Escrow Officers, Property Managers, or Landlords at the beginning of the transaction.

2. DO NOT EVER WIRE OR ELECTRONICALLY TRANSFER FUNDS PRIOR TO CALLING TO CONFIRM THE TRANSFER INSTRUCTIONS. ONLY USE A TELEPHONE NUMBER YOU WERE PROVIDED PREVIOUSLY. Do not use any different telephone number or account number included in any emailed transfer instructions.

3. Orally confirm the transfer instruction is legitimate and confirm the bank routing number, account numbers and other codes before taking steps to transfer the funds.

4. Avoid sending personal information in emails or texts. Provide such information in person or over the telephone directly to the Escrow Officer, Property Manager, or Landlord.

5. Take steps to secure the system you are using with your email account. These steps include creating strong passwords, using secure Wi-Fi, and not using free services.

29. Mobile Home Park Conversion - Disclosure Regarding Prices

Prior to filing a notice of intention to sell or lease subdivided lands, the subdivider of a mobile home park that will be converted to resident ownership must, by written notice, disclose to homeowners and residents of the mobile home park the tentative price of each lot that will be subdivided and either sold or leased.

30. Water Heater Bracing Statement of Compliance

Owners of new or replacement water heaters and owners of existing residential, including used mobile homes, manufactured homes, and used multi-family manufactured housing with fuel gas-burning water heaters must brace, anchor, or strap water heaters (usually with a readily-available pre-engineered strapping kit that has two straps) to resist

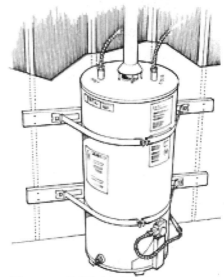

Figure 9.8 Water Heater

falling or horizontal displacement due to earthquake motion. Water heaters located in closets are also subject to the law.

The seller of real property must certify in writing to a prospective purchaser that the seller has complied with this section of the law and applicable local code requirements.

Figure 9.9 Carbon Monoxide Detector

31. Carbon Monoxide Detector Disclosure & Compliance

The Carbon Monoxide Poisoning Prevention Act of 2010 requires a carbon monoxide (CO) detector device (battery or hard-wired) to be installed in all dwelling units.

32. Gas and Hazardous Liquid Transmission Pipeline Notice

The Gas and Hazardous Liquid Transmission Pipeline Notice applies to every contract for the sale of residential real property. The Notice informs the buyer that information about the general location of these pipelines is available to the public online via the National Pipeline Mapping System (NPMS) and provides the web address.

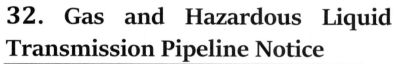

33. Megan's Law Disclosure (Registered Sex Offender Database)

Since 2004, the public has been able to view information on sex offenders required to register with local law enforcement under California's Megan's Law. Previously, the information was available only by personally visiting police stations and sheriff offices or by calling a 900 number. The law was given final passage by the Legislature on August 24, 2004 and signed by the Governor on September 24, 2004.

The Megan's Law Disclosure is required for the sale or lease/rental of all residential real property of any size, with no exemptions except for never-occupied properties in which a public report is required or properties exempted from a public report.

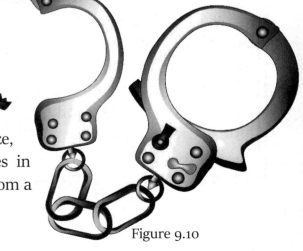

Figure 9.10

Every sales contract and lease or rental agreement is required to include a statutorily-defined notice regarding the existence of public access to database information regarding sex offenders. The law is not intended to punish the registrant and specifically prohibits using the information to harass or commit any crime against a registrant.

California has required sex offenders to register with their local law enforcement agencies since 1947. California's Megan's Law provides the public with certain information on the whereabouts of sex offenders so that members of our local communities may protect themselves and their children. Megan's Law is named after seven-year-old Megan Kanka, a New Jersey girl who was raped and killed by a known registered sex offender who had moved across the street from the family without their knowledge. In the wake of the tragedy, the Kanka's sought to have local communities warned about sex offenders in the area. All states now have a form of Megan's Law.

34. Rent Control

Rent Control: Laws that limit rental increases and have "just cause for eviction" ordinances.

Certain cities in California may have adopted **rent control** laws that limit rental increases and have "just cause for eviction" ordinances. Some cities may include tenant relocation assistance and possibly interest on security deposits.

California cities with rent control may include: Berkeley, Beverly Hills, Campbell, East Palo Alto, Fremont, Hayward, Los Angeles, Los Gatos, Oakland, Palm Springs, San Francisco, San Jose, Santa Monica, Thousand Oaks, and West Hollywood.

Tales from the Trade

The Story of the Berkeley Attic Dweller

One intrepid Berkeley apartment owner decided to circumvent Berkeley's rent control ordinances by renting his attic to a tenant. Even though his four apartment units were under rent control that limits the amount he can charge residents to rent each unit in the property, his attic was not considered a habitable space and he could not legally rent it to a tenant.

Of course, with Berkeley rental properties under rent control, finding a place to live was a big challenge for many residents, so the apartment owner was able to compile a list of people who wanted to rent the attic. He rented it to a tenant and started collecting rent. At some point in time the Berkeley Rent Stabilization Board will catch up with him because he hasn't been paying his annual fee to them for the unpermitted attic. Remember, always follow the money.

35. Private Transfer Fee

If a property has a **private transfer fee** that was imposed by the homebuilder, a fee must be paid to some specified party every time the property is transferred (sold or otherwise conveyed). Private transfer fees are an attempt by single-family home builders to use future private transfer fees to pay for many of the upfront costs incurred by homebuilders. These costs may include off-site improvements, impact fees, mitigation fees, and other development costs that reduce homebuilder profits.

> **Private Transfer Fee:** A fee imposed by homebuilders to help pay for off-site improvements and other development costs.

In response to the use of private transfer fees, homebuyers who purchase a property from a homebuilder, must record a separate document with the grant deed (that transfers title to the property) that informs future buyers of the private transfer fee requirements. In addition, Fannie Mae will not purchase loans that have private transfer fees and the Federal Housing Administration (FHA) will not insure loans made by lenders that make loans on properties with private transfer fees.

These government entities will effectively make owner-occupied, low-interest rate, low down payment, and high loan-to-value loans unavailable to properties with private transfer fees, thus significantly reducing the value of properties with private transfer fees on them.

36. Supplemental Assessment/Supplemental Property Tax Notice

When a buyer purchases a property that has a low assessed value as determined by the county tax assessor, and the new assessed value is significantly higher than the seller's former assessed value, then a supplemental assessment may be mailed to the buyer several months after close of escrow.

The reason for the supplemental assessment is that the escrow agent must prorate property taxes at close of escrow on *what is* and *not what will be* in the future. The escrow officer must prorate property taxes on the seller's existing low property tax bill, rather than the buyer's new high property tax bill. The buyer will pay an amount that is much lower than the buyer should really be paying for their property taxes. Several months down the road the buyer will receive a supplemental assessment bill that requires the buyer to pay the difference between what was paid at close of escrow and the higher property taxes that are due with the buyer's new higher assessed value.

37. Water Conserving Fixtures Compliance and Disclosures

The seller or transferor must disclose in writing to the prospective transferee that the law requires that noncompliant plumbing fixtures must be replaced with water-conserving plumbing fixtures and the required date, and also whether the real property includes any noncompliant plumbing fixtures.

Noncompliant plumbing fixtures must be replaced by water conserving plumbing fixtures. However, this is a requirement of owning real property regardless of whether or not the property is being sold. It is not a point of sale requirement.

Exemptions include: registered historical sites, properties that are certified not technically feasible by a licensed plumber, and a water service that is disconnected.

Figure 9.11 Modern Plumbing Fixtures

38. Window Security Bars and Safety Release Mechanism

The seller must disclose the existence of any window security bars and any safety release mechanisms on those window security bars.

39. Acrylonitrile Butadiene Styrene (ABS) Pipe Disclosure

Acrylonitrile butadiene styrene (ABS) pipe is rigid, black, non-pressurized plastic pipe used to drain sinks, tubs, showers, toilets, washing machines and dishwashers commonly used in residential construction as waste, drain, and vent pipe. According to the ABS pipe class action suits, during certain periods of time between the years 1984 and 1990, ABS pipe manufactured by Polaris Pipe Co., Gable Plastics, Inc., Centaur Mfg., Inc., DBA (Doing Business As/Fictitious Business Name) Phoenix Extrusion Co., and Apache Plastics, Inc. contained plastic resin that could cause the ABS pipe to crack and ultimately leak.

Each manufacturer used allegedly unsuitable resin during different periods. Plaintiffs claimed that this allegedly defective ABS pipe could crack circumferentially (around the pipe) at the glue line where the pipe was cemented into the socket of the fitting, and that such cracks could ultimately result in leaks. Due to these facts, the seller must disclose if their home has the defective ABS pipe.

40. Commercial Industrial Disclosure

California-mandated natural hazard disclosures required in commercial and industrial property transactions include: flood, seismic, brushfire, former military ordnance sites, airport influence areas, airport noise proximity, toxic mold, radon, leaking and permitted underground and above ground fuel tanks, landfills, hazardous materials generators, and notices of a special tax, special assessment, and supplemental assessment.

Real estate agents must understand each of the required disclosures and know when to use them while helping clients buy and sell real estate in California.

Chapter Nine Summary

Part II of the real estate disclosures include: Energy Rating Program and Booklet, Lead-Based Paint Disclosure/Lead Hazard Pamphlet, Smoke Detector Compliance, Alquist-Priolo Special Studies Zones, Subdivision Map Act and Subdivided Lands Law, Common Interest Subdivision Conversion, Mello-Roos Disclosure, Military Ordnance Disclosure, Seller Financing Disclosure, Loan Broker Disclosure, Appraisal - Disclosure of Fair Market Value in Loan Transactions, Advertising of Loan - License Disclosure, Advertising Disclosure, Disclosure of Compensation for Obtaining Financing, Disclosure of Intent to Make Sales Presentation, Notice of No Policy of Title Insurance, Blanket Encumbrance on Subdivisions, Possible Representation of More than One Buyer or Seller, Wire Fraud Advisory, Mobile Home Park Conversion - Disclosure Regarding Prices, Water Heater Bracing Statement of Compliance, Carbon Monoxide (CO) Detector & Compliance, Gas and Hazardous Pipeline Notice, Megan's Law (Registered Sex Offender Database), Rent Control, Private Transfer Fees, Supplemental Assessment/Supplemental Property Tax Notice, Water Conserving Fixture Compliance/Water Conserving Fixture Disclosure, Window Security Bars and Safety Release Mechanisms, Acrylonitrile Butadiene Styrene (ABS) Pipe Disclosure, and Commercial Industrial Disclosure.

Chapter Nine Quiz

1. If a property owner replaces a heating, ventilating, and air conditioning (HVAC) unit for a home located in California, a(n) _____ may be required to obtain a building permit for the new unit.
(A) duct test
(B) home inspection
(C) injunction
(D) zoning change

2. Homes that were built prior to 1978 and are regulated by the lead-based paint regulations are called:
(A) uninhabitable
(B) target housing
(C) red tag housing
(D) super fund sites

3. All existing real property dwelling units must have a smoke alarm centrally located outside each sleeping area (bedroom or group of bedrooms). This includes:
(A) used manufactured homes
(B) used mobile homes
(C) used multi-family manufactured housing
(D) all of the above are correct

4. California has enacted the Alquist-Priolo Special Studies Earthquake Zones Act to control development of homes:
(A) located near hazardous earthquake faults
(B) that may experience surface fault rupture
(C) Both (A) and (B) are correct
(D) Neither (A) nor (B) is correct

5. The minimum time required for an owner to give notice to the tenants in an apartment building (when that building is being converted by the owner to a condominium form of ownership) is:
(A) 90 days
(B) 180 days
(C) 270 days
(D) one year

6. A seller of any one-to-four unit residential property must make a good faith effort to obtain a disclosure notice concerning the special tax from each local agency under the _____ on the property being transferred.
(A) Mello-Roos Community Facilities Act
(B) supplemental assessment
(C) county building department
(D) county board of supervisors

7. In any loan transaction in which a fee is charged to a borrower for an appraisal of real property that will serve as security for a loan, a copy of the appraisal report must be given to:
(A) only the borrower
(B) only the lender
(C) both the borrower and the lender at or before the closing of the loan transaction
(D) none of the above are correct

8. A _____ is a loan that blankets several lots in a subdivision. When the developer sells one of the lots, a release clause or partial release clause is used to remove the lot from under it.
(A) blanket encumbrance
(B) subordinated loan
(C) seller carry loan
(D) Both (B) and (C) are correct

9. The Carbon Monoxide Poisoning Prevention Act of 2010 requires a carbon monoxide (CO) detector device (battery or hard-wired) to be installed in:
(A) all dwelling units
(B) only commercial office buildings
(C) only retail centers
(D) most industrial properties

10. When a buyer purchases a property that has a low assessed value as determined by the county tax assessor, and the new assessed value is significantly higher than the seller's former assessed value, then a _____ may be mailed to the buyer several months after close of escrow.
(A) special assessment
(B) Mello-Roos bond
(C) supplemental assessment
(D) none of the above are correct

Answers: 1. A, 2. B, 3. D, 4. C, 5. B, 6. A, 7. C, 8. A, 9. A, 10. C

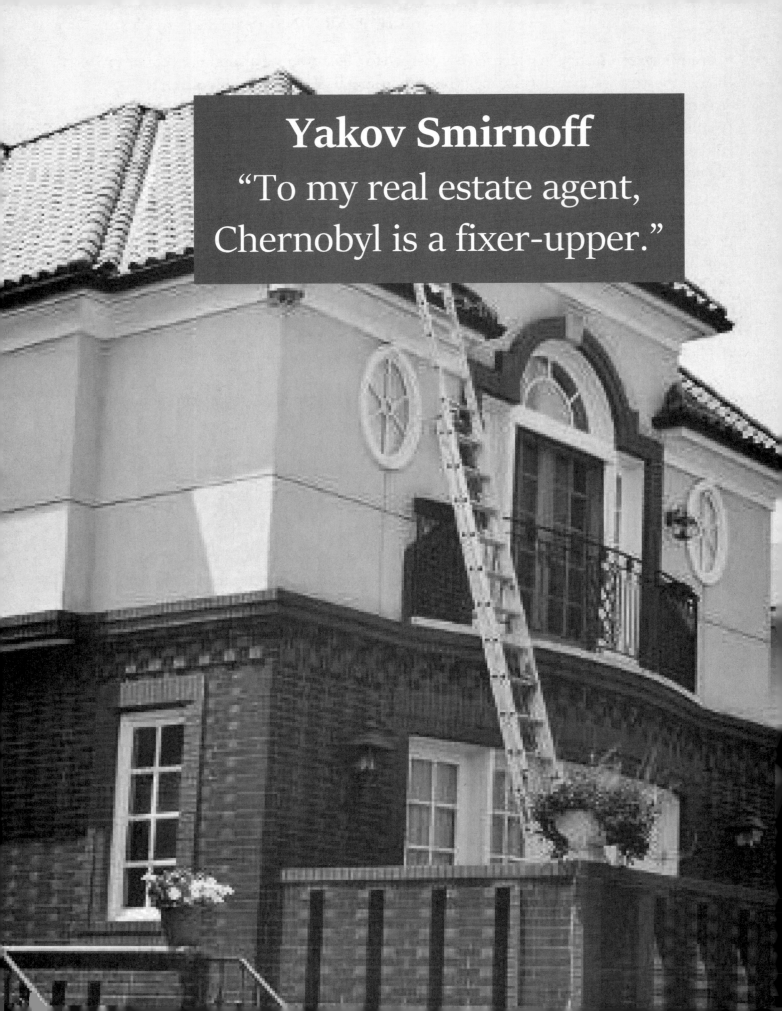

10

Chapter

TEN

Physical Inspection Contingencies

Real estate purchase agreements typically have contingencies to the contract that allow the buyer to not go forward with the purchase and have their earnest money deposit returned by the escrow agent. There are three contingencies that are commonly used with residential single-family real estate purchases in California, they include a(n): physical inspection contingency, appraisal contingency, and financing contingency. A fourth contingency is estoppel certificates that are used with commercial leased investments to verify lease information and discussed in the California Real Estate Practice textbook.

Physical inspection contingencies allow a buyer adequate time, usually seventeen (17) days in CAR contracts, to thoroughly inspect a single-family home and have experts inspect it prior to moving forward with the purchase transaction. Possible inspectors may include a home inspector, roof inspector, HVAC inspector, structural pest inspector, pool inspector, pool equipment inspector, soil inspector (compaction), hazardous material inspector, lead-based paint inspector, and mold inspector.

Most residential purchases utilize a home inspector to inspect the entire house including the roof and HVAC system(s). If the home inspector finds the roof, HVAC system(s), or any other items to be in disrepair, the home inspector may

267

recommend a specialized inspection from a roofing company, HVAC company, or other company to determine if the item needs to be repaired or replaced. Buyers usually pay $400 or more for a home inspection, depending upon the type and size of the home. Separate lead-based paint, mold, or radon inspections may be used if lead, mold, or radon is suspected in the property.

Due to the more specialized nature of commercial property inspections, commercial properties may use a much longer physical inspection contingency period with earnest money deposit increases as contingencies are removed. For example, an industrial property many need a phase one environmental inspection to look for hazardous materials on the property site.

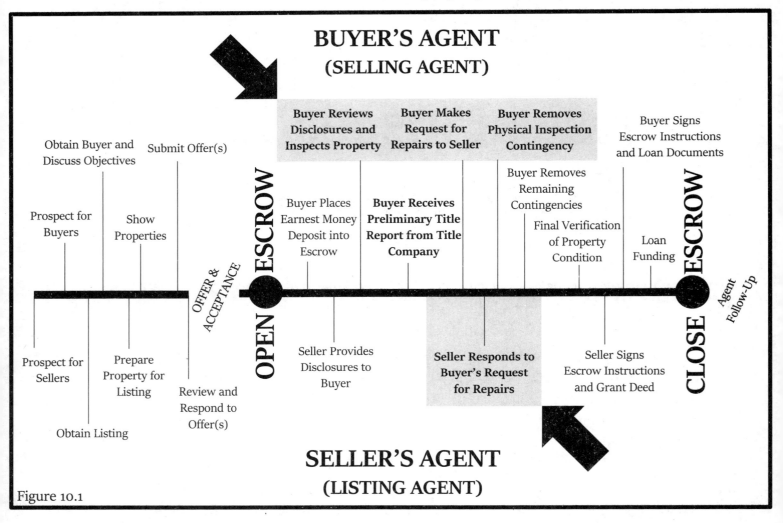

Figure 10.1

1. Buyer's Investigation of Property Condition and Home Inspections

The buyer's acceptance of a property's condition is usually a contingency to the agreement and is removed along with the physical inspection contingencies set forth in the contract. A buyer usually has the right, at the buyer's expense, to conduct inspections, investigations, tests, surveys, and other studies. In addition, a buyer usually has the right to inspect a property for lead-based paint, other lead-based paint hazards, and wood destroying pests and organisms (pest inspection).

Thus, a prudent homebuyer will get a home inspection during the due diligence period prior to close of escrow. A home inspection is a complete evaluation of the home. The home inspector is looking for items that should be repaired due to health and safety concerns, along with other cosmetic issues that may detrimentally affect the value of the property.

The seller is generally required to make the property available for all inspections. In addition, the seller will generally be required to have the water, gas, and electricity turned on for the buyer's inspections. At the seller's request, the buyer must give the seller (at no cost to the seller) complete copies of all inspection reports.

Moreover, once a home inspection report has been issued for a property, items in the home inspection report become material facts and must be disclosed to the buyer of the property, *and any future buyers as well.*

A home inspector usually advises the buyer to investigate the square footage, room dimensions, lot size, age of improvements, and property boundaries. Fences, hedges, walls, retaining walls, and other natural and man-made barriers and markers do not necessarily identify the true property boundaries.

A. Swimming Pools

A swimming pool is usually a much sought-after amenity for single-family homes and condos located in hot dry areas. In temperate areas like San Francisco, the residents who live there might consider a swimming pool an "eccentric addition" that is not necessary, due to San Francisco's mild climate. A pool might need to be heated to be used with any regularity, even in the summer. Mark Twain summed it up best when he said, "The coldest winter I ever spent was a summer in San Francisco."

Figure 10.2 Swimming Pool

With the beginning of cost-effective solar heating systems in single-family homes, many swimming pools are now installed with solar heating that extends the time when a pool can be used by owners or tenants. They may get an extra month on each end of the summer, and it usually makes the kids happy too.

A built-in swimming pool can increase or decrease the intrinsic value of a single-family home. It depends upon the age of the pool, neighborhood where the property is located, and desires of owners and tenants.

A built-in swimming pool constructed in a newer existing tract home is probably worth approximately 50% of the cost to build the pool. For this reason, it may not be a good financial decision to have a built-in pool installed within a property. The smart person buys a home that already has a built-in pool to take advantage of the previous homeowner(s)' resulting financial loss.

An older pool located in an older neighborhood may actually reduce the value of a home because of a needed renovation of the pool itself, as well as inevitable deterioration of pool equipment.

Tales from the Trade

THE STORY OF THE OLD BUILT-IN SWIMMING POOL

Homebuyer Lori was considering buying a home that was built in the early 1960s. The home had a built-in swimming pool that had been constructed at about the same time as the home. Lori made an offer to purchase the property and it was accepted by the seller. According to the purchase contract between her and the seller, she had seventeen days to inspect the property and make a decision whether to buy the home or look for another property.

Lori scheduled a home inspection with a professional home inspector during the seventeen-day physical inspection contingency period. The home inspector thought the home was in good condition; however, the pool was a major area of concern. The home inspector recommended that Lori hire a professional pool inspector to look at the pool and make a separate report.

A professional pool inspector informed Lori that she would need to refinish the pool exterior in the very near future—if she intended to use the pool at all. The professional pool inspector recommended hiring a professional pool equipment inspector to examine the older pool equipment and determine its projected useful life.

The pool equipment expert informed Lori that she would probably have to replace the pool equipment in the very near future. With the reports from the home inspector, pool inspector, and pool equipment inspector, Lori realized that the pool would have to be extensively renovated.

Having thorough inspections prior to purchasing a single-family home can save a lot of headaches in the long run. Buyers will understand the true condition of the home before it is purchased and discover problems with the property *before* close of escrow.

The buyer's options for the old swimming pool were:
1. Renovate the pool
2. Fill in the pool with soil or concrete
3. Do nothing and use it as an eyesore

THE STORY OF THE OLD BUILT-IN SWIMMING POOL

Since Lori's pool was rectangular-shaped, a common shape for pools built many years ago in the U.S. and still a common shape in many countries around the world, it has some functional obsolescence (styling) issues causing a reduction in value.

Most modern swimming pools located in the U.S. have curved sides, whereas this pool was obviously rectangular, old, and outdated. Lori negotiated a much lower purchase price than the home would have been worth if it had a modern swimming pool built in the backyard. The negotiated price was less than what Lori believed the home was worth without the pool! Due to the age of the pool, the home's intrinsic value declined by as much as $75,000.

Tales from the Trade

THE STORY OF THE HOME WARRANTY POLICY

A seller decided to sell a semi-custom single-family home located in a high socio-economic neighborhood. The home had a fine built-in swimming pool located in the backyard. The house, pool, and pool equipment were approximately twenty-five years old.

The buyer was wise to obtain a home warranty policy for the home, HVAC, and pool equipment prior to close of escrow. The pool equipment stopped working after close of escrow. The home warranty policy had an endorsement that covered the pool equipment, so the buyer ended up with new pool equipment.

As mentioned earlier, it is generally best to purchase a newer home that already has a built-in swimming pool constructed on the property. The previous owner—and not the buyer—will take the loss of approximately 50% of what was paid to construct the pool.

For example, if a buyer paid $50,000 to install a built-in swimming pool, the resale value of the pool will be approximately $25,000. Therefore, a buyer would probably receive approximately $25,000 more for the property than a person who owned the same property and did not have a built-in swimming pool.

In large super custom homes located in dry Mediterranean-type climates, such as Southern California and Northern California's inland areas, a pool may be an expected amenity by an owner-occupied homebuyer. Many large homes will come with a pool, and if not, the buyer may look elsewhere for a home that does have one. Unfortunately, an above ground pool adds virtually no value to a single-family home.

B. Pest Report and Repairs

Another area of concern for single-family homebuyers is pest infestation and dry rot. Extensive pest infestation caused by subterranean termites and dry rot caused by bacterial decay are two of the most common problems experienced by homeowners in California.

Pest Infestation: Subterranean termites and bacterial decay (dry rot) tend to destroy the wood in a home.

(1) Pest Infestation and Dry Rot

A pest inspector generally looks for signs of **pest infestation** within a single-family home. Two primary areas of concern are subterranean termites and dry rot

(bacterial decay). Termites are particularly active in warm, wet areas such as the coastal areas of California. However, termites are prevalent throughout most of the state. Cold, high elevation areas in California usually do not have termites. Everywhere else they seem to be a continual problem for real estate homeowners, investors, and agents.

Figure 10.3 Subterranean Termite

When there is earth-to-wood contact, termites may be able to eat the wood in the home. Even if the wood is a reasonable distance from the soil, termites can build tubes between the soil and the wood and travel up them into the home. However, they generally have difficultly consuming wood without the direct earth-to-wood contact.

When a builder leaves wood scraps in the crawl space under a single-family home, his action can attract termites. The earth-to-wood contact may allow termites to enter through the soil and eat the wood scraps. From there, the termites may be able to build mud tubes from the soil to the wood in the house. These scraps may be removed from the crawl space to prevent this potential downward spiral of termite destruction.

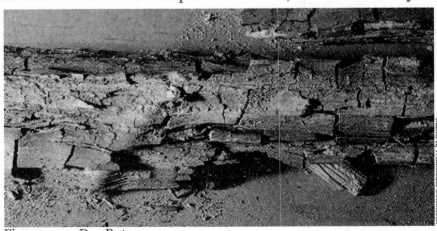

Figure 10.4 Dry Rot

(2) Pest Infestation Report

A **pest infestation report** is a written report indicating whether a home has termite damage or dry rot. The pest inspector may look within and under bathrooms and kitchen areas for signs of termite infestation, as well as dry rot damage under the eaves of the home. Older homes with raised foundations are particularly susceptible to dry rot damage under the bathroom(s) and kitchen areas.

Pest reports are usually comprised of Section 1 and Section 2 items. Section 1 items are items that are in existence at the time of the report. Section 2 items are items that are "deemed likely" to lead to infestation.

The seller can limit the amount of money that will be paid for each section of the report. However, pest repairs are usually agreed upon in the Request for Repairs addendum. If the buyer and seller cannot come to an agreement, then the buyer may decide not to go forward with the purchase of the property.

> **Pest Infestation Report:** A pest inspector checks a home for termite damage and dry rot and issues a pest report that can be used by the buyer to ensure the property is clear of termites and dry rot damage.

(3) Structural Pest Control Board

The **Structural Pest Control Board** was originated in 1935 and is comprised of seven members of which, by law, four are public members, and three are members of the pest control industry. The Governor appoints two public members and three licensed industry members. The Senate Rules Committee and the Speaker of the Assembly each appoint one public member. Board Members may serve up to two four-year terms. Board members fill non-salaried positions but are paid per diem for each Board meeting, committee meeting, and other meetings approved by the President of the Board. Travel expenses are also reimbursed.

> **Structural Pest Control Board:** Regulates structural pest control companies in California.

Structural pest control is the control of household pests (including but not limited to rodents, vermin, and insects) and wood-destroying pests and organisms or such other pests which may invade households or structures.

According to the Structural Pest Control Board, the practice of structural pest control includes the, "Engaging in, offering to engage in, advertising for, soliciting, or the performance of any of the following:

- Identification of infestations or infections;
- The making of an inspection for the purpose of identifying or attempting to identify infestations or infections of household or other structures by such pests or organisms;
- The making of inspection reports; recommendations, estimates, and bids, whether oral or written, with respect to such infestation or infections; and
- The making of contracts, or the submitting of bids for, or the performance of any work including the making of structural repairs or replacements, or the use of pesticides, insecticides, rodenticides, fumigants, or allied

chemicals or substances, or mechanical devices for the purpose of eliminating, exterminating, controlling or preventing infestations or infections of such pests, or organisms."

(4) When to Order a Pest Report

Many real estate agents wait until they have an accepted contract before ordering a pest inspection report. If the buyer does not request a clear pest report in the purchase agreement, then the seller may not need to obtain a pest report for the property.

a. New Homes and Newer Homes

Pest inspections are usually not needed with new homes. Accordingly, with newer homes that are only a few years old and have a concrete slab foundation, there will probably not be very much corrective work required to obtain a clear report.

b. Older Homes

Older homes, especially with raised foundations, may contain a considerable amount of pest infestation and dry rot. The repairs could easily total $5,000 to $10,000 or more.

During a hot upward-trending sellers' market, the seller may be dealing with multiple offers for their single-family home and the "cleaner" the offer the better the chances it will be accepted. Some buyers may not include any pest inspection and repair contingencies to the purchase agreement, while other buyers may include a required clear pest report (both Section 1 and Section 2). If the seller is not aware of the amount of pest work required to obtain a clear pest report, it will be easier to accept an offer that does not require a clear pest report as a requirement in the purchase agreement.

Figure 10.5 Older Home

(5) Pest Repairs

If the buyer would like a clear pest report or certain items from the pest report to be repaired, the buyer may use an addendum or request for repairs addendum to the purchase agreement. A clear pest report describes a home as being free of pest infestation, including termite damage and dry rot/bacterial decay. However, if there is a significant amount of pest infestation, the seller may agree to repair only a few items that were specified in the pest report. It is also common for a seller to give a buyer a monetary credit in lieu of making pest repairs to the property.

Referrals from a real estate agent can be a good way to select a pest inspection company. Since the agent may be using the pest company on a frequent basis, the pest company will probably have future pest reports and (possibly) pest repair work riding on agent referrals. Homeowners, on the other hand, may be a "one-shot deal." They do not represent future business to the pest company and will probably be treated accordingly—if they don't have a real estate agent's future business backing them up.

a. The Rabbit in Charge of the Lettuce Patch

Many pest inspection companies perform inspections and do the corrective work as well. Pest inspectors are usually paid a commission based on the amount of pest work they can generate from their own pest reports, which is similar to the rabbit being in charge of the lettuce patch. For this reason, agents really need to refer an honest pest inspector, or at least one whose future business income will be adversely affected by gouging your client on this particular inspection and resulting corrective work.

b. The Home Sprayer Mistake

One home seller mistake is to use the same pest spraying company that has been spraying the home for pests on a regular basis to do the pest inspection. On the surface this seems like a good idea. However, the pest spraying company most likely specializes in pest spraying, not pest inspections. Also, the owner may hope they will not find any pest infestation because, after all, they have been spraying the rental property for years. On the contrary, they may actually find *more* infestation than a company that specializes in pest inspections and repairs. In addition, they may not be able to perform the corrective work themselves, so the owner may need to find a contractor to perform the work. The pest spraying company may make it difficult to obtain a clearance, especially when the pest spraying company realizes how much liability they have generated—with little return.

c. The "Your Relative the Contractor" Mistake

Pest inspection companies normally charge an inspection fee of between $100 and $150, however, this varies by geographical market. Pest inspectors usually make their big money from the commission income generated from pest repairs, not from pest inspection fees. Thus, pest inspectors prefer homeowners to use their repair services along with their inspection services.

Figure 10.6 Termite Damage

For example, a seller hires a contractor who is one of their relatives to repair five items on a pest inspection report. These items need to be repaired before the seller can obtain a clear pest report from the pest inspector. The relative completes all five items, and then the seller calls the pest inspector for a re-inspection. This will cost another pest inspection fee and the inspector determines that three items on the report have been repaired, however, there are two items that remain to be "satisfactorily" completed. The relative returns and completes the two items and the seller orders another re-inspection and pays the fee for a third time. The pest inspector finds one of the items is still not satisfactorily completed and the seller must call the relative back out to the property...and the process continues. The pest inspector may be penalizing the seller for not using his company to do the pest repair work and causing him to lose the resulting commission income.

The inspector may be trying to increase his inspection income to compensate for the loss of revenue caused by the relative doing the corrective work—instead of using his company. More importantly, the inspector may delay the close of escrow. If a clear pest report is required in the purchase contract and the pest clearance causes a delay in escrow, the buyer's loan lock may expire. If interest rates have increased during the rate lock period, usually in place for 30 to 45 days, the buyer's loan payment may increase. This may cause the buyer to not qualify for the anticipated loan, escrow closing may be delayed, and the transaction may fall apart.

Hence, it can be advantageous for the homeowner to use the same pest company for inspection and repair work.

d. During a Downward-Trending Buyers' Market

During a downward-trending buyers' market, there may be a large number of homes in pre-foreclosure, foreclosure, and post foreclosure. Pre-foreclosure homes have not had a notice of default (NOD) recorded against them. The seller may or may not be late with loan payments and may be attempting to obtain a loan modification or short sale for the home.

Foreclosure homes are homes that have had NODs recorded against them and are on the way to foreclosure. In California, this is usually through a trustee's sale. Post Foreclosure homes have already been foreclosed and are being held by the foreclosing lender as a "Real Estate Owned" or REO.

Banks many times employ professional executives who know how to negotiate during a downward-trending buyers' market. The bank generally will not pay for any pest inspections or repairs during this type of market. If an owner-occupied homebuyer includes a request for a pest inspection and clear pest report in the purchase agreement, the lender will most likely not agree to pay for this pest report or clearance. Therefore, if the buyer is *not* able to pay for the inspection and resulting corrective work, the purchase may not go through. For this reason, real estate investors have a better chance of purchasing distressed properties (e.g., pre-foreclosure, short sales, REOs) when they are in poor physical condition.

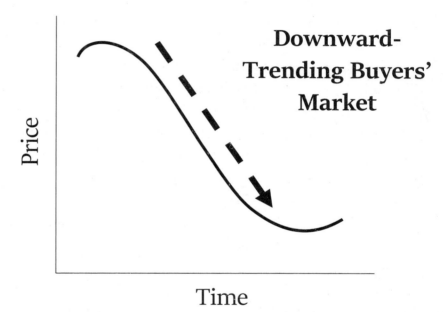

Figure 10.7 Downward-Trending Buyers' Market

Tales from the Trade

Story of Simon

Simon owned a single-family home located in a lower socio-economic neighborhood. The property had 3 bedrooms and 1 bathroom and had a detached two car garage that was not connected to the home.

The property was an REO (Real Estate Owned) that a bank had in its portfolio of foreclosed properties and wanted to sell it for the highest possible price.

Story of Simon

The property had sold five years earlier for $310,000 and the bank had made a 100% loan-to-value loan for the purchase. Five years later the bank had listed the property with a real estate agent for $82,950.

Simon placed an offer for $83,000 to purchase the home. The bank accepted the offer and Simon closed the deal thirty days later. He was elated. He had purchased a home for over $200,000 less than its sale price only a few years earlier.

Simon rehabbed the property with new paint inside and out, new carpet, new flooring in the kitchen, new appliances, repaired the roof, and cleaned up the backyard. His payments were $445/month principal and interest, $80/month property taxes, $45/month homeowner's insurance, totaling $570/month PITI. This same house five years earlier would have cost Simon $1,665/month principal and interest, $300/month property taxes, and $45/month homeowner's insurance, totaling $2,010/month.

Simon purchased this older property, that was located in a lower socio-economic neighborhood, because of the attractive price. The price had declined so dramatically since the market had peaked five years earlier, he could now afford to buy the home. Simon's gross income was $2,500 per month. After taxes, his net income was approximately $1,800/month. After paying his loan payment of $570/month plus water/sewer/garbage which was another $125/month, electricity, natural gas, telephone, and cable TV he was actually able to afford the home and have some discretionary income left over for entertainment and fun.

Simon could also expect to see slow appreciation over a long period of time. The appreciation of his home may not be as fast as homes located in higher socio-economic neighborhoods; however, he bought the home for such a good price, he could really afford to wait out the market while paying his really low loan payments.

Eight years later Simon's home was worth $275,000.

e. The Tale of Two Pest Control Reports

Some sellers try the "I'll call another pest company and get a second opinion" routine. Remember, the first pest report must be disclosed to all future buyers. There are several court cases in California to confirm this requirement.

The sellers who try the "two pest report routine" will many times remove the first pest inspector's date of inspection sticker from the garage wall, so the next inspector will not know about the existing report. Removing the pest inspection sticker off the garage wall is illegal in California. The Structural Pest Control Board in California is supposed to keep pest reports on file for two years, so it is easy to obtain a copy of the first inspector's report.

2. Seller to Disclose Material Facts and Buyer Has Right to Request Repairs

Based upon information resulting from the home inspection, other inspections, and disclosures, the buyer may ask the seller to make certain repairs. If the buyer elects to submit a Request for Repairs addendum to the seller, then the seller can respond to the Request for Repairs addendum with one of the following:

- Agree to the terms by repairing requested items and/or providing financing concessions (price reduction or seller credits buyer in escrow)
- Counter with a Response to the Request for Repairs addendum
- Reject the Request for Repairs addendum

If the seller elects not to make the requested repairs, the buyer may decide not to remove the physical inspection contingency and not proceed with the purchase of the property. However, the buyer may not immediately receive the earnest money deposit back from the escrow agent unless the seller mutually agrees to terminate the escrow by signing an escrow rescission form. The buyer may have paid $400 for a home inspection and possibly $500 for an appraisal of the property and may not have any money left over to buy another property.

Repairs required by an agreement or addendum to an agreement usually must be completed prior to close of escrow (unless otherwise specified in writing). Many repairs are completed and noted by the buyer during the walk-thru inspection prior to close of escrow. If required repairs are not completed prior to close of escrow, the escrow holder can hold back as much as 1 ½ to 2 times the estimated amount for the repairs. Holding back funds in escrow has become less common-place in recent years, some escrow officers will not hold back funds for repairs that were not completed prior to close of escrow.

Repairs that are paid by the seller usually may be performed by the seller or through others, providing the work complies with applicable laws, government permits, inspections, and approvals. Repairs generally

Figure 10.8

must be performed in a skillful manner with materials of a quality and appearance comparable to existing materials. A seller is usually required to:

1. Obtain receipts for repairs performed by others
2. Prepare a written statement indicating the date of repairs performed by the seller
3. Provide copies of receipts and statements to the buyer prior to final verification of condition.

In addition, work performed by service providers, that is referred by the agents in the transaction, is generally not guaranteed by the agents. Furthermore, a buyer and seller may choose any outside entity to perform required work or inspections on a property.

Real estate agents sometimes refer lenders, title insurance companies, escrow companies, home inspectors, structural pest control companies, contractors, and home warranty companies for buyers and sellers to complete required repairs and inspections necessary to a transaction.

3. Physical Inspection Contingency Removal

The physical inspection contingency must be removed before the buyer can move forward and close escrow. Two methods of contingency removal are active contingency removal and passive contingency removal.

A. Active Contingency Removal

Active contingency removal requires the buyer to actively sign a physical inspection contingency removal form that removes all physical inspection contingencies contractually agreed upon in the purchase agreement. Residential transactions commonly use the active contingency removal method. Accordingly, commercial transactions also use the active contingency removal method, but may trigger a deposit increase and "non-refundable" earnest money deposit requirement not normally seen in single-family home purchases.

B. Passive Contingency Removal

Passive contingency removal occurs when a buyer inspects the property and then does nothing, thereby passively removing the physical inspection contingency and moving forward with the transaction. This method was used with single-family residential properties in the past; however, today the active contingency removal method is the most commonly used contingency removal method in California. The physical inspection contingency generally must be removed before the buyer can move forward and close escrow.

4. Home Construction Basics (From the Ground Up)

A. Soils Report/Soils Engineering Report

A **soils report** or **soils engineering report** shows the type of soil lying beneath a home and whether it is a type that will shrink and swell, thus causing cracks in the walls of a home. For example, a residence located on a hillside is being appraised. There are cracks in the foundation and doors and windows do not close properly. The appraiser would most likely recommend a soils engineering report, also called a geotechnical report.

> **Soils Report/Soils Engineering Report:** Report that indicates whether the soil underneath a proposed building construction will support it.

A geotechnical report can be used by builders to confirm the soil is stable enough to hold the foundation of a new single-family home. Geotechnical engineers perform the analysis by digging a hole to a predetermined depth, examining the soil horizons (soil layers) under the surface, and then producing a geotechnical report with recommendations whether the builder can safely build a home on the parcel of land.

In steep, hilly country one of the greatest concerns for home builders is slope stability and the potential for landslides. The geotechnical engineer examines how a new foundation will react to landslides, earthquakes, liquefaction (solid soil liquifies during an earthquake), erosion, weathering, and other environmental factors that may affect a new single-family home. Thus, a geotechnical report usually costs $1,500 or more and examines how natural earth materials will interact with a single-family home's foundation system.

> **Backfill:** Soil that fills in around foundations, retaining walls, or other excavations.

(1) Soil Conditions

Soil conditions may include expansive, adobe, and alkalinity. All three soil types have a high clay content that can absorb a large amount of water. This causes shrinking and swelling as the water is absorbed and then released from the clay soils.

(2) Backfill

Backfill is soil that is used to fill in around foundations, retaining walls, and other excavations. An example of an excavation is when soil is removed from a lot in order to build a house on the site.

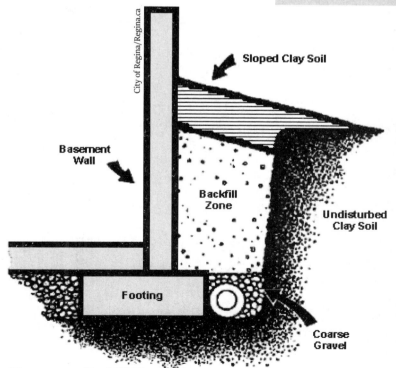

Figure 10.9 Backfill Illustration

B. Foundations

Many newly constructed homes in California use a concrete slab foundation that places the home on a concrete slab that does not have a crawl space underneath the floor. In contrast, a raised foundation has a crawl space located between the soil and floor and is commonly found in modern custom homes and older homes in California. The Federal Housing Administration's (FHA) minimum crawl space height is 18 inches.

It is easier to make plumbing changes to a single-family home that is built on a raised foundation than one that is located on a concrete foundation. A plumber can crawl into the home's crawl space and make plumbing changes (e.g., a bathroom added) without significant excavation costs.

Older homes with raised foundations can be a problem, however, because floor supports tend to deteriorate over time and a defective foundation may be expensive for a homeowner to repair in the future.

A concrete slab foundation is less expensive to build than a raised foundation and lends itself well to the predominant soil types seen in California. Accordingly, a heavy concrete course placed into the ground where a concrete foundation is set is called a footing and is the spreading element of the foundation wall.

Foundation Plan: Plan that indicates the location of the foundation that supports the house.

A plan that refers to piers, columns, and footings is called a **foundation plan.** A concrete slab foundation may be placed on top of the soil. Concrete footings that support the entire home are usually located on the outside edge of the foundation, and under bearing walls throughout the interior of the home. Attached on top of the footings and concrete slab is a sole plate. The sole plate is generally comprised of 2" x 4" or 2" x 6" boards lying horizontally on the floor. Studs are then attached to the sole plate on sixteen-inch (16") centers (center of the small edge of the board). The studs are the vertical structural members that hold up the house.

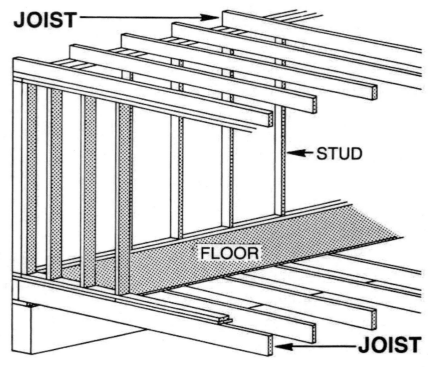

Figure 10.10 Joists and Studs Illustration

C. Other Construction Terms

(1) Plot Plan

A **plot plan** shows where the building will be located on a parcel of real property. Thus, an architect's plot plan is a drawing showing the location and dimensions of improvements on a parcel.

(2) Orientation

A map that shows the house and its location relating to other plants, buildings, and streets is an example of **orientation**.

Figure 10.11 Plot Plan

(3) Topography

Topography relates to hilly or irregular land and a topographical map shows the steepness of a parcel of real property. Single-family homes that are built on hilly or irregular land usually have greater value than homes built on flat land.

(4) Elevation Plan

An **elevation plan** shows an exterior front and side views of the building(s) being placed on a parcel of real property.

(5) R-Value

R-Value represents the amount of heat or cooling resistance insulation provides in a home. For example, R-38 insulation would be a better insulator than R-10 insulation. The higher the R-Value the greater the resistance to the passage of heat flow.

(6) Energy Efficiency Ratio (EER Ratio)

EER is defined as **energy efficiency ratio**. The higher the EER ratio, the better the energy efficiency rating. So, when an air conditioning unit has a higher energy efficiency ratio (EER), the unit is more efficient.

(7) Joist

Parallel wooden members used to support floor and ceiling loads are called **joists**. Therefore, joists are located in the ceiling and floors of a house.

Plot Plan: Shows where the house is located on the lot.

Orientation: Shows where the lot is located in relation to surrounding amenities.

Topography: A map that shows the hills and valleys within a parcel of real property.

Elevation Plan: The front and side views of a proposed construction.

R-Value: Represents the amount of insulation in a wall or ceiling of a home.

Energy Efficiency Ratio (EER Ratio): Indicates the energy efficiency of an appliance.

Joist: Boards in the ceiling or floor of a home.

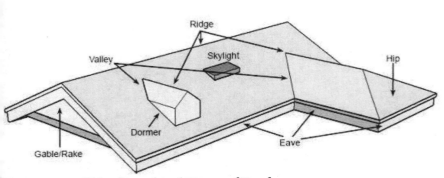

Figure 10.12 Ridge Board and Types of Roofs

(8) Hip Roof

A **hip roof** slopes on all four sides.

(9) Ridge Board

A **ridge board** is the peak of the roof and the highest member of a frame house.

(10) Flashing

Flashing is the metal material placed in the valleys of a roof to prevent water seepage into the home. In other words, the name of the sheet metal which is used to protect a building from water seepage is called flashing.

(11) Wood Shingles

Wood shingles are nailed to the sheathing on the roof of a house.

D. Alternative Energy Sources and Programs

(1) Solar

The **Solar Rights Act of 1978 (Act)** is concerned with certain rights relating to the installation and maintenance of solar energy systems. The Act generally prohibits the use of CC&Rs and contracts to restrict the installation and use of solar energy systems. Any deed, contract, or security instrument that does this will cause these restrictions to become void and unenforceable. However, condominium homeowner associations can limit *common area* solar use.

(2) Wind Turbines

Wind turbines operate on a simple principle. The energy in the wind turns two or three propeller-like blades around a rotor. The rotor is connected to the main shaft, which spins a generator to create electricity.

So how do wind turbines make electricity? Simply stated, a wind turbine works the opposite of a fan. Instead of using electricity to make wind (like a fan), wind turbines use wind to make electricity. The wind turns the blades, which spin a shaft, which connects to a generator that makes electricity.

E. Residential and Commercial Construction

(1) Building Permit

A **building permit** allows a builder to construct a building or improvement on a property. If a builder would like to construct a residence, the builder will secure

Hip Roof: A roof that slopes on all four sides.

Ridge Board: Highest member of a frame house.

Flashing: Metal that is in the valley of a roof and keeps water from seeping into the home.

Wood Shingles: Nailed to the sheathing on the roof of a home.

Building Permit: Issued by the local building department to allow the construction or remodeling of a home.

a building permit from the local building department. An application for a building permit is submitted by the builder to the local building department.

(2) Turnkey Property

A **turnkey property** or project is a single-family home ready for the buyer to move into or new construction that is ready to move into.

F.   Differences among Rehabilitation, Renovation Restoration, and Remodeling

Four possible improvements to real property may affect the value and overall desirability of a property. These include rehabilitation, renovation, restoration, and remodeling.

(1) Rehabilitation

A **rehabilitation** (rehab) is defined as the restoration of a property to satisfactory condition without drastically changing the plan, form, or style of architecture.

(2) Renovation

A **renovation** brings the property back to a new condition, while making changes in style and function to today's living standards.

(3) Restoration

A **restoration** occurs when a property is brought back to its exact form. Historical restorations occur in Victorian-era homes in San Francisco.

(4) Remodeling

The opposite of restoration is **remodeling**. Remodeling changes the actual use and/or rooms in a property. Modernizing an old San Francisco Victorian home would be considered remodeling.

Sometimes a property owner may be better off tearing down the home, rather than renovating it. In expensive areas of California, homebuyers may tear down the existing home and build a new home on the property.

A "California Remodel" occurs when a real estate owner tears down all the walls in the home, except one that is left standing, and then rebuilds the rest of the house. The reason homeowners tend to like California Remodels is because they *may* not require building permits for the work being completed. It is generally considered a rehabilitation of an existing property and no walls or additional square footage property additions have been added that will require a building permit.

However, it is best to have clients check the local laws before starting a California Remodel.

Chapter Ten Summary

The chapter discusses physical inspection contingencies, including active and passive contingency removal methods, time periods for removal or cancellation, home inspections, buyer's investigation of property condition, swimming pool inspections, pest inspections, pest reports and repairs, and the Structural Pest Control Board. Additional topics include the seller disclosing material facts, the buyer's right to request repairs, and service provider networks.

Home construction basics are discussed including soils reports, soil conditions, backfill, foundations, foundation plans, piers, columns, and footings, plot plan, orientation, topography, elevation plan, R-value, energy efficiency ratio, joist, hip roof, flashing, wood shingles, ridge boards, and alternate energy sources including solar and wind turbines.

Lastly, building permits and turnkey properties are covered, along with the differences among rehabilitation, renovation, restoration, and remodeling.

Chapter Ten Quiz

1. Once a home inspection report has been issued for a property, items in the home inspection report:
(A) becomes material facts
(B) must be disclosed to the buyer of the property
(C) must be disclosed to any future buyers as well
(D) all of the above are correct

2. A primary concern of a pest inspector is:
(A) subterranean termites
(B) dry rot
(C) Both (A) and (B) are correct
(D) Neither (A) nor (B) are correct

3. Structural pest control is the control of household pests which include:
(A) rodents
(B) vermin
(C) insects
(D) all of the above are correct

4. A seller usually must complete repairs prior to:
(A) the final verification of condition
(B) the contract date
(C) open of escrow
(D) the home inspection

5. Real estate agents may refer:
(A) lenders
(B) title insurance companies
(C) escrow companies
(D) all of the above are correct

6. Soil conditions may include:
(A) expansive
(B) adobe
(C) alkalinity
(D) all of the above are correct

7. _____ shows where the building will be located on a parcel of real property.
(A) Orientation
(B) A plot plan
(C) Topography
(D) An elevation plan

8. Parallel wooden members used to support floor and ceiling loads are called:
(A) joists
(B) ridge boards
(C) rafters
(D) flashing

9. A _____ is defined as the restoration of an older home to its original condition without changing its floor plan or style.
(A) renovation
(B) rehabilitation
(C) restoration
(D) remodel

10. A _____ brings the property back to a new condition, while making changes in style and function to today's living standards.
(A) renovation
(B) rehabilitation
(C) restoration
(D) remodel

Answers: 1. D, 2. C, 3. D, 4. A, 5. D, 6. D, 7. B, 8. A, 9. B, 10. A

Unknown

"By the time you pay for a home in the suburbs, it isn't."

11

Chapter

ELEVEN

Appraisal
Contingencies

Correctly pricing a single-family home for sale is one of the most important requirements for a successful real estate transaction. The loan may not be funded if the property's appraised value is less than the purchase price. Lenders want to verify that a property is sufficient collateral before funding a loan. In other words, lenders need to ensure there is a way to get their money back if the buyer defaults on future loan payments and the property goes into foreclose. Hence, lenders order an appraisal to verify a property's value. The buyer usually pays for the appraisal and is entitled to receive a copy of the report. Thus, real estate agents must understand appraisal principles to effectively help their clients buy and sell real estate in today's rapidly changing economic environment.

1. Real Estate Agents and the Appraisal

Real estate agents use the same appraisal techniques as real estate appraisers to help price a property for sale. Agents perform a comparative market analysis to help sellers determine an appropriate list price. If the list price is greater than the property's market value, and a buyer makes a full-price offer that is accepted by the seller, the agreed upon purchase price will be greater than the market value of the property, and it will not appraise for the purchase price. In this case, the lender

289

will usually not fund the loan and the purchase transaction will fall apart. For these reasons, finding the correct listing price is crucial to happy clients, closed real estate transactions, and consistent commission income.

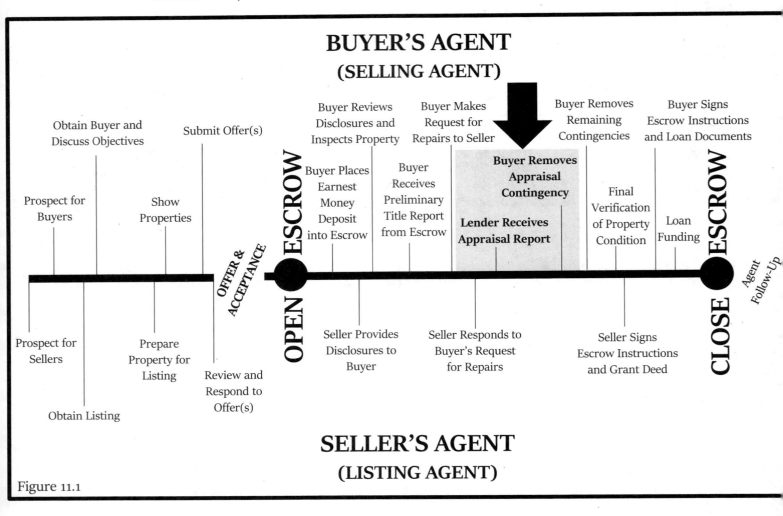

Figure 11.1

There are three possible outcomes resulting from the appraisal valuation: above purchase price, at purchase price, or below purchase price.

Figure 11.2

Appraisal Valuation Outcomes	
Appraisal valuation **ABOVE** purchase price	buyer happy
Appraisal valuation **AT** purchase price	both seller and buyer happy
Appraisal valuation **BELOW** purchase price	lender not happy because property is not sufficient collateral for the loan

A. Appraisal Valuation Above Purchase Price

If a property's appraised value comes in above the purchase price, the buyer will be happy to know the property's market value is above the purchase price. The seller usually does not see the appraisal report that was provided to the lender and buyer, so the seller is happy to sell the property at full list price.

B. Appraisal Valuation At Purchase Price

An ideal situation for both buyer and seller is for the property to appraise at the purchase price. Thus, the buyer is only paying what the property is truly worth in an open and competitive market and the seller is not leaving any money on the table. In addition, the lender is willing to make the loan because the property's loan-to-value ratio is low enough to allow the lender to recoup most of the loan amount in the event of a foreclosure.

C. Appraisal Valuation Below Purchase Price

If the appraised value of the property comes in below the purchase price, the lender will usually not fund the loan. Consequently, there are four possible actions that can be taken at this point:

1. Buyer increases down payment
2. Buyer and seller agree to a purchase price reduction
3. Buyer challenges appraisal valuation
4. Transaction cancelled

(1) Buyer Increases Down Payment

If a property appraises for less than the purchase price, the lender may require the buyer to increase the down payment to maintain the same loan-to-value ratio. Loan-to-value ratio is calculated as the loan amount divided by the purchase price or appraised value—whichever is lower. If the borrower is not willing to increase the down payment, then the lender will not be willing to make the loan and the borrower will not remove the appraisal contingency to the contract and not go forward with the purchase.

(2) Buyer and Seller Agree to a Purchase Price Reduction

Another alternative is to ask the seller to reduce the purchase price down to the appraised value. If the seller agrees to do this, then the buyer's existing down payment will be sufficient to maintain the appropriate loan-to-value ratio required by the lender.

(3) Buyer Challenges Appraisal Valuation

Appraisers are licensed by the Office of Real Estate Appraisers (OREA) and are required to use Uniform Standards of Professional Appraisal Practice (USPAP) when performing property appraisals. For this reason, their valuations are usually indicative of the true market value of a property. However, sometimes the appraised value may not reflect the property's true market value because the appraiser made an honest mistake. When this occurs, the buyer may ask for a copy of the appraisal report and forward it to the selling agent for review. The agent will then use appraisal principles to verify the appraisal amount and determine if there are better and more recent sales comparables the appraiser may not have considered in the analysis. In addition, there may be incorrect property information that was used by the appraiser. The lender can then request an appraisal update – taking into account the new sales comparables and/or information.

Tales from the Trade

The Story of the Agent
Challenging the Appraised Valuation

A real estate agent was representing the seller and buyer (dual agency) in the sale of a twenty-two year old single-family home. The buyer was obtaining a loan to finance the sale, so the lender ordered an appraisal to verify the property was worth the $350,000 purchase price. However, the appraiser's opinion of value was only $329,000. Therefore, the buyer would have to do one of the following to keep the transaction on track to close escrow: (1) increase the down payment, (2) get the seller to agree to reduce the purchase price to $329,000, (3) challenge the appraiser's opinion of value (valuation), or (4) cancel the transaction. The buyer was not willing to increase the down payment and the seller would not reduce the agreed upon purchase price. Thus, the buyer would have to challenge the appraisal or cancel the transaction.

During the transaction, the agent was stunned to see the low appraised value for the property. She had completed an extensive comparative market analysis (CMA) when helping the seller to price the property. In addition, it is important to note that the dual agency was fully disclosed and had the consent of both the buyer and seller. The buyer provided a copy of the appraisal report to the agent and, after review, the agent found the appraisal to be an inaccurate representation of the property's true market value. The sales comparables used by the appraiser were not comparable to the subject property because they were not similar in size, construction, amenities, or proximity to the subject property.

There were many factors affecting the appraised valuation, but the biggest issue was one certain property used as a sales comparable. This comparable property had sold for $360,000

The Story of the Agent
Challenging the Appraised Valuation

about 90 days earlier and was smaller in size, completely remodeled, and the year of construction was *incorrectly* stated as four years earlier. The appraiser assigned a $330,000 valuation for this specific comparable. Plus, the appraiser assigned the greatest weight to this comparable property, so the appraiser's final valuation was $21,000 below the purchase price.

The selling agent researched the sales comparable and found it to be riddled with inaccuracies. The comparable property was actually over 100 years old! It had been completely remodeled (with permits) four years ago. When the property being used as the sales comparable had been listed for sale, the listing agent had input into the MLS the renovation date as the year the property was built. Thus, when the appraiser was compiling his research, he exported the data field from the MLS listing without realizing the county tax records stated the property was 100 years old. The selling agent informed the lender of this inaccuracy and after the buyer requested an appraisal update, the appraiser revised the appraised valuation to $350,000.

The agent saved the deal by understanding how to read a real estate appraisal and apply the principles of appraisal to challenge the appraiser's opinion of value. If the agent had not assisted with challenging the appraiser's findings, the transaction would have been canceled. The buyer was not going to increase the down payment and the seller was not going reduce the purchase price. Thus, by the agent being knowledgeable about appraisal principles, the seller maximized his profits, the buyer only paid what the property was truly worth, the lender funded the loan, and the agent received a nice commission (dual agency) and happy clients for repeat business and many future referrals.

(4) Transaction Cancelled

If the first three methods are not feasible, then the buyer and seller may agree to cancel the transaction. The appraisal contingency to a real estate purchase agreement allows a buyer to decide not to move forward with the purchase of the property if it does not appraise for the purchase price. In other words, if the property does not appraise for the purchase price, the buyer will have a way to get out of the deal by not removing the appraisal contingency to the contract and not moving forward to close escrow. The buyer and seller will sign the escrow rescission form and the buyer will receive his or her earnest money deposit from escrow. If the seller is not willing to sign the escrow rescission form, the escrow agent cannot reimburse the buyer for the amount of the earnest money deposit and must file an interpleader action in court, asking the courts to determine what to do with the buyer's earnest money deposit.

Due to the situations mentioned above, a real estate agent must understand the principles of appraisal. The rest of the chapter will discuss appraisal principles and how they relate to an appraiser's opinion of value.

2. Appraisal Principles

A real estate appraisal is an estimate of the value of a parcel of real property. Appraisals are used mostly by lenders to determine whether a parcel of real property will be sufficient collateral (security) for a loan.

In other words, when a lender forecloses a loan secured by a parcel of real property, the lender must be able to obtain the entire loan amount (or as much as possible) returned at the trustee's sale (foreclosure auction). The lender must be assured that the property is worth the sale price, so the lender will use the appraised value of the property as a basis for calculating the loan-to-value ratio. Lenders also use appraisals for property owners who want to refinance an existing loan (replace one loan with another one—usually at a lower interest rate). For these reasons, real estate appraisers and their appraisals are crucial to the real estate lending process.

Value: Relationship between a thing desired and the potential purchaser or desirous person, maximum utility of available resources, present worth of future benefits, and ability of one commodity to command another commodity in exchange.

Elements of Value: Demand, utility, scarcity, and transferability.

A. Value

Value is relative to each person and is the:
- Relationship between a thing desired and the potential purchaser or desirous person
- Maximum utility of available resources
- Present worth of future benefits
- Ability of one commodity to command another commodity in exchange

(1) Elements of Value

Elements of Value	
D	Demand
U	Utility
S	Scarcity
T	Transferability

Figure 11.3 Elements of Value

Elements of value include **d**emand, **u**tility, **s**carcity, and **t**ransferability. The acronym "DUST" is sometimes used to help remember the elements of value.

a. Demand
Demand occurs when buyers want to purchase properties in a given geographical area. This relates to personal income, land available for development, commute time to the central business district, along with many other factors. When demand for real properties increases and supply stays the same, prices

will usually increase. Conversely, when demand for real properties decreases and supply stays the same, prices will usually decrease.

b. Utility

Utility is the ability to use a property for a desired use. For example, if a homebuyer can use a property to live in, then the utility value of the property has served its purpose. However, if other factors cause the property to not be suitable as a home (e.g., crime, violence, etc.), then the utility of the property will be reduced and the value of the property will decrease accordingly.

c. Scarcity

Scarcity occurs when there are few properties available for purchase in a specific geographical area. For example, there are not enough homes available for purchase considering the number of aspiring home buyers (demand) in the Silicon Valley of Northern California. This scarcity of housing has driven housing prices to extremely high levels. As the supply of real estate decreases and demand stays the same, property prices will increase. Conversely, as the supply of real estate increases and demand stays the same, property prices will decrease.

d. Transferability

Transferability is the ability to transfer a property to someone else. If the property cannot be sold or willed, then the value of the property will decrease when the existing property owner cannot transfer it. In determining the worth of a parcel of real property for a specific reason as of a definite date, the real estate appraiser is making a valuation. In doing so, an appraiser will consider the size and physical characteristics of a property, bundle of rights, utility of the property, property identification, and property rights when establishing market value.

(2) Value Variables

Value Variables: Price, terms, condition, market timing, and location.

There are five variables that will generally affect the value of a home: price, terms, condition, market timing, and location. Price, terms, and condition can be immediately changed. Market timing can usually be changed by waiting for the real estate market to move from a downward-trending buyers' market to an upward-trending sellers' market. Location, however, cannot be changed and is the most critical factor that determines whether a home will increase in value in the future. In other words, the *most important factor* in the decision to purchase real property is always location.

Price, terms, and condition of a single-family home can usually be changed. Price and terms of the property purchase can be negotiated with the seller. If the buyer does not like the price and terms of the transaction, the buyer can elect not to go forward with the purchase. The condition of the home can be changed by the buyer performing a rehabilitation or renovation of the property, thus increasing its value. Turnkey properties are in good condition and are ready for the buyer to move in. However, fixer properties are in disrepair and require a considerable amount of work to get them into a livable condition.

Market timing is important because single-family homes in California typically are cyclical, moving up and down over a long period of time. The value of the land that sits under the single-family home moves up and down due to supply and demand of land in California, prevailing wages, and interest rates. In contrast, the value of the single-family home itself (building) does not move up and down as much as the land value because it is based on the cost of labor and materials. Therefore, if a single-family homebuyer buys a home during a downward-trending buyers' market–in which prices of homes are declining–the homebuyer may be able to wait for the real estate market to turn into an upward-trending sellers' market and increase the value of the property.

Location, on the other hand, cannot be changed. There is an old saying, "Location, location, and location," meaning that location is the most important variable to consider when acquiring a parcel of real estate property. This is why many homeowners consider location to be the most important long-term factor affecting price appreciation of a property and are very careful where they purchase real estate.

(3) Market Value

Market Value: Primarily based upon the willing buyer and willing seller concept.

In real estate appraisal, **market value** is primarily based upon the *willing buyer and willing seller concept*. It is what the market believes a property is worth and is the value an appraiser tries to determine when making an appraisal. In other words, market value is the value a buyer (under no duress) places on a parcel of real property.

a. Marketability and Acceptability

Marketability and Acceptability: A property can be sold and is acceptable to the target market. Marketability is the ultimate test of functional utility.

Marketability is the ability to sell a parcel of real property. **Acceptability** is a measure of how acceptable the property will be to the general buying public. Therefore, when an appraiser begins to determine the value of a residential property the appraiser will consider its marketability and acceptability. The ultimate test of functional utility is marketability.

(4) Principles of Value

a. Principle of Highest and Best Use

Highest and best use is defined as the use for a parcel of real property that will provide the highest return to a property owner. For example, an appraiser will perform a site analysis on a parcel of vacant land to determine the best type of building to place on the parcel. This use will be its highest and best use.

> **Highest and Best Use:** The use of a parcel of real property that will provide the greatest return to the owner.

1. Subtract Demolition Costs

For example, an appraiser determines that a building on a parcel of real property adds no value to the land. When considering the highest and best use for the property in determining value, the appraiser would subtract the demolition costs from the value of the property.

Figure 11.4 Building Demolition

2. Interim Use

When the highest and best use of a property is expected to change, the current use is called the **interim use**. For example, an interim use is a single-family home that is sitting on a parcel of land that is zoned for a retail shopping center. The existing use as a single-family home is the interim use, while tearing down the single-family home and building a retail strip center (**strip commercial development**) on the property is its highest and best use.

> **Interim Use:** The present use of a property before it is converted to its highest and best use.
>
> **Strip Commercial Development:** Strip of retail stores along a business corridor.

b. Principle of Conformity

When homes are similar in size and construction materials, they conform to a well-planned community that will help maintain property values. Therefore, in a

Principle of Conformity: Conformity helps a well-planned community to maintain property values.

well-planned residential community, **conformity** to proper land use objectives contributes the most to the maintenance of value.

c. Principle of Contribution

Principle of Contribution: Occurs when an improvement increases the value of a property more than the cost of the improvement.

An owner is considering modernizing an income-producing building. In making this decision, the owner would rely most on the *effect on net income*. Therefore, when a property owner adds a swimming pool to an apartment building, and the pool increases the value of the property more than the cost of the swimming pool, this is called **contribution**.

For example, competing apartment buildings that surround a subject property can charge $50 per month more in rent because they have a swimming pool, whereas the subject property does not have one. If the subject property adds a swimming pool for a cost of $50,000, the increase in rents would equate to an increase in property value of $70,000 (calculated using the income/capitalization appraisal approach discussed elsewhere in the book), thus the swimming pool has contributed to an increase in value of the property by $20,000.

In contrast, a swimming pool added to an owner-occupied single-family home generally does not contribute value to the home in excess of the cost of the pool. Usually, it will only add 1/2 of the cost of the swimming pool to the value of the home. For this reason, it is usually best to purchase an existing single-family home that already has a built-in pool constructed on the property.

d. Principle of Regression

Principle of Regression: Occurs when a substandard building causes the properties around it to sustain a loss in value.

The appraisal principle that describes the best property in a neighborhood being adversely affected by the presence of a substandard property is called **regression**. In other words, when a house of greater value is adversely affected by houses of comparably lesser value, this is described as regression.

For example, a homeowner adds 1,000 square feet to the homeowner's existing 1,000 square foot home—totaling 2,000 square feet. The surrounding neighborhood is comprised of 1,000 square foot homes valued at $100,000 (1,000 square feet x $100 per square foot). The homeowner may think the newly expanded home is now worth $200,000 (2,000 square feet x $100 per square foot); however, because of the principle of regression, the home is probably worth $125,000 (2,000 square feet x $62.50 per square foot). The homeowner has lost $75,000 ($37.50 per square foot) in value because the neighborhood is not comprised of 2,000 square foot homes. The value of the 2,000 square foot home will regress to the level of the 1,000 square foot homes surrounding it.

Tales from the Trade

The Story of the Crazy Lady and the Junk Man

A home seller decided to sell his single-family home. His neighbor across the street was a problem because his home was a real mess. His wife was locally known as "The Crazy Lady" because of her frequent trips to the mental hospital. All the neighbors were convinced that her husband "The Junk Man" was the cause of all her troubles. The Junk Man was a real character. One of his goals in life was to own a junkyard, and he was successful–his own backyard! He liked to store old, beat-up used tires in his backyard. His one apparent ambition in life was to one-up the notorious Wesley Tire Fires that occasionally occur east of San Francisco.

He always kept at least five old jacked-up cars in his front yard because, according to him, he didn't have room in the backyard because of all the tires. He also kept an old beat-up RV in the front yard where his relatives could stay, and frolic, and maybe never go home.

It was impossible to determine the outside color of The Junkman's home—because it had been so long since it had been painted–if ever, and it was built during the 1960s. The Junkman also liked to keep a couple of incredibly huge, mangy, and vicious mongrel dogs running around to protect his treasure trove from "thieves." This was another name for the county authorities who were constantly trying to get him to clean things up.

With neighbors like The Crazy Lady and the Junk Man you might think that some stiff CC&Rs might be used to get him to clean up his place—or sell it and move away. However, the subdivision where he was located had been built many years ago and had very weak covenants, conditions, and restrictions (CC&Rs). There was also no homeowner's association (HOA), or provision for one, to enforce the CC&Rs. The Crazy Lady and the Junk Man's neighbors had a difficult time enforcing the CC&Rs to get him to clean up his home. The Crazy Lady and the Junk Man's mess caused a lot of homes located in the area to lose value because of the appraisal principle of regression. Houses located around The Crazy Lady and the Junk Man tended to seek the level of the Junk Man's house and reduce in value. The local authorities repeatedly asked him to clean up his place, but he ignored their requests and was as stubborn as ever.

The authorities next tried to get his attention by levying fines against him for his infractions. Since he didn't have any money to pay the fines, he laughed at that too. The last straw was when the authorities placed liens against his home. He still did nothing and let the fines accumulate. He said he wasn't intending to sell the property anyway, so who cares about a bunch of pesky little fines? The neighbors were never able to get The Crazy Lady and the Junk Man to clean up their property. As far as anyone knows, their home still remains in the same dilapidated condition. Someone said, "Death and taxes are the only two certain things in life." It appears the Junkman has so far been able to escape both.

e. Principle of Assemblage

The act of placing two (or more) properties under one ownership with the resulting value of the combined parcel being greater than the total purchase price of the two parcels is called **assemblage**. Accordingly, the primary purpose of combining lots is to create assemblage in anticipation of **plottage increment**. Plottage increment is the increase in value that results from combining lots through assemblage.

Any increase in property value that is *not* due to the owner's actions but occurs through market forces out of the owner's control, is called an **unearned increment**. For example, when real property increases in value because of an increase in population in the local area, this is called an unearned increment.

f. Principle of Anticipation

Within the income/capitalization approach, the **principle of anticipation** occurs when an investor purchases an income property in anticipation of a future income stream. For example, an investor is willing to pay $1,000,000 to obtain an annual income of $70,000 over the holding period of a property. This is a 7% annual return and is called the capitalization rate.

g. Principle of Substitution

The appraisal **principle of substitution** is defined as substituting one property for another. When a property that has sold is substituted (compared) with the subject property that is being appraised, a comparison of the two properties can be made and this is commonly used in appraising single-family homes. The comparable property is commonly called a sales comparable or "sales comp."

h. Principle of Balance

The **principle of balance** refers to the relationship between cost, added cost, and the value it returns. For each dollar invested, the value should increase by more than one dollar.

3. Appraisal Approaches

There are three appraisal approaches that are used to value real property:

- Comparison Approach/Market Data Approach
- Income Approach/Capitalization Approach
- Cost Approach

Appraisal Approaches

Comparison Approach / Market Data Approach	Uses the principle of substitution; most readily adaptable and useable approach	Most often used with single-family homes and unimproved land
Income Approach/ Capitalization Approach	Used to appraise the value of income producing properties by converting an income stream into value	Commonly includes multi-unit residential apartment buildings and leased investments
Cost Approach	Looks at the cost to build a building (e.g., house) on a parcel of land and adds it to the land value to determine the overall property value	Good for special purpose and service buildings, new residences, new construction, and older homes

Figure 11.5 Comparison of Appraisal Approaches

A. Comparison Approach/Market Data Approach

The **comparison approach** or **market data approach** of appraising properties uses the principle of substitution. It is most often used with *single-family homes* and *unimproved land* and is the most readily adaptable and useable approach for real estate agents. However, it is hindered most by rapidly changing economic conditions when property prices are rising or falling at a very fast rate.

Comparison/Market Data Approach: Compares properties that have recently sold to the subject property being appraised. Commonly used for single-family homes and vacant land.

Sales Comparables: Similar properties that have recently sold near the subject property.

(1) Sales Comparables

An appraiser uses **sales comparables** (sales comps) to value a subject property. Sales comparables are similar properties that have recently sold near the subject property. The closer the sales comparables are to the subject property in relation to location, size, amenities, and other characteristics, the better suited they are to be used to value the subject property. Moreover, when appraising a home, the greatest consideration should be given to the current prices paid for other similar homes in the same neighborhood.

An appraiser makes adjustments between the subject property and each of the sales comparables. For example, a sales comparable may have a swimming pool and the subject property does not have one. If this occurs, the appraiser will reduce the sales comparable by the value of the swimming pool and then substitute it for the subject property to help determine its market value.

After the appraiser has collected all the data, the next step in the appraisal process is to reconcile or correlate the adjusted sales prices of the sales comparables.

(2) Rental Comparables

Rental Comparables: Similar properties that have recently rented near the subject property.

The market data method of real property appraisal is most often used to determine rents for apartment buildings and leased investments (shopping centers, office buildings, and industrial properties).

These are called **rental comparables** and are used to determine market rents for a subject property. Even though income properties use the income approach/capitalization approach to determine their value, they use the comparison approach/market data approach to help determine market rents for a property.

B. Income Approach/Capitalization Approach

Income/Capitalization Approach: Appraises the value of income producing properties by converting an income stream into value.

The **income approach** or **capitalization approach** is used to appraise the value of income producing properties by converting an income stream into value. These commonly include multi-unit residential apartment buildings and leased investments, which include retail shopping centers (e.g., strip centers), office buildings, and industrial buildings.

Appraisers, real estate brokers, and investors use the income approach/capitalization approach to determine the value of an income property. They use the I/R=V formula (income divided into the rate equals value). "I" indicates annual income, "R" indicates the capitalization rate which is the percentage return the property generates if the buyer uses all cash and no loan to purchase the property, and "V" is the value of the property. "IRV" can be used to remember the I/R=V formula.

For example, if an investor pays $1,000,000 for an apartment building and receives an annual income stream of $70,000, the investor has obtained a 7% return on investment. This return is the capitalization rate. Capitalization rate is the rate of return an investor receives if he or she pays all cash to purchase an income property.

$$\frac{\text{Income}}{\text{Rate}} = \text{Value}$$

Figure 11.6 IRV Formula

The following calculation is used to derive net operating income (which is the "I" in the IRV formula).

Net Operating Income

Gross (Scheduled) Income (income with no vacancy)

      less Vacancy

      less Bad Debts*

      less Rent (Collection) Losses*

= Effective Gross Income (income actually collected)

      less Operating Expenses

= Net Operating Income (income "I" used in IRV)

      less Mortgage Interest/Debt Service/Mortgage Debt

= Cash Flow**

*Used by appraisers only, not included in broker and investor calculations

**Used by appraisers only, brokers and investors refer to it as "Before Tax Cash Flow"

Figure 11.7 Net Operating Income Calculation

(1) Gross Scheduled Income

The gross scheduled income (also called scheduled gross income) is the total amount of rents an owner will collect from an income property that is completely rented and has no vacancy.

The actual or contracted rent received from a rental property is called **contract rent**. For example, a developed lot (that has a single-family home built on it) receives contract rent when it is rented to a residential tenant. In contrast, **economic rent** is the rent received for a comparable space in the open market and is the *highest and best use* for the property. Therefore, if the zoning for the developed lot allows a shopping center to be built on the property, the economic rent will be much higher for a shopping center than the existing use of a single-family residential rental (contract rent).

> **Contract Rent:** Actual rent collected from an income property.

> **Economic Rent:** Rent received for a comparable space in the open market and is the highest and best use for the property.

(2) Effective Gross Income

Effective gross income is the income that is collected by the property owner, after vacancy, bad debts, and rent collection losses have been deducted from the gross scheduled income. In the Figure 11.7 illustration, effective gross income is defined as gross schedule income minus vacancy, bad debts, and rent (collection) losses equals effective gross income. It is the income actually collected by the property owner.

> **Effective Gross Income:** Actual rent collected from an income property.

(3) Operating Expenses

Operating expenses are the costs associated with operating a property and include both fixed and variable expenses. Fixed expenses are expenses that do not change each month (e.g., property taxes and property insurance). Variable expenses generally include water, sewer, garbage, maintenance expenses (e.g., cost to replace a water heater), property management fees, and other expenses. Variable expenses change each month depending on tenant usage, occupancy rates, and other factors.

(4) Net Operating Income

Net operating income is defined as gross scheduled income less vacancy, bad debts, rent collection losses, and operating expenses equals net operating income. It is the annual income a property produces each year and is represented by "I" in the IRV formula.

(5) Capitalization Rate

Capitalization rate is the return an investor will receive when all cash is used to purchase an income property. It is represented by "R" in the IRV formula: net operating income (I) divided by capitalization rate (R) equals value (V).

The capitalization approach is based primarily on the appraisal concept of *anticipation* and places the greatest emphasis on the present worth of future benefits. Capitalization rate is a measure of risk. A lower capitalization rate indicates lower risk and an investor will accept less income for the price paid to purchase the property. Conversely, a higher capitalization rate indicates greater risk and an investor will require more income for the price paid to purchase the property.

(6) Gross Rent Multiplier

Gross rent multiplier is the number of times the annual gross scheduled income of a multi-unit residential income property will divide into the price of the property. Real estate brokers and investors use an annual gross rent multiplier to help value medium to large size (5+ unit) multi-unit residential apartment buildings. Single-family homes and small one-to-four unit residential income properties usually rely on the comparison/market data approach to estimate value because they can be used (and financed) as owner-occupied, and an owner-occupant will generally pay more money for a home than an investor will pay for the same property as an investment.

In contrast to real estate broker and investor calculations, *appraisers* may use an *annual* gross rent multiplier for five-or-more unit (medium to large) apartment buildings and a *monthly* gross rent multiplier to appraise single-family rental properties and small one-to-four unit multi-unit residential income properties.

C. Cost Approach

The **cost approach** is the third and last appraisal approach. The land is valued using the comparison approach/market data approach and then the cost to build a building (e.g., a house) on the land using the cost approach is added to the land value to obtain an overall value for the existing property. The cost approach is good for special purpose and service buildings, new residences, new construction, and older homes.

Cost Approach: Land is valued using the market data approach and then the cost to build a building on the land using the cost approach is added to the land value to obtain an overall value for the existing property.

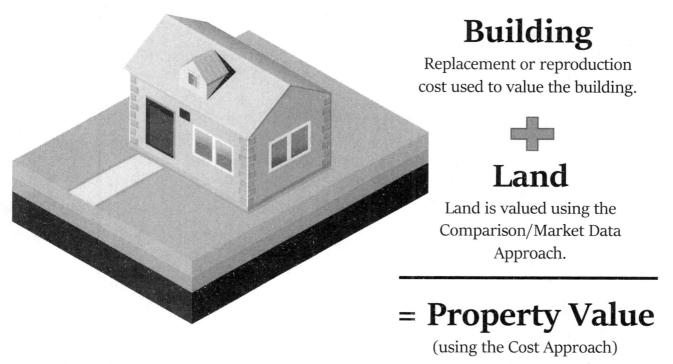

Building

Replacement or reproduction cost used to value the building.

Land

Land is valued using the Comparison/Market Data Approach.

= Property Value

(using the Cost Approach)

Figure 11.8 Diagram of the Cost Approach

The cost approach considers either replacement cost or reproduction cost when valuing a building that is located on the land. **Replacement cost** considers the cost to replace the building with a comparable structure that has the same *utility* but uses today's materials and building methods. **Reproduction cost**, on the other hand, considers the cost to reproduce the building with an exact replica of the subject property.

Replacement Cost: The cost to replace a structure with another structure having the same utility.

Reproduction Cost: The cost to replace a structure with another structure that is an exact replica.

| **Replacement Cost** | = | **Same Utility** |
| **Reproduction Cost** | = | **Exact Replica** |

Figure 11.9 Replacement vs. Reproduction Cost

(1) Methods Used to Determine Replacement Cost of a Building

The cost approach uses three methods to determine the replacement cost of a building: quantity survey method, unit-in-place method, and square foot/cubic foot method.

a. Quantity Survey Method

Quantity Survey Method: Considers every unit of material that goes into construction and totals them up to determine the total cost to build the property.

The **quantity survey method** of calculating the value of a building, that is sitting on a parcel of land, considers every unit of material (e.g., board, nail, plaster, brick, etc.) that goes into the construction and totals them up to determine the total cost to build a building on the land. Thus, quantity survey is the most accurate method of determining the cost to build a replacement building on a parcel of land.

b. Unit-in-Place Method

Unit-in-Place Method: Totals up each component (e.g., wall) to reach a cost to build a replacement building.

The **unit-in-place** method considers each component (e.g., wall) of the structure and totals up each component to reach a cost to build a replacement building on the property. Unit-in-place is the fastest method to calculate the cost to build a building on a parcel of land.

c. Square Foot/Cubic Foot Method

Square Foot/Cubic Foot Method: Considers the cost to build a similar building on a square foot basis for residential and most commercial construction.

The **square foot** or **cubic foot** method considers the cost to build a similar building on a square foot basis for residential and most commercial construction; and a cubic foot basis for warehouses. For example, an appraiser selects an estimated cost per square foot to build an apartment building on a parcel of land and multiplies it by the total square feet in the apartment building to arrive at an estimated cost to build a replacement building on the land. Please note, however, warehouses are rented or leased by the square foot, but may be appraised by the cubic foot because of varying ceiling heights.

(2) Applicability of the Cost Approach

The cost approach is used to appraise special property and service buildings (such as a firehouse or library), new residences, new construction, and older homes.

a. Special Purpose Properties/Special Service Buildings

The cost approach is used to appraise special use or special purpose buildings such as libraries and fire houses. There are usually very few firehouses and libraries selling at any one time, so sales comparables are difficult to find for these property types. In addition, they generally do not produce income. Therefore, the only possible appraisal approach that can be used to appraise special purpose and service buildings is the cost approach.

b. New Residence/New Construction

The cost approach is the most accurate when the property is new. It has recently been built and appraisers are able to obtain the exact costs to build the building on the land.

c. Older Home

The cost approach is also the best appraisal method for older homes. Older homes can be difficult to appraise because of the effects of depreciation (loss of value for any reason or any cause). By using the cost approach to value older homes, the appraiser can consider the property's condition in light of physical deterioration, functional obsolescence, and economic obsolescence.

(3) Depreciation

Depreciation, from an appraisal standpoint, is loss of value for any reason or from any cause. Depreciation is described through physical deterioration, functional obsolescence, and economic obsolescence.

Depreciation: From an appraisal standpoint, it is loss of value for any reason or from any cause.

Figure 11.10 Diagram of Depreciation for Appraisal Purposes

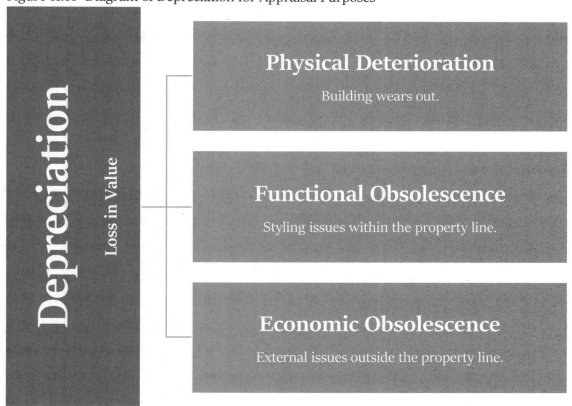

a. Physical Deterioration

Physical deterioration occurs when a building wears out. Appraisers look at a building's economic life versus its physical life, as well as effective age versus actual age when appraising a property using the cost approach.

1. Economic Life vs. Physical Life

Economic life is the number of years a property can be used and/or provide income. In contrast, the **physical life** of a property is the number of years the property is standing and has not fallen to the ground. For these reasons, the economic life is generally shorter than the physical life of a property.

2. Effective Age vs. Actual Age

The **actual age** of a property is its age from the time it was built until present. The **effective age** of a property is based on the actual condition of the property (which could be more or less than the actual age). For example, if the owner has performed good and consistent maintenance on the property and the property looks like it is 6 years old, when in fact it is really 12 years old, its effective age is 6 years old and its actual age is 12 years old.

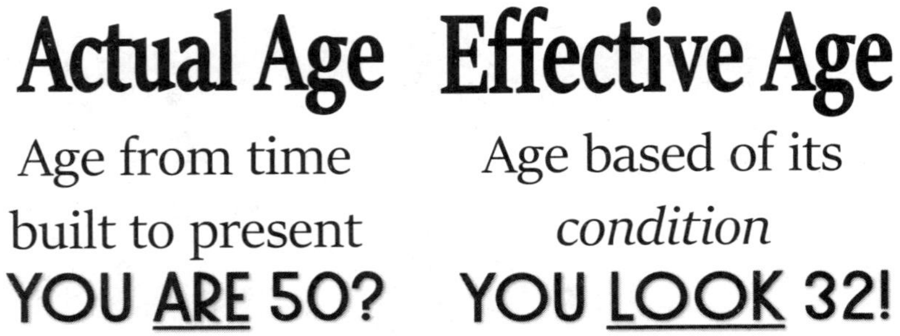

Actual Age

Age from time built to present

YOU ARE 50?

Effective Age

Age based of its *condition*

YOU LOOK 32!

Figure 11.11 Actual vs. Effective Age

b. Functional Obsolescence

Functional obsolescence is the loss in value a property receives from styling factors within the property lines. In other words, anything that is within the property lines and causes a loss in value due to outdated styling is considered functional obsolescence.

For example, a home that has 3 bedrooms and only 1 bathroom will be considered to have functional obsolescence, especially when all the other homes in the neighborhood have 3 bedrooms and 2 bathrooms. The loss in value due to having only 1 bathroom is due to functional obsolescence.

1. Layout and Floor Plan

Real estate buyers should start their analysis by examining a property's floor plan to determine how well it flows between rooms. Does the master bedroom open directly into the living area? If so, there should be a hallway between the two spaces. Is there an entry foyer, or does the front door open directly into the front yard? The front door should be set back from the front of the home, otherwise the property may look like a mobile home or manufactured home, rather than a more desirable "stick built" home that was built from the ground up.

2. Number, Type, and Size of Rooms in Relation to Square Footage of Living Space

A single-family home should have the correct number, size, and room types considering the total square footage of the home. Garage space is generally *not* included in house square footage estimates in California. However, the size and number of spaces in the garage are usually important considerations for appraisers, buyers, and tenants and will affect the overall desirability and value of the property.

a. 1,200 to 1,400 Square Foot Single-Family Home

Smaller single-family homes with floorplans between 1,200 and 1,400 square feet are usually single-story construction with three bedrooms, two bathrooms, and a standard-size 400 square foot two-car garage. The master bedroom may be smaller in size than those seen in larger single-family homes, however, it will usually have an ensuite private bathroom. Accordingly, the home is not large enough to offer a formal living room or formal dining room; instead, it may have a great room concept with the family room and kitchen combined into one living space.

b. 1,800 Square Foot Single-Family Home

Single-family homes in the 1,800 square foot size range may be large enough to accommodate a large open floorplan. Two story single-family homes start to become more prevalent, along with four-bedroom homes, in this square footage range. In addition, the overall size of the lot may be approximately 5,000 square feet, and two-story homes built on such small lots are commonly called "patio homes" because they may have a **zero lot line** where the next door neighbor's home is actually a part of the subject property's fence line.

Zero Lot Line: The next door neighbor's home is actually a part of the subject property's fence line.

c. 2,500 Square Foot Single-Family Home

As homebuyers reach the 2,500 square foot range, they may find a single-family home that contains close to everything an owner-occupied buyer might desire in a home. It may include a formal living room, formal dining room, large open family room, nook area, laundry room, and storage areas throughout the home. A fourth bedroom is usually attainable in this square footage range, and 600 square foot three car garages are common. In recent years, houses in this square footage range and larger have moved to more open floorplans with high ceilings.

d. 3,500+ Square Foot Single-Family Home

As real estate homebuyers move into the 3,500+ square footage range, they find single-family homes with five or more bedrooms, three or more bathrooms, a bonus room, and larger rooms in general. The master bedroom is usually large with a big walk-in closet and master bathroom with separate tub and shower. Double sinks located in the master bathroom tend to be very common. Three car garages are a must and four or more car garages are common.

The size and style of a single-family home generally indicates the type of person who is going to buy or rent it. Homes with a large number of bedrooms tend to attract families with children. Smaller single-story homes, with two or three bedrooms, may be popular with empty nesters. Each market segment generally requires a different type of single-family home to fit their needs.

Typically, four bedroom homes will sell and rent for a greater amount than three bedroom homes. Home buyers and renters see greater utility with a four bedroom home because it allows a master bedroom and separate bedrooms for up to three children or a master bedroom, office, and separate bedrooms for up to two children.

In an attempt to overcome the possibility of a single-family home becoming out-of-style or dated, three and four bedroom homes with two or three bathrooms have been popular during recent years. An additional fourth bedroom is generally a big plus, and so is a third bathroom. It may result in higher rents, and possibly a higher sale price because of its greater desirability for large-size families.

Many one-bathroom single-family homes have become functionally obsolete, making the second bathroom a key feature. However, at the top of an upward-trending sellers' market, older one-bathroom single-family homes located in lower socio-economic neighborhoods may sell very close to the price of two-bathroom properties located in the same geographical area. This is because of the extreme competition for single-family homes that occurs as the market nears the top of an upward-trending sellers' market. Buyers may be willing to overlook the absence of one of the bathrooms and appraisers may understand this fact and appraise the home close to the values of two-bathroom homes. Again, it all comes down to market timing.

Homebuyers should be aware that builders who build homes near the top of an upward-trending sellers' market may try to pass off large-size homes built with only two car garages. This may be a styling (functional obsolescence) issue if other new homes in the area have three-car garages and may reduce the future value of the home. However, if most of the homes in the local area have two car garages, then a new home with a two-car garage may not cause it to lose much value.

c. Economic Obsolescence / Social Obsolescence / External Obsolescence / Environmental Obsolescence

Economic Obsolescence: Anything outside the property line that causes a loss of value to the property.

Social, external, and environmental obsolescence are all terms used to represent **economic obsolescence.** Economic obsolescence is a loss in value due to *external* factors occurring outside the property lines of the subject property. For example, when an airport is placed very near to a single-family home, this external factor may cause a loss in value to the subject property because of excessive jet engine noises. Economic obsolescence is the hardest form of depreciation to correct because it is outside the property line and usually out of the property owner's control.

Figure 11.12

1. Noise

A single-family home located in an area where loud noises affect the tranquility of tenants and homeowners can cause a loss in both rents and property values. Noise issues may be caused by airports, busy roads, and traffic congestion near the home.

2. Greenbelts

A greenbelt adjacent to a home can be a very desirable amenity because of the visual aesthetics homeowners enjoy when using the backyard. It may provide the home with a "woodsy" feel and builders like to charge lot premiums (higher prices) for lots located adjacent to a greenbelt. Unfortunately, burglars may have an easier time burglarizing this type of property because they can enter and exit the property through the greenbelt. For this reason, a good alarm system and a big dog may be a good idea.

A greenbelt may be a problem if snakes and other undesirable critters do not receive the memo that a new home has been built in their neighborhood. This may result in unwanted visits by the old-time "neighbors" during the first few years of a new home's existence. In addition, field mice and other rodents will have direct access to the home through the greenbelt.

Tales from the Trade

THE HUNGRY MOUNTAIN LION STORY

One homeowner had a disturbance in his backyard and went to investigate. He found his Brittany Spaniel cowering in a corner of the yard with a large mountain lion sizing him up for a meal. This was in a suburban area and was a disclosure issue, especially when the homeowner told all the neighbors about it.

4. Appraisal Practice

A. Fee Appraiser

Fee Appraiser: An appraiser who charges a fee.

A **fee appraiser** is an appraiser who is self-employed and appraises properties for the payment of a fee. If there is a new loan being placed on the property, the lender will usually require an appraisal before funding the loan.

B. Reconciliation of all Three Appraisal Approaches

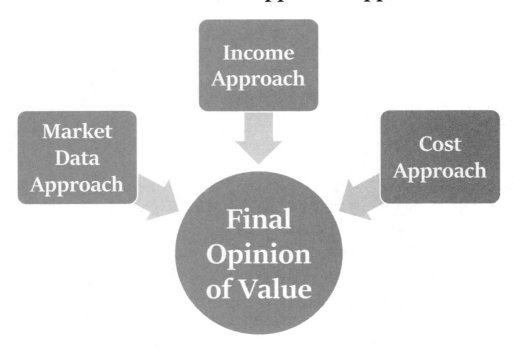

Figure 11.13 Diagram of Reconciliation of Appraisal Approaches

An appraiser will **reconcile** all three of the appraisal approaches to determine an opinion of value for the subject property. This is a total reconciliation of all three appraisal approaches which include the comparison approach/market data approach, income approach/capitalization approach, and cost approach. This reconciliation is different than an appraiser reconciling only sales comparables or rental comparables under the comparison/market data appraisal approach.

> **Reconciliation:** When an appraiser reconciles all three appraisal methods (comparison, income, and cost approaches) to determine a final estimate of value.

C. Appraisal Reports

An appraisal report provides an opinion of value for the subject property being appraised. There are two types of appraisal reports that are normally used in the real estate industry: form report and narrative report.

(1) Form Appraisal Report

Most single-family residential appraisers utilize a **form report** called the Uniform Residential Appraisal Report (URAR) to provide appraisal reports to lenders and buyers. It is also called a short form report.

> **Form Appraisal Report:** Form used to appraise single-family homes.

(2) Narrative Appraisal Report

Appraisers normally use a **narrative appraisal report** for commercial properties. It is the most complete appraisal report and may comprise several pages of pertinent information related to a subject property's value. This information may include headings of "Introduction," "Site and Improvement," "Property Description," "Supporting Data," and "Final Value Estimate."

> **Narrative Appraisal Report:** Form used to appraise commercial properties.

D. Who Else Uses Appraisals?

County tax assessors use appraisals to help determine the value of a parcel of real property. The assessed value of the land and assessed value of the building are determined separately and then multiplied by the property tax rate that is determined by the *county board of supervisors* or other regulatory body in the county where the property is located. The tax rate is usually 1.15% to 1.25% of the total assessed value, but it does vary by county. A real estate appraiser does *not* consider the assessed value of a property when making a real estate appraisal for lending purposes.

Insurers use appraisals to help determine the amount of coverage needed to replace the structure(s) built on a parcel of real property. The insurer establishes a value for the home and its contents and determines the amount and type of insurance needed to return the property owner to the same position the property owner was at before the calamity occurred.

5. Appraisal Contingency Removal

Contingencies are used to allow the buyer to not move forward with the transaction if the buyer does not remove the contingency to the contract. Appraisal contingencies are used to ensure the property appraises for the purchase price. If the property does not appraise for the purchase price, then the buyer may not remove the appraisal contingency to the purchase agreement and not move forward with the purchase.

The appraisal contingency ties in with the financing contingency because the lender usually will not fund a loan in which the appraised value is not at least at the purchase price of the property. In other words, if the property does not appraise for the purchase price, the lender will not be willing to make the loan, and the loan contingency cannot be removed because the buyer will not be able to obtain a loan to purchase the property. Therefore, both appraisal and loan contingencies allow the buyer to terminate the contract if they are not removed in a timely fashion as specified in the purchase agreement. The next chapter looks at financing contingencies.

Chapter Eleven Summary

The chapter covers appraisal contingencies, including the appraisal principles of value (demand, utility, scarcity, and transferability or DUST). Value variables include price, terms, condition, market timing, and location. Principles of value include marketability and acceptability, principle of highest and best use, principle of conformity, principle of contribution, principle of regression, principle of assemblage, principle of anticipation, principle of substitution, and the principle of balance.

The three appraisal approaches are discussed, including the comparison/market data approach, income/capitalization approach, and the cost approach. Under the cost approach, physical deterioration, functional obsolescence, and economic obsolescence are presented. Lastly, appraisal reports are considered, including form reports and narrative reports.

Chapter Eleven Quiz

1. _____ is calculated as the loan amount divided by the purchase price or appraised value—whichever is lower.
(A) Loan-to-value ratio
(B) Debt coverage ratio
(C) Debt-to-income ratio
(D) Financing contingency

2. Value is relative to each person and is the:
(A) relationship between a thing desired and the potential purchaser or desirous person
(B) maximum utility of available resources
(C) present worth of future benefits
(D) all of the above are correct

3. In real estate appraisal, _____ is primarily based upon the willing buyer and willing seller concept.
(A) commission amount
(B) market value
(C) list price
(D) none of the above are correct

4. _____ are similar properties that have recently sold near the subject property.
(A) Rental comparables
(B) Sales comparables
(C) Pending sales
(D) Listed properties

5. The _____ is used to appraise the value of income producing properties by converting an income stream into value.
(A) income approach
(B) capitalization approach
(C) Both (A) and (B) are correct
(D) Neither (A) nor (B) is correct

6. Operating expenses include:
(A) fixed expenses
(B) variable expenses
(C) Both (A) and (B) are correct
(D) Neither (A) nor (B) is correct

7. The cost approach uses:
(A) replacement cost
(B) reproduction cost
(C) Both (A) and (B) are correct
(D) Neither (A) nor (B) is correct

SECTION III: During the Real Estate Transaction

8. _____ is the number of years a property can be used and/or provide income.
(A) Physical life
(B) Economic life
(C) Effective age
(D) Actual age

9. A fee appraiser is an appraiser who (is):
(A) self-employed
(B) appraises properties for the payment of a fee
(C) Both (A) and (B) are correct
(D) Neither (A) nor (B) are correct

10. Appraisal reports include:
(A) narrative report
(B) form report
(C) Both (A) and (B) are correct
(D) Neither (A) and (B) are correct

Please use this space for notes.

12

Chapter
TWELVE

Financing
Contingencies

Most real estate agents will agree that financing drives deals. Almost all owner-occupied real estate buyers use financing to buy a home. For this reason, obtaining a loan is usually the determining factor in whether a transaction will be completed.

One must understand *why* loans are originated to fully understand the lending process. Borrowers can include a first-time homebuyer wanting to purchase a home for the family, a homeowner looking to refinance an existing home loan, or an ultra-sophisticated commercial investor using financing to leverage an income property and increase the return on investment. Each has similar lending requirements, but all have different reasons for obtaining a loan.

First-time homebuyers are looking to purchase a home for the family. Obtaining a loan may be the only way this type of buyer will be able to purchase a home. A refinancing homeowner usually wants to replace an existing home loan with a new one that has a lower interest rate. An understanding of loan amortization schedules is important when making this kind of decision because if a homeowner is far enough out on the amortization curve (e.g., twenty years out on a thirty-year amortized loan or ten years out on a fifteen-year amortized loan), refinancing may not be in the borrower's best interest. The borrower may have paid off so much of the principal balance of the loan that keeping the loan and paying it off may be a better strategy. An ultra-sophisticated commercial real estate investor is usually looking for a return on investment. The investor wants to purchase an asset that will return a desired amount (cash flow and price appreciation) over a projected holding period.

An owner-occupied homebuyer is the most prevalent type of borrower a real estate agent will encounter in the marketplace and will be discussed at length in this chapter. Existing homeowners, who refinance an existing home loan, experience very similar loan requirements as a homebuyer obtaining a new home loan, so they are discussed together in the chapter. Commercial investors are discussed elsewhere in the book.

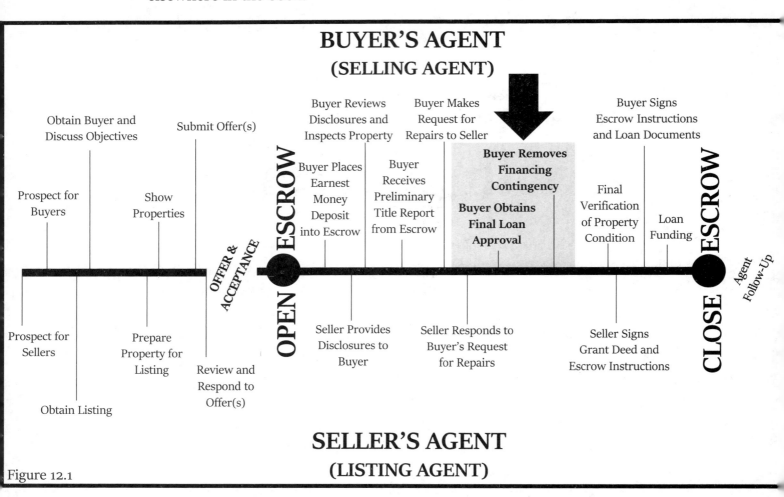

Figure 12.1

Why is someone willing to loan money to a borrower who is purchasing a home? What type of collateral does a lender require to be comfortable making a loan to a home buyer? Collateral is something a borrower places with a lender as security for repayment of the loan. Since it is very difficult for a new homebuyer to pay (for example) $160,000 cash as collateral for a $160,000 loan, lenders have allowed borrowers to use the *home itself* as security for the loan.

Placing a home as security for repayment of a loan is called **hypothecation** and comes in two forms: **mortgages** and **deeds of trust** (also called a trust deeds). Both mortgages and deeds of trust hypothecate a parcel of real property as security for a loan. Mortgages are used in many states, but they are *not* normally used in California. California usually uses deeds of trust/trust deeds to secure real property. If a borrower does not repay the loan (with interest), then the lender will foreclose the loan that is securing property and sell the property (through the trustee) to collect the debt.

An appraisal is generally required by the lender when a property is purchased. It is important to the lending process because it assures the lender of the property's value. Otherwise, the lender will lose the difference between the value of the home (less the costs of a trustee's sale) and the existing loan amount in the event of **foreclosure.**

A borrower is usually required to pay a part of the purchase price known as a down payment. For example:

Sale Price	$200,000
• 20% Down Payment	$40,000
• 80% Loan-to-Value Loan	$160,000

If the down payment is substantial (e.g., 20% or more of the purchase price or appraised value, whichever is lower) the lender may feel somewhat secure that the borrower will make every attempt to make the loan interest payments and not lose their initial $40,000 down payment. In other words, the borrower has enough money at stake not to walk away from the debt obligation at the first sign of financial trouble.

As the down payment decreases to less than 20%, the lender will become more nervous and worried that the borrower will walk away from the debt obligation because there is not enough of their own money at stake. The borrower may stop making scheduled loan payments and allow the lender to foreclose the loan.

Hypothecation: Places a house as collateral for a loan.

Mortgage: Places the house as security for the loan. Not normally used in California.

Deed of Trust: An instrument placing the real property being purchased or refinanced as collateral for the loan. Secures a promissory note.

Foreclosure: Procedure whereby property pledged as security for a debt is sold to pay the debt in the event of default in payments or terms.

1. Interest

Interest is rent a person pays for the use of money and is usually a percentage of the amount of money that is borrowed. Interest on real estate loans is simple interest. This means that interest is only charged on the principal balance of the loan that has not yet been paid. In contrast, compound interest results in interest being paid on the principal balance that has not been paid *and* any deferred interest that is owed but not yet paid by the borrower. In other words, the borrower pays interest on the principal amount of the loan that is due and interest on the interest that is due but has not yet been paid. For this reason, simple interest is generally used in most real estate loans made in today's real estate market.

A. Nominal Interest Rate

The **nominal interest rate** is the actual interest rate named in the promissory note (evidence of the debt). The nominal rate does not include loan fees that are charged by lenders when making a loan, nor discount points which allow a borrower to pay money upfront to the lender and reduce the loan interest rate.

B. Effective Interest Rate

The **effective interest rate** is the actual rate of interest the borrower pays including loan fees, discount points, and other loan costs. For example, the nominal rate (named in the note) is 5%. However, when all the loan fees, discount points, and loan costs are considered, the effective rate (what the borrower actually pays) is 7%. Therefore, the effective interest rate is usually greater than the nominal rate for most real estate loans.

(1) Annual Percentage Rate

The effective interest rate is expressed as the annual percentage rate (APR) in advertising placed by lenders. This allows borrowers to compare one loan to another using the annual percentage rate for each loan. Borrowers can compare "apples to apples" rather than comparing nominal interest rates with differing loan fees, discount points, and other loan costs.

(2) Discount Points

Discount points allow a borrower to pay a certain amount of money upfront to reduce the loan interest rate. For example, a borrower is quoted a 5.00% interest rate from a lender for the purchase of a home. However, the borrower would like a 4.50% interest rate. The lender then informs the borrower that if the borrower will pay discount points to the lender, the lender will provide the borrower with a 4.50% interest rate loan. In this example the lender requires the borrower to pay one discount point (1% of the loan amount) to reduce the interest rate by $1/8^{th}$ of one percent. Therefore, the borrower will be required to pay four discount point to be able to reduce the interest rate from 5.00% to 4.50%. This is calculated as: 4 discount points = buyer pays 4% of the loan amount to reduce the interest rate by 4/8% = ½ of one percent. Therefore, the 5.00% interest rate – ½% = 4.5% interest rate paid by the borrower. The break-even for discount points is usually between five and seven years (not considering net present value), so if the borrower plans to keep the loan longer than five to seven years, paying discount points can be a good idea. There are also some tax ramifications as well.

2. Fixed and Adjustable Rate Loans

A. Fixed Rate Loan

Fixed rate loans have a fixed interest rate throughout the life of the loan. The monthly principal and interest payment is the amount the borrower will pay throughout the life of the loan. The interest rate stays the same, so there are no surprises with fixed rate loans. It usually is best to acquire a fixed rate loan during times of low interest rates.

> **Fixed Rate Loan:** The monthly principal and interest payment is the amount the borrower will pay throughout the life of the loan.

B. Adjustable Rate Loan

An **adjustable rate loan** (**ARM**) is a loan that adjusts to some predetermined index (Monthly Treasuries Average or MTA, Cost of Savings Index, London Inter-Bank Offered Rate or LIBOR, and the Secured Overnight Financing Rate or SOFR) that measures the cost of money and changes over the life of the loan. The SOFR rate measures overnight loans collateralized by U.S. government debt.

> **Adjustable Rate Loan:** A loan that adjusts to some predetermined index that measures the cost of money and changes over the life of the loan.

Lenders look favorably upon adjustable rate loans because they place the market risk of rising interest rates on the borrower and not the lender. Lenders usually offer attractive initial low interest rates (lower than fixed rate loans) to entice borrowers to accept this type of loan and the market risk that accompanies it. Commercial lenders call these loans variable interest rate loans (VIR).

3. Equity and Debt

Equity is defined as the fair market value of a property minus the loans against it. It can also be defined as the amount of cash a buyer has in a property when existing loans are paid off. Real estate loans are called **debt** and most owner-occupied single-family homes are usually acquired by using equity funds and debt funds. Thus, equity is the amount of cash a buyer uses to purchase a parcel of real estate.

> **Equity:** Fair market value of a property minus the loans against it.

> **Debt:** That which is due from one person or another; obligation, liability (e.g., money that is owed by a borrower to a lender).

In fact, the best way to assure that a borrower will not default on a real estate loan is to have high equity in the property. Moreover, many successful real estate purchases are initiated and put into place using equity funds (down payment) and mortgage (loan) funds.

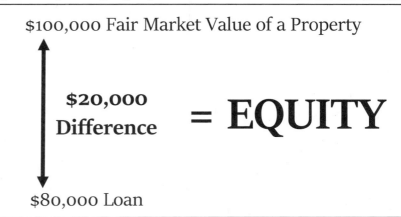

$100,000 Fair Market Value of a Property

$20,000 Difference = EQUITY

$80,000 Loan

Figure 12.2 Equity Diagram

A. Loan-to-Value Ratio

Loan-to-Value Ratio (LTV): The loan amount divided by a property's purchase price or appraised value – whichever is lower.

A **loan-to-value ratio (LTV)** is defined as the loan amount divided by the price of the property. Lenders will usually use either the purchase price or appraised value, whichever is lower to calculate the loan-to-value ratio. For example, if a property sells for $100,000 and the lender makes an $80,000 loan, the loan-to-value ratio is 80%. Loan-to-value ratio is a lender's first line of defense against loan default because the borrower has a significant amount of money in the property.

$$\frac{\text{Loan Amount}}{\text{Price of Property}} = \text{Loan-to-Value Ratio}$$

Figure 12.3 Loan-to-Value Ratio Calculation

B. Leverage

Leverage is defined as using the maximum amount of borrowed funds to purchase real property. During an upward-trending sellers' market, homeowners may find their home increasing in value. Since many homeowners use low down payment and high loan-to-value ratio loans to purchase a home, they may find a significant increase in value over time. The problem homeowners have in capturing this price appreciation is that homeowners need a place to live. If they sell the property and capture the increase in equity, they still must find a place to live and most homeowners are not willing to become renters again. Real estate investors, on the other hand, can ride an upward-trending sellers' market upward until it is near the top-of-the-market and then sell without having to find another place to live.

C. Private Mortgage Insurance

Private Mortgage Insurance (PMI): Used to insure a lender for the loan amount made above the 80% loan-to-value ratio.

Lenders generally do not like to make loans above an 80% loan-to-value ratio (LTV). So, when a borrower needs a loan that is greater than 80% LTV, the lender may not be comfortable making the loan. Thus, **private mortgage insurance** can be used to insure a lender for the loan amount made above the 80% loan-to-value ratio. The borrower pays a private mortgage insurance (PMI) company who will (in return for an up-front fee and/or monthly payments to the PMI company) insure the additionally loaned funds that are above the 80% maximum LTV.

For example, if a borrower only has a 5% down payment (15% less than the 20% down payment required by most lenders), lenders may not recoup all their money if the property is foreclosed in the future. For this reason, private mortgage insurance (PMI) companies have stepped in and may be willing to insure the portion of the loan between the 80% loan (the amount the lender is comfortable making) and 5% down payment the borrower is able to make. Therefore, the lender makes a 95% LTV loan to the borrower and the lender will incur any losses up to the 80% LTV amount. The additional 15% of the loan amount, that the PMI company insures, will be paid to the lender if there is a foreclosure and the proceeds from the trustee's sale are not enough to reimburse the lender for their loss. The PMI company must pay the difference between the 95% LTV loan that was made by the lender and the 80% LTV loan the lender was comfortable making. In other words, the PMI company must pay the lender for the 15% loss which is the difference between 80% LTV and 95% LTV.

Borrowers have some financing options when using PMI because several lenders may be willing to make a 95% LTV loan, providing the PMI company is willing to pay for the loss incurred between 80% LTV and 95% LTV. Thus, borrowers may be able to negotiate a better loan interest rate and PMI costs by shopping around for a lender.

D. 80-10-10 Loans

An **"80-10-10" loan** is used when the buyer only has a 10% down payment and does not want to pay private mortgage insurance (PMI). For example, a seller sells a property for $100,000 and the buyer makes a 10% down payment. The buyer obtains a new conventional first deed of trust loan in the amount of $80,000 at 7% interest and amortized over 30 years. The seller then agrees to carry a second deed of trust loan in the amount of $10,000 at 9% interest-only, due in two years.

> **80-10-10 Loan:** 80% first deed of trust, 10% owner-carry second deed of trust, and 10% down payment.

The buyer will pay $532 per month for thirty (30) years to pay off the first deed of trust loan that was made by an outside conventional lender. The buyer will also pay $75 per month for 24 months to the seller who carries (becomes the lender) the $10,000 second trust deed loan. On the 24th month, the buyer will pay the last remaining $75 interest-only payment to the seller—along with the entire $10,000 loan balance that is due (to the seller) at that time. Hence, when a buyer obtains an 80% first deed of trust loan from a conventional lender, the seller carries a 10% second deed of trust loan (made by the seller to the buyer), and the buyer pays a 10% down payment, this is called an "80-10-10."

E. Impounds

Impounds are reserves for property taxes and property insurance that a lender usually collects from a borrower who has a greater than 80% loan-to-value loan. The lender then, on behalf of the borrower, pays the property taxes and property insurance as they become due each year.

4. Types of Real Estate Loans

Types of real estate loans include: interest-only, fully amortized, partially amortized, negative amortization, shared appreciation, and reverse mortgages.

$10,000 Loan, 9% Interest-Only, Due in 2 Years

0

1 ← $75 Interest-Only Payment

12 Months

23 ← $75 Interest-Only Payment

24 Months

$75 Interest-Only Payment + Entire $10,000 Loan Balance

Figure 12.4 Interest-Only Loan/Straight Note Example

A.   Interest-Only Loan/Straight Note

A **straight note** is an **interest-only loan** in which only interest is paid during the term of the loan. The borrower pays interest each month until the last payment that is due. At that time, the last interest only payment will be paid, along with the entire principal balance of the loan.

Interest Only/Straight Note: Only interest is paid during the term of the loan.

B. Amortization and Fully-Amortized Loans

When a borrower pays off a loan with principal and interest payments over the life of the loan, this is called amortization. Accordingly, a loan that is completely repaid by a series of regular equal installment payments of principal and interest is called a fully-amortized loan.

Specific amortization schedules must be used to establish an amortization curve in which the buyer pays the same payment each month for 360 months and pays off the loan.

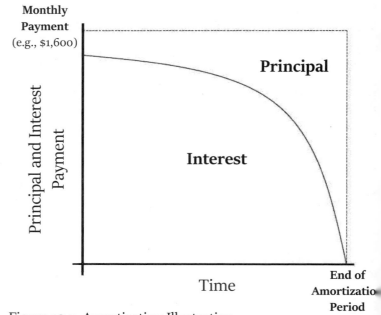

Figure 12.5 Amortization Illustration

326

With each payment, the principal balance of the loan is decreased, so even though the total principal and interest payment stays the same, the portion of the payment that is principal increases and the portion that is interest decreases with each payment.

(1) Amortization Tables

Amortization tables are used to determine the monthly payment of a loan. They help determine the amount of each payment that goes toward interest and the amount that goes toward principal reduction. As mentioned earlier, with each payment, the interest portion of the payment decreases and the principal portion increases. However, these changes are non-linear and favor the lender early in the amortization period, while favoring the borrower later.

In other words, when a loan is fully amortized by equal monthly payments of principal and interest, the amount applied to principal increases while the amount of interest paid decreases. Therefore, when reading an amortization table or chart, the amount shown as the payment, based on a given loan amount, rate of interest, and loan term indicates both principal and interest.

Partial Amortization: Loan that is paid off like a fully amortized loan, except the loan becomes due and payable sometime before the end of the amortization period.

Balloon Payment: Lump sum that is due at the end of a partially amortized loan.

C. Partially-Amortized Loan

A **partially-amortized loan** is a loan that is paid off in a very similar fashion to a fully amortized loan, except the loan becomes due and payable sometime before the end of the amortization period. This is usually five to seven years from the loan origination date. This lump sum payment that is due is called a **balloon payment**.

Residential lenders may provide a borrower with a lower-than-market interest rate to induce them to accept a partially amortized loan with a balloon payment. The balloon payment allows the lender to get their loan funds back from the borrower within a reasonable length of time and re-loan the funds at current market interest rates. Therefore, the borrower is bearing the market risk associated with a rise in interest rates. The borrower will be required to obtain another loan after the balloon payment becomes due, and this loan may have a higher interest rate if there has been an increase in market interest rates between the loan origination date and the balloon payment date.

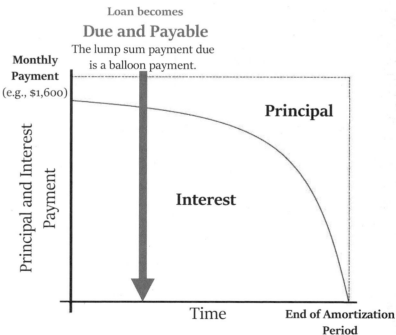

Figure 12.6 Partially-Amortized Loan Diagram (e.g., 30 years)

D. Negative Amortization

A **negative amortization** loan requires monthly payments that are *not* sufficient to cover the monthly interest that is due. The borrower pays such a small payment that it does not reduce any principal and pays only part of the interest that is due to the lender. The principal balance of the loan actually *increases* over the life of a negative amortization loan. Negative amortization loans may be used when a real estate market is appreciating (increasing) in value and a real estate investor would like to obtain as much cash flow from a property as possible–while stabilizing rents, rehabilitating or renovating the property, and selling it at a substantial profit. Unfortunately, because of their volatility (principal balance of the loan goes up), negative amortization loans do not work very well for owner-occupied homebuyers.

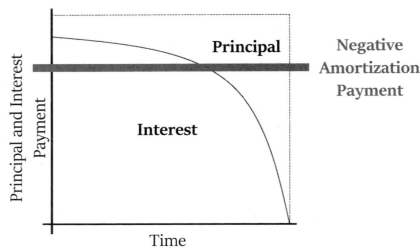

Figure 12.7 Negative Amortization Diagram

E. Shared Appreciation Loan

A **shared appreciation loan** allows the lender to participate in the increase in value of a borrower's property. It is usually a below-market fixed rate loan that provides for contingent interest to be paid to the lender when the property increases in value. The lender is able to participate in an upward-trending sellers' market and increase their returns accordingly.

F. Reverse Mortgages

A **reverse mortgage** allows a senior citizen to stay in their home while taking the equity out of the home each month through a reverse mortgage.

5. Promissory Notes and Security Devices

A. Promissory Notes

A **promissory note** is evidence of a debt obligation and is an unconditional promise to pay the loan back—with interest. In plain terms, it is an "IOU" ("I owe you") that specifies the amount and terms of the loan, but there is no collateral securing a promissory note that is by itself.

A promissory note is usually secured by a deed of trust (also called trust deed). A trust deed places the property itself as collateral for the loan. If a borrower defaults when making specified loan payments, then the lender may accelerate the loan balance to become due and payable immediately and proceed with a foreclosure action. The lender can force the sale of the property through a nonjudicial trustee's sale (or occasionally judicially through the courts) and get reimbursed for the funds that were loaned to the borrower—along with applicable interest, fees, and expenses incurred during the trustee's sale.

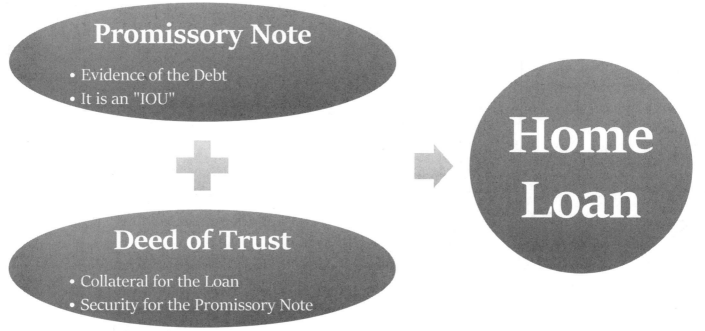

Figure 12.8 Promissory Note and Deed of Trust Illustration

(1) Seasoned Note

A **seasoned note** is a promissory note that has a previous history of prompt loan payments. Seasoned notes can be purchased (assigned) from the lender that originated the loan to another lender that wishes to add the loan to their portfolio of performing loans. The loan company that purchases the promissory note from the original lender is called a holder in due course. Lenders may sell a loan several times over the life of the loan. The maker of the note (borrower) has less defenses against a holder in due course than against the original lender.

Seasoned Note: A promissory note with a prompt payment history.

(2) Holder in Due Course

A **holder in due course** is a lender or person who purchases a loan (promissory note and usually deed of trust) from the original lender or someone the original lender sold the loan to (subsequent holder). For example, when a lender makes a loan and then sells it (assigns it) to another lender who takes over the loan, this new lender is called a holder in due course. A holder in due course takes a

Holder in Due Course: Loan company that purchases the promissory note from the original lender.

promissory note in good faith without notice of dishonesty or any defenses against it.

(3) Note Endorsements

A **note endorsement** transfers a promissory note from one person or entity to another. A promissory note can be endorsed (signed) as a blank endorsement, restricted endorsement, or a qualified endorsement. For example, Able sold his home and carried back a $150,000 first deed of trust (seller made the loan to the buyer). Later, the seller sold the promissory note to Baker endorsing it "without recourse." If the borrower defaults on the loan, Baker could not ask Able for reimbursement for the loss. Baker must foreclose on the loan secured by the property to collect the balance due.

(4) Joint and Several Note

A **joint and several note** makes each borrower responsible jointly and severally for the promissory note. In other words, each borrower is responsible together with the other borrowers on the note, along with each borrower severally (which means separately). Thus, each borrower is responsible together and individually for repayment of the promissory note. This is used by lenders to increase their collateral position in a property.

(5) Negotiable Instrument

A **negotiable instrument** is a document that can be used as an item of exchange and therefore, negotiated. Examples include checks, drafts, and installment notes. However, trust deeds and mortgages are *not* considered negotiable instruments.

(6) Promotional Note

Promotional notes are sometimes used by subdividers to help sell vacant or improved lots in a subdivision. Promotional notes provide borrowers with attractive financing to stimulate sales in the subdivision. However, promotional notes are typically subordinate (in second position) to existing blanket encumbrances (blanket trust deeds that secure all the lots in the subdivision) existing on the property. For this reason, the California Business and Professions Code, California Corporations Code, and the California Corporations Commissioner's Regulations require promotional notes to be up to and including 36 months (3 years) in duration. Therefore, a promotional note must not exceed 36 months in length, and thus a promissory note that is 37 months in duration would *not* be considered a promotional note.

B. Deeds of Trust/Trust Deeds

A deed of trust or trust deed is an instrument placing the real property being purchased or refinanced as collateral for the loan. A promissory note is evidence of the debt and a trust deed is used to secure the promissory note and collateralize the loan.

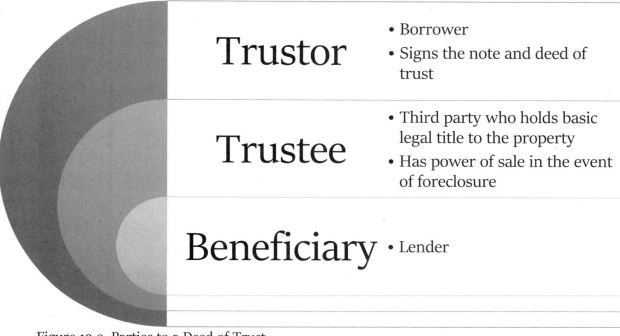

Trustor	• Borrower • Signs the note and deed of trust
Trustee	• Third party who holds basic legal title to the property • Has power of sale in the event of foreclosure
Beneficiary	• Lender

Figure 12.9 Parties to a Deed of Trust

A deed of trust (trust deed) is the main security device for real estate loans in California. Many states use mortgages as their primary security device; however, deeds of trust are used in California and have many distinct advantages over mortgages. It should be noted that lenders in California are commonly called "mortgage companies" even though they use deeds of trust and not mortgages to secure the loans they originate.

There are three parties to a deed of trust: *trustor, trustee,* and *beneficiary.* The **trustor** is the borrower who signs the note and deed of trust for the amount of the loan.

The **trustee** is a third party who holds basic legal title to the property securing the loan and has power of sale in the event of foreclosure. The trustor and beneficiary rely upon the trustee to hold the basic legal title to the property.

The **beneficiary** is the lender. An owner who gives a trust deed as security for repayment of a debt has borrowed money from the beneficiary. When a loan is being paid off, a **beneficiary statement** is issued by the lender to the borrower. It shows the loan balance and identifies the current status of the loan. This is usually requested by an escrow officer who will pay off an existing loan at close of escrow. Thus, a beneficiary statement is a statement sent by the beneficiary (lender) to

Trustor: Borrower who signs the note and deed of trust.

Trustee: Third party who holds basic legal title to a property.

Beneficiary: Lender

Beneficiary Statement: Issued by the lender to the borrower identifying the current status of the loan.

escrow informing the escrow officer of the exact amount that must be paid out of the seller's proceeds to pay off the seller's existing loan.

Lenders usually charge a small fee to provide the beneficiary statement. The escrow officer receives the beneficiary statement and then pays the existing lender the amount that is needed to pay off the loan. The lender then authorizes the trustee to reconvey the basic legal title back to the trustor. The property owner (former trustor) then owns the property without a loan and can freely transfer it to a buyer.

Please Note: Trust Deed vs. Grant Deed

Even though a deed of trust (trust deed) has the word "deed" in its name, it is used differently than both grant deeds and quitclaim deeds. Grant deeds convey a property's title to someone else. Quitclaim deeds remove someone from title. Trust deeds do neither. Trust deeds are used with real estate loans. A trust deed is used to place the house as collateral for a real estate loan being made to the borrower who owns the property. The lender is called the beneficiary who makes a loan to the trustor (borrower). A third party (trustee) is used to hold the basic legal title to the property.

An acceleration clause in a deed of trust allows the lender to accelerate the loan amount due and payable immediately upon borrower loan default. If the trustor (borrower) stops making required debt service (loan) payments to the beneficiary (lender), the beneficiary can instruct the trustee to sell the property and get their money back from the sale of the property. This is called a foreclosure. A deed of trust can be foreclosed either through a trustee's sale (non-judicial foreclosure) or through the courts (judicial foreclosure). However, trust deeds in California are normally foreclosed non-judicially through a trustee's sale.

The trustee will sell the defaulted property to a buyer at a non-judicial trustee's sale (auction) and get as much money back for the beneficiary (lender) as possible. A deed of trust is merely a *lien* (money encumbrance that limits the title to real property) on the property. If the borrower (trustor) does not make the scheduled loan payments on time, the beneficiary can accelerate the entire loan balance due and payable immediately, direct the trustee to sell the property through the power of sale provision in the deed of trust, and get their money back (or as much as possible).

(1) Parties to a Deed of Trust

A deed of trust or trust deed is an instrument placing the real property being purchased (or refinanced) as collateral for the loan. A promissory note is evidence of the debt and uses the deed of trust to collateralize the loan. In other words, the deed of trust places the home as security for repayment of the promissory note. If the trustor stops making debt service payments, the lender can foreclose and (hopefully) get most of their money back. A promissory note can exist by itself. A deed of trust must have a promissory note to secure.

a. Trustor

A trustor is the borrower who is borrowing the money. In the creation of a purchase money trust deed loan (trust deed that is used to *buy* a property, not a refinance), the trustor is the one who signs the promissory note and deed of trust for the amount of the loan. In other words, the trustor signs the promissory note as maker of the promissory note and is obligated to pay the balance of the promissory note plus interest. The trustor also signs the deed of trust which secures the promissory note.

b. Trustee

A trustee is a third party who holds the basic legal title to the property until the trustor pays off the loan. This is usually with a sale of the property, refinance that pays off the existing loan and replaces it with a new one, or the trustor pays off the loan with cash.

c. Beneficiary

The beneficiary is the lender who makes a loan to the trustor.

(2) Loan Clauses
a. Alienation/Due-on-Sale Clause

An **alienation clause** or **due-on-sale clause** in a trust deed provides that the principal amount of the loan plus accrued interest is due in the event of the sale of the property. If the owner conveys the property, it allows the lender to call the entire loan balance immediately due and payable. The term "alienate" means to convey and an alienation clause is considered an acceleration clause.

> **Alienation Clause/Due-on-Sale Clause:** Provides that the principal amount of the loan plus accrued interest is due in the event of the sale of the property.

Figure 12.10 Alienation Clause Diagram

b. Prepayment Penalty

Prepayment Penalty: Provides for a certain sum to be paid by the trustor (borrower) if the loan is paid off before it matures.

Prepayment of a loan (paying the loan off early) is a privilege and not a right. If a loan has a prepayment penalty clause and is paid off before it matures (becomes due), the trustor (borrower) may be required to pay a predetermined amount to the lender. This is called a **prepayment penalty** and may be placed on a loan by a to prevent the loan from being paid back early. A common prepayment penalty is six (6) months loan interest (as a penalty) if the loan is paid back while the prepayment penalty remains in effect. Government-insured and government-guaranteed loans do *not* allow prepayment penalties.

c. Formal Loan Assumption

Formal Loan Assumption: Assigns all loan rights, obligations, and responsibilities of the seller to the buyer.

A **formal loan assumption** by a buyer assigns all rights, obligations, and responsibilities of the seller to the buyer. The buyer steps into the seller's shoes regarding loan payments to the lender and the seller is completely relieved of all responsibilities for repayment of the loan.

d. Taking a Property "Subject To" an Existing Loan

Subject To: Lender does not approve the assumption and the seller continues to remain primarily liable for repayment of the loan for five years.

When a borrower takes over an existing loan "**subject to**" that loan, the lender does *not* approve the assumption and the seller continues to remain primarily liable for repayment of the loan for five years after the "subject to" sale date. Therefore, if a buyer takes a property subject to the existing loan, "subject to" most nearly means the buyer will *not* be personally liable for the loan and the seller remains liable for five years.

For example, if Buyer Able buys Blackacre from Seller Baker, taking title to the property subject to the existing loan, the person primarily responsible for the repayment of the loan will be Seller Baker.

e. Open-End Mortgage

Open-End Mortgage: A loan that allows additional borrowing at a later date.

An **open-end mortgage** is a loan that allows additional borrowing at a later date and is similar to an equity line of credit in which the additional funds are collateralized by the existing deed of trust. When an open-end mortgage is used, the trustor could borrow more money if it is needed. In other words, when a mortgage secures an initial loan and then sums later loaned, this is called an open-end mortgage.

f. Seller Financing

Seller Financing: A loan made by the seller to the buyer.

When a seller owns a property with a large amount of equity, the seller may be willing to "carry" a loan on the property. This means the seller will extend credit to the buyer, rather than the buyer having to go to a conventional lender to get a loan to purchase the property. This is called seller financing or an owner carry.

1. All-Inclusive Trust Deed/Wraparound Mortgage

An **all-inclusive trust deed (AITD)** or **wraparound mortgage** is used when prevailing interest rates are higher than the interest rate a property owner is presently paying on a property loan. The property owner institutes an AITD for an amount that is greater than the existing loan on the property, while keeping the existing loan in place.

For example, Property Owner Able owns a property that is worth $100,000. There is an existing loan of $50,000 on the property at 4% interest only, due in five (5) years. Property Owner Able is paying $166.67/month interest-only to the lender of this loan.

Shortly thereafter, Property Owner Able decides to sell the property. Property Owner Able found Buyer Baker who was interested in buying the property. Buyer Baker paid $30,000 to Property Owner Able as a down payment (which Property Owner Able kept) and Property Owner Able carried a loan (seller carry) in the amount of $70,000, at 6% interest-only, due in five (5) years. Therefore, Property Owner Able collected $30,000 from Buyer Baker as a down payment and collected $350.00 per month interest-only payments from Buyer Baker for five (5) years.

Property Owner Able collects $350.00 each month from Buyer Baker, and then pays the $166.67 principal and interest loan payment that is due on the existing loan (that continues to be in Property Owner Able's name). Property Owner Able keeps the difference between $350.00 - $166.67 = $183.33.

The example illustrates an all-inclusive trust deed (AITD) because it wraps around the existing loan. In addition to the $30,000 down payment, Property Owner Able receives 6% interest on the $20,000 credit that is being extended to Buyer Baker ($70,000 AITD minus $50,000 existing loan), along with 2% more interest on the $50,000 existing loan (6% AITD interest rate minus 4% existing loan interest rate = 2% margin).

The existing $50,000 loan most likely has an alienation/due-on-sale clause in the deed of trust that makes the entire loan balance due and payable when the property is sold. For this reason, when the property is conveyed to Buyer Baker, the existing lender will be notified of the sale and call the loan immediately due and payable. Lenders do not like Property Owner Able receiving the 2% increase in interest rates, when they can call the loan due, get their money back, and then re-loan to funds to another buyer at the higher 6% interest rate.

Some sellers may use an unrecorded land contract (real property sales contract that is covered later in the chapter) to accomplish this without

All-Inclusive Trust Deed (AITD)/ Wraparound Mortgage: Used when prevailing interest rates are higher than the interest rate a property owner is presently paying on a property loan.

actually transferring legal title to the property. A real estate attorney should be consulted anytime an AITD or unrecorded land contract is used.

g. Subordination Clause

Subordination: Allows a loan or lien to take priority over another loan or lien that was recorded prior to it. It is used for both construction loans and the refinancing a first deed of trust when there is an existing second deed of trust already on the property.

A **subordination clause** allows a first deed of trust to change positions with a second deed of trust with regard to priority of recording. It is commonly seen with construction loans and when a property owner wants to refinance a first deed of trust when there is a second deed of trust existing on the property.

1. Example #1: Construction Loan

Buyer Baker wants to purchase vacant land. To do so, Baker obtains a purchase money first trust deed loan to finance the purchase. Afterwards, Baker intends to place a construction loan on the land. Thus, the first trust deed used to purchase the land will most likely contain a subordination clause. The subordination clause permits Baker to place a future loan (second trust deed) that will have priority if there is a foreclosure in the future. In other words, the purchase money first trust deed loan to purchase the land is allowing the second trust deed construction loan to trade places and take priority over it. The subordination clause permits the second trust deed construction loan to take priority even though it was made *after* the first trust deed purchase money loan that was used to obtain the land.

Subordination Clause and a Construction Loan

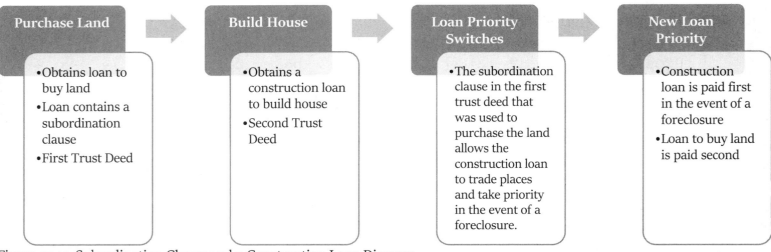

Purchase Land
- Obtains loan to buy land
- Loan contains a subordination clause
- First Trust Deed

Build House
- Obtains a construction loan to build house
- Second Trust Deed

Loan Priority Switches
- The subordination clause in the first trust deed that was used to purchase the land allows the construction loan to trade places and take priority in the event of a foreclosure.

New Loan Priority
- Construction loan is paid first in the event of a foreclosure
- Loan to buy land is paid second

Figure 12.11 Subordination Clause and a Construction Loan Diagram

2. Example #2: Refinance First Deed of Trust

If an owner wants to refinance a first deed of trust when a second deed of trust exists on the property, the lender on the first deed of trust will probably require the second deed of trust to contain a subordination clause.

Therefore, when the first deed of trust is refinanced and recorded, it will keep its priority over the junior (second) deed of trust.

(3) Other Loan Terms

a. Late Payment

From a legal standpoint, a trustor (borrower) may be assessed a late charge if loan payments are made ten days after the due date. Most lenders, however, allow a borrower fifteen days before the loan payment becomes late and the trustor is assessed a late charge.

b. Discounting

When a lender sells a promissory note (loan) for less than the unpaid balance, this is called **discounting** the note. If a lender of a deed of trust sells all the lender's interest in the note for less than the unpaid balance, this is called discounting.

Discounting: Selling a promissory note for less than the face value of the note. The buyer of the note waits until the note is due and then collects the face value.

For example, if Able sells a $15,000 promissory note secured by a second deed of trust to Investor Baker for $7,500, this is called discounting. The promissory note may be due in two years, however, Able is willing to accept $7,500 now, as payment for the note. Investor Baker pays $7,500 now and receives a note valued at $15,000 in two years. Investor Baker waits two years until the note is due and then collects $15,000. Therefore, a lender on a deed of trust that sells their interest in a note for less than the unpaid balance has discounted the note.

c. After-Acquired Title

When a property owner adds a barn or other structures to the property and then defaults on the loan, the lender that forecloses on the property will receive the additional improvements (barn and other structures) in the foreclosure. In other words, the owner loses the money spent on the improvements and the lender receives **after-acquired title** to the property.

After-Acquired Title: Buildings that are built on a property that is already encumbered by a loan will be acquired by the lender if the property is foreclosed in the future.

d. Deed of Reconveyance

A **deed of reconveyance** transfers the basic legal title held by the trustee back to the trustor. This occurs when a loan is paid off.

Deed of Reconveyance: Transfers the basic legal title held by the trustee back to the trustor.

e. Blanket Trust Deed/Blanket Encumbrance

A **blanket trust deed** (blanket deed of trust) or **blanket encumbrance** "blankets" several parcels of land under one trust deed. It is commonly used in subdivisions, so the subdivider can finance the purchase of several lots (vacant parcels) and other off-site improvements (streets, curbs, etc.). As each lot in the

Blanket Trust Deed/Blanket Encumbrance: Several parcels of land under one trust deed.

subdivision is sold, it is released from the blanket trust deed with a release clause or partial release clause.

For example, Able sold six unencumbered properties to Baker. Able carried a loan as part of the purchase price and secured all six properties with one deed of trust. This document is called a blanket encumbrance.

f. Release Clause/Partial Release Clause

A **release clause** or **partial release clause** allows the subdivider to sell lots within a subdivision and remove them from under an existing blanket encumbrance (blanket trust deed or blanket deed of trust) covering all the lots in the subdivision. When a subdivider sells a lot that is presently under a blanket encumbrance, the escrow officer will use a release clause or partial release clause to remove the lot from under the blanket encumbrance. This allows the buyer to purchase the lot free and clear of the blanket encumbrance. The buyer can then place a loan on the lot that is in first position (first trust deed) and not encumbered by the blanket encumbrance.

(4) Foreclosure Procedures for a Deed of Trust

a. Power of Sale

The trustor (borrower) gives the trustee (third party that holds basic legal title to the property) the power to sell the property if the trustor defaults on the scheduled loan payments. The trustee has the **power of sale**. Therefore, a default will result in a trustee's sale (foreclosure auction).

b. Acceleration Clause

An **acceleration clause** in a deed of trust makes the loan due and payable upon the happening of a certain event. The event most commonly associated with an acceleration clause is a loan default by the borrower. When the borrower stops making payments on the loan, the acceleration clause takes effect and makes the entire loan balance immediately due and payable.

1. Notice of Default

A **notice of default** is recorded by the trustee when the trustor defaults on loan payments made to the beneficiary. When this occurs, the trustee (through the power of sale) moves forward with foreclosure proceedings. The first thing the trustee does is record a notice of default. The trustee must then wait three months and then publish a notice of the trustee's sale in a newspaper of general circulation once per week for three

Release Clause/Partial Release Clause: Clause that allows the subdivider to sell lots within a subdivision and remove them from under an existing blanket encumbrance.

Power of Sale: The trustor gives the power of sale in a deed of trust to the trustee.

Acceleration Clause: Makes the loan due and payable upon the default of the borrower.

Notice of Default: Recorded by the trustee when the trustor defaults on loan payments made to the beneficiary.

weeks prior to the trustee's sale. Therefore, the trustee's sale can take place 3 months + 21 days (about four months) after recording the notice of default.

2. Request for Notice of Default

A **request for notice of default** alerts a holder (beneficiary/lender) of the second trust deed when the trustor has defaulted on the first trust deed. If this occurs, then the holder (beneficiary/lender) of the second trust deed can move in, pay off the first trust deed, and take over the property. Thereby attempting to preserve their collateral position for the second trust deed. The beneficiary (lender) on the second deed of trust should record a request for notice of default so they will be notified if the first trust deed goes into foreclosure.

Request for Notice of Default: Alerts a holder (beneficiary/lender) of the second trust deed when the trustor has defaulted on the first trust deed.

3. Reinstatement

The trustor has up to five days before the trustee's sale to pay up the back interest due on the loan, as well as other fees and costs incurred by the lender, and **reinstate** the loan. If the trustor does not reinstate prior to the five days, then the trustee can move forward with a trustee's sale and sell the property to the highest qualified bidder.

Reinstatement: Trustor has up to five days before the trustee's sale to pay up the back interest due on the loan and other lender fees and costs.

5 Days Prior

Trustor pays back interest due on the loan + other fees and costs incurred by the lender

TRUSTEE'S SALE

Loan Reinstatement

Figure 12.12 Loan Reinstatement Illustration

4. Deficiency Judgment

Foreclosure by trustee's sale cannot have a **deficiency judgment**. In other words, if the property does not produce enough money to the lender from the foreclosure to pay off the loan, the lender cannot go after the trustor's personal assets for the difference. Although not common in California, a lender could foreclose a non-purchase money trust deed through the courts and obtain a deficiency judgment.

Deficiency Judgment: A judicial foreclosure allows a lender to pursue a deficiency judgment against the borrower.

5. Redemption Period

If a deficiency judgment occurs (foreclosed through the courts), then the trustor has a **one-year right of redemption period** to pay all back interest, fees, and costs and redeem the property anytime up to one year after the judicial foreclosure. The situation places a lender in a poor position to dispose of the asset, since the lender must wait until the one-year redemption period is over before they can sell and transfer clear title to the property. This is the reason why lenders usually foreclose a deed of trust through a non-judicial trustee's sale that does not allow a deficiency judgment. The lender can dispose of the non-performing asset quickly and not have to wait a year for the redemption period to end.

6. Deed in Lieu of Foreclosure

When a trustor informs the beneficiary (lender) that he or she does not want to go through with the foreclosure process, the trustor will deed the property directly to the beneficiary/lender. This is called a **deed in lieu of foreclosure**.

One pitfall lenders face with this arrangement is the lender who accepts a deed in lieu of foreclosure also accepts any existing junior trust deeds (2nd, 3rd, 4th, etc. trust deeds) that may exist on the property. For this reason, it is in the lender's best interest to verify there are no additional junior loans or liens existing on the property prior to accepting a deed in lieu of foreclosure.

c. Trustee's Sale

An involuntary foreclosure in California usually has the lender foreclosing through a **trustee's sale**. This is a non-judicial foreclosure which is not through the courts. The beneficiary (lender) usually bids the amount of money the beneficiary/lender already has out on the property. This is usually the loan amount plus costs of the trustee's sale and arrearages (back interest that is due). At the trustee's sale, real estate investors bid above the loan amount—if the property is valued more than the loan. Sometimes the lender places the starting bid well below the loan amount. If this occurs, the lender has made the decision to sell the property and take the loss in value at the trustee's sale.

If the property is upside down or underwater (i.e., the loan amount is greater than the value of the property), real estate investors will usually not bid above the property's current market value at the trustee's sale. When this occurs, the property will usually be sold to the lender for the loan amount and other costs and expenses they have already incurred. At this point the property will usually be placed in the lender's REO portfolio and sold as an REO property.

Redemption Period: When a lender forecloses using a deficiency judgment, the borrower has a one-year redemption period to redeem the property.

Deed in Lieu of Foreclosure: A trustor informs the beneficiary (lender) that he or she does not want to go through with the foreclosure process, so the trustor deeds the property directly to the beneficiary/lender.

Trustee's Sale: Nonjudicial foreclosure of a deed of trust.

d. Short Sale

When the loan balance is greater than the value of the home, the borrower may ask the lender to voluntarily take a loss *before* the trustee's sale. This is called a pre-foreclosure or **short sale**. The owner usually finds a buyer who is willing to buy the property at or within 10% of the property's market value. The borrower then asks the existing lender(s) to voluntarily take the loss now rather than in the future. If the lender(s) wait until the trustee's sale, especially during a downward-trending buyers' market, the loss may be significantly more than if they had sold it earlier as a short sale. In other words, take the loss now rather than later and save some money in the process.

Pricing of short sales is usually accomplished when the real estate listing agent comes up with a price the agent thinks will move (sell) the property. If the price is considerably below the present actual market value of the home, the bank may not accept it and the short sale may not go through.

As mentioned earlier, with REOs the bank usually has already considered the price and has made a decision to sell the property at that price. Conversely, with short sales the lender has *not* made a decision at what price they will sell it. Deliverability of short sales comes into question at this point.

Buying short sales generally takes several months to complete and can be quite tedious dealing with uncooperative lender(s) and an anxious seller. The seller's lender generally informs the real estate broker of the amount they will accept for the property.

A general time line for the short sale process is as follows:

- 7-10 days after sending the short sale package to the lender, the lender will acknowledge receipt of the package.
- 30-45 days after submitting the short sale package, the lender will find a local broker to perform a Brokers Price Opinion (BPO).
- 2-3 weeks after the BPO is completed, the lender will review and approve or disapprove the terms of the short sale. If the loan was previously sold to an investor, the investor must approve the terms of the short sale. The investor is usually motivated to recoup as much money as possible.
- Approval of the short sale may be name specific to one buyer or a general approval that can be used by anyone. As lenders move through a downward-trending buyers' market, they generally become more efficient in handling short sales and more of their approvals tend to become non-name specific and can be sold to anyone. A real estate buyer may be able to obtain a good deal if the buyer can close fairly quickly on an "approved" short sale.

> **Short Sale:** When the loan balance is greater than the value of the home, the borrower may ask the lender to voluntarily take a loss before the trustee's sale.

If there is more than one loan existing on the property, the short sale may not go through at all. This is especially true if the lender on the second loan (e.g., junior lien holder) is different than the lender on the first loan. The junior loan holder may not be willing to accept a small amount of money to voluntarily release the loan and complete the short sale.

Of course, the lender on the second loan may receive nothing if the property goes into foreclosure. It becomes a negotiation among all the parties involved, which is why a good short sale negotiator is worth their weight in gold during the short sale process.

Some advantages to the homeowner regarding a short sale are:

- Seller is in control during the short sale process.
- There may not be a "foreclosure" on the seller's credit report when a short sale is used. Foreclosures may need to be disclosed on future employment and loan applications, short sales may be able to escape this requirement.
- The seller may not be required to be late on loan payments; however, many lenders require the seller to be delinquent or at least have a "hardship" prior to allowing a short sale. This can generally be:
  - Property underwater
  - Adjustable Rate Loan (ARM) adjustment
  - Unexpected major home maintenance expenses (sewer line breaks, etc.)
  - Unemployment/Loss of second income
  - Job demotion/Pay cut
  - Death/Death in the family
  - Divorce
  - Illness/Medical emergency
  - Excessive debt obligations/Bankruptcy (Chapter 7 liquidation or Chapter 13 restructuring)

In short, a hardship could cause a 30% or more drop in a seller's credit score. The seller may not be able to purchase another home for three to five years in the future. This time requirement tends to change over time, so a short sale seller should consult a lender to determine the loan underwriting guidelines for conventional and FHA loans at the time.

e. Bank Owned Real Estate: Real Estate Owned (REOs)

Real Estate Owned (REO): Occurs when a lender receives a property through a trustee's sale.

If there are no bids above the starting bid price set by the lender at a trustee's sale, the lender will generally receive the property as a **"Real Estate Owned"** or **REO** property. Lenders are not required to pay the amount to the trustee because the lender has already paid the money when the loan was made. Lenders are usually motivated to sell REOs to recoup as much money as possible from the sale of the property. This is especially true during downward-trending buyers' markets.

Lenders, however, do not want to flood the surrounding real estate sales market with REO properties and cause market values to decline even further. For this reason, lenders may trickle REO properties onto the real estate market in an attempt to keep supply at a constant level, thus keeping property prices up by matching the demand for single-family purchases with the supply of listings coming on the market.

Lenders generally make their money originating real estate loans, not as real estate investors holding REO properties in their portfolio. The REO mechanics involved in selling real estate properties being held in a lender's portfolio of non-performing assets is discussed next.

Figure 12.13

1. REO Mechanics

The lender's asset manager may list a property for sale with a real estate broker. The broker is usually required to submit a resume and application to the asset manager, thus ensuring that the real estate broker is experienced and able to effectively handle the sale of REO properties. REO listing agents usually must do a high volume of transactions to be able to make a decent profit. They may have an organization of licensed assistants who do all the busy work during the listing and selling process, while the real estate broker oversees the entire operation. The real estate broker is usually required by the lender to list the property for sale in the local MLS to obtain the maximum exposure for the property.

Single-family homebuyers and investors may favor REO properties because the lender has already made the decision to take a loss on the real estate loan when it is listed for sale with a local real estate broker. REO properties are generally more deliverable than short sale properties because short sale lenders have not made the decision to take a loss on the property.

The pricing decision has already been made by the lender for an REO property and a buyer is usually able to close escrow within thirty to sixty days. Both owner-occupied and non-owner occupied buyers may be drawn to REO properties because of their greater deliverability over short sale properties.

After the REO property has an accepted contract, the buyer generally has seventeen days (this varies) to remove the physical inspection contingency to the contract. This is a common physical inspection time-period seen in purchase contracts provided by the California Association of Realtors or CAR. The actual time period for contingencies to a contract vary at the discretion of the buyer (with seller's approval) and can be longer or shorter depending upon the real estate market and property type.

During an upward-trending sellers' market, multiple offers may occur with every property that comes on the market. This, in turn, may cause smart buyers to tighten up (reduce) contingency periods to entice the seller to take their offer. It should be noted (once again) that commercial properties generally have much longer contingency periods due to their price, size, and complexity.

During the seventeen-day physical inspection contingency period for single-family homes, the buyer should perform due diligence inspections to determine the true physical condition of the property. A home inspection, pest inspection, and other specialized inspections may be used to provide the buyer with critical information used to decide whether to move forward with the purchase or not remove the physical inspection contingency and not purchase the property.

If the property is going to be financed with a loan, the buyer's loan contingency period may be written into the contract, so it coincides with the physical inspection contingency period or until the loan is funded. Smart buyers will negotiate a financing contingency period that is removed when the loan is funded. However, some real estate contracts have allowed the financing contingency to remain in effect only for a period of time before the close of escrow. This tightening of the contingency period tends to benefit the seller more than the buyer, thus providing the buyer with fewer avenues of escape from the purchase contract and/or escrow instructions when nearing the end of the escrow period. If there are multiple offers on a property, a homebuyer may be forced to tighten up the loan contingency period to entice the lender (seller of the property) to accept their offer. However, it really depends on the situation.

If the financing contingency can be removed right up until the loan is funded, the buyer may have the ability to escape the contract right up until the very last moment before funds are wired into escrow. Anything that will cause the borrower's lender to not make the loan (e.g., change in credit score resulting from the buyer buying a new car during the escrow period) may cause loan funding problems from the lender.

The buyer may want to consider noting in the purchase contract that, "The loan contingency will remain in effect until the buyer's loan is funded." The buyer will have more time to arrange financing and it also provides the buyer with a possible way to get out of the deal—especially if a deal-breaker is discovered after the seventeen-day physical inspection contingency period has been removed.

Therefore, savvy real estate homebuyers and investors like to keep their loan contingency in effect until the loan is funded, thereby not risking their earnest money deposit until the buyer or investor's lender has actually funded the loan.

2. Factors to Consider When Purchasing an REO Property

Some factors to consider when purchasing an REO property include: deliverability, good title, title insurance, property condition, potential renovation costs, faster close of escrow, REOs may have a higher purchase price than short sales, less REOs are available on the market, and large real estate investors may buy REOs directly from the lender.

REO properties tend to be more deliverable than short sales. REO properties have already been foreclosed by the lender and the bank is holding them in their REO portfolio. Since lenders are in the business of lending, they do not generally like to become property managers for their own portfolio of foreclosed properties.

Lenders are usually motivated to sell their REO properties to get them off the books and move forward making money—rather than losing it. The lender has made the decision to sell the property and has gone through the BPO (broker price opinion) process and understands the property's market value and potential loss that will be incurred when it is sold.

Consequently, during the early stages of a downward-trending buyers' market, REO properties have more deliverability than short sales. Short sale lenders must go through a similar process and voluntarily decide to take a loss on the sale of the property. Conversely, lenders have already made this decision with REO properties and may be more inclined to sell the property and take their losses.

Purchasing single-family REO properties located in California is similar to a normal real estate transaction and **good title** is usually accomplished through a grant deed and insured by a policy of title insurance. In other states, title may be conveyed using a warranty deed or special warranty deed, however, they are seldom used in California.

When a real estate homebuyer or investor buys a single-family home at a trustee's sale, a **trustee's deed upon sale** may be used to convey title from the trustee to the buyer. Researching existing liens and other encumbrances prior to purchase continues to be a buyer's greatest concern when buying properties through a trustee's sale.

Furthermore, one advantage REO properties have over trustee's sale properties is the ability to obtain a title insurance policy. This is a major advantage for real estate buyers who purchase REO properties. At a trustee's sale, the buyer may need to perform their own research and try to determine if there are outstanding loans, liens, and other encumbrances existing on the property. The title search will usually start with a search of property records on the internet, then proceed to a physical check of records at the county recorder's office, county courthouse, or other locations where recorded documents may exist in the county where the property is located.

In addition, due to the poor condition of many REO properties caused by a lack of maintenance, in some cases REOs may not qualify for FHA insured, VA guaranteed, or even conventional financing. When this occurs, it drastically reduces the number of competing buyers for a property and adversely affects the price. When supply goes up and demand does down, this usually results in a lower purchase price. Most buyers of REOs that

Good Title: Accomplished with a grant deed and title insurance.

Trustee's Deed Upon Sale: Deed used to convey title from the trustee to the buyer.

Figure 12.14

are in poor physical condition will be all-cash real estate investors rather than owner-occupied homebuyers.

Low sale prices impact sales comparables surrounding a subject property and reduce property values. It may become a downward spiral as more distressed properties come on the real estate market and depress values even further—with lenders losing money at every turn. Lenders may lose money through short sales, trustee's sales, and REO properties.

Tales from the Trade

THE STORY OF THE TRIPLE HURT

A real estate investor decided to purchase an REO property from one of the big national lenders. The lender had made a $320,000 loan on the property. Five years later, the real estate investor purchased the REO property for $80,000, so (Hurt #1) the lender lost more than $240,000 on the property. In addition, the real estate investor paid all cash to purchase the REO and (Hurt #2) withdrew funds from the same lender (bank) who was selling the property! So, the lender lost the interest rate margin between the interest rate paid to the real estate investor for money on deposit in the bank and the interest rate charged on one of their real estate loans. As if this weren't bad enough, (Hurt #3) the national lender was not asked to make the new loan on the property. Of course, many REO lenders in the past did not want to make loans on their own REOs—no use placing salt on an open wound and possibly lending good money after bad. Nine years after the investor purchased the REO property, it was worth $275,000.

REOs are usually much faster to close than short sales. The average REO usually requires between 30 and 60 days from the contract date to close of escrow. However, this varies due to many factors out of a buyer's control. The largest obstacle is escrow and title. The escrow officer must arrange all the documents, so the terms and conditions of the escrow have been met.

The title insurer usually investigates the liens and other encumbrances affecting the property and issues a policy of title insurance. The title insurance company may provide one or more updated preliminary title reports as more encumbrances are discovered during the escrow period.

Some lenders and asset managers may "require" a real estate homebuyer or investor to use an escrow company and title insurance company selected by them. Legally, they cannot do this. However, to expedite close of escrow many REO homebuyers and investors will go ahead and use their selected company or companies—since they most likely already have many of the documents needed to close escrow and issue a policy of title insurance. It will probably speed up the closing process as well.

A buyer can use anyone they choose to handle escrow and title services. This can be difficult, however, when a seller receives multiple offers on a property. Buyers generally do not like to negotiate for escrow and title services. Price and other more tangible issues may be a better place to negotiate.

Escrow and title insurance prices are usually fairly uniform throughout California. The quality of the work can be anywhere from awesome to horrible, depending upon the professionalism of the company.

According to the real estate law, the REO lender is generally not required to provide a Real Estate Transfer Disclosure Statement (TDS) for the sale of REO properties. However, the REO lender remains obligated by common law (court cases) to disclose any material facts (facts that would cause the buyer to not buy the property) they are aware of existing in the property. Since most REO lenders have not physically seen or been inside the property, they generally have nothing to disclose to a new buyer.

Real estate agents, however, must make a visual inspection of accessible areas and note their findings. REO properties do not require the TDS, so the agent will usually use the Agent Visual Inspection Disclosure (AVID) to perform the visual inspection.

C. Mortgages

Mortgagor: Borrower for a mortgage.

Mortgagee: Lender for a mortgage.

Mortgages are generally not used in California. California uses deeds of trust (or trust deeds). The **mortgagor** in a mortgage is the borrower and the **mortgagee** is the lender. Foreclosure of mortgages is usually accomplished through the courts.

D. Real Property Sales Contract / Land Contract / Installment Contract

Real Property Sales Contract/Land Contract/Installment Contract: The seller sells the property to a buyer and extends credit to the buyer using a real property sales contract.

Vendor: Seller for a real property sales contract. Holds legal title to the property.

Vendee: Buyer/ borrower for a real property sales contract. Holds equitable title (possession) to the property.

A good example of a **real property sales contract** is when a seller owns the property free and clear without a loan encumbering it. The seller then sells the property to a buyer and the seller extends credit to the buyer using a real property sales contract. When this occurs, the seller becomes the **vendor** (holds legal title to the property) and the buyer becomes the **vendee** (owns equitable title, which is possession of the property). The vendee makes monthly payments to the vendor, and when the property has been paid off, the vendor uses a grant deed to transfer legal title to the vendee. This eliminates the land contract and the vendee now owns the property free and clear without any loans against it.

6. Loan Types

Loan types include hard money loans, purchase money loans, conventional loans, government loans, and construction loans.

Loan Types

TYPE	DESCRIPTION
Hard Money	• Usually secured by real estate and given to a third party to obtain a cash loan • Generally have very high interest rates, many discount points, and low LTV ratios • No restrictions regarding how the loan will be used
Purchase Money	• A loan made to purchase a property
Conventional	• Loans made by institutional lenders (e.g., commercial banks and savings banks) that do not have government insurance or guarantees • Usually comfortable making up to 80% LTV loans
Government	• FHA Insured • VA Guaranteed • CalVet • CalHFA • USDA
Construction	• A loan used during the construction of a property

Figure 12.15

A. Hard Money Loans

A **hard money loan** is usually secured by real estate and given to a third party to obtain a cash loan. They generally have very high interest rates, many discount points, and low loan-to-value ratios. The borrower has no restrictions regarding how the loan will be used. When a lender charges an interest rate that is higher than allowed by law, this is called **usury**.

B. Purchase Money Loans

A **purchase money loan** is a loan made to purchase a property. Refinances are not purchase money loans. A purchase money transaction may be a conventional loan, government insured or guaranteed, seller-carry back loan, or a loan from a private individual lender.

Hard Money Loan: Usually secured by real estate and given to a third party to obtain a cash loan.

Usury: When a lender charges an interest rate that is higher than allowed by law.

Purchase Money Loan: A loan used to purchase real property.

As mentioned earlier, purchase money loans are loans that are used to purchase a property. So, when a homebuyer uses a loan to purchase a home, this is called a purchase money loan. In contrast, non-purchase money loans are loans that are not used to purchase a property. An example of a non-purchase money loan is when a homeowner refinances an existing loan securing a parcel of real property. The refinance replaces an existing loan with a new one, with usually a lower interest rate.

C. Conventional Loans

Conventional Loan: Loans made by institutional lenders such as commercial banks and savings banks that do not have government insurance or guarantees.

Loans made by institutional lenders (e.g., commercial banks and savings banks) that do *not* have government insurance or guarantees are considered **conventional loans**.

Conventional lenders are usually comfortable making up to 80% loan-to-value (LTV) loans. However, since an 80% LTV loan is not insured or guaranteed by the government, a conventional lender is usually not comfortable making a loan above this amount (i.e., above an 80% LTV). For this reason, private mortgage insurance is commonly used to protect conventional lenders who makes loans above 80% LTV.

D. Government Loans

Federal Housing Administration (FHA) Loan: High loan-to-value government-insured loans.

Department of Veteran's Affairs (VA) Loan: High loan-to-value government-guaranteed loans for veterans.

Government loans include FHA insured loans, VA guaranteed loans, CalVet loans, CalHFA loans, and USDA loans.

(1) Federal Housing Administration Loans

The **Federal Housing Administration (FHA)** is under the U.S. Department of Housing and Urban Development (HUD). FHA insures loans made by approved lenders and charges mutual mortgage insurance (MMI or MIP) to pay the mortgage insurance for these high loan-to-value loans. Therefore, the main purpose of FHA is to promote homeownership by insuring home loans.

(2) Department of Veterans Affairs (VA) Loans

Veteran's Administration (VA) loans are under the U.S. Department of Veterans Affairs. The VA guarantees loans made by approved lenders, and one of the advantages to veterans who qualify for a VA guaranteed loan is no money down 100% financing.

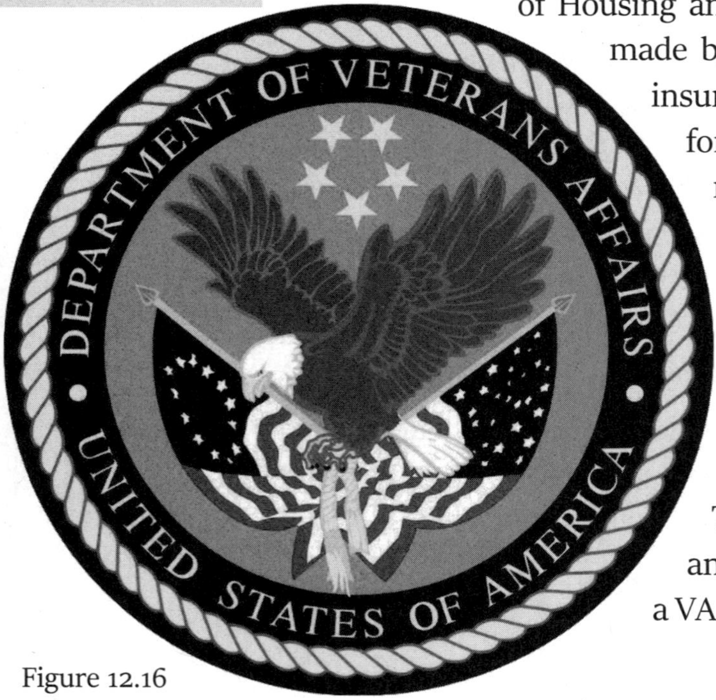

Figure 12.16

(3) California Veterans Farm and Home Purchase Program (CalVet) Loans

In recognition of veterans' sacrifice and service, the California legislature enacted the **California Veterans Farm and Home Purchase Program (CalVet)** in 1921. This act provides low-cost, low-interest financing for eligible veterans who purchase a home, farm, or mobile home as a primary residence in California.

CalVet purchases the home that is selected by the veteran and then sets up a real property sales contract (land contract) for repayment of the loan. CalVet is the vendor (holds legal title) and the veteran is the vendee (holds equitable title, which is possession). CalVet always has an adjustable interest rate and may use a variable amortization period. Therefore, CalVet loans may experience interest rates that increase or decrease during the term of the loan.

When a buyer buys a home with a CalVet loan, the seller of the home executes a grant deed in favor of the California Department of Veterans Affairs (CalVet). CalVet collects funds through issuing bonds and uses the funds to purchase the home. A real property sales contract is a purchase contract and security device (all in one) between CalVet and the veteran. Therefore, legal title to a CalVet home is in the name of the Department of Veteran's Affairs (CalVet) until it is paid off in full, then it will be transferred into the name of the veteran through a grant deed.

> California Veterans Farm and Home Purchase Program (CalVet) Loan: Provides low-cost, low-interest financing for eligible veterans who purchase a home, farm, or mobile home as a primary residence in California.

(4) California Housing Finance Agency (CalHFA) Loans

For more than 40 years, the **California Housing Finance Agency (CalHFA)** has supported the needs of renters and homebuyers by providing financing and programs so that low to moderate income Californians have a place to call home. Established in 1975, CalHFA was chartered as the state's affordable housing lender.

The Agency's Multifamily Division finances affordable rental housing through partnerships with jurisdictions, developers and more, while its Single-Family Division provides first mortgage loans and down payment assistance to first-time homebuyers. CalHFA is a completely self-supporting state agency, and its bonds are repaid by revenues generated through mortgage loans, not taxpayer dollars.

> California Housing Finance Agency (CalHFA) Loan: Supports the needs of renters and homebuyers by providing financing and programs so that low to moderate income Californians can buy a home.

(5) U.S. Department of Agriculture (USDA) – Farmers Home Administration

The **U.S. Department of Agriculture (USDA)** is called the Farmers Home Administration has primary responsibility for providing financial assistance to farmers and others living in rural areas where financing is not available on reasonable terms from private sources.

> U.S. Department of Agriculture (USDA) Loan: Providing financial assistance to farmers and others living in rural areas where financing is not available on reasonable terms from private sources.

E. Construction Loans

Construction Loan: A loan used during construction of a property.

A **construction loan** (also called an interim loan or loan for obligatory advances) is a loan used during the construction of a property. It is usually short-term and is usually replaced after completion of the project with a permanent, long-term take-out loan.

Figure 12.17 Property Construction

(1) Take-Out Loans

Take-Out Loan: Long-term financing used after a home has been built on a property.

A **take-out loan** is a long-term loan taken out after construction of a property. It is usually a conventional loan with a long-term amortization schedule.

(2) Standby Loans

Standby Loan: A commitment from a lender to provide funds if needed by the borrower.

When a buyer receives a commitment from a lender to provide funds if needed by the buyer, this is called a **standby loan**. In other words, it is an agreement by a lender to provide a loan upon the demand of a borrower.

7. Types of Lenders in the Primary Mortgage Market

Primary Mortgage Market: Lenders that make loans to borrowers.

A. Federal Savings and Loan Associations (Federal Savings Banks)

Federal Savings and Loan Associations (Federal Savings Banks) have been a major source of loans for the single-family residential lending market. Therefore, for financing the purchase of residential properties, a principal lender of money is federal savings and loan associations (federal savings banks).

B. Insurance Companies

Insurance companies have traditionally made very large multi-million-dollar loans. They may require the assistance of mortgage companies to place the loans.

C. Private Individual Lenders

A private individual lender is a private person who extends credit to a borrower. Private Individual lenders are a primary source of secondary financing (second trust deeds).

D. Institutional Lenders

Institutional lenders include commercial banks, insurance companies, and savings banks. Mortgage bankers and mortgage brokers are *not* considered institutional lenders.

E. Mortgage Companies

(1) Mortgage Bankers

Mortgage bankers loan their own funds and participate directly in the secondary mortgage market.

> **Mortgage Bankers:** Lenders that loan their own funds and sell them on the secondary mortgage market.

(2) Mortgage Brokers

Mortgage brokers do *not* loan their own funds but sell originated loans to mortgage bankers and other institutional lenders who operate on the secondary mortgage market.

> **Mortgage Brokers:** Lenders that do not loan their own funds but sell originated loans to lenders that operate on the secondary mortgage market.

8. Secondary Mortgage Market

Most lenders do not want to tie up their money for a long period time and incur the interest rate risk inherent with market interest rate fluctuations. In other words, lenders do not want to make a long-term fixed rate loan at (for example) 4% interest, when interest rates may increase in the future. If this happens, the lender will be collecting interest on a 4% loan when the lender could be collecting a significantly higher interest rate (e.g., 8%) on loans that are originated in the future. For this reason, lenders tend to enjoy making short-term rather than long-term loans.

In response to this, the **secondary mortgage market** was instituted in the 1930s to promote home ownership. Long-term 30-year amortized loans were a product of Franklin Delano Roosevelt's new deal. Lenders made loans up to 30-years in length and then, rather than holding them for 30 years, sold them to lenders that operated on the secondary mortgage market.

> **Secondary Mortgage Market:** Primary market lenders sell their loans to lenders that operate on the secondary mortgage market.

A. Types of Lenders in the Secondary Mortgage Market

Secondary market lenders include the Federal National Mortgage Association (FNMA, called Fannie Mae), Federal Home Loan Mortgage Corporation (FHLMC, called Freddie Mac), Government National Mortgage Corporation (GNMA, called Ginnie Mae), and Farmer Mac.

Secondary Mortgage Market

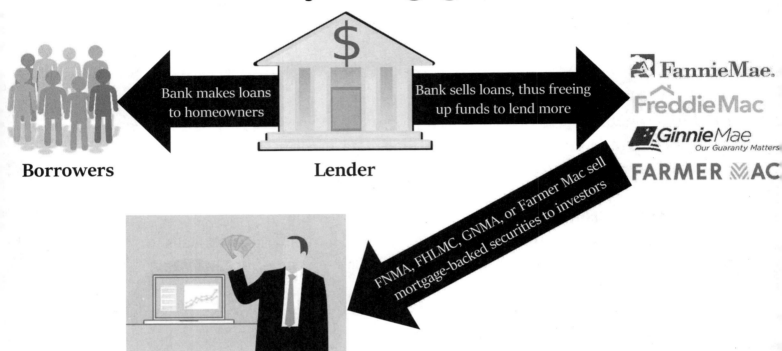

Figure 12.18 Secondary Mortgage Market Illustration

Secondary market lenders purchase pools of mortgages from primary mortgage market lenders (who make loans directly to borrowers), securitize them through the issuance of mortgage-backed securities (securities that are collateralized by home loans and traded on the stock exchanges), and then sell these securities to investors all over the world. This allows cash poor areas of the U.S. to have the same access to low-interest rate, long-term mortgage loans as do cash-rich areas.

Institutional lenders and mortgage bankers originate loans in the primary mortgage market and then sell them on the secondary market. Prior to selling the loans, primary mortgage market lenders will warehouse (hold onto) the loans for a period of time to season them prior to sale in the secondary mortgage market. After the loans have been seasoned, which means they have a history of prompt loan payments, they are sold to such entities as Fannie Mae, Freddie Mac, Ginnie Mae, and Farmer Mac on the secondary mortgage market.

(1) Federal National Mortgage Association (FNMA or Fannie Mae)

Fannie Mae was established in 1938 to expand the secondary mortgage market through the securitization of mortgage loans in the form of mortgage-backed securities (MBS). According to Fannie Mae, "Fannie Mae serves the people who house America. We are a leading source of financing for mortgage lenders, providing access to affordable mortgage financing in all markets at all times. Our financing makes sustainable homeownership and workforce rental housing a reality for millions of Americans. We also help make possible the popular 30-year, fixed-rate mortgage, which provides homeowners with stable, predictable mortgage payments over the life of the loan. Our tools and resources help homebuyers, homeowners, and renters understand their housing options."

Fannie Mae: Lender that operates on the secondary mortgage market.

(2) Federal Home Loan Mortgage Corporation (FHLMC or Freddie Mac)

Freddie Mac was chartered by Congress in 1970 to keep money flowing to mortgage lenders in support of homeownership and rental housing. Freddie Mac's mission is to provide liquidity, stability and affordability to the U.S. housing market. Freddie Mac purchases loans on the secondary market in a very similar fashion to Fannie Mae. For this reason, Fannie Mae and Freddie Mac have been merged into one entity that will issue a common security called the Uniform Mortgage-Backed Security (UMBS). The UMBS will be issued through a joint venture between Fannie Mae and Freddie Mac called Common Securitization Solutions (CSS).

(3) Government National Mortgage Association (GNMA or Ginnie Mae)

The Government National Mortgage Association (GNMA), also known as "Ginnie Mae," guarantees securities backed by pools of mortgages. Securities holders receive pass-throughs of principal and interest payments from the pool. GNMA guarantees that monthly payments will be made on time.

(4) Farmer Mac

Farmer Mac was originated under the Agricultural and Lending Act of 1987. According to Farmer Mac, "Farmer Mac is a vital part of the agricultural credit markets and was created to increase access to and reduce the cost of capital for the benefit of American agriculture and rural communities. As the nation's premier secondary market for agricultural credit, we provide financial solutions to a broad spectrum of the agricultural community, including agricultural lenders, agribusinesses, and other institutions that can benefit from access to flexible, low-cost financing and risk management tools. Farmer Mac's customers benefit from our low cost of funds, low overhead costs, and high operational efficiency. In fact, we are often able to provide the lowest cost of borrowing to agricultural and rural borrowers. For more than a quarter-century, Farmer Mac has been delivering the capital and commitment rural America deserves."

B. Secondary Mortgage Market Lending Terms
(1) Loan Correspondents and Loan Portfolio

Some mortgage companies may act as **loan correspondents** when they institute loans and then sell them to institutional lenders such as insurance companies, commercial banks, and savings banks who either hold the loans in their own **loan portfolio** (buy the loans with depositor's money and hold them while collecting interest payments) or sell them on the secondary mortgage market.

Mortgage companies that act as loan correspondents usually receive a loan brokerage commission when the loan is funded, and they can also service the loans for a fee by collecting the debt service payments for the lender, along with property taxes and property insurance impounds from borrowers and paying them as they become due.

(2) Mortgage Yield

Mortgage yield is the return an investor will receive from a loan. It includes loan origination fees and other fees charged by a lender to specifically increase their yield. Mortgage yield is best described as the effective interest return obtained from a first trust deed by an investor.

(3) Portfolio Risk Management

When a lender looks at their entire loan portfolio and tries to minimize the risks inherent in non-performing loans, this is called portfolio risk management. A lender considers liquidity (the loan can be easily sold on the secondary mortgage market), loan loss reserves (money held by the lender to cover non-performing loans), and diversification (not too many loans made in one property type or to one borrower) when considering portfolio risk management.

(4) Borrower Qualification

Investors in the secondary mortgage market require some way to measure the default risk of loans they are purchasing. For this reason, they have instituted loan qualification criteria that primary lenders must follow to insure their loans will be purchased on the secondary mortgage market. Two of these criteria are debt-income ratio and liquidity.

Loan Correspondent: A lender that makes loans and sells them to lenders that operate on the secondary mortgage market.

Loan Portfolio: The loans a lender keeps and continues to collect interest.

Mortgage Yield: The return an investor will receive from a loan.

a. Debt-Income Ratio

Debt-income ratio is defined as either: Monthly Principal + Interest divided by the borrower's gross monthly income; or Monthly Principal + Interest + Taxes + Insurance + Homeowner Association Dues + PMI + other recurring costs divided by gross monthly income. Thus, lenders are referring to a loan qualifying tool when they mention "debt-income ratio."

b. Liquidity (Relating to Borrower Qualification)

The **liquidity** of a borrower is generally determined by a loan officer in considering current assets to current liabilities. It refers to how many assets can be easily converted into cash and used to purchase a property or pay debt service on a loan.

(5) Loan Commitment

The real estate loan application correlates the characteristics of the borrower, the loan amount, and the property to help lenders arrive at a **loan commitment**.

> **Debt-Income Ratio:** Monthly Principal + Interest divided by the borrower's gross monthly income; or Monthly Principal + Interest + Taxes + Insurance + Homeowner Association Dues + PMI + other recurring costs divided by gross monthly income.
>
> **Liquidity:** The ability of a borrower to convert assets into cash.
>
> **Loan Commitment:** A lender makes a formal commitment to make a loan to a borrower.

9. Loan Estimate and Closing Disclosure

A. Overview

The Dodd-Frank Wall Street Reform and Consumer Protection Act (Dodd-Frank Act) directed the Bureau of Consumer Financial Protection (Bureau) to publish rules and forms that combine certain disclosures that consumers receive in connection with applying for and closing on a mortgage loan under the Truth in Lending Act and the Real Estate Settlement Procedures Act.

The Bureau is amending Regulation X (Real Estate Settlement Procedures Act) and Regulation Z (Truth in Lending) to establish new disclosure requirements and forms in Regulation Z for most closed-end consumer credit transactions—which include most real estate home loans, except it does not apply to home equity lines of credit, reverse mortgages, or mortgages secured by a mobile home or by a dwelling that is not attached to real property.

B. Background

For more than 30 years, Federal law has required lenders to provide two different disclosure forms to consumers applying for a mortgage. The law also has generally required two different forms at or shortly before closing on a loan.

Two different Federal agencies developed these forms separately, under two Federal statutes: Truth in Lending Act (TILA) and Real Estate Settlement Procedures Act of 1974 (RESPA).

The information on these forms was overlapping and the language inconsistent. Not surprisingly, consumers often found the forms confusing. It is also not surprising that lenders and settlement agents found the forms burdensome to provide and explain. In response to this, the Bureau requires the use of two new forms: Loan Estimate and Closing Disclosures.

C. Loan Estimate

The first new form (the **Loan Estimate**) is designed to provide disclosures that will help consumers to understand the key features, costs, and risks of the mortgage for which they are applying. This form must be provided to consumers within three business days after they submit a loan application. (The Loan Estimate form replaces two current Federal forms. It replaces the Good Faith Estimate designed by the Department of Housing and Urban Development (HUD) under RESPA and the "early" Truth in Lending disclosure designed by the Board of Governors of the Federal Reserve System under TILA.)

Recognizing that consumers may work more closely with a mortgage broker, either a mortgage broker or creditor is required to provide the Loan Estimate form upon receipt of an application by the mortgage broker. However, even if the mortgage broker provides the Loan Estimate, the creditor remains responsible for complying with all requirements concerning provision of the form.

The creditor or mortgage broker must give the form to the consumer no later than three business days after the consumer applies for a mortgage loan. An "application" consists of the consumer's name, income, social security number to obtain a credit report, the property address, an estimate of the value of the property, and the mortgage loan amount sought.

The creditor generally cannot charge consumers any fees until after the consumers have been given the Loan Estimate form and the consumers have communicated their intent to proceed with the transaction.

There is an exception that allows creditors to charge fees to obtain consumers' credit reports. Creditors and other persons may provide consumers with written estimates prior to application. The rule requires that any such written estimates contain a disclaimer to prevent confusion with the Loan Estimate form. This disclaimer is required for advertisements as well.

D. Closing Disclosure

The second form (the **Closing Disclosure**) is designed to provide disclosures that will be helpful to consumers in understanding all the costs of the transaction. This form must be provided to consumers at least three business days before they close on the loan.

The forms use clear language and design to make it easier for consumers to locate key information, such as interest rate, monthly payments, and costs to close the loan. The forms also provide more information to help consumers decide whether they can afford the loan and to compare the costs of different loan offers, including the cost of the loans over time. The final rule applies to most closed-end consumer mortgages but does not apply to loans made by a creditor that makes five or fewer mortgages in a year.

The Closing Disclosure form replaces the HUD-1 (Uniform Settlement Statement), which was designed by HUD under RESPA. It also replaces the revised Truth in Lending disclosure designed by the Board under TILA.

The Closing Disclosure form contains additional disclosures required by the Dodd-Frank Act and a detailed accounting of the settlement transaction. The creditor must give the Closing Disclosure form to consumers so that they receive it at least three business days before the consumer closes on the loan.

If the creditor makes certain significant changes between the time the Closing Disclosure form is given and the closing – specifically, if the creditor:

- Makes changes to the APR above 1/8 of a percent for most loans (and 1/4 of a percent for loans with irregular payments or periods),
- Changes the loan product, or
- Adds a prepayment penalty to the loan,

then the consumer must be provided a new form and an additional three business day waiting period after receipt of the new form.

This requirement will provide the important protection to consumers of an additional three-day waiting period for these significant changes but will not cause closing delays for less significant costs that may frequently change.

Charges for the following services cannot be increased:

- the creditor's or mortgage broker's charges for its own services;
- charges for services provided by an affiliate of the creditor or mortgage broker; and
- charges for services for which the creditor or mortgage broker does not permit the consumer to shop.

Charges for other services can increase, but generally not by more than 10 percent, unless an exception applies. Exceptions include, for example, situations when:

- the consumer asks for a change,
- the consumer chooses a service provider that was not identified by the creditor,
- information provided at application was inaccurate or becomes inaccurate, or

- the Loan Estimate expires

When an exception applies, the creditor generally must provide an updated Loan Estimate form within three business days.

10. Equal Credit Opportunity Act (ECOA)

The Equal Credit Opportunity Act (ECOA) became effective on October 28, 1975 and aims to give individuals an equal opportunity to apply for loans from financial institutions and other organizations. It prohibits discrimination on the basis of race, color, religion, national origin, sex, marital status, or on the grounds of receipt of income from a public assistance program. In other words, lenders cannot discriminate against individuals upon factors that do not deal with their creditworthiness.

The law also requires that a lender/creditor that denies an application for credit must provide the applicant with a statement of reasons or a written notification of the applicant's right to obtain a statement of reasons.

California state law regulates the issuance of consumer credit reports, access by the consumer to such reports, and the obligations of credit reporting agencies. Also, users of consumer credit reports are subject to the requirements of California state law and must provide notice to the consumer when credit is denied.

11. U.S.A. Patriot Act

U.S.A. Patriot Act: A loan applicant is to be identified to determine if there exists an association with terrorism, narcotics trafficking and/or money laundering.

According the U.S. Department of Treasury regarding the **U.S.A. Patriot Act**, "An applicant is to be identified to determine if there exists an association with terrorism, narcotics trafficking and/or money laundering. This is accomplished by utilizing the lists published by the Office of Foreign Asset Control.

"The information regarding the persons or nation-states that identify with such an association is known as the U.S. Treasury Department's Specially Designated Nationals (SDN) and Blocked Persons list. This list also includes nation-states that have been placed on non-favored nation status. If the applicant is either specifically named or is from one of the nation-states appearing on the list, the financial institution (depository institution) or licensed creditor/lender, including MLB/MLO, cannot proceed with a loan application or with other financial services."

According to DRE, "The Office of Foreign Assets Control (OFAC) administers a series of laws that impose economic sanctions against hostile targets to further U.S. foreign policy and national security objectives. The list identifies 'pariah' countries, as well as certain groups, such as narcotics traffickers and terrorists, who threaten the security, economy, and safety of the United States and its citizens."

Chapter Twelve Summary

Financing drives deals. Lenders use the property itself as collateral for a loan they have agreed to make on a specific property. In California, this is normally accomplished using a promissory note and deed of trust. If the borrower does not pay scheduled loan interest payments, the lender may be able to foreclose the loan through the power of sale provision in the deed of trust. Lenders many times require a significant down payment before they will fund a loan. Private mortgage insurance and mutual mortgage insurance can be used to reduce the amount of down payment required by lenders.

Loans can be paid off over the life of the loan using an amortization schedule for both fixed rate and adjustable rate loans. If a borrower would like to reduce the interest rate on their loan, they usually can pay discount points that are based on a percentage of the loan amount. Most real estate contracts have a financing contingency that allows the buyer to not go forward with the transaction if they cannot qualify for a loan to purchase the property. For this reason, many sellers require a buyer to be preapproved by a lender prior to accepting an offer from them. The chapter also looks at seller financing, loan assumptions, the secondary mortgage market, loan origination, and loan documents.

Chapter Twelve Quiz

1. Real estate loans are normally:
(A) Compound interest
(B) Simple interest
(C) Negative interest
(D) Effective interest

2. What type of loan is used when a borrower only has a 10% down payment and does not want to pay for private mortgage insurance (PMI)?
(A) Conventional loan
(B) FHA insured loan
(C) VA guaranteed loan
(D) 80-10-10 loan

3. What is used to determine the monthly payment of a loan?
(A) Amortization tables
(B) Appraisal cost
(C) Title insurance cost
(D) Escrow cost

4. Which of the following is an index that is commonly used with adjustable rate loans?
(A) Monthly Treasuries Average (MTA)
(B) Federal Home Loan Bank Board's 11th District Cost of Funds Index
(C) London Inter-Bank Offered Rate (LIBOR)
(D) All of the above are correct

5. A beneficiary is a:
(A) borrower
(B) lender
(C) third party
(D) mortgagor

6. A(n) _____ is a loan that allows additional borrowing at a later date.
(A) conventional loan
(B) FHA insured loan
(C) open-end mortgage
(D) jumbo loan

7. When a lender sells a promissory note (loan) for less than the unpaid balance this is called:
(A) discounting the note
(B) a capital loss
(C) an operating loss
(D) Both (B) and (C) are correct

8. An involuntary foreclosure in California usually has the lender foreclosing through a:
(A) judicial foreclosure
(B) trustee's sale
(C) quiet title action
(D) quitclaim deed

9. The seller when using a real property sales contract is called the:
(A) vendor
(B) vendee
(C) quitor
(D) quitee

10. Government loans include:
(A) FHA insured loans
(B) VA guaranteed loans
(C) Both (A) and (B) are correct
(D) Neither (A) nor (B) is correct

Answers: 1. B, 2. D, 3. A, 4. D, 5. B, 6. C, 7. A, 8. B, 9. A, 10. C

Please use this space for notes.

Robert Grandinetti

"I had a house where a guy showed up with envelopes of cash for the down payment. I was like, 'Well, that's not how it works at all.'"

13

Chapter
THIRTEEN

Taking Title to Real Property and Close of Escrow

Most real properties in California use a grant deed to convey legal title from the seller to the buyer. Understanding how this process occurs is important to the real estate brokerage business and real estate agents must have a working knowledge of title transfer in California. In addition, when listing and selling real property it is important for real estate agents to understand how their clients are hold title to the real property. Whether they hold title in severalty, tenancy in common, joint tenancy, or any of the other ways of holding title to real property may affect the entire transaction. Real estate agents, however, should be careful not to give clients advice regarding how to take title to real property. Clients should consult a real estate attorney and tax advisor (such as a Certified Public Accountant or CPA) prior to any real estate endeavor. The reason real estate agents do not provide assistance to their client when taking title to real property is because the agent may be guilty of practicing law, providing tax advice, or possibly causing discrimination against the client.

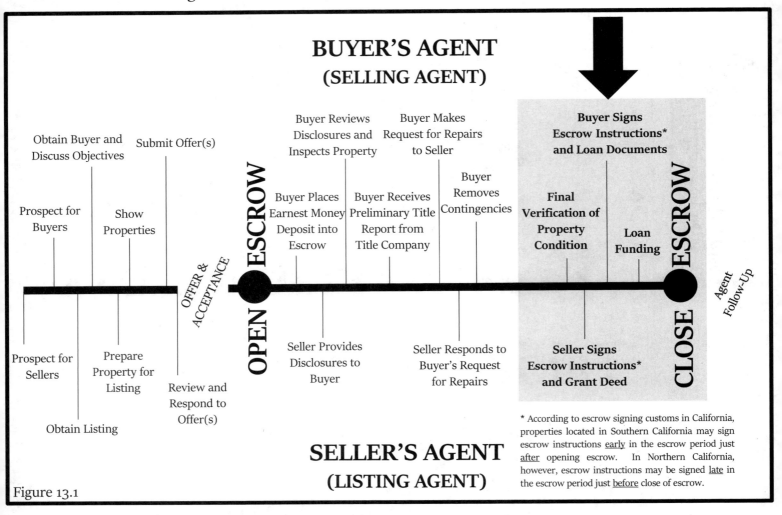

BUYER'S AGENT
(SELLING AGENT)

Obtain Buyer and
Discuss Objectives

Submit Offer(s)

Buyer Reviews
Disclosures and
Inspects Property

Buyer Makes
Request for Repairs
to Seller

Buyer Signs
Escrow Instructions*
and Loan Documents

Prospect for
Buyers

Show
Properties

Buyer Places
Earnest Money
Deposit into
Escrow

Buyer Receives
Preliminary Title
Report from
Title Company

Buyer
Removes
Contingencies

Final
Verification of
Property
Condition

Loan
Funding

OFFER &
ACCEPTANCE

OPEN ESCROW

CLOSE ESCROW

Agent
Follow-Up

Prospect for
Sellers

Prepare
Property for
Listing

Review and
Respond to
Offer(s)

Seller Provides
Disclosures to
Buyer

Seller Responds to
Buyer's Request
for Repairs

Seller Signs
Escrow Instructions*
and Grant Deed

Obtain Listing

SELLER'S AGENT
(LISTING AGENT)

* According to escrow signing customs in California, properties located in Southern California may sign escrow instructions early in the escrow period just after opening escrow. In Northern California, however, escrow instructions may be signed late in the escrow period just before close of escrow.

Figure 13.1

1. Final Verification of Condition: Walk-Thru Inspection

Just prior to close of escrow, the buyer will make a walk-thru inspection that is a final verification of condition for the property being purchased. The walk-thru inspection is used to verify nothing has changed with the property being purchase (e.g., house burned to the ground). It is also used by the buyer, if the seller agreed to repair certain items during the escrow period using a Request for Repairs Addendum, to verify the agreed upon work has been completed by the seller.

The buyer will usually complete a home inspection of the property during the physical inspection contingency period in the purchase agreement. As a result of this inspection, the buyer may ask the seller to repair certain items in the property. If the seller agrees to make repairs to the requested items, then the buyer will usually verify the repairs have been completed during the buyer's walk-thru inspection that occurs just prior to close of escrow. If the repairs have not be completed by the time of the buyer's walk-thru inspection, the buyer will be required to inform the seller of this fact and either wait for the seller to make the repairs or ask the seller to credit the buyer in escrow for the estimated amount needed to make the repairs. The escrow officer may decide to withhold 1.5 to 2 times the amount of the repairs from the seller's proceeds and then pay for the repairs out of these withheld funds after close of escrow. It is generally better to have the repairs completed by the seller *prior* to close of escrow, than to obtain a credit from the seller because of the uncertainty that the credited funds will be enough to complete the repairs after close of escrow.

For example, during the walk-thru inspection the buyer discovers several repairs that have not been completed. The agent should inform the seller about the uncompleted repairs before close of escrow (and ask for them to be repaired) or credit the buyer (from the seller's proceeds and with the seller's consent) for the repairs in escrow.

In another example, the day before escrow closes the buyer asks for the gate to be repaired. If the seller agrees to repair the gate but does not have time to do so, the seller may have escrow credit funds to the buyer for the repairs.

In yet another example, prior to close of escrow the buyer would like to make repairs to the property, the agent should obtain the seller's written approval before the buyer makes the repairs. A buyer making repairs prior to close of escrow is generally a very bad idea. If escrow does not close, the buyer could lose the money spent on the repairs.

2. Closing Costs

Closing costs are the costs incurred by the buyer and seller in the escrow closing process. There are many closing costs associated with a real estate transaction. The buyer will become aware of them when the loan estimate is delivered by the lender to the buyer within three business days of applying for a loan to purchase the property. The seller will become aware of the seller's closing costs when the listing agent provides an estimated seller proceeds sheet at the time the property is listed and/or when an offer to purchase the property has been received. Closing costs are usually grouped into recurring and non-recurring closing costs.

Figure 13.2

A. Recurring Closing Costs vs. Non-Recurring Closing Costs

Recurring closing costs occur more than once. Examples include property taxes and homeowner's insurance. In contrast, non-recurring closing costs occur only once. Examples include escrow and title insurance fees. The following are some common closing costs.

B. Common Lender-Related and Non-Lender-Related Closing Costs

(1) Loan Origination Fee

Real estate transactions incorporating a new loan may contain a **loan origination fee** that can be 1% or more of the loan amount. In other words, one percent (1%) of the loan amount is paid to a loan originator as a commission for making the loan. Loans originated by mortgage brokers and mortgage bankers commonly contain loan origination fees; however, some institutional lenders do not charge a loan origination fee because their higher loan interest rates compensate for this fact.

(2) Discount Points

If a buyer would like to reduce the interest rate on a loan the buyer is using to purchase a home, the lender may allow the buyer to reduce the loan interest rate by paying up-front money to the lender. This up-front money is called discount points or "points."

For example, a buyer can pay a lender one percent (1%) of the loan amount (one discount point) for every one-eighth of one-percent (1/8%) reduction in the loan interest rate.

In contrast, if a buyer is willing to pay a slightly *higher* interest rate for the loan being used to purchase the property, the lender is willing to pay all the buyer's closing costs–along with the mortgage broker's commission for originating the loan. The "points" received from the lender are called yield spread or rebate pricing. Therefore, funds received from the lender can be used to pay the borrower's closing costs.

(3) Appraisal Fee

Most lenders require an independent appraisal performed on a property prior to purchase. The mortgage broker usually selects a licensed real estate appraiser who is approved by the lender that will be funding the loan. Single-family home appraisals usually cost approximately $475 or more, depending on the type, size, and price of the property. Commercial narrative appraisals can cost several thousand dollars.

(4) Credit Report Cost

Lenders usually require a prospective borrower's credit score to help determine the person's attitude toward debt. Loan underwriters place a considerable amount of emphasis on a buyer's attitude toward past debt obligations. Accordingly, a borrower's credit score can be used to help determine default risk and whether it is a good idea to make a loan to a particular borrower. Borrowers typically pay a lender to "pull" their credit report.

(5) Tax Service Fee

Lenders generally require a borrower to provide a tax service to keep track of property taxes that become due. A tax service protects a lender's interest in a property and usually costs a one-time charge of $55-$100.

(6) Private Mortgage Insurance (PMI)

Lenders usually require private mortgage insurance (PMI) for high loan-to-value (LTV) loans. These are loans that are over 80% LTV and may require up-front fees in addition to annual renewal premiums.

(7) Mortgage Insurance Premium (MIP)

Mortgage Insurance Premium, also called MIP is the mortgage insurance paid for FHA insured loans. MIP can be paid up-front or financed with the loan. FHA also charges a monthly MIP premium. MIP is also called Mutual Mortgage Insurance (MMI).

(8) Veterans Administration (VA) Funding Fee

The Department of Veterans Affairs, also called VA, guarantees loans made by approved lenders. VA loans generally require a funding fee of between one to three percent (1%-3%) of the loan amount to guarantee a VA loan. Some of their loans allow a veteran to place no money down (100% financing). A VA appraiser must appraise the property for at least the sale price (Certificate of Reasonable Value or CRV) or the veteran may terminate the transaction without penalty.

> **VA Funding Fee:** Fee charged by the VA to guarantee a VA loan.

(9) County Transfer Tax

County transfer tax is also called a **documentary transfer tax**. This tax is decided by the county where the property is located. The maximum amount is

> **County Transfer Tax:** $.55 per $500 tax charged by county tax assessor to transfer real property in the county. Charged on new money in the transaction, not loan assumptions.

$.55 per $500 (or $1.10 per $1,000) of all new money coming into a transaction. Cash and new loans are taxed, loan assumptions are not taxed.

Documentary Transfer Tax Example

Seller sells a property for $200,000. An existing $100,000 loan is assumed by the buyer. The buyer obtains a $50,000 second trust deed from an outside lender and pays $50,000 cash. The documentary transfer tax is calculated:

~~$100,000~~ (old/existing money)

$100,000 (new money = $50,000 second trust deed + $50,000 cash)

x $.55 per $500 (or, $1.10 per $1,000)

= $110 Documentary Transfer Tax paid to the county where the property is located.

Figure 13.3

(10) City Transfer Tax

Some cities in California levy a transfer tax for all properties located within the city limits. Amounts vary, usually as a percentage of the purchase price.

(11) Recording Fees

The county recorder where a property is located will record a grant deed conveying the property and a trust deed for the loan (if applicable). Costs average around $10 per document and are usually split between the buyer and seller. The seller usually pays for recording the grant deed and the buyer usually pays for recording the trust deed.

(12) Home Warranty Policy

A home warranty policy is many times split between the buyer and seller; however, this is negotiable. A home warranty policy usually takes effect at close of escrow and usually costs $400 to $600 or more, depending on coverage.

(13) Commissions

Real estate sales commissions usually range between 5% and 6% of the sale price of a property. A commission may be split between cooperating brokers and their salespersons. The sales commission is usually paid by the seller. The broker sends a broker demand to escrow specifying the amount of commission to be paid to the broker. Escrow companies generally wait until confirmation of the grant deed being recorded before releasing commission funds to the broker. After the commission check has been received by the broker, the broker pays the salesperson their portion of the commission.

(14) Tax and Insurance Impounds

Some lenders require funds to be impounded each month to pay a buyer's property taxes and homeowner's insurance. Loans with greater than 80% LTV's usually require impounds.

Twice per year property taxes are paid by the lender from the impound account. Homeowner's insurance is paid once each year from the same impound account. Lenders may require additional impound reserves in the first year of the loan.

(15) Wire Transfer Fee

A wire transfer fee pays wire charges for wiring funds from the lender to the escrow holder. Fees can be $50 or more.

(16) Notary Fee

An escrow holder is many times also a notary public who can acknowledge and verify (notarize) signatures. A photo ID and thumbprint are usually required to notarize documents. Notary fees usually average $10-$20. However, mobile notaries can be more expensive.

Figure 13.4

(17) Prepaid Interest

Interest on real estate loans is paid in arrears. It is the opposite of rent, which is paid in advance. For example, when a borrower makes a loan payment on June 1st, the borrower is paying the mortgage interest for *May*, not June. Whether a buyer closes at the end of the month or at the beginning of the month matters only in the time value of money and whether a buyer has enough funds to close escrow.

(18) Other Fees

- **Drawing Fee** is a fee charged to draw loan documents.
- **Prepayment Penalty** is a penalty that a lender may impose on a borrower if the borrower sells or refinances a property within a certain specified period of time. Residential loans may have prepayment fees of six months interest if the loan is paid off prior to two or three years from the original loan date—however, this varies. Commercial loans can have huge prepayment penalties.
- **Beneficiary Demand Fee** is charged when a lender of an existing loan sends a payoff amount to escrow and escrow pays off the loan. A beneficiary

statement is a statement sent by the beneficiary (lender) to escrow informing the escrow officer of the exact amount that must be paid (from escrow) to pay off the existing loan. The escrow officer receives the beneficiary statement and then pays the existing lender the amount stated in the demand. The lender then authorizes the trustee to reconvey the basic legal title back to the trustor, thereby eliminating the deed of trust. The trustor may then sell the property or refinance it and place another trust deed on the property through a different lender and the process continues. A beneficiary demand usually costs $50 to $100.

- **Deed of Reconveyance/Reconveyance Deed** is a deed a trustee sends to a trustor when a loan has been paid off. It moves basic legal title from the trustee back to the trustor (borrower) and eliminates (removes the lien) the deed of trust from title.

Prorated Rents: Seller already collected rents for the month. Close of escrow is in the middle of the month, part of the rents must be paid to the buyer.

- **Prorated Rents** (used for income properties) are rents that have already been paid in advance to a seller and must be credited to a buyer at close of escrow. These can be quite substantial if the property is large and close of escrow is in the middle of the month.

- **Homeowner's Transfer Fee** may be charged by a homeowner's association to transfer ownership from a seller to a buyer. Fees can be $200+.

Flood Certification: Identifies whether a property is in a flood zone.

- **Flood Certification Fee** may be charged to determine whether a property is located in a flood zone. FHA insured loans sometimes require a flood certification. Flood zone disclosures are normally included in the Natural Hazards Disclosure.

- **Roof Certification Fee** may be charged by a roofing contractor to certify that the roof will not leak for two years or more from the date of close of escrow.

- **Wire Fee/Courier Fee/Federal Express Fee** may be incurred when sending documents. Examples include inter-spousal grant deeds and power of attorney forms.

Other closing costs may also be needed. Knowing all the closing costs *before* they are incurred will reduce mistakes made by the agent and eliminate surprises for buyers.

3. Methods of Holding Title to Real Property (Vesting)

After a buyer understands the amount of closing costs involved in the purchase of real property, a decision must be made how to take title to the real property. Title to real property is placed on the grant deed that transfers legal title from the seller to the buyer. Vesting is an extremely important area that buyers tend to decide on the spur of the moment, when they should enlist the services of a real estate attorney and CPA to decide how to take title to the property. This can impact future tax planning and inheritance taxes.

A real estate agent should *not* give legal advice regarding how a buyer should take title to a parcel of real property. Estate planning attorneys provide this type of advice.

Forms of real estate ownership include sole ownership (one person holds title to real property) called severalty. Forms of concurrent ownership (more than one person holds title to real property) include tenancy in common, joint tenancy, community property, tenancy in partnership, co-ops, limited liability companies (LLC), domestic corporations, foreign corporations, non-profit/not-for-profit associations, and revocable and irrevocable living trusts.

A. Form of Sole Ownership

Sole ownership is comprised of real property owned by one person. The vesting on the grant deed (that transfers title to the buyer) may read, "Jane Doe, a single woman as her sole and separate property."

(1) Severalty

Sole ownership is held in **severalty**. Severalty means to sever out one person who owns the property. Therefore, when one person holds title to real property it is being held in severalty.

Severalty: A person owns a parcel of real property as sole ownership.

B. Forms of Concurrent Ownership
(1) Tenancy in Common/Tenants in Common

Concurrent ownership by two or more persons, each with an undivided interest—but not necessarily equal—and without right of survivorship is the definition of **tenancy in common (TIC)**. The owners of a property held as tenancy in common are called tenants in common and each has possession of the property.

Tenancy in Common: Concurrent ownership by two or more persons, each with an undivided interest—but not necessarily equal—and without right of survivorship.

For example, Fred Jones and Beth Ramirez hold title as Tenants in Common. Fred owns 30% of the property and Beth owns 70%. Both have possession of the property and each can either sell their portion of the property or will it to their heirs.

In other words, tenancy in common (TIC) occurs when two of more people own a property together and can will each of their portions to their own heirs. They both have possession of the property, own *unequal* shares with the right of possession, and can will their ownership portion to their heirs (no right of survivorship).

TICs have been a popular way for individual owners to come together to buy large properties and maintain the tax advantages of an Internal Revenue Code 1031

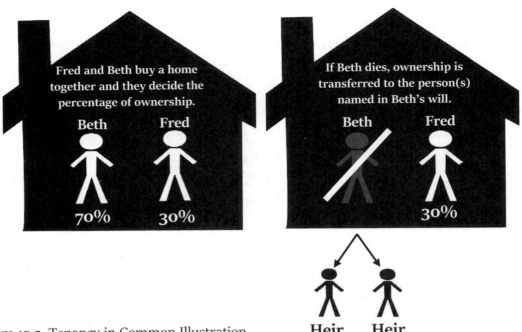

Figure 13.5 Tenancy in Common Illustration

tax-deferred exchange (discussed in Chapter 15). TICs that have usage rights include:

- Space-Assignment Co-Ownerships (SACOs) assign specific rooms, apartments, houses, retail, offices, and storage space to each owner.
- Time-Assignment Co-Ownership (TACOs) assign specific usage times or intervals to each owner. In the past these were called "timeshares," but today they are called "fractionals."
- Equity Shares include one or more owners who get usage rights and one or more owners who are purely investors.

(2) Joint Tenancy/Joint Tenants

Joint Tenancy: Form of concurrent ownerships in which two or more people own a parcel of real property with the unities of time, title, interest, and possession. Also, it has a right of survivorship.

Joint tenancy is a form of concurrent ownership in which each joint tenant has four common unities: time, title, interest, and possession. The joint tenants must: take title at the same time, with the same title instrument (usually a grant deed), their interests must be equal, and they must have equal possession.

Joint tenancy provides the property owners with a right of survivorship. When one of the joint tenants dies, his or her portion of ownership goes to the other joint tenant(s) and *not* to the deceased person's heirs. This can be an important distinction when performing estate planning, so clients should always be encouraged to consult proper legal and tax advice prior to any investment endeavor.

Each joint tenant is also free of the other joint tenants' debts. For example, a property is owned in joint tenancy with two joint tenants, Joint Tenant A and Joint Tenant B. Joint Tenant A takes out a loan on the property in Joint Tenant A's own

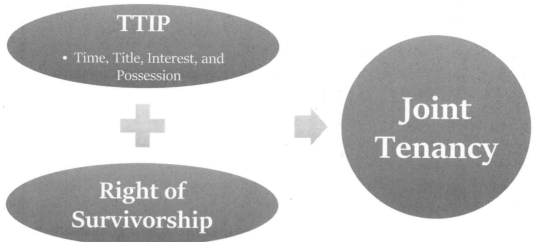

Figure 13.6 Joint Tenancy Unities and Right of Survivorship

name and not with the consent or signature of Joint Tenant B. If Joint Tenant A (who took out the loan) dies, Joint Tenant B is *not* responsible for the debt. For this reason, lenders usually require both Joint Tenant A and Joint Tenant B to sign the promissory note with *"joint and several liability."* This means that Joint Tenant A and Joint Tenant B are responsible for the debt jointly (together), along with each severally (by themselves).

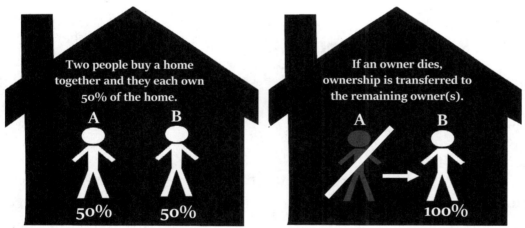

Figure 13.7 Joint Tenancy Illustration

(3) Community Property

Community property is property held by husband and wife (or two spouses). Property acquired by a husband and wife during marriage is considered community property and is therefore owned by both parties. Exceptions to community property include property that is willed to one spouse or property taken in severalty by one of the spouses is not considered community property. The husband and wife must have equal interests if real property is held as community property and there is no right of survivorship. Vesting will be: Husband and Wife, as Community Property.

Both husband and wife need to sign for a contract to be enforceable. An agreement to sell property held as community property that is signed by only one spouse is unenforceable until the other spouse takes action (within one year) to set aside the sale and rescind the contract.

California is a community property state; however, in states that are not community property states, a husband and wife can take title to real property as tenancy by the entireties. This signifies that title is held by husband and wife, but is not considered community property. Tenancy by the entireties usually has a right of survivorship and may be used in states that do not have community property laws. Again, tenancy by the entireties is normally not used in California.

(4) Tenancy in Partnership

A **tenancy in partnership** may be in the form a general partnership or limited partnership. A **general partnership** creates unlimited liability for the partners. In contrast, a **limited partnership** limits an investor's liability only to the amount invested in the property. A limited partner is only taxed once at the personal income tax level, rather than twice like a corporation that is taxed at the corporate level and dividend level (double taxation).

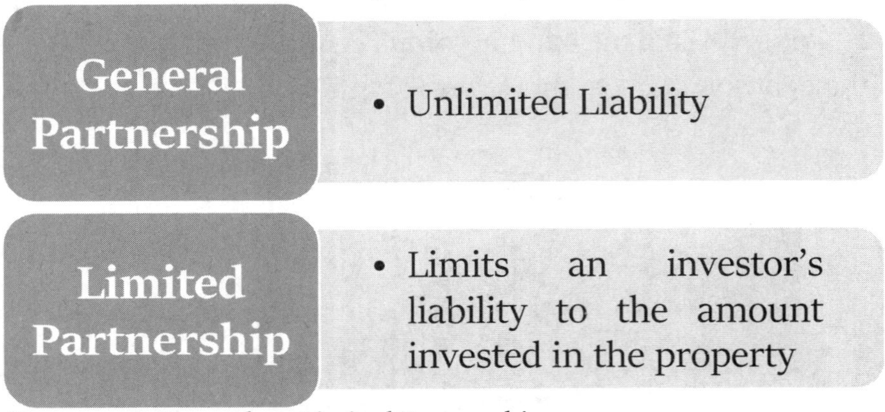

General Partnership	• Unlimited Liability
Limited Partnership	• Limits an investor's liability to the amount invested in the property

Figure 13.8 General vs. Limited Partnership

a. General Partnership

Tenancy in Partnership: Two or more people own a parcel of real property as a partnership.

General Partnership: Partnership that exposes the partners to unlimited liability, including other assets besides the partnership property.

Limited Partnership: Partnership that only exposes the partners to the liability of the partnership property.

Two or more people who come together to purchase an investment property may use a general partnership as a vehicle to hold title to real property. A general partnership is a way for partners to share in profits. However, it has one very strong drawback as each partner has unlimited liability for their investments in the property.

For example, General Partner A and General Partner B purchase a single-family home as an investment property. During the time they own the rental home (holding period), a tenant slips and falls on a wet walkway leading to the home. If the injured tenant sues the general partnership for damages, and the courts believe the general partners should have foreseen the possibility that someone would fall on the walkway and should have had it repaired before the tenant was harmed, the tenant could go after the money in the general partnership (property) along with both general partners personal assets to satisfy the claim. This can be devastating to high net worth individuals who have a large amount of assets at risk.

In contrast, if the two partners had held the property as a limited partnership, the injured tenant could have only gone after the property itself and *not* after the limited partners personal assets.

b. Limited Partnership

A limited partnership minimizes an investor's liability exposure because the investor can only lose what was invested in the property. Personal assets are not at risk. It is important to note that a limited partnership requires one general partner and at least one limited partner. In addition, a limited partnership has traditionally been a good income tax shelter. A real estate investor will usually only be taxed once at their personal income tax level when a limited partnership is used to hold title to real property.

c. Syndicate Venture/Syndication

When real estate investors come together to buy a parcel of real property, they may use a **syndicate venture** or "**syndication**." A syndicate venture may have two entities: a general partner and limited partners (although limited liability companies and corporations are used as well). The general partner has unlimited liability for the syndication, while the limited partners can only lose what they invest in the syndicate venture. For this reason, a syndicator may use a corporation as the general partner.

> **Syndication:** Real estate investors come together to buy a parcel of real property.

A "blind pool" syndicate venture is a syndication in which the property investors have no property information and have given the general partner money to find and acquire an appropriate property.

(5) Stock Cooperatives/Coops

A **stock cooperative** is a corporation that owns an entire property. Each shareholder owns a portion of shares in the corporation and has the right to occupy a specific unit. If an owner wants to sell the unit, the owner transfers his or her ownership in stock to the new buyer, rather than using a deed. One problem with stock cooperatives is if the other owners do not pay their debt service and go into default, a foreclosure may cause *every* owner to lose their unit as well. Stock cooperatives are very common in New York City and have had some use in San Francisco.

> **Stock Cooperative:** A corporation that owns an entire property. Each shareholder owns a portion of shares in the corporation and has the right to occupy a specific unit.

In comparison to stock cooperatives, condominiums (condos) allow the owner to own the airspace within the condo separately along with the common areas in common with all the other condo owners. Condos are transferred with a grant deed and are much more common in California than stock cooperatives.

(6) Limited Liability Company

A **limited liability company (LLC)** shields personal assets from property liability, has flexible management structure and tax reporting, separates business and personal finances, and is accepted in all states of the United States.

Limited liability companies have taken over for limited partnerships, corporations, and syndications as a major concurrent ownership vehicle in California. A limited liability company limits each principal owner's liability and files tax returns similar to a corporation.

(7) Corporations

A **corporation** has a separate capacity to deal with property independently from its members (separate legal entity), centralized control in a board of directors, liability of shareholders normally limited to the amount of their investment, freely transferable shares, and continued existence regardless of death or retirement of its shareholders.

Although a corporation may take title to real property in its own name, it is an "artificial person" created by law and must function through human agents. Accordingly, corporate control is vested in the board of directors and so it becomes important to have some evidence of the board's decision in connection with the proposed property transaction. The corporation may enter into contracts as well as acquire and dispose of real or personal property in its own name. Liability arises if the corporate veil is pierced due to fraud or other legal infraction.

a. Domestic Corporations

Domestic corporations are corporations established in the United States. A corporation can choose between filing taxes as a C corporation ("C corp") or as an S corporation ("S corp"). Both C corporations and S corporations are considered separate legal entities and individual investors are protected against liability by the corporate veil. Investors personal assets are protected and are not at risk when a corporate entity is used to own real property. However, if the corporate veil is pierced (e.g., usually caused by fraud), then individual investors may find their personal assets at risk.

A C corporation is double taxed at the corporate level and at the stockholder's personal income tax level (dividend). An S corporation is only single taxed at the stockholder's personal income tax level.

1. C Corporation

Income is double taxed at the corporate level, and, if dividends are distributed, at the individual level as well. Businesses taxed as C corporations are not pass through entities because the business must pay corporate income tax on its earnings *and* owners must pay personal income tax on dividend income.

2. S Corporation

An S corporation is considered a "pass-through entity," which means the business itself is not taxed and all business income/loss is passed through to the owners each year. Income is reported on the owners' personal income tax returns.

A C corporation may be taxed at the property level and at the dividend (stockholder's personal income tax) level. Conversely, an S corporation will only be taxed once at the investor's personal income tax level. S corporations have the advantage of shielding an investor's liability along with limiting their personal income tax.

b. Foreign Corporations

Before a foreign corporation can transact intrastate business within California, the business must first qualify/register with the California Secretary of State. Foreign corporations can qualify/register to transact business in California by filing the applicable form with the California Secretary of State and attaching a valid certificate of good standing by an authorized public official of the foreign jurisdiction under which the foreign corporation is incorporated.

(8) Joint Venture

A **joint venture** occurs when two or more people enter into a real estate venture for one specific property. It is for one property and is not designed to continue to other properties.

Joint Venture: Two or more people enter into a real estate venture for one specific property.

(9) Nonprofit and Not-for-Profit Associations

According to DRE, "Sometimes transactions in real property will involve nonprofit associations: loosely knit, unincorporated associations of natural persons for religious, scientific, social, educational, recreational, benevolent or other purposes. Members of such associations are not personally liable for debts incurred in acquisition or leasing of real property used by the association, unless they specifically assume such liability in writing. These nonprofit organizations may, by statute, hold such property in the group name as is necessary for business objects and purposes."

(10) Revocable and Irrevocable Living Trusts

Revocable and irrevocable living trusts are another way to hold title to real property. Revocable living trusts are used to avoid probate and are very popular in California. Irrevocable living trusts are used to protect assets from liability and avoid probate as well.

4. Transfer of Title to Real Property

Once the buyer decides how title will be vested, title will normally be transferred in California using a grant deed. However, there are five different ways to acquire title to real property in California. The most common way is transfer through a deed. The other ways include will, succession, accession, and occupancy.

Methods of Acquiring and Transferring Title

Transfer	Will	Succession	Accession	Occupancy
• Deeds	•Written instrument used to dispose of real and personal property after a person's death	•When a person dies without a will but has heirs, the law provides for disposition of the person's property to their heirs	• Annexation • Accretion	• Adverse Possession • Government Patent

Figure 13.9 Methods of Acquiring and Transferring Title

A. Transfer

Transfer of real property is accomplished when title is conveyed to another person through a deed. The person conveying real property by deed is called a **grantor** and the person receiving real property by deed is called a **grantee**. There are two major types of deeds used to convey real property in California: grant deeds and quitclaim deeds.

(1) Grant Deed

A grant deed is normally used in California to convey real property from a seller to a buyer. The seller is called the grantor and the buyer is called the grantee. The grantor must be at least 18 years of age (or married, divorced, in the military, or emancipated by the courts). A grant deed requires a granting clause (i.e., "grants to") that conveys the parcel of real property from the grantor to the grantee. A grant deed must be in writing, requires a property description, and must be signed by the grantor (seller). Lastly, a grant deed must be **delivered** to the grantee

Grantor: Person who is conveying real property to another person (grantee).

Grantee: Person who is receiving real property from the grantor.

Delivery: Grant deeds (and quitclaim deeds) require delivery of the document from the grantor (seller) to the grantee (buyer). Recordation presumes delivery.

(buyer). Delivery can be accomplished by physically delivering the grant deed to the grantee or by recording it at the county recorder's office in the county where the property is located. Recording presumes delivery to the grantee, so the grantor is *not* required to physically deliver it to the grantee and have the grantee accept it.

Specifically, if the grantor (seller) has the grant deed acknowledged (notarized by a notary public) and then recorded at the county recorder's office in the county where the property is located, then the recordation presumes delivery to the grantee (buyer). This means that the grantor (seller) is not required to physically deliver the grant deed to the grantee (buyer) because recordation of the grant deed presumes this delivery.

Grant deeds convey a parcel of real property and contain two implied warranties: (1) the grantor has not conveyed the property to someone else (fraud) prior to signing the grant deed, and (2) there are no undisclosed encumbrances on the property.

Grant Deed

Two Implied Warranties

The grantor has not conveyed the property to someone else (fraud) prior to signing the grant deed

There are no undisclosed encumbrances on the property

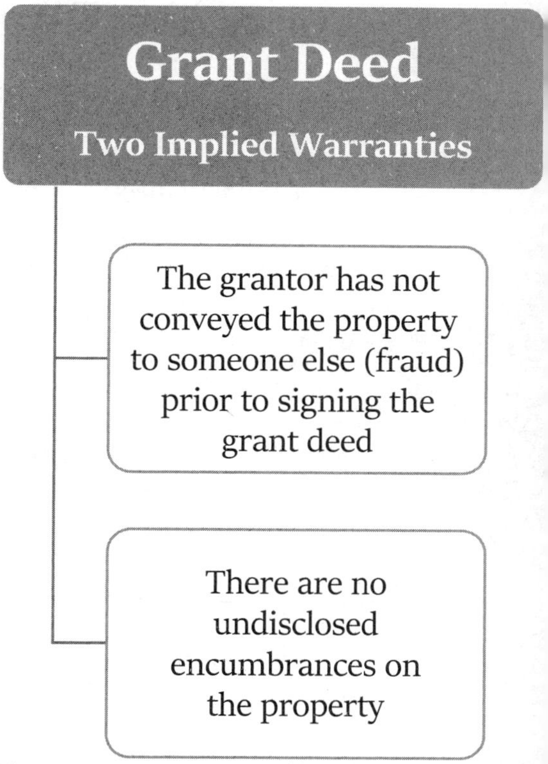

Figure 13.10 Grant Deed Implied Warranties

There are several types of grant deeds such as a trustee's deed, sheriff's deed, and patent deed. All three are types of grant deeds.

Requirements for a valid grant deed are:

- The grant deed must be in writing
- It must identify the grantor and grantee
- It must have a granting clause ("I deed." "I grant." "I convey." etc.)
- It must adequately describe the property and be signed by the grantor
- It must be delivered by the grantor to the grantee. Although not required, a grant deed is usually recorded in the county where the property is located and presumes delivery.

Although a grant deed does not require acknowledgement, it must be acknowledged if it is to be recorded. A notary public "notarizes" a grant deed by acknowledging who the grantor is and verifying that the grantor really owns the property. A grant deed is usually recorded in the county where the property is located and presumes delivery to the buyer (grantee). A grant deed cannot be assigned.

Even though grant deeds have the above two implied warranties, prudent buyers usually always obtain title insurance to ensure they are receiving clear title to the property. However, if the chain of recorded title to a property is broken with an unrecorded grant deed, or there are other irregularities in the title, the title insurance company may not be willing to issue a policy of title insurance.

a. Minimum Property Description

When a grant deed transfers real property from the grantor (seller) to grantee (buyer), one of the requirements is a legal description of the property. In other words, the property must be adequately described to be a valid transfer. Accordingly, there are three primary land description methods used in California: 1. Lots, Blocks, and Tracts; 2. Government Survey; and 3. Metes and Bounds.

1. Lots, Blocks, and Tracts Land Description Method

Lots, Blocks, and Tracts Land Description Method: Land description method that utilizes recorded subdivision maps to describe real property.

The **Lots, Blocks, and Tracts Land Description Method** utilizes recorded subdivision maps to describe real property. The Subdivision Map Act requires the mapping of all new subdivisions, so each parcel in the subdivision is delineated and identified. When accepted by county or city authorities, the map is filed in the county recorder's office in the county where the property is located. Documentation can then describe any lot in the subdivision by indicating the lot number, the block, and the map. The description also includes the name of the city, county and state. For example (not related to Figure 13.11): "Lot 18, Block B, Parkview Addition (as recorded July 17, 1956, Book 2, Page 49 of maps), City of Sacramento, County of Sacramento, State of California."

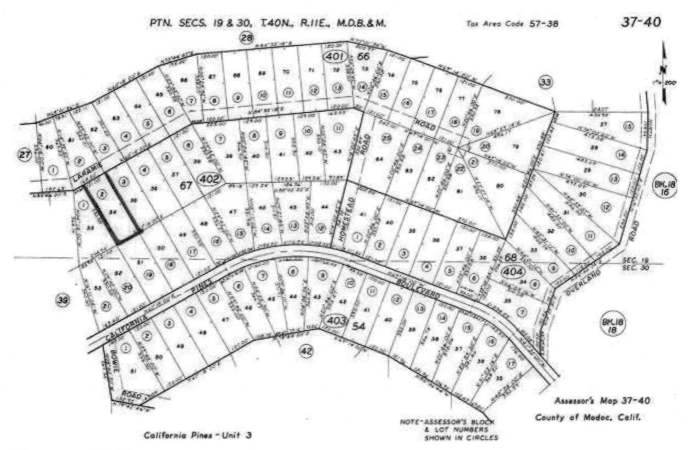

Figure 13.11 Plat Map

2. Government Survey Land Description Method

The **Government Survey Land Description Method** is used for large parcels of rural acreage. California has three principal base and meridian line intersections. They include the Humboldt, Mt. Diablo, and San Bernardino principle base line and meridian line intersections. Starting from the intersection of (for example) the Mt. Diablo base line and meridian, there are squares that spread out in all directions from the point of intersection. Each one of these squares is called a township that is 6 miles square (6 miles on each side) or 36 square miles. Each township is comprised of 36 sections that are one square mile in size. One section is one square mile and equals 640 acres. An **acre** is 43,560 square feet.

Parcel/lot square footage information commonly uses acres to describe the amount of square footage for a property. Of course, one acre is 43,560 square feet; so, a residential lot that is 8,000 square feet may be listed in the multiple listing service (MLS) and county tax record database as .18 acres +/- (more or less).

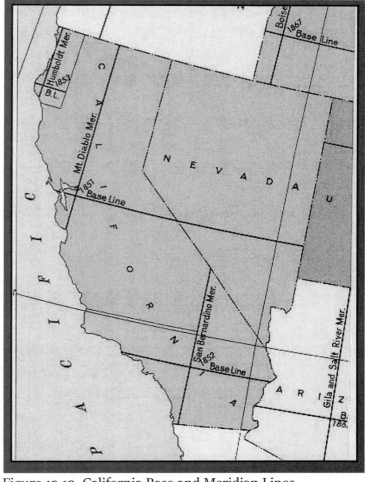

Figure 13.12 California Base and Meridian Lines

A **commercial acre** is an acre of land less the amount of land dedicated for public improvements (sidewalks, alleys, etc.). Therefore, a commercial acre can be much less than the 43,560 square feet in an acre of land.

Figure 13.13

Important numbers to remember:	
43,560 square feet	= 1 acre
640 acres	= 1 square mile
5,280 linear feet	= 1 linear mile
1 section	= 1 mile x 1 mile
36 sections	= 1 township
1 township	= 6 miles x 6 miles
1 township	= 6 miles square
1 township	= 36 square miles

Government Survey: Land description method used for large parcels of rural acreage.

Acre: 43,560 square feet

Commercial Acre: An acre of land less the amount of land dedicated for public improvements.

3. Metes and Bounds Land Description Method

Metes and Bounds: Land description method that utilizes measurements and boundaries.

The **Metes and Bounds Land Description Method** describes the measurements of distances (metes) and boundaries (bounds) from a predetermined point, usually a monument.

An example of a metes and bounds land description (not related to Figure 13.14): "Beginning at a point on the southerly line of "T" Street, 150 feet westerly of the SW corner of the intersection of "T" and 8th Streets; running thence due south 300 feet to the northerly line of "P" Street; thence westerly along the northerly line of "P" Street, 100 feet; thence northerly and parallel to the first course, 300 feet, to the southerly line of "T" Street; thence easterly along the southerly line of "T" Street, 100 feet, to the point or place of beginning."

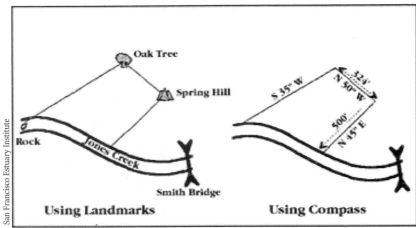

Figure 13.14 Metes and Bounds Illustration

b. Race Restrictions on a Deed

Regarding the conveyance of a deed including race restrictions, the deed is valid (lawful and effective), but the race restrictions are unenforceable because they violate the United States Constitution. The conveyance is unaffected because the race restriction covenant is unlawful and therefore, unenforceable.

(2) Quitclaim Deed

Quitclaim Deed: Document used to remove a person from the title to real property.

A **quitclaim deed** is used to remove someone from title to a parcel of real property and has no warranties or covenants both expressed or implied. Both a grant deed and quitclaim deed use the terms grantor (person granting the property) and grantee (person receiving the property) to denote the parties to the deed.

Quitclaim deeds have the same requirements as a grant deed: a quitclaim deed must be in writing, identify the grantor and grantee, have a granting clause, adequately describe the property, be signed by the grantor, and delivered to the grantee—usually through recordation that presumes delivery to the grantee.

For example, Fred and Mary Smith decide to get a divorce. They own a home together and it is agreed that Mary will keep the property. Fred executes a quitclaim deed removing him from title to the property. Mary will then hold the property in severalty as sole and separate property.

(3) Inter-Spousal Deed

An **inter-spousal deed** is a type of grant deed that transfers title between a married couple. It may be used during a divorce in lieu of a quitclaim deed.

(4) Warranty Deed

A warranty deed guarantees clear title to real property. It goes all the way back to the beginning of the chain of recorded title. Warranty deeds are *not* normally used in California, but are used in many other states in the United States.

(5) Special Warranty Deed

A special warranty deed guarantees clear title only back to the time the present owner took title to the property. Special warranty deeds are *not* normally used in California, but are used in many other states in the United States.

B. Wills

A **will** is a written instrument used to dispose of real and personal property after a person's death. To **devise** is to leave real property by will. A **devisor** is the person who wills real property to their heirs after death. A **devisee** receives real property by will and is usually an heir.

(1) Holographic Will

A holographic will is a will that is handwritten, dated, and signed by the testator (person making the will) in the testator's own handwriting and is not witnessed.

(2) Witnessed Will

A witnessed will usually has two witnesses who subscribe their names as witnesses to the will. A witness usually is someone other than a beneficiary who is receiving something by will.

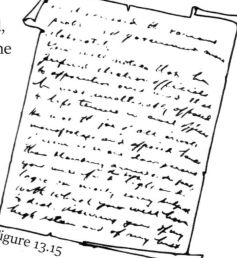

Figure 13.15

(3) Executor

An executor is a person appointed by the testator (person leaving property by will) to carry out the testator's requests in the will. This includes disposing of real and personal property according to the will. If the person appointed is male, then he is called an executor. If the person appointed is female, she is called an executrix (pronounced like grand "prix").

(4) Administrator

The devisor usually appoints an executor (male) or executrix (female) to handle the disposition of the devisor's will. If the devisor does not appoint an executor or executrix, then the court will appoint an administrator to perform the duties of handling the disposition of the will.

(5) Probate, Conservatorship, and Guardianship

Probate: Process of administering a deceased person's will or estate.

Probate is the process of administering a deceased person's will or estate. It is used to verify the validity of a will. The minimum period of time for probate is six months, however, a possible heir has up to four months to file a claim for probate. The real estate commission for a property that is in probate is set by court order.

Conservatorship is a court-appointed person or entity who manages the financial affairs, health, and assets of a person who does not have the mental or physical capacity to care for him or herself.

Guardianship occurs when someone other than the parent is appointed by the courts to have custody of a child and/or manage the child's property or estate.

C. Succession

Intestate Succession: When a person dies without a will (however, they do have heirs), the law provides for disposition of the person's property.

When a person dies without a will (however, they do have heirs), the law provides for disposition of the person's property. This is called **intestate succession**. There are many specialized circumstances surrounding the division of property under intestate succession, the most basic situations are described below.

(1) Separate Property

If separate property is divided equally between a surviving spouse and surviving child, then 50% goes to the spouse and 50% to the child. If separate property is divided equally among a surviving spouse and two children, then 33 1/3% goes to the spouse, 33 1/3% to the first child, and 33 1/3% to the second child.

(2) Community Property

One-half of community property belongs to the surviving spouse, and the other half is subject to disposition by the decedent's will. There is no right of survivorship. If there is no will, the decedent's half of the community property remaining after payment of the debts goes to the surviving spouse.

Intestate Succession
(dies without a will but with heirs)
Separate Property: Surviving Spouse and Two Children

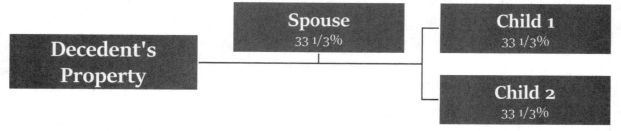

Separate Property: No Surviving Spouse, Two Surviving Children

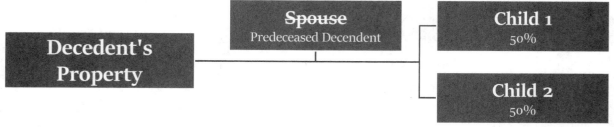

Community Property: Held between Decedent and Spouse

If the decedent had a will, the decedent's one-half of community property would be disposed per the decedent's will.

Figure 13.16 Intestate Succession Illustrations

(3) Escheat

When a person dies without a will and without heirs, the property will escheat to the State of California. Since it is presumed there are some heirs in existence to claim the property, escheat is not automatic and may take some time to complete. Escheat proceedings may be initiated by the probate court or the State Attorney General.

Escheat
(dies without a will and no heirs)

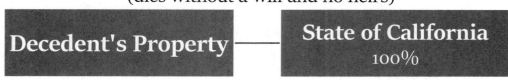

Figure 13.17 Escheat Illustration

D. Accession

Accession is the extension of an owner's title to real property through either annexation (man-made) or accretion (naturally occurring). Annexation occurs when a property owner combines parcels of land. One parcel is annexed (added) to the other parcel. Accretion occurs when a property owner acquires land from a gradual build-up by natural causes. For example, accretion occurs when a riparian owner (property located next to a moving river or stream) or littoral owner (property located next to a body of water such as a lake, pond, or ocean) acquires title to additional land by the gradual build up or accumulation of land (soil) deposited on the owner's property by the shifting of the river or lake's action.

(1) Avulsion

When a stream suddenly tears land away from its bank (rapid washing away of the land), this is called **avulsion**.

(2) Alluvium

The brown material that flows down a river is called **alluvium**. Alluvium is the land that accumulates due to the splash-up action of water.

Figure 13.18

Accession: Extension of an owner's title to real property through either annexation (man-made) or accretion (naturally occurring).

Avulsion: Rapid tearing away of the land by a stream.

Alluvium: Land that accumulates due to the splash-up action of water.

Adverse Possession: A person can acquire land by use that is open and notorious, uninterrupted for five years, a claim of right, hostile to owner's intent, and pays property taxes.

E. Occupancy

There are two ways to acquire title to real property through occupancy: adverse possession or government patent.

(1) Adverse Possession

A property can be acquired by **adverse possession** when a person uses another person's property while fulfilling the following requirements:

1. **O**pen and notorious to the owner's intent
2. **U**ninterrupted (continuous) use for a period of 5 years or more
3. **C**laim of right
4. **H**ostile to the owner's title and intent, PLUS
5. **Taxes:** Payment of all real property taxes for a period of 5 years or more

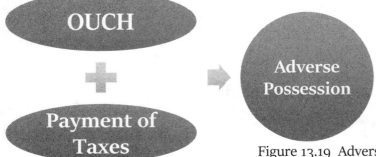

Figure 13.19 Adverse Possession Diagram

(2) Government Patent

A patent is an instrument that conveys real property from the state or federal government to an individual. A transfer of ownership from the Sovereign (government) to a member of the general public is called a **government patent**.

Government Patent: Conveys real property from the state or federal government to an individual.

5. Loan Funding and Close of Escrow

Loan documents are submitted to escrow by the lender and the buyer signs the loan documents. The buyer's signature is usually required to be notarized by a notary public. The escrow officer is usually a notary public and can complete this task. A mobile notary can be used to perform the same task. The mobile notary comes to the buyer's home and obtains signatures while at the home. Some lenders may require the buyer to use their own mobile notary, even though the escrow officer is a notary public. It really depends on the lender. After the loan documents have been signed, the lender will fund the loan. Lenders are very careful about wire fraud and may require several security measures to be completed prior to wiring the funds into the escrow officer's bank account.

The escrow officer makes sure all the terms and conditions to the escrow have been satisfied (including the funds received from the lender), then moves forward and closes escrow. This is when the escrow is considered perfected.

Figure 13.20

Chapter Thirteen Summary

The chapter investigates final verification of condition, closing costs, and methods of holding title to real property. These include severalty, tenancy in common, joint tenancy, community property, tenancy in partnership, syndications, co-ops, limited liability companies, corporations, joint ventures, non-profit and not-for-profit associations, and revocable and irrevocable living trusts.

An investigation of the methods of acquiring and transferring title to real property is discussed through transfer, wills, succession, accession, and occupancy. Deeds are covered, including grant deeds, quitclaim deeds, interspousal deeds, warranty deeds, and special warranty deeds. Property description methods are discussed in light of deed requirements and include lots, blocks, and tracts method, government survey method, and metes and bounds. The last part of the chapter discusses loan funding and close of escrow.

Chapter Thirteen Quiz

1. Recurring closing costs include:
(A) property taxes
(B) homeowner's insurance
(C) Both (A) and (B) are correct
(D) Neither (A) nor (B) are correct

2. Non-recurring closing costs include:
(A) escrow fees
(B) title insurance fees
(C) Both (A) and (B) are correct
(D) Neither (A) nor (B) are correct

3. Concurrent ownership by two or more persons, each with an undivided interest—but not necessarily equal—and without right of survivorship is the definition of _____.
(A) joint tenancy
(B) community property
(C) severalty
(D) tenancy in common (TIC)

4. A _____ is normally used in California to convey real property from a seller to a buyer.
(A) grant deed
(B) trust deed
(C) mortgage
(D) bill of sale

5. Regarding the conveyance of a deed including race restrictions, the deed is _____, but the race restrictions are _____.
(A) void, unenforceable
(B) valid, unenforceable
(C) void, enforceable
(D) void, unenforceable

6. A(n) _____ transfers title between a married couple.
(A) bill of sale
(B) security agreement
(C) inter-spousal deed
(D) none of the above are correct

7. _____ is a court-appointed person or entity who manages the financial affairs, health, and assets of a person who does not have the mental or physical capacity to care for themselves.
(A) Guardianship
(B) Conservatorship
(C) Executor
(D) Executrix

8. _____ occurs when someone other than the parent is appointed by the courts to have custody of the child and/or manage the child's property or estate.
(A) Guardianship
(B) Conservatorship
(C) Executor
(D) Executrix

9. _____ is the extension of an owner's title to real property through either annexation or accretion.
(A) Transfer
(B) Accession
(C) Occupancy
(D) Will

10. A transfer of ownership from the Sovereign (government) to a member of the general public is called a(n) _____.
(A) government patent
(B) adverse possession
(C) will
(D) holographic will

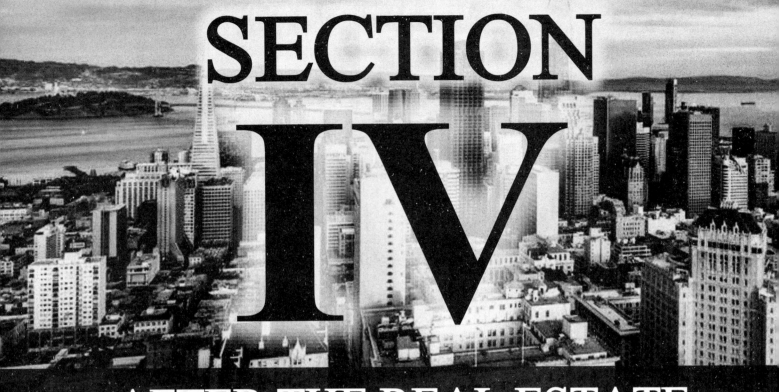

SECTION IV

AFTER THE REAL ESTATE TRANSACTION

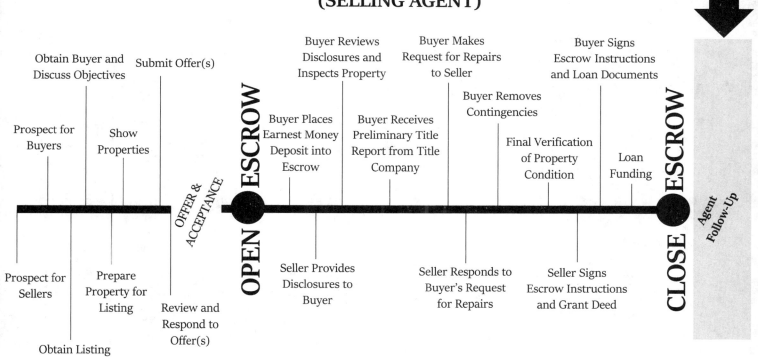

Real Estate Transaction Overview
BUYER'S AGENT
(SELLING AGENT)

Obtain Buyer and Discuss Objectives

Submit Offer(s)

Buyer Reviews Disclosures and Inspects Property

Buyer Makes Request for Repairs to Seller

Buyer Signs Escrow Instructions and Loan Documents

Prospect for Buyers

Show Properties

Buyer Places Earnest Money Deposit into Escrow

Buyer Receives Preliminary Title Report from Title Company

Buyer Removes Contingencies

Final Verification of Property Condition

Loan Funding

OFFER & ACCEPTANCE

OPEN ESCROW

CLOSE ESCROW

Agent Follow-Up

Prospect for Sellers

Prepare Property for Listing

Review and Respond to Offer(s)

Seller Provides Disclosures to Buyer

Seller Responds to Buyer's Request for Repairs

Seller Signs Escrow Instructions and Grant Deed

Obtain Listing

SELLER'S AGENT
(LISTING AGENT)

Robert Kiyosaki

"Real estate investing, even on a very small scale, remains a tried and true means of building an individual's cash flow and wealth."

14

Chapter
FOURTEEN

After Close of Escrow

There are several items that occur after close of escrow. One of the most satisfying for real estate brokers and salespersons is getting paid for their work. The real estate broker submits a broker demand form to escrow directing the escrow officer to pay the negotiated commission amount. The real estate broker then pays the salesperson the amount that was negotiated in their employment agreement.

Another item that may occur after close of escrow is a rent-back provision that allows the seller to occupy the property after close of escrow. This is common with large single-family homes in which the seller has a significant amount of furniture and other belongings that must be moved out of the property after close of escrow.

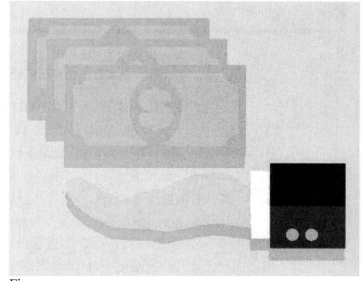

Separately, after close of escrow the real estate agent will need to remove the MLS lockbox and for sale sign from the property. The agent will update the MLS database indicating that the property is sold and add the client to the agent's follow-up email list.

The agent may also run into liability issues if there are defects in the property that were not disclosed by the seller. In addition, the agent may

Figure 14.1

notice that certain items have become inoperable after close of escrow. Hopefully, a home warranty policy will cover the buyer for these inoperable items.

Lastly, defects in the chain of recorded title may be discovered after close of escrow and may detrimentally affect the marketability of the property. Title insurance may cover title defects if they arise after close of escrow.

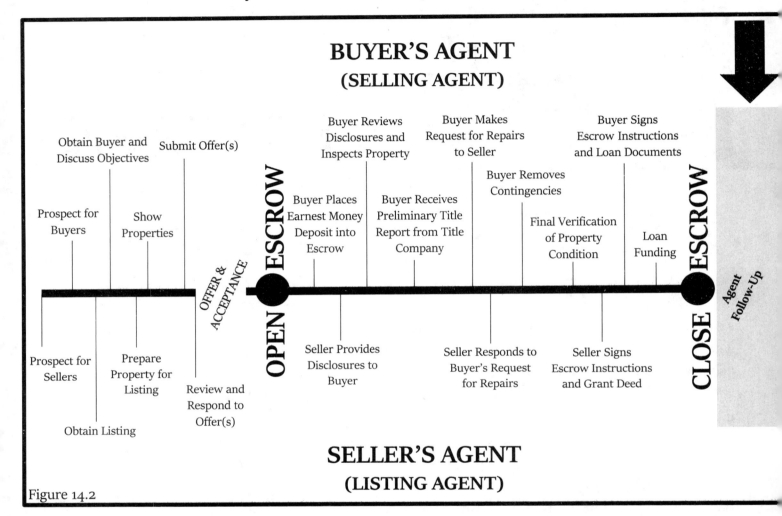

Figure 14.2

1. How Real Estate Brokers and Salespersons Get Paid

A. Real Estate Broker and Salesperson Commissions

An exclusive authorization and right to sell listing agreement normally specifies the commission amount that has been negotiated between the seller and real estate broker. Brokers usually get paid this commission at close of escrow after recordation of the grant deed that transfers title from the seller to the buyer. When the escrow officer receives confirmation of recording of the grant deed, the broker's commission can be paid by the escrow agent to the broker. The broker receives the commission check and then disburses the portion due to the salesperson at that time.

B. Referral Fees

A **referral fee** is paid by one agent to another agent for referring a client. When escrow closes, the referring agent may be paid a referral fee to compensate for the referral. Average referral fees for single-family homes are 20% to 25% of the broker's commission; while commercial properties usually have referral fees of 10% or less.

> **Referral Fee:** Fees paid from a real estate broker to another real estate broker for referring a client.

The Real Estate Settlement Procedures Act (RESPA) does not allow referral fees to be paid between loan officers and agents if the property is a one-to-four unit owner-occupied dwelling. Some companies have affiliated business arrangements that may allow them some flexibility in this area.

C. Finder's Fees

A **finder's fee** is paid from an agent to a non-licensee for introducing the agent to the client. A non-licensee cannot solicit clients for the agent, the non-licensee can only introduce the agent to a potential client.

> **Finder's Fee:** Fees paid from a real estate broker to a member of the general public for referring a client to them.

D. Advance Fee Agreements

An **advance fee agreement** allows a real estate agent to accept a payment in advance (i.e., prior to services rendered) with no guarantee of a successful outcome. An advance fee contract does not guarantee that the sale, lease, or exchange will be completed.

> **Advance Fee Agreement:** Allows a real estate agent to accept a payment in advance (i.e., prior to services rendered) with no guarantee of a successful outcome.

"Advance fee" contracts must include:

- Total amount of compensation or fee to be paid to the broker
- A complete description of the services to be provided by the broker
- Date and terms for payment of the compensation

E. Funds Illegally Paid Directly to a Real Estate Salesperson

Commission income and referral fees cannot be paid directly to a real estate salesperson. The monies must be paid to the salesperson's broker and then the salesperson's broker pays the salesperson. If a salesperson is receiving referral fees directly from anyone, this is illegal and both the salesperson and broker must immediately notify the Real Estate Commissioner in writing of the circumstances of the infraction.

For example, a broker has discovered that one of his salespersons received a referral fee directly from a lender. Salespersons cannot directly receive compensation but must be paid by their broker. Consequently, both the salesperson and broker are subject to disciplinary action by the Commissioner.

F. Funds Paid to Buyer or Seller

If a real estate agent advertises that he will give a seller a $50 credit in escrow from his commission to any seller who lists with him and he will pay $50 to any buyer who purchases a property from him, this type of advertising is legal if disclosure is made to all parties to the transaction. *Real estate salespersons should always consult with their real estate broker before paying money to a buyer or seller.*

G. Out-of-State Broker

A broker in California can pay a commission to an out-of-state broker. For example, you are a California real estate broker. A prospect is referred to you by an out-of-state broker and a sale is consummated by you. You want to split your commission with the cooperating broker. Under the California Real Estate Law you may pay a commission to a broker from another state.

H. Broker Profit

A real estate broker submits a broker demand to escrow for the amount of commission that is due. After confirmation of recording of the grant deed the escrow officer will then "cut a check" to the real estate broker for the amount in the broker demand. The real estate broker then pays the real estate salesperson his or her commission split (as per the written employment and commission agreement between the real estate broker and real estate salesperson). The real estate broker pays all the expenses of running a real estate brokerage office and the money left over is the real estate broker's profit.

(1) Company Dollar/Office Operating Cash

Company Dollar/Office Operating Cash: The amount of money a real estate broker has after paying commissions to other brokers and the real estate broker's salespeople.

Company dollar is the amount of money the broker has after paying commissions to other brokers (cooperative arrangements through the MLS) and to salespersons and associate brokers in the broker's office. The real estate broker collects the company dollar and then pays the desk cost for each salesperson and associate broker. The remaining amount is the real estate broker's profit.

For example, a real estate broker hires a real estate salesperson and places the salesperson's real estate license under the real estate broker's license. The broker negotiates a commission split with the salesperson. Real estate commission splits between real estate brokers and real estate salespersons can be anywhere from 50% broker/50% salesperson to as high 0% broker/100% salesperson. A real estate broker who keeps 50% of the commission and pays 50% to the salesperson, usually recruits brand new agents who have no experience in the real estate brokerage business. The broker must train the agents, so the broker expects an appropriate commission split.

As the salesperson becomes trained and gains more experience, the 50%/50% broker may raise the commission split for the salesperson up to as high as 90% or more to the salesperson and 10% or less to the broker. Some real estate brokers specialize in experienced agents and provide a very high commission split for this type of real estate agent. In fact, some real estate brokerages collect 0% commission and pay the real estate agent all (100%) of the commission. The broker collects income from desk fees charged to agents, secretarial and computer service fees, and other fees that make up the real estate broker's profit from the business.

Tales from the Trade

THE STORY OF THE COMMISSION SPLIT

A single-family home was priced at $300,000 with a 5% commission agreed to by the seller in the listing agreement. Therefore, $300,000 x 5% = $15,000 total commission paid by the seller. The $15,000 total commission is usually split between the listing broker (broker who represents the seller) and selling broker (broker who represents the buyer). Therefore, 2.5% of the sale price ($300,000 x 2.5% = $7,500) is paid to the listing broker and 2.5% of the sale price ($300,000 x 2.5% = $7,500) is paid to the selling broker.

The listing real estate broker then splits the listing side commission ($7,500) with the real estate salesperson who is working under the listing broker to sell the property. If, for example, the listing broker and listing salesperson (who is working under the listing broker's license) have a commission split providing the real estate salesperson to receive 80% of the commission and the real estate broker receives 20% of the commission paid to the listing real estate broker, then the salesperson will receive $6,000 ($7,500 x 80% = $6,000) and the broker will receive $1,500 ($7,500 x 20% = $1,500). High commission splits are normally seen with very experienced real estate agents. Therefore, the real estate salesperson will receive 80% of the $7,500 commission ($6,000) that was paid to the listing broker and the listing broker will keep 20% of the $7,500 commission ($1,500).

The real estate salesperson then pays personal expenses incurred while listing the property for sale and the remaining amount of funds is the salesperson's profit. The real estate salesperson will then pay their own federal and state income taxes that are due each year. However, since real estate salespersons may receive large commission checks over the course of a year, the Internal Revenue Service or IRS (collects federal income tax) and California Franchise Tax Board (collects California state income tax) will most likely require the real estate salesperson to pay income taxes on a quarterly basis during the year the income is earned, rather than at the end of the year like most wage earners. For this reason, it is advisable for new real estate agents who anticipate substantial commission income to see a certified public

▼

THE STORY OF THE COMMISSION SPLIT

accountant (CPA) and set up quarterly tax payments to avoid potential penalties in the future.

The other half of the commission ($300,000 x 2.5% = $7,500) is paid to the selling broker who is representing the buyer in the transaction. Of the $7,500 commission paid to the selling broker, part of the real estate commission is paid to the real estate salesperson who represented the buyer and the other part of the real estate commission is paid to the selling real estate broker (the broker under which the real estate salesperson has placed his or her license). In this case, the real estate salesperson is new to the real estate brokerage business and the starting commission split between the selling real estate broker and selling real estate salesperson is 50% to the salesperson and 50% to the broker. In this instance the real estate salesperson will receive $3,750 ($7,500 x 50%= $3,750) commission and the real estate broker will receive $3,750 ($7,500 x 50% = $3,750) commission.

However, if the real estate salesperson is new and requires training, the real estate broker may ask an experienced real estate salesperson to act as a mentor to the real estate salesperson and help close the first few transactions. For this help, the mentor may ask for 50% of the real estate salesperson's commission. Thus, a $1,875 commission is paid to the selling real estate salesperson (calculated as 50% of the $3,750 paid to the salesperson that came from their 50% commission split with the broker) and $1,875 is paid to the mentor (who is another real estate salesperson who is working under the same real estate broker) for helping the new salesperson close their first deal.

New real estate salespersons need to learn the real estate brokerage business and the costs of mentor training tend to consume a significant amount of their commission income during the first two or three real estate transactions. Once the real estate salesperson learns the real estate business and can operate on their own, then the salesperson can start to receive higher commissions without needing to pay a mentor to help close future deals.

(2) Desk Cost

The total costs to run a real estate brokerage office is called a real estate broker's **desk cost**. Desk cost may include space rent, common area maintenance (CAM) charges (used on triple net leases to pass through expenses to be paid by the tenants in the building), electrical, janitorial, and other overhead costs necessary to run a business. The real estate broker's total expenses are divided into the number of salespersons and associate brokers working under the broker. The result is the cost per salesperson/associate broker the real estate broker incurs each month. This is subtracted from the company dollar and the difference is the real estate broker's profit.

> **Desk Cost:** Total costs are divided by the number of agents in the office to derive the desk cost per agent.

The real estate broker incurs a desk cost for each real estate salesperson and broker associate working under their license, however, it is usually much less than an employer will incur while paying a salary or hourly wage to a worker (employee).

2. Buyer Receives Possession of the Property

There are some additional details that need to be completed after close of escrow. One of them is getting the house keys, mail box key, and other keys that provide property access to the buyer. Selling agents sometimes access the MLS lockbox after confirmation of recording of the grant deed and present the keys to the buyer. If they cannot arrange a meeting with the buyer, the selling agent may take the keys out of the lockbox and place them in a hidden location where the buyer can easily find them. Some agents have been known to place the keys inside the electrical box on the side of the home. Others may place the keys under the doormat. It depends on the desires of the buyer. Selling agents usually suggest that their buyers have the locks changed as soon as possible.

Figure 14.3

A. Seller Occupies the Property After Close of Escrow

Close of escrow is technically when all the terms and conditions of the escrow have been met; yet, for possession purposes close of escrow usually occurs after confirmation of recording of the grant deed. Possession is normally provided to the buyer at 5pm on the date of closing. However, a buyer can legally take possession of a property anytime the parties agree.

Furthermore, with large, owner-occupied properties in which the seller has a large amount of furniture, some agents believe that one or two days after close of escrow is an appropriate time to transfer possession to the buyer. A seller rent-back arrangement prevents a bottleneck on the day of close of escrow and provides less stress for both buyer and seller.

The buyer usually institutes a *seller occupancy addendum* to the purchase agreement for the one or two days the seller is "renting" the property from the buyer. The buyer should consider the home insurance ramifications of having a tenant (seller) in the property for a period after close of escrow. The buyer's homeowner's insurance policy that usually covers the structure for fire, and contents up to a given dollar amount, will not be the correct policy for a landlord who is renting the property to a tenant (even if it is for a short period of time). A landlord's rental policy usually covers the structure for fire and owner's liability insurance in the event of injury to the seller while occupying the property. Many homeowner's insurance policies do not provide coverage for the personal contents of the tenant (seller in this case). Therefore, the buyer/landlord may consider an Owner–Landlord–Tenant (OLT) policy for the seller's short occupancy period.

The amount of rent paid by the seller is usually negotiated in the contract and can be paid inside or outside of escrow. Many escrow officers prefer that rent be paid outside of escrow because of the many potential problems that are out of the control of the escrow officer and real estate agent(s). A common amount of rent paid by the seller is the interest, property taxes, and homeowner's insurance being paid by the buyer prorated over the one or two days the seller occupies the property. Principal reduction is not included because it is not a buyer expense.

However, the buyer should obtain a significant security deposit from the seller. This will take care of any problems that may arise from a seller leaving the property in worse condition than it appeared at the buyer's walk-thru inspection prior to close of escrow. A security deposit will also provide some leverage if the seller does not move out of the home on the agreed upon date. The buyer may be forced to evict the seller from the property, which can be expensive and time-consuming.

Conversely, what happens when the buyer moves in early? A buyer can legally take possession of a property when both the buyer and seller agree. This can be at close of escrow, before close of escrow, or after close of escrow. An interim occupancy agreement (i.e., a short lease) is used when a buyer will move in prior to the close of escrow, and a seller occupancy addendum is used when the seller will move out after the close of escrow. No addendum is usually needed if the buyer moves in at close of escrow.

If a real estate agent sells a property in which the buyer will take possession prior to transferring title, the document the buyer and seller will execute is called an **interim occupancy agreement**. An interim occupancy agreement is used when a buyer will take possession of the property prior to close of escrow. When this happens, the buyer becomes the tenant of the seller. If the buyer is unable to obtain financing for the property, the sale may fall out of escrow and the seller is stuck with a person living in the property. The seller will have to use formal eviction procedures to move the tenant out of the property. The seller may or may not have a security deposit from the former buyer who is now a tenant.

Interim Occupancy Agreement: Agreement that allows the buyer to move into the property before close of escrow.

If the buyer and seller agree to have the buyer move in early, prior to close of escrow, the seller should consider the home insurance ramifications also. The buyer may destroy the property and then not close escrow, or the buyer may be injured while living there and sue the seller. In addition, if the buyer is unable to purchase the property, the seller may be forced to evict the potential buyer, who is now a tenant. The potential buyer may have painted the walls some interesting colors, as well as made some "improvements" to the property during their occupancy period. Thus, a large security deposit is advisable for this type of situation as well. Many agents will advise their sellers not to move a buyer in early because of the inherent problems associated with early possession and potential future eviction problems.

3. Lockbox and For Sale Sign Removed

The listing agent usually goes by the property after confirmation of recording and removes the lockbox from the home. The for sale sign is removed either by the listing agent sending a sign removal request to the sign company or the listing agent personally picking up the sign at that time. Both the MLS lockbox and sign should be removed promptly from the property.

4. MLS Updated

The listing agent must also remember to update the MLS as sold, which entails going into the MLS and changing the listing status from pending sale to sold. The agent may include the sale price, type of financing, whether any seller concessions were provided and the amount, escrow company, escrow number, and recording date. The information is very useful to other agents because the property is a recent sales comparable and can be used by other agents to help potential sellers price their properties for sale. This is especially useful in a rapidly changing real estate market that is increasing or decreasing at a fast rate. The tax record database may take several months to add the sale price information to their database. In contrast, sales comparables are accessible to MLS participants

Figure 14.4

immediately after the listing agent enters the sale information in the MLS database.

5. Client Added to Follow-Up Email List

Real estate agents should add their clients to their follow-up email database. Social media is an excellent way to keep in contact with past clients and continually remind them that the real estate agent is in the real estate business and loves referrals and repeat business.

6. Real Estate Agent Liability Issues

Real estate agents must keep in mind that the real estate brokerage business does come with some professional liability to the agent. This is especially true during a downward-trending buyers' market when real estate property prices are decreasing. Real estate buyers will see the value of their purchase decreasing in the months and years after the purchase. Some of these buyers may try to get someone else (and not them) to take the loss by finding something wrong with the property and use it as a way to obtain a settlement from the seller. Even though the listing and selling agents knew nothing of the issue being contested by the buyer, they may be added to the lawsuit as well. For this reason, real estate brokers usually carry errors and omissions (E&O) insurance to cover these types of eventualities.

E&O insurance usually covers the real estate salesperson and broker for negligent misrepresentation in which the agent merely missed the item in question. E&O insurance, however, usually does not cover the real estate salesperson and broker for intentional misrepresentation which is fraud (a nice word for lying).

A buyer must have been harmed by the seller and/or real estate agent(s) to collect damages. The amount of harm may be a

Figure 14.5 Errors and Omissions (E&O) Insurance Diagram

loss in value to the property and is called compensatory damages. When this occurs, the real estate broker has vicarious liability for the actions of the real estate salesperson who is working under their real estate broker's license.

If the agent knew about the issue in question and did not disclose it to the buyer, then the agent may be guilty of fraud and the buyer may be able to collect punitive damages against the real estate salesperson and broker. Punitive damages are considered punishment damages and may be calculated by the amount the seller (and possibly the real estate salesperson and broker) have in assets (i.e., their net worth) rather than the severity of the misrepresentation.

7. Items in the Home Become Inoperable After Close of Escrow

A home warranty insurance policy (home warranty) are used to provide the buyer with a means of repairing broken mechanical items that occur *after* close of escrow. A home warranty policy insulates the seller and the real estate agent(s) from any potential liability that may be asserted by the buyer against the seller, listing agent, and even the selling agent for nondisclosure of material facts (i.e., mechanical items, such as a stove or dishwasher going out during the first year after close of escrow). Home warranty companies will generally *not* pay for preexisting conditions if the item was already in disrepair prior to close of escrow.

8. Title Defects are Discovered After Close of Escrow

During the close of escrow, the buyer and lender normally obtain title insurance for the home. This insures that the seller is delivering good title to the buyer and there are no encumbrances or breaks in the chain-of-title that will cause the property to become unmarketable in the future.

If a title defect is discovered after close of escrow, the title insurance company may be required to pay for the buyer's (and/or lender's) loss. Even though grant deeds have two implied warranties (the seller not having sold the property to someone else and there are no undisclosed encumbrances), title insurance allows the buyer to be compensated for their loss without using the courts for restitution.

Title insurance is a contractual obligation by a title insurance company to the buyer and/or lender to protect them against losses that may occur when title to a property is not free and clear of defects (e.g., liens, encumbrances, and defects that were known when the title policy was issued). Good, marketable title is title that a reasonable person would accept as free and clear from challenge.

Title insurance policies are issued at close of escrow and protect the buyer and/or lender from title defects that occurred before the buyer owned the property, yet, may cause a loss in value to the property now or in the future. The title insurer will reimburse the property owner for losses that are covered, up to the face amount of the policy, and any related legal expenses. This protection is effective as of the issue date of the policy and covers defects arising prior to ownership.

Before issuing a title insurance policy, title companies search and examine public records and, in certain circumstances, survey the property to identify liens, claims, or encumbrances that relate to the property, and alert the new buyer to possible title defects. A title insurance company obtains data from their own title plant (that researches titles to real property), federal court clerk, and tax agencies.

The title insurance premium cost is a one-time charge payable at the time of escrow closing.

Some encumbrances are apparent when looking at a property, while others will need a title search to be uncovered. In either case, title defects are extremely important for a buyer to discover during the due diligence period prior to close of escrow.

A. Chain of Title

Chain of Title: Every person who has owned a property all the way back to the Spanish Land Grants in California.

The **chain of title** (chain of recorded title) is the recorded history of ownership interests that affect the subject parcel of real property, including encumbrances and other matters relating to the title to a property. Each change of ownership is chronologically placed to form a "chain" representing all the owners of the property from the beginning of recorded title (Spanish Land Grants in California) to the present. If there are any breaks in the chain of title, there is a cloud on the title and the present owners may not have valid title to the property.

B. Blockchain Technology and Distributed Ledger Systems

Blockchain Technology and Distributed Ledger Systems place information on multiple computers that are located all over the world. Each computer can be used to check the other computers to verify the information stored on each of the computers. For this reason, blockchain technology and its distributed ledger system may be the future for recorded documents such as real estate title information.

C. Abstract of Title

Abstract of Title: A list of every person who has owned a property. *Not* normally used in California.

Every recorded change of ownership and/or claim of ownership for a property is in the abstract of title. In other words, an **abstract of title** is a history of conveyances and encumbrances affecting title to real property. An abstract of title is typically *not* used in California but is used in other states that use attorneys to handle real estate closings.

D. Cloud on Title

Quiet Title Action: Court action to remove a cloud on the title to real property.

A **quiet title action** is a court action designed to quiet the title of a parcel of real property that has a cloud on the title. For example, Anna Able recorded title to her existing property as "a single woman." Later, she married Bob Baker and changed the name on the deed to read, "Anna Baker, a married woman." This would create a cloud on the title.

Tales from the Trade

The Story of the Deed of Reconveyance

An elderly woman owned a single-family home for many years. There were two deeds of trust that had been paid off many years ago; however, there had not been deed of reconveyances instituted to remove the two deeds of trust from title to the property. The woman decided to sell the property but was not able to do so because the existing deeds of trust appeared on the preliminary title report. The preliminary title report showed the two deeds of trust existing on the title to the property and the title insurance company would not insure the title to the property for this reason. Most astute all-cash buyers will only purchase a property if they can get title insurance. Accordingly, if a buyer is obtaining a loan to purchase the property, then the lender will require title insurance.

So, the woman was stuck with a property that had a defective title. The two old loans had been private party loans, so when both beneficiaries (lenders) died, it was impossible to have them sign the deed of reconveyance and remove them from the chain of recorded title to the property.

The woman considered a quiet title action in court to clear the cloud on the title. However, quiet title actions are expensive and time consuming. She could have asked a judge to rule on it through a summary judgment since there was no one to contest the loans, however, that remained expensive and time consuming as well.

She asked the title insurance company to allow her to indemnify them against loss in the future from the old loans remaining on title to the property. The title company agreed and required her to sign an affidavit indemnifying them against loss in the future if anything surfaced regarding the two loans. She was able to sell the home and the buyer was able to obtain title insurance for the property.

Chapter Fourteen Summary

Real estate commissions, referral fees, finder's fees, and funds paid to the buyer or seller are discussed in light of real estate license requirements. Advance fee agreements allow a real estate agent to charge a fee before the work in completed, with no guarantee of the result. Company dollar and desk costs include the real estate broker's commission income (company dollar) less the costs to operate the business (desk costs) to derive the broker's profit. The chapter then discusses the illegal payment of money directly to the real estate salesperson and not through their broker. Funds paid to the buyer or seller are considered, along with getting the house keys to the buyer, removing the MLS lockbox and for sale sign, updating the MLS, and adding the client to the real estate agent's follow-up email list are discussed. Agent liability is covered in light of negligent and intentional misrepresentation. Lastly, items becoming inoperable and title defects after close of escrow are discussed.

Chapter Fourteen Quiz

1. A(n) _____ specifies the commission amount that has been negotiated between the seller and real estate broker.
(A) exclusive authorization and right to sell listing agreement
(B) power of attorney
(C) novation
(D) none of the above are correct

2. _____ is the amount of money the broker has after paying commissions to other brokers (cooperative arrangements through the MLS) and to salespersons and associate brokers in the broker's office.
(A) Desk cost
(B) Company dollar
(C) Both (A) and (B) are correct
(D) Neither (A) nor (B) is correct

3. The real estate broker incurs a(n) _____ for each real estate salesperson working under their license, however, it is usually much less than an employer will incur while paying a salary or hourly wage to a worker (employee).
(A) company dollar
(B) office operating cash
(C) desk cost
(D) all of the above are correct

4. A buyer can legally take possession of a property:
(A) anytime the parties agree
(B) when only the seller agrees
(C) never before close of escrow
(D) only if the California Real Estate Commissioner approves it

5. With large, owner-occupied properties in which the seller has a large amount of furniture (e.g., lived in the property for a long period of time and accumulated a large amount of personal property) some agents believe that _____ is an appropriate time to transfer possession to the buyer
(A) one or two days before close of escrow
(B) three weeks before close of escrow
(C) one of two days after close of escrow
(D) none of the above are correct

6. The listing agent usually goes by the property after _____ and removes the lockbox from the home.
(A) the physical inspection has been removed
(B) the financing contingency has been removed
(C) the appraisal contingency has been removed
(D) confirmation of recording

7. The listing agent must also remember to update the MLS as sold, which entails going into the MLS and changing the listing status from pending sale to sold. The agent may include the:
(A) sale price and type of financing
(B) whether any seller concessions were provided and the amount
(C) escrow company, escrow number, and recording date
(D) All of the above are correct

8. Real estate agents must keep in mind that the real estate brokerage business does come with some professional liability to the agent. This is especially true during a _____ when real estate property prices are _____.
(A) upward-trending buyers' market; increasing
(B) downward-trending buyers' market; decreasing
(C) upward-trending sellers' market; decreasing
(D) downward-trending sellers' market; increasing

9. Blockchain Technology and Distributed Ledger Systems:
(A) place information on multiple computers that are located all over the world
(B) place information on one computer that is locked up in vault
(C) have no future with real estate titles
(D) None of the above are correct

10. A _____ is an action designed to quiet the title of a parcel of real property that has a cloud on the title.
(A) quitclaim deed
(B) grant deed
(C) warranty deed
(D) quiet title action

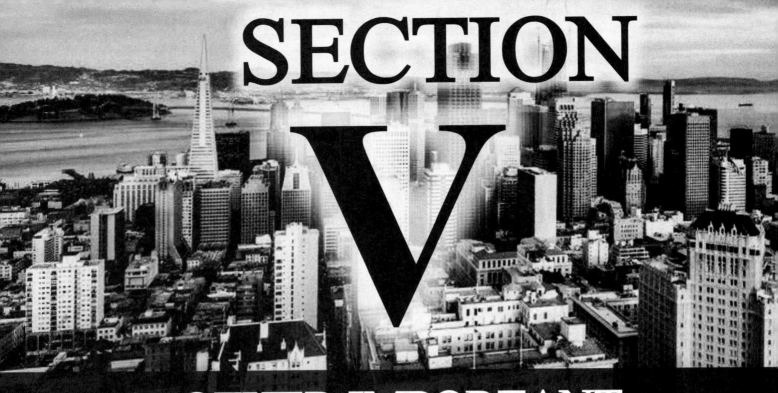

SECTION V

OTHER IMPORTANT REAL ESTATE AREAS

SECTION FIVE
Other Important Real Estate Areas

Working with Real Estate Investors

Acquisition	Holding Period	Disposition
Investment	Income	Capital

Investors

and Real Estate Taxation

Buyer	Assessor	Auditor	Tax Collector
Purchases new home	Determines the new assessed value after the deed is recorded	Applies tax rates to new assessed value to determine property tax	Mails tax bills and collects property tax payments

Will Rogers

"The only difference between death and taxes is that death doesn't get worse every time Congress meets."

15

Chapter
FIFTEEN

Working with Real Estate Investors and Real Estate Taxation

An owner of real property may be able to separate a property's freehold and leasehold estates. When the owner rents out a property to a tenant, the owner is giving possession for a short period of time (leasehold estate) to the tenant in exchange for the tenant paying rent to the owner. In other words, the tenant receives the leasehold estate in the property (possession) in return for paying rent to the owner (who continues to hold the freehold estate).

This process allows property owners to obtain rental income from a property by giving up possession in return for rent. The property owner keeps the freehold estate (considered real property) during the entire rental process and then regains possession when the tenant moves out and relinquishes possession back to the property owner. The property owner then owns both the freehold estate, which has been held all along by the owner, and the leasehold estate (possession and considered personal property) of the property. The leasehold estate is extinguished at this time because the property is not rented to a tenant.

The property owner then finds another tenant to take possession of the property, signs a rental agreement, the tenant pays rent, and the process repeats.

This is one of the reasons why real estate is such a good investment over the long-term. Property owners can rent their properties to a tenant and obtain income (net operating income), while at the same time enjoying the benefits of possible price appreciation over the holding period. In addition, the property owner can deduct depreciation for the property over the holding period, even though the property may actually be increasing in value at the time. **Depreciation** is a paperwork loss the IRS allows investors to take on their income tax returns. The IRS allows property owners to depreciate the improved (building) portion of the property over a set depreciation schedule. Residential income properties are depreciated over 27.5 years straight line (evenly depreciated each year), and commercial income properties are depreciated over 39 years straight line.

Depreciation: From a taxation standpoint, it is a paperwork loss the IRS allows a person to take on their taxes.

Lastly, property owners may be able to leverage their investment during an upward-trending sellers' market by using real estate loans–rather than using all cash (equity)–to purchase the property.

Cost of Homeownership: Equity is stuck in the home and cannot be used to provide income from other investments.

The **cost of homeownership** is the loss of interest on the owner's equity. For example, the property owner could have the down payment collecting interest in a mutual fund, thus creating a yield on the money. Instead, it is in the house not producing any cash flow.

1. Residential Income Properties

Residential income properties encompass tenant-occupied single-family rental homes (a single-family home that has been rented to a tenant); small multi-unit residential properties containing two (duplex), three (triplex), or four (fourplex or quadraplex) rental units; and all the way up to the largest multi-unit residential properties that are comprised of hundreds of rental units.

A. Single-Family Homes

Real estate investors generally have different alternatives than owner-occupied homeowners. They can buy and sell, not based upon their own home and where they live, but strictly by market timing. When the real estate market nears the top of an upward-trending sellers' market, many investors perform a 1031 tax-deferred exchange and move their equity into another real estate market in the U.S. that has not yet peaked.

Figure 15.1

Allan Ferguson/Wikimedia Commons

Single-family homes tend to be the most desirable property type for tenants, with halfplexes, townhouses/townhomes, and condominiums following on the desirability continuum. If an investor purchases single-family rental properties at the right time, they may be in a good position to take advantage of future price appreciation.

The financial analysis of single-family rental properties can be accomplished through the investigation of sales comparables and rental comparables.

(1) Sales Comparables

A sales comparable or "sales comp" is the documented sale price, terms, and other pertinent information for the sale of a specific parcel of real property. For a sales comparable to be effective, it should be as close as possible in geographic location, size, condition, and construction to the subject property. It should also be as recent as possible.

Sales comparables can generally be obtained from the county recorder in the county where the property is located, the county property tax database, a local title insurance company's title plant, and/or a local Multiple Listing Service (MLS) database. Many title insurance companies are willing to perform customer service work for real estate agents at no charge. The title information generated from computerized databases is usually fairly accurate and tends to make sales comparables easier to locate.

A real estate investor usually bases sales price on the market data appraisal method, which uses sales comparables. The income approach is generally not appropriate for use with single-family income properties. This is because a real estate investor is usually competing with owner-occupied homebuyers who have different financing terms and psychological motivations for purchasing a single-family home. When a real estate investor sells a single-family home at the end of its holding period, the investor most likely will sell it to an owner-occupied buyer who can and will pay more money for the property than another real estate investor.

Owner-occupied homebuyers are usually buying on emotion and generally have lower interest rates and higher loan-to-value ratios than real estate investors. For these reasons, they can and will pay more money for a single-family home than a real estate investor who is not emotional and is looking at the property strictly as an investment vehicle.

Owner-occupied buyers tend to drive the prices of homes up and down due to the availability of housing in the local geographic area, employment sources, prevailing wages, and owner-occupied single-family loan interest rates.

Tales from the Trade

The Story of the Crooked Husband and His Fraudulent Girlfriend

There was one occasion when a man tried to have his girlfriend pose as his wife while conveying a single-family home to a buyer. His wife had divorced him, remarried, and then died; yet she remained a joint tenant with him on the title to the property. He was not knowledgeable about real estate closing procedures and did not realize that this fraud would surface when the notary public asked for his "wife's" driver's license and thumb print. The girlfriend may have been able to produce a forged driver's license, but the thumbprint would most likely have produced a very long "rap sheet."

Real estate investors generally look at single-family rental properties as an investment vehicle that will derive a projected rate of return at an acceptable level of risk over a projected holding period. Therefore, a real estate investor may base his or her investment decisions on projected appreciation of single-family homes in a particular geographic area and NOT on projected increases in income derived from increased rents. This is one of the main differences between single-family and multi-unit residential investment properties.

(2) Rental Comparables

To perform a rental comparable analysis, a single-family investor may physically inspect the local geographic area around the subject property. A few calls to "For Rent" signs or advertisements online will usually provide a general idea of the rental range for the property. Calls to a few local property management companies may be helpful in determining market rents as well. A conservative estimate is usually the best course. Savvy single-family home investors usually plan for the lower end of a rental range and then are pleasantly surprised when they receive higher rents for the property.

(3) A Single-Family Home is Converted into a Rental Property

When an owner-occupied homeowner decides to purchase a new home and rent their present home to a tenant, they may be able to use part of the rental income from the existing home to qualify for a loan on the new home. This really depends on the loan underwriting guidelines of the lender for the new home.

The existing home, that will become a rental property, may have a high loan-to-value ratio because it was purchased with owner-occupied financing. Lenders generally regard owner-occupied buyers as having less default risk than real estate investors. Owner-occupied homebuyers need a place to live and will usually try to avoid foreclosure more frequently than investors—who look at a home strictly as an investment.

If the single-family investment has not worked out, real estate investors typically make a business decision to cut their losses and walk away from the property. For this reason, lenders generally charge real estate investors a higher interest rate and require a larger down payment than they do homeowners buying owner-occupied properties.

For example, a home was originally purchased with owner-occupied financing and the homeowner turned the home into a rental property. The homeowner (now turned real estate investor) may have paid as little as 5% down payment and financed the remaining 95%. This is considered a 95% loan-to-value (LTV) loan and is well above the 80% maximum LTV most lenders feel comfortable loaning to owner-occupied buyers in a normal real estate market.

If an owner-occupied borrower has an exceptionally good credit rating and stable income, a private mortgage insurance (PMI) company may step in and insure the 15% (95%-80%= 15%) the lender does not want to loan. PMI covered loans are generally used for owner-occupied single-family home loans and may not be available for non-owner occupied home loans.

An owner-occupied lender is usually comfortable with 80% LTV exposure; however, the 15% insured by the PMI company must be paid to the lender by the PMI company if these is a foreclosure. PMI companies are generally fairly active during upward-trending sellers' markets—because property values are increasing, and they have less risk than exists in a declining market.

Conversely, PMI companies may be practically nonexistent in a downward-trending buyers' market. PMI companies ask themselves, "Why insure a 95% LTV loan when the market is heading downward?"

A loan with PMI insurance will allow the owner to lose their 5% down payment; however, the lender may actually come out in fairly good shape as the PMI company must pay for the lender's loss-up to 15% of the loan amount (the amount of the down payment the borrower was not required to pay because the PMI

Private Mortgage Insurance (PMI)

company insured it). This amount, of course, is the amount of the down payment that the borrower did not make and the lender did not want to lend. So, the PMI insurer usually pays for this loss.

However, if the homeowner had originally purchased the property as a rental property, most lenders would have required at least 20-30% down and charged a higher interest rate than owner-occupied borrowers. Most lenders want the borrower to have some "skin in the game," so if there is a foreclosure, the borrower will have enough equity at stake to make an honest attempt to keep the property—rather than walk away at the first sign of trouble. Thus, it is sometimes advantageous to purchase a property with owner-occupied financing and then convert it into a rental property in the future.

Example #1: Wealth Building

Year 1

A husband and wife purchase a $110,000 single-family home located in Chico, California. The buyers can qualify for $180,000, however, their loan payments will be greater than what the house will rent for in the future (when the property becomes a rental). Therefore, the husband and wife purchase less house, put their egos on the back burner, and plan for the future. They pick a middle socio-economic neighborhood, instead of the more affluent neighborhoods where their friends live, and their income qualifies them as a dual income household.

Property Purchase:

$ 11,000	Down payment (10%)
$99,000	Promissory note secured by a first deed of trust, 7% fixed rate (example only), 30-year amortization schedule, due in 30 years.
$110,000	Purchase price

Monthly Payment:

$658.65	Principal and Interest
$ 92.00	Property Taxes
$ 30.00	Homeowner's Insurance
$ 40.00	Private Mortgage Insurance (PMI)
$ 41.25	Property Management Fee (5% of gross collected rents paid when the property becomes a rental, but may be as high as 10% of gross collected rents plus one month's rent as a lease up fee.)
$861.90	PITI plus PMI and Property Management Fee

The husband and wife must first perform a market rental analysis for single-family homes in the area where they intend to purchase.

Break-Even Analysis:

Scheduled Gross Income (annual)		$10,200
less Vacancy (5% is normal, but is not considered here)		N/A
Effective Gross Income		$10,200
less Operating Expenses		
Property Taxes (1.15-1.25% of sale price)	$1,104	
Property Insurance	$ 360	
Private Mortgage Insurance (PMI)	$ 480	
Property Management Expenses	$ 495	
Total Operating Expenses		$ 2,439
Net Operating Income		$ 7,761
less Debt Service (no principal reduction considered)		$ 7,903 (annual)
Before Tax Cash Flow		($ 142)

This is very close to a break-even cash flow.

If the husband and wife do not achieve a break-even cash flow, they will generally continue to bring the purchase price downward and increase the down payment until this balance is achieved.

If the single-family homes they purchase are located in too low of a socio-economic neighborhood, they may expect destructive tenants in the future, so they may want to consider halfplexes, townhouses, and condominiums located in higher socio-economic neighborhoods.

Year 4

The husband receives a promotion and must move to the San Fernando Valley in Southern California. The real estate market nationally has rebounded, but not in Southern California. It is two years or more behind the rest of the United States and still trying to recover from earthquakes, floods, fires, and tsunamis.

The single-family residential property the investors bought in Year 1 may have lost some of its value because of the economic recession. However, since they purchased an entry-level home, their devaluation is not nearly as severe as the homes in the higher $180,000 price range.

The new value of this Chico home is $100,000. Since their loan is $99,000 (less four years of principal reduction which is not considered in this example), the employer may step in and purchase the house from the husband and wife, sell it, and pay the difference (loss). The difference can be significant because closing costs and sales commissions will be approximately $10,000. Total out of pocket costs to the employer will be approximately $11,000.

When the employer purchases the employee's home, the employee will go to Southern California with more salary income, but without any equity in his pockets nor control of any assets that may produce equity in the future. He and his wife will be starting over. They will be relegated to renters once again. Independent wealth and early retirement will remain the same distance away as it was in Year 1.

The other alternative is to turn the Chico home into a rental property. By purchasing below their means and not making the usual homeowner over-improvements, they may be able to rent the property near a break-even cash flow and in a basic rentable condition. Many improvements do not increase the rental value of a home.

Interior and exterior paint and trimmed landscape are usually the most cost-effective improvements a landlord can make to a property. It might be best to make all the major renovations (new carpet, appliances, and fixtures) just prior to selling the home at the end of the holding period many years down the road. As mentioned earlier, if the property owner times the market correctly, the owner may be able to sell the property at the top-of-the-market *without* performing an extensive rehabilitation of the home at all.

In addition, it is usually a good idea to purchase a home built after 1978 because of potential hazardous materials that may exist in the home. Many pre-1978 homes have asbestos in their ceiling material and lead-based paint throughout the interior walls of the home. This can be a potential liability problem for both sellers and real estate agents. Homes built in 1978 and later usually have less maintenance costs than other older homes. Older homes tend to have increasingly more expensive maintenance costs as appliances, sinks, fixtures, HVAC systems, and other items wear out over time and must be replaced.

Furthermore, since the husband and wife have been living below their means in Chico, they may have been able to save some of their income.

Thus, during year 4, when the husband and wife move to Southern California, they may have enough money for a down payment on a new Southern California home. In addition, loan qualification may be enhanced as the husband's new position probably pays more money and the wage scale for the wife's job is much higher in Southern California.

Since the husband and wife's intent is a long-term hold for the property, they should look at loan interest rates. Since interest rates were 7% fixed (example) in

Year 1 and may go up in the future, a fixed rate loan may have been a good idea in Year 1. If they thought interest rates were going to go down, an adjustable rate loan may have been the answer. It really depends upon the husband and wife's tolerance for interest rate risk.

At this point 4 years later, interest rates have (for example) increased to 11%. They should do a cash flow analysis over the holding period and possibly purchase the property.

Year 8

The executive husband is promoted again, but this time to San Francisco. The cost of living index in Chico is 100 (examples), San Fernando Valley 130, and San Francisco 235. Even with the one spouse's incredible income, the husband and wife can only afford to purchase a home three hours commuting time from the office location in San Francisco. The husband pays for this promotion with commuting time and stress. The husband and wife may be able to purchase their third home with owner-occupied financing. They will probably not have enough income available to purchase a fourth home with this type of financing in the future. They will probably be forced to purchase future homes through non-owner occupied financing, seller financing, or other types of creative financing.

Year 12

The husband is promoted again. This time to San Diego. The national economy is peaking. The husband and wife purchase their fourth home with a large down payment and a seller-carry loan at the prevailing market interest rates.

Year 16

The husband and wife's loans have started to amortize with significant principal reduction (especially true if they used 15-year amortization schedules instead of 30 years, although the higher payments may not have been practical) and additional equity has built up through price appreciation in the homes.

If the husband and wife can acquire ten homes over their careers, they could have close to $1 million in equity as they reach age 55. This is in addition to retirement accounts and other more passive securities investments. This strategy is not a walk in the park, however. Even with a professional property manager managing the property, the husband and wife will still have to deal with the headaches of being a landlord.

Example #2: Inexpensive Home Located in a Lower Socio-Economic Area

A real estate investor paid $65,000 all cash to purchase a 3 bedroom/1 bathroom home located in Northern California. The home was built in 1953 with a concrete slab foundation, thus making it difficult to add a second bathroom to the property. However, the concrete slab foundation may have more durability than a raised foundation because the wood piers and columns in the raised foundation may wear out over time. Consequently, the concrete slab foundation may not have as many water leakage issues in the bathroom and kitchen versus a raised foundation.

The property is located near Sacramento. It has good proximity for State of California workers, easy freeway access, and a predominately blue-collar neighborhood. Plus, the long-term economic outlook is good as job sources include the State of California, High Tech Industries, Medical, and Service businesses.

The home rents for $1,000 per month, with rents projected to increase in the future as demand for single-family homes increases and supply stays the same. This will probably be due to projected population growth resulting from a high quality of life and solid median household income levels. Furthermore, this tends to cause long-term increases in rents and price appreciation for single-family homes in the area.

Tenants living in lower socio-economic neighborhoods, however, are generally more difficult to manage than higher-end tenants living in higher socio-economic neighborhoods. This is because lower socio-economic tenants typically have less income than tenants living in higher socio-economic neighborhoods, so feeding the family may come before paying the rent.

Figure 15.3 Older Home in a Lower Socio-Economics Neighborhood

The Numbers:

$65,000	All cash purchase price
$12,000/year rents	$1,000/month rents x 12 months/year

Net Operating Income Calculation:

Scheduled Gross Income	$12,000
less Vacancy	$ 0
Effective Gross Income	$12,000

less Operating Expenses

Property Taxes (1.25% of purchase price)	$ 813	
Insurance (Owner Liability and Tenant Policy or OLT)	$ 425	
Water, Sewer, & Garbage ($125 per month)*	$1,500	
Maintenance (based on age of property)	$1,000	
Total Expenses		$ 3,738
Net Operating Income		$ 8,262

*Water, sewer, and garbage may become a lien on a property if the tenant does not pay the bill. This means that the landlord will be stuck paying this bill no matter what happens with the tenant. Thus, some landlords pay the water, sewer, and garbage bills themselves and increase the rental amount accordingly to cover it. Water meter usage is sometimes billed to the tenant.

Capitalization Rate:

The real estate investor's return is the capitalization rate when all cash is used to purchase the property. Therefore, Price x Capitalization Rate = Net Operating Income. In other words, capitalization rate is the return a real estate investor receives if all cash is paid to purchase the property.

Value (V)   x   Rate (R)   =   Income (I)
$65,000 (price)   x   ?% (capitalization rate)   = $8,262 (NOI)

Therefore, V x R = I   **OR**   I/V = R (income divided by value equals rate)

Thus,

$$\frac{\$8,262 \text{ (Income)}}{\$65,000 \text{ (Value)}} = 12.71\% \text{ Rate}$$

Therefore, the capitalization rate is 12.71%.

To verify the calculation, $65,000 (V) x 12.71% (R) = $8,262 (I).

In addition to a 12.71% return on the buyer's all cash investment, the buyer may also experience price appreciation (increase in the value of the property) during the holding period. If the buyer purchased the home during an upward-trending sellers' market, the buyer may experience an increase in value that will increase the overall return when the property is sold in the future.

The buyer may receive depreciation, which is a paperwork loss the IRS may allow the buyer to take on the buyer's income taxes, from the property over the holding period. The IRS generally allows real estate investors to depreciate residential income properties over a 27.5 year straight-line period (an equal amount of deprecation is taken over 27.5 years). Of course, buyers and sellers should always see their CPA or tax attorney before making any real estate investment.

If single-family homes start to appreciate (increase) in value over the holding period, clients may decide to pull out some of their equity through a cash-out refinance. This allows homeowners to leverage their investment with financing and purchase more properties in the future. It really depends on market timing. This strategy tends to work well during a strong upward-trending sellers' market. However, it generally does not work very well during a downward-trending buyers' market.

The single-family home investor can pay off some of the loan through amortization. This is the systematic liquidation of a debt obligation over a period of time. The total principal and interest payment for a fixed rate loan never changes. Each payment is part principal and part interest. The portion of the total payment that is principal increases and the portion that is interest decreases with each payment over the life of the loan.

Single-family homes have been the most desirable type of property in which both tenants and owners enjoy living. Sometimes single-family home prices are so expensive, that many tenants and homeowners cannot afford to live there. This leads to tenants renting a less-expensive unit in a multi-unit residential property (apartment building). For this reason, real estate investors may decide to purchase a duplex, triplex, or fourplex in lieu of a single-family home.

B. Small Multi-Unit Residential Properties: Duplex, Triplex, and Fourplex

A duplex is a building that is comprised of two residential units located on one parcel of real property. Owners of duplexes can rent each of the units to a separate tenant or occupy one of the units and rent the other unit to a tenant. A triplex is three apartment units

Figure 15.4 Duplex

located in one building. An owner can occupy one unit and rent the other two units to tenants or rent all three units to tenants. A fourplex (also called quadraplex in some markets) is four apartment units in one building. An owner can occupy one unit and rent the other three units to tenants or rent all four units to tenants. When the owner lives in one unit and rents the other unit(s) in a duplex, triplex, or fourplex to tenants, the owner may be eligible for owner-occupied financing for the *entire* property–even though part of the property is rented to tenants and producing income.

Figure 15.5 Fourplex

Sometimes a builder will build a building comprised of two residential units with each adjoining unit having its own parcel of real estate. Thus, each half of the two residential unit building is comprised of one unit and is called a halfplex.

Tales from the Trade

The Story of a Fourplex Short Sale

A real estate investor found a fourplex (apartment building with four units) that was being sold as a short sale. A short sale occurs when the seller's existing loan is greater than the value of the property. The seller asks the lender to allow a short sale in which the lender accepts less than the total amount of the loan when the property is sold.

The fourplex was listed for sale at $94,000. It was hoped that the lender would accept $94,000 in lieu of the outstanding balance of the loan that was $325,000. At the time, $94,000 was the value of the fourplex in the neighborhood where it was located.

The real estate investor made an offer to purchase the fourplex for $94,000 all cash. The real estate investor had fourteen (14) days to inspect the property (physical inspection contingency period) and thirty days (30) days to close escrow. The purchase agreement required the real estate investor to place $5,000 as an earnest money deposit.

The seller accepted the real estate investor's offer and escrow was opened with an escrow officer who was referred by the listing agent (agent of the seller). The real estate investor looked at the condition of the property and realized that it was a major fixer. It needed new windows, new flooring, painted inside and out, new kitchens in two of the units, ranges and refrigerators in all of the units, and new central heating, ventilating, and air conditioning (HVAC) systems in all of the units. The real estate investor thought he could get away with not replacing the roof for a few years. The estimated rehabilitation cost was $50,000 or more–depending on the company that performed the work and the quality of materials used to complete the rehab. ▼

The Story of a Fourplex Short Sale ▲

The real estate investor decided to remove the physical inspection contingency at the end of the fourteen (14) day period and move forward with the purchase. At the end of thirty (30) days the lender had not fully approved the short sale and had not decided whether to accept $94,000 (less a 6% commission and closing costs) instead of the $325,000 that was owed by the seller.

Thirty days after the contractual date to close escrow had expired, the lender finally approved the $94,000 sale price and accepted the loss ($325,000 loan amount owed by the seller minus $94,000 lender-approved purchase price). The listing agent and selling agent had extended the contract for another thirty days at the end of the first thirty (30) day period that was stated in the contract. This required the seller and buyer to sign an addendum extending the contract. The lender did not sign the addendum because the lender did not own the property. The seller continued to own the property and the lender was merely accepting less than the full amount owed on the existing loan that was secured by the fourplex. Thus, the real estate investor was able to stay "in contract" during the entire period from contract acceptance until close of escrow.

Escrow closed sixty (60) days after the effective date of the contract. The real estate investor immediately started the rehabilitation of the property back to a rentable condition. Thirty days later the rehab was completed, and a professional property manager was hired to lease the property and manage it during the real estate investor's holding period. The property manager charged 10% of the effective gross income (actual rents collected) and was able to find four solid tenants to occupy the property. The tenants had good rental histories in which they had paid their rent on time, not destroyed the property while living there, and stayed there for a significant period of time. The real estate investor decided to keep the property long-term because it was such a good investment.

C. Large Multi-Unit Residential Properties

Apartment buildings with five (5) or more units are described as large multi-unit residential properties and are not generally used for owner-occupied use. They are strictly income properties that are purchased for their income stream, price appreciation, leverage, and depreciation (tax purposes).

Five or more-unit apartment buildings are considered residential income properties by lenders who make loans for these types of properties and, therefore, a home buyer who intends to move into a multi-unit residential property of five or more units will usually not be able to obtain favorable financing from lenders. Lenders will see greater loan default risk with large residential income properties than they do with single-family rentals, duplexes, triplexes, and fourplexes and charge the buyer a higher interest rate than owner-occupied loans to compensate for the added risk.

For this reason, large 5+ unit apartment buildings usually do not move from owner-occupied use to a rental property and then back again (like one-to-four unit residential properties). They are never considered to be owner-occupied, but to always be residential income properties.

Figure 15.6 Large Apartment Building

Some areas of interest to a large multi-unit residential investor include down payment, gross rent multiplier, debt coverage ratio, operating expenses, before-tax cash flow, and cash-on-cash return.

For example, a 32-unit multi-unit residential property is priced a $1,195,000 with a $315,000 down payment. The property's annualized operating information is posted below.

Scheduled Gross Income	$155,196
less Vacancy	$ 7,760
Effective Gross Income	$147,436
less Expenses (35%)	$ 55,420
Net Operating Income	$ 92,016
less Debt Service	$ 81,149
Before-Tax Cash Flow	$ 10,867

(1) Down Payment

The larger the down payment, the more comfortable the lender is in making a loan on the property. In the 32-unit example, the down payment is $315,000, which is a 26% down payment and normal for this type of income property.

(2) Gross Rent Multiplier

Gross rent multiplier (GRM) is defined as the Scheduled Gross Income (SGI) divided into the sale price. The Scheduled Gross Income is the amount of income a property will produce in a year if all units are rented with no vacancy for the entire year. GRM is merely an indicator of the number of times the SGI will divide into the sale price, hence, "times the gross." In the 32-unit example:

$$\frac{\$1,195,000 \quad \text{Sale Price}}{\$115,196 \quad \text{Scheduled Gross Income}} \quad = \quad 7.7 \text{ GRM or times the gross}$$

(3) Debt Coverage Ratio for Multi-Unit Residential Properties

Debt Coverage Ratio (DCR): Before funding a loan, lenders may calculate the DCR to ensure the net operating income covers the borrower's debt service (i.e., loan payments). It is calculated as the NOI divided by debt service.

Commercial variable interest rate and fixed rate loans typically have a **debt coverage ratio (DCR)** associated with them. Before funding a loan for a multi-unit residential property, lenders calculate the DCR to ensure the net operating income covers the borrower's debt service (i.e., loan payments). This is calculated as the annual net operating income divided into the annual debt service.

$$\frac{\$92,016 \quad \text{Net Operating Income}}{\$81,149 \quad \text{Debt Service}} \quad = \quad 1.13 : 1 \text{ Debt Coverage Ratio}$$

The Debt Coverage Ratio (DCR) is required by lenders and varies by property type, riskiness of the investment, down payment, and points charged for the loan. Apartment buildings may have 1.00:1 to 1.05:1 or higher DCRs. In contrast, commercial leased investments may have 1.10:1 or higher DCRs.

(4) Operating Expenses

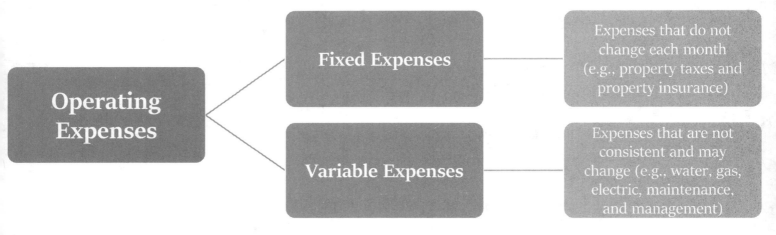

Figure 15.7 Operating Expenses Diagram

Operating expenses include both fixed and variable expenses. Fixed expenses are expenses that do not change each month and generally include property taxes and property insurance. Property taxes are usually based on the sale price of the property. This price is multiplied by a specified factor (usually 1.15% to 1.25% in California) to obtain the annual property taxes for the property. Property insurance can be estimated through an insurance quote by a reputable carrier.

Variable expenses are expenses that are not consistent and may change. Variable expenses include water, sewer, garbage, gas, electric, maintenance and repair, on-site and off-site management, and other miscellaneous items.

(5) Before-Tax Cash Flow and Cash-on-Cash Return

Before-tax cash flow is a function of potential rents less vacancy, expenses, and debt service to reach an actual monetary return before taxes. Accordingly, Cash-on-cash return is the return the investor achieves on the equity invested. It is calculated by dividing the before-tax cash flow by the down payment (cash invested).

$$\frac{\$10,867 \quad \text{Before-Tax Cash Flow}}{\$315,000 \quad \text{Cash Invested}} = 3.45\% \text{ Cash-on-Cash Return}$$

These measures should not be the only bottom-line financial factors the investor should consider in making an informed investment decision. The investor should look at the tax implications and an excellent source of tax information is a CPA and/or tax attorney. It is recommended that clients consult with both entities prior to any investment decision.

2. Real Estate Taxation

Knowledge of real estate taxation can be advantageous to a real estate agent. Real property taxes, mortgage interest deductions, and capital gains taxation are important considerations that California property owners should consider prior to purchasing owner-occupied or investment real estate. A real estate agent should not give tax advice because the agent is not a CPA or tax attorney and should not advise in these matters. However, knowing tax

Figure 15.8

ramifications and how they motivate clients can be advantageous to a real estate agent.

A. Property Taxes

In California, property owners pay annual property taxes on all privately held real property in the state. These taxes are paid in two installments during the fiscal property tax year and amount to approximately 1.15-1.25% of the assessed value. The assessed value of a property is determined by the county tax assessor in the county where the property is located. The tax rate is determined by the county board of supervisors (or other county entity) in the county where the property is located.

Figure 15.9

According to the California Legislative Analyst's office, "Property tax revenue remains within the county in which it is collected and is used exclusively by local governments. However, state laws control the allocation of property tax revenue from the 1 percent rate into more than 4,000 local governments, with K–14 districts and counties receiving the largest amounts. The distribution of property tax revenue, however, varies significantly by locality. The California State Board of Equalization administers the allocation of property tax revenue for the State.

"Although the property tax is a local revenue source, it affects the state budget due to the state's education finance system—additional property tax revenue from the 1 percent rate for K–14 districts generally decreases the state's spending obligation for education. Over the years, the state has changed the laws regarding property tax allocation many times in order to reduce its costs for education programs or address other policy interests."

(1) County Tax Assessor

The county tax assessor assesses the value of each individual property and collects property taxes that are due each year. The property's land and buildings are valued separately, and then combined to determine the total assessed value. This assessed value is multiplied by the tax rate for the county (usually 1.15% to 1.25%) to arrive at the total property taxes to be paid by the property owner each year.

(2) Property Tax Year

The fiscal property tax year starts on July 1st and continues through June 30th. The first installment of property taxes is due on November 1st and delinquent on December 10th. The second installment of property taxes is due on February 1st and delinquent on April 10th. Hence, No Darn Fooling Around is a good way to remember these dates.

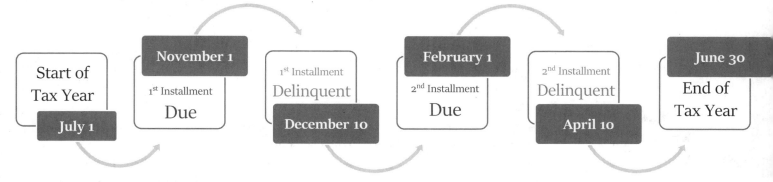

Figure 15.10 Due and Delinquent Property Tax Diagram

(3) Over-Assessed

When a parcel of real property has been over-assessed by the county tax assessor, the property owner can make an appeal to the assessment appeals board. The property owner must send three recent sales comparables to the board during a specified time-period and the assessment appeals board will review the assessment and make changes as necessary.

(4) Reassessment

When a property is sold it is reassessed by the county tax assessor. In addition, when a long-term lease is created, or a gift/inheritance is given, each may cause a reassessment of a property. Inter-spousal transfers will generally not trigger a reassessment.

(5) Supplemental Assessment

When a person purchases a property that has not been sold in many years, the seller is probably paying very low property taxes under Proposition 13. When a buyer closes escrow, the escrow officer usually prorates the property taxes based upon the seller's existing tax bill (which may be a lot less than what the buyer will be paying in the future). After close of escrow, the buyer will receive a supplemental assessment from the county tax assessor collecting the taxes that should have been paid in escrow but could not be collected because of the seller's very low tax bill. Therefore, the escrow officer must *prorate on what is, not what will be.*

For example, Seller Olds sold her home for $1,000,000. She paid $17,000 for the home in 1961 and has lived in it during that time. She pays $195.50 per year in property taxes. If the close of escrow occurs in the middle of the tax year, then the escrow officer will prorate the property taxes paid ahead of time by the seller as a credit (paid to) to the seller and debit (paid from) the buyer for the same amount. Since the amount debited (paid from) the buyer is not nearly as much as she will pay with her new assessed value (based on the new sale price of $1,000,000 x 1.15% = $11,500 per year in property taxes), she will receive a supplemental tax bill from the tax assessor to make up the difference. This bill will usually arrive one to six months or more after close of escrow.

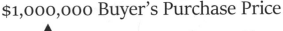

$1,000,000 Buyer's Purchase Price

$983,000 Difference

Buyer paid property taxes in escrow based on the seller's existing property taxes that were due up until the time of sale. In other words, property taxes are prorated on what IS, not what WILL BE. This means the buyer pays property taxes in escrow based on the *seller's existing assessed value* of $17,000 and not on the buyer's purchase price of $1,000,000. A supplemental tax bill will arrive within approximately six months for the property taxes on the difference of $983,000 the buyer should have paid at close of escrow.

$17,000 Seller's Property Tax Assessed Value

Figure 15.11 Supplemental Tax Assessment Example

New homes in a subdivision will usually have a supplemental assessment that will be sent to the buyer within six months of close of escrow. The reason is because the builder paid a low price for the vacant lot that the home sits on and then builds a house on the lot that significantly increases the value of the property. The escrow officer will prorate the property taxes based on the seller's (builder's) existing low property tax bill for the vacant land and not for the new value of the property with a home built on it. A supplemental assessment will arrive several months later with the rest of the tax bill that the buyer should have paid at close of escrow but could not do so because the escrow officer had to prorate the taxes based on the existing low property tax assessment and not on the new sale price of the property.

For new home sales and homes that have not been sold for a long time, real estate agents should make their buyers aware of the supplemental assessment and supplemental tax bill that will be arriving in the mail in the future and understand that it is part of the property taxes the buyer did not pay in escrow. This will save a lot of buyer misunderstandings and preserve happy clients for future transactions.

(6) Delinquent Property Taxes

When property taxes are not paid on time, they become a lien on real property. However, when an owner becomes delinquent in the payment of real estate property taxes, the owner may remain in the property undisturbed for five years. If the property is not redeemed (delinquent property taxes paid including possible penalties) during the five years statutory redemption period, it will be deeded to the State of California.

(7) Ad Valorem

Real property in California is taxed "ad valorem" which means *according to value.* So, when a property is sold, its value is established for property tax purposes. Accordingly, the addition of an improvement may increase the assessed value of a property. Assessment rolls reflect a California policy of basing property taxation on 100% of a property's true market value.

> **California Land Conservation Act of 1965 (Williamson Act):** Local governments enter into contracts with private landowners for the purpose of restricting specific parcels of land to agricultural use.

a. California Land Conservation Act of 1965 (Williamson Act)

The **California Land Conservation Act of 1965**–commonly referred to as the **Williamson Act**–was originally drafted to slow the loss of prime agricultural land, regardless of soil quality. It enables local governments to enter into contracts with private landowners for the purpose of restricting specific parcels of land to agricultural or related open space use. The Act authorized local governments and property owners to commit land to specified uses of twenty years or more under a binding contract. Once committed, the land is to be valued as open space land.

In return, landowners receive property tax assessments which are much lower than normal because they are based upon farming and open space uses as opposed to full market value for its highest and best use.

Figure 15.12 Agricultural Land

(8) Tax Base

A tax base is a tax assessor's tax roll of all the property owners who pay property taxes in a county. The tax roll is a great way to obtain property owner names and contact addresses for prospecting activities because whoever is paying the property taxes is most likely the owner of the property.

(9) Special Assessment

When a community would like to place street lights and other improvements within their neighborhood, it would not be fair to tax all the taxpayers in the entire county. Thus, a special assessment is established to tax only the property owners who benefit from the street lights. Special assessments provide for many different specific local improvements.

(10) Mello-Roos Community Facilities Act/Mello-Roos Municipal Bonds

A Mello-Roos bond is a private bond issue used by developers to finance the costs of schools, sidewalks, and other off-site improvements. A seller is responsible to disclose to the buyer any Mello-Roos Bonds that exist on a property.

(11) Homeowner's Property Tax Exemption

Homeowner's Property Tax Exemption: Owner-occupied properties in California may qualify for a $7,000 homeowner's property tax exemption.

Each homeowner in California (who lives in their property) is eligible for a property tax exemption of $7,000 deducted from the assessed value of their home. For example, if a home is assessed at $100,000, the homeowner will pay property taxes on only $93,000 of the assessed value ($100,000 - $7,000 home owner's exemption = $93,000). Therefore, 1.15% annual property tax rate x $93,000 = $1,069 per year paid in property taxes, versus $1,100 per year in property taxes without the homeowner's exemption.

B. Transfer Taxes

Transfer taxes are imposed on the transfer of real property and include a documentary transfer tax/county transfer tax, city transfer tax, and private transfer fees.

(1) Documentary Transfer Tax/County Transfer Tax

Each county in California can collect a tax on the transfer of real property. The county collects a documentary transfer tax of $.55 for every $500 of new money in a transaction. Therefore, the documentary transfer tax applies to a buyer's down payment, a new loan being placed on the property (first and second deeds of trust— and other junior loans), and all cash purchases. Documentary transfer tax is *not* imposed on loan assumptions.

For example, a seller sells a property for $600,000. An existing $500,000 loan is assumed by the buyer. The buyer obtains a $50,000 second trust deed from an outside lender and pays $50,000 cash. The documentary transfer tax will be:

$~~500,000~~	loan assumption (old/existing money)
$100,000	$50,000 second trust deed + $50,000 cash (new money)
x $.55 per $500	
= $110	Documentary Transfer Tax
	(paid to the county where the property is located)

(2) City Transfer Tax

Some cities in California impose a city transfer tax. This is in addition to a documentary transfer tax/county transfer tax. Some cities that may have a city transfer tax include Alameda, Albany, Berkeley, Hayward, Oakland, Piedmont, San Leandro, Richmond, Culver City, Los Angeles, Pomona, Redondo

Figure 15.13

Beach, Sacramento, Santa Monica, San Rafael, Riverside, San Francisco, San Mateo, Mountain View, Palo Alto, San Jose, Vallejo, Petaluma, Santa Rosa, and Woodland.

(3) Private Transfer Fees

According to DRE, "AB 980 (Calderon) Real estate transfer fees: residential property. Some home builders have instituted the use of private transfer fees to fund the maintenance of amenities, improvements or open space. The funds generated by the transfer fee are typically paid to a third-party entity, not associated with the developer or homeowner association. These fees are generally imposed upon initial sale of a newly constructed home and upon the *'transfer' or subsequent sales of the home.* Existing law does not impose any limits on the amount, duration or use of the transfer fees.

"AB 980 requires the disclosure of the existence of a transfer fee for properties that are subject to such a fee. Disclosure will generally be in the form of a recorded notice and a requirement that a seller provide a buyer with a statement indicating, among other things, the amount of the transfer fee based on the asking price and how the fee is calculated." Many lenders will *not* make a loan on a property that has a private transfer fee.

C. Sales Tax (Successor's Liability)

It is important for the buyer of a business opportunity to verify the seller's sales tax has been paid to the California State Board of Equalization and there are no monies due at close of escrow. Otherwise, the *buyer takes responsibility for the tax liability.* Therefore, the buyer is responsible for sales taxes collected prior to the sale and not yet paid to the State Board of Equalization. This is called successor's liability.

D. Capital Gains Tax

(1) Personal Owner-Occupied Residence

A single person may take up to $250,000 of the home sale proceeds and a married couple can take up to $500,000 of the sale proceeds *tax free* (no capital gains tax on this amount). One stipulation is that homeowner(s) must have lived in the residence at least two years out of the last five years. It is always best to refer clients to a CPA or tax attorney for advice regarding all tax matters.

(2) Residential and Commercial Income Properties

Real estate investors are normally concerned with deferring capital gains taxes into the future. For this reason, knowledge of taxation can help an agent understand investor buying and selling motivations.

a. Operational Loss

An investor may take an annual loss if an income property loses money during the year. For example, if an apartment building receives $100,000 in revenue during the year and incurs operational costs of $120,000, it would show an operational loss of $20,000. This passive loss may be deductible against other income the investor may receive from other sources.

For example, if Able owns an apartment building and sustained a $3,000 operational loss for the tax year, for income tax purposes he may deduct the full amount from his ordinary income. In addition, prepayment penalties, mortgage interest payments, and property taxes are all usually deductible for federal income tax purposes.

b. Tax Shelter

Tax shelter refers to income tax. One form of tax shelter is a limited partnership. Limited partnerships have traditionally been a good way to shelter income. A limited partnership minimizes an investor's liability exposure because the investor can usually only lose what has been invested in the property. The investor's personal assets are *not* at risk.

436

In addition, a limited partnership enjoys single taxation, rather than the double taxation of a corporation. A limited partnership passes the income directly to the limited partner without taxing it and the limited partner then pays partnership income tax on their personal income tax return.

A general partnership may exist when two or more people come together to invest in a parcel of real property. The general partners have unlimited liability and are usually risking *all* their personal assets. Therefore, the type of ownership that would minimize tax obligations for the individual investor and limit their personal liability would be a limited partnership and not a general partnership.

Limited liability companies have become a preferred vehicle for investment in today's litigious society. They generally utilize many of the characteristics of a limited partnership, with similar liability protection of a corporation.

c. Sale of an Income Property

Investors have different rules to consider when buying and selling real estate. Differences include a shorter rollover time, ability to write-off capital losses, and ability to incur expenses on an annualized basis.

For federal income tax purposes, the change in market value identified in the sale of a property could be identified as a capital loss or gain in disposing of a capital asset. A capital gain occurs when the property increases in value and the investor makes a profit on the sale of the property. A capital loss occurs when the investor loses money on the sale of the property. The formula:

Formula for Calculating Capital Gains or Capital Losses

        Unadjusted Cost Basis

        + Acquisition/Settlement Costs

        + Capital Improvements

        - Accrued Depreciation

        ADJUSTED COST BASIS

        Selling Price

        − Acquisition/Settlement Costs

        ADJUSTED SELLING PRICE

        ADJUSTED SELLING PRICE

        − ADJUSTED COST BASIS

        CAPITAL GAIN OR CAPITAL LOSS

Figure 15.14

Next is a look at the sale of a parcel of real property and its subsequent capital gains calculation using the above formula.

Calculating Capital Gains Example

The Details:

Investor Judi purchased a house for $100,000. The acquisition costs to purchase the property was $10,000 and the investor improved the property with a patio at a cost of $10,000. The property value is $100,000, but the land has a value of $20,000. Therefore, the building value is $80,000. Investor Judi held the property for ten (10) years and then sold it for $200,000. The acquisition costs to purchase the property was $10,000 and the settlement costs to sell the property were $10,000.

The Calculation:

Unadjusted Cost Basis	$100,000
+ Acquisition/Settlement Costs	$ 10,000
+ Capital Improvements	$ 10,000 (patio)
- Accrued Depreciation	$ 29,090 (10 years x $2,909/year)
ADJUSTED COST BASIS	$ 90,910
Selling Price	$200,000
– Acquisition/Settlement Costs	$ 10,000
ADJUSTED SELLING PRICE	$190,000
ADJUSTED SELLING PRICE	$190,000
– ADJUSTED COST BASIS	$ 90,910
CAPITAL GAIN	**$ 99,090**

The Calculation Explanation:

1. Adjusted Cost Basis Calculation

Unadjusted Cost Basis

For federal income tax purposes, the unadjusted basis of a property would include the original sale price or original cost. In the above example, the unadjusted cost basis is $100,000.

+ Acquisition/Settlement Costs

Real estate commissions and closing costs are added to the adjusted cost basis. This helps to reduce the amount of capital gains the investor will pay to the IRS. The acquisition/settlements costs in the above example are $10,000 and are added to the unadjusted cost basis.

+ Capital Improvements (Permanent Improvements)

For federal income tax purposes, capital expenditures for improvements of an income property are added to the cost basis of the property. In the above example, the patio was a capital improvement at a cost of $10,000.

- **Accrued Depreciation**

Depreciation for income tax purposes is very different than depreciation for appraisal purposes. Depreciation for income tax purposes is a paperwork loss allowed by the Internal Revenue Service (IRS). To calculate depreciation of an income property, the building portion only (land is NOT depreciated) is divided into a predetermined number of useful years on a straight-line basis.

The property value in the above example is $100,000, but the land value is $20,000. Thus, the building value is $80,000 (property value of $100,000 − land value of $20,000 = $80,000 building value). The building portion ($80,000) is divided by 27.5 years to obtain the amount the property depreciates each year.

Therefore,

$$\frac{\$80,000 \text{ (Building Value)}}{27.5 \text{ Years}} = \$2,909 / \text{year}$$

Hence, the property depreciates $2,909 each year. At the end of 27.5 years the property is completely depreciated. When the investor sells the property and capital gains are calculated, the accrued depreciation is the total amount of depreciation deducted by the owner over the holding period (between purchase and sale). In the above example, the property was depreciated for ten years at $2,909 each year. Thus, the accrued depreciation totaled $29,090.

It is extremely important to note that only the improved portion of a property can be depreciated, which is usually the building. Land cannot be depreciated, only the improved portion. For federal income tax purposes, an estimated life of 27.5 years is used for capital improvements made to residential income property after 1986. All residential properties (single family homes, duplexes, up to huge apartment buildings) use a 27.5 year straight line depreciation schedule. All other commercial properties use a 39 year straight line depreciation schedule.

= Adjusted Cost Basis

Adjusted cost basis is the cost actually used in calculating capital gains and losses for a property.

Regarding the example, the adjusted cost basis calculation is as follows:

Unadjusted Cost Basis	$100,000
+ Acquisition/Settlement Costs	$ 10,000
+ Capital Improvements	$ 10,000 (patio)
- Accrued Depreciation	$ 29,090 (10 years x $2,909/year)
ADJUSTED COST BASIS	$ 90,910

2. Adjusted Selling Price Calculation

Selling Price

When the investor sells the property, the purchase price is the selling price. In the above example, the selling price was $200,000.

- Acquisition/Settlement Costs

Real estate commissions and closing costs are subtracted from the selling price. This helps to reduce the amount of capital gains the investor will pay to the IRS. In the example, the settlement costs to sell the property are $10,000 and are subtracted from the selling price.

= Adjusted Selling Price

The adjusted selling price is the price used when determining if a property has a capital gain or loss.

The adjusted selling price calculation in the above example is as follows:

Selling Price	$200,000
– Acquisition/Settlement Costs	$ 10,000
ADJUSTED SELLING PRICE	$190,000

3. Capital Gain or Capital Loss Calculation

When an investor purchases a real estate investment property and then resells it in the future, the investor may incur capital gains or capital losses. A **capital gain** occurs when the property increases in value and an investor receives a profit on the sale of the property. A **capital loss** occurs when the investor loses money on the sale.

Capital Gain: Increase in value of a parcel of real property from purchase to sale.

Capital Loss: Decrease in value of a parcel of real property from purchase to sale.

Under provisions of the federal income tax rules and regulations, a taxpayer may deduct a loss on the sale of residential real property when the property was acquired as an investment that was rented or leased to others. In other words, the owner of a parcel of real estate which is held by the taxpayer for investment purposes, would be permitted to deduct a loss suffered in the sale of the property. It should be noted that a person cannot take a capital loss on the sale of a home that was used as their personal residence.

Regarding the above example, Investor Judi ended up with a $99,090 capital gain.

ADJUSTED SELLING PRICE	$190,000
– ADJUSTED COST BASIS	$ 90,910
CAPITAL GAIN	**$ 99,090**

d. Exchanges: IRC 1031 Tax-Deferred Exchange

Capital gains can be deferred through a **1031 tax-deferred exchange** or "Starker." It allows an investor to rollover capital gains if the investor purchases an acquired property within 180 days from the date of the sale of the relinquished property. The investor must identify the replacement property within 45 days from the date of sale of the relinquished property.

> **1031 Tax-Deferred Exchange:** Allows real estate investors to sell an existing income property and move the funds into another income property thus deferring capital gains taxes.

An investor's acquired property must be higher in value than the relinquished property and the investor must also incur as much or more debt than exists on the relinquished property. Many investors use this technique to build very large real estate empires, thus deferring capital gains taxes into the future.

The commercial real estate investment business revolves around 1031 exchanges. Without these exchanges, many investors would refinance investment properties rather than exchange them. Real estate taxation is a driving force behind the real estate business. Knowledge of tax laws and rules can help a real estate practitioner increase earnings and reduce risks in this rapidly changing business environment.

1031 Exchange Process

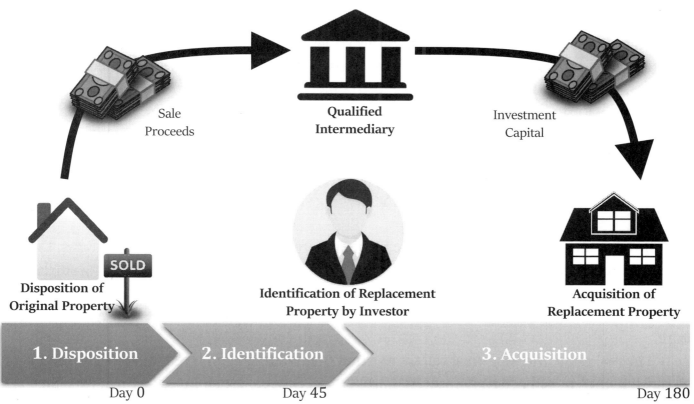

Sale Proceeds — **Qualified Intermediary** — Investment Capital

Disposition of Original Property — SOLD

Identification of Replacement Property by Investor

Acquisition of Replacement Property

1. Disposition | 2. Identification | 3. Acquisition

Day 0 | Day 45 | Day 180

Figure 15.15 1031 Exchange Illustration

1. Reasons for the 1031 Exchange Law

As properties age, they lose value through physical deterioration, functional obsolescence, and economic obsolescence. As they age, they become underutilized and underinvested because the owner does not want to sell the property and incur the huge federal and state capital gains taxes that will occur if the property is sold. The 1031 exchange allows the owners of these properties to move the capital gains (increase in value of the property over the investor's holding period) into another asset that is fully utilized with possibly some leverage (loans) that will help the lending industry and the overall U.S. economy. The 1031 exchange law allows property owners who hold onto these properties over a long period of time, exchange them for another property, and defer the capital gains taxes until the property is sold (not exchanged) in the future and federal and state capital gains taxes will be paid at the time of sale.

Tales from the Trade

THE STORY OF A 1031 EXCHANGE

A real estate investor purchased a single-family residential rental property, rented it to a tenant for eight years, and then decided to sell the property.

The real estate investor listed the property for sale with a real estate agent. The real estate agent placed the property in the local multiple listing service (MLS) and immediately received multiple offers from several qualified buyers. The real estate investor accepted the best offer (greatest net proceeds to the seller and the highest likelihood of closing the deal) and opened escrow for the sale of the property.

While the property was in escrow, the real estate investor asked the real estate agent to help find a property in which to exchange the proceeds from the sale of the single-family home into a larger real estate property. The real estate investor wanted to purchase a larger single-family home that was of greater value than the existing single-family home investment that was being sold.

If the real estate investor follows prescribed federal and California state procedures, the real estate investor will be able to move the capital gains (increase in value of the existing single-family residential property) over to the acquired single-family residential property and *defer both federal and state capital gains taxes* (taxes on the increase in value to the property) into the future.

The real estate investor must sell the existing single-family home (relinquished property) and buy a higher-priced property (acquired property). The real estate investor must exchange property that is of a *like kind*. This means the real estate investor must exchange real estate for real estate. This is generally any type of real estate for any type of real estate. The real estate investor is required to identify the acquired property within 45 days and close it within 180 days

THE STORY OF A 1031 EXCHANGE

of the close of escrow of the relinquished property. In addition, if the real estate investor's income taxes become due during the 180-day period, this may terminate the entire 1031 exchange.

Accordingly, there are specific rules that must be followed, so a real estate agent should advise their clients who are looking to perform an Internal Revenue Code 1031 tax-deferred exchange to consult with a Certified Public Accountant (CPA) or tax attorney prior to starting the exchange process.

The real estate investor must follow all required 1031 exchange rules, then the real estate investor may be able to move the capital gains from the existing relinquished single-family residential property into the acquired single-family residential property and defer the capital gains taxes into the future.

As long as the real estate investor acquires a property that is of equal or greater value than the relinquished property and incurs at least the same amount of debt on the property, the real estate investor may be able to defer the capital gains taxes into the future.

The real estate investor usually must keep the acquired property for at least one year, before considering performing another IRC 1031 exchange. There are many rules to a 1031 tax-deferred change, so (again) a real estate agent should refer their clients to tax professionals who can guide them through the exchange process.

Next is a look at the numbers. The real estate investor purchased a small single-family rental property in for all cash. It was a 3 bedroom/1 bathroom, 1,000 square foot home that was purchased for $100,000. The real estate investor rented the property to a tenant for $1,000 per month. The real estate investor paid $100 per month for water, sewer, and garbage for the property. Property taxes were 1.15% of the purchase price and property insurance was $500 per year.

The following is an analysis of the annual income and expenses for the property:

Scheduled Gross Income (Annual)		$12,000
less Vacancy		N/A
Effective Gross Income		$12,000
less Operating Expenses		
Fixed Expenses		
Property Taxes	$1,150 ($100,000 x 1.15%)	
Property Insurance	$ 500	
Variable Expenses		
Water, Sewer, & Garbage	$1,200 ($100 per month x 12)	
Total Operating Expenses		$ 2,850
Net Operating Income		$ 9,150

THE STORY OF A 1031 EXCHANGE

Therefore, the real estate investor is receiving a 9.15% annual return on the initial $100,000 cash investment. The I/R=V formula is used to calculate the capitalization rate and is set up as $100,000 price x ?% = $9,150 NOI. The $9,150 NOI is divided by $100,000 price which equals a 9.15% capitalization rate.

Furthermore, eight years after purchasing the property, the real estate investor listed the property for sale with a real estate agent who sold it for $200,000. The real estate investor was allowed by the Internal Revenue Service (IRS) to depreciate the building portion of the property during the eight-year holding period. Therefore, the $100,000 purchase price x 80% building/land ratio = $80,000 (value of the building). The improved value of the property of $80,000 is divided by 27.5 years straight line depreciation which equals an annual depreciation of $2,909. This amount may possibly be used by the real estate investor (with some restrictions) to reduce income tax liability each year. However, when the property is sold in the future, the IRS will recapture the yearly tax savings the real estate investor received from depreciation deductions and get some of their money back. Accrued depreciation (total amount of depreciation taken over the real estate investor's holding period) is $2,909/year x 8 years of depreciation (taken by the real estate investor) equals $23,272 total depreciation taken over the real estate investor's eight-year holding period.

The adjusted cost basis calculation is as follows:

Unadjusted Cost Basis	$100,000
+ Acquisition/Settlement Costs	N/A (not considered in the analysis)
+ Capital Improvements	N/A (not considered in the analysis)
- Accrued Depreciation	$ 23,272
= ADJUSTED COST BASIS	$76,728

Therefore, the capital gains on the sale of the property is $123,272.

Selling Price	$200,000
– Adjusted Cost Basis	$ 76,728
CAPITAL GAIN	**$123,272**

The total capital gains on the sale of the property is $123,272 and multiplied by the real estate investor's capital gains tax (percentage determined by the real estate investor's annual income tax bracket) to obtain the amount of capital gains taxes the real estate investor must pay to the IRS for the sale of the property. If the real estate investor's tax bracket requires the capital gains tax to be 15% of the amount of the capital gains realized from the sale of the property, then approximately $18,490 in capital gains taxes ($123,273 x 15%= $18,490) will be paid by

THE STORY OF A 1031 EXCHANGE

the real estate investor to the IRS for the sale of the property. However, it should be noted that the depreciation is recaptured at a 25% rate (rather than 15% paid by the real estate investor), so the actual capital gains tax paid will be a little more than $18,490.

In addition to federal capital gains taxes, the real estate investor must pay California state capital gains taxes. The amount is determined by the real estate investor's tax bracket. And of course, clients should always see a CPA or tax attorney when buying or selling any parcel of real property.

Instead of paying capital gains taxes to the federal government (IRS) and California state government, the real estate investor decided to do an Internal Revenue Code 1031 tax-deferred exchange. The real estate investor placed the proceeds from the sale of the single-family residential income property with an exchange intermediary to hold the funds while the real estate investor looked for a property to acquire. The real estate investor found a single-family residential property to purchase, made an offer that was accepted by the seller, and placed the property into contract. The real estate investor directed the exchange intermediary to use the proceeds from the sale of the relinquished property to purchase the acquired single-family residential property.

The real estate investor had 45 days from the sale of the relinquished property to identify the acquired property and 180 days to close escrow. If the real estate investor's income taxes had become due during the 180 period, this would have terminated the exchange. Fortunately, this did not occur during the exchange period.

Therefore, the real estate investor sold the relinquished home and performed a 1031 tax-deferred exchange into the acquired property. Thus, deferring the payment of any capital gains taxes to the IRS and the State of California into the future.

The real estate investor can continue performing 1031 tax-deferred exchanges. However, if the real estate investor decides to sell the property in the future and not move the capital gains into another 1031 exchange property, then the real estate investor will pay capital gains taxes on *all* the deferred capital gains taken from the very first acquisition of the property for $65,000 until the present. This amount can be quite substantial.

e. Taxation for International Clients: Foreign Investment in Real Property Tax Act (FIRPTA)

According to DRE, "The **Foreign Investment in Real Property Tax Act** requires that a buyer of real property must withhold and send to the Internal Revenue Service (IRS) 15% of the gross sales price if the seller of the real property is a 'foreign person.' The primary grounds for exemption from this requirement

Foreign Investment in Real Property Tax Act (FIRPTA): Requires that a buyer of real property must withhold and send to the Internal Revenue Service (IRS) 15% of the gross sales price if the seller of the real property is a "foreign person."

are: (1) the seller's nonforeign affidavit and U.S. taxpayer I.D. number; (2) a qualifying statement obtained through the IRS attesting to other arrangements resulting in collection of, or exemption from, the tax; or (3) the sales price does not exceed $300,000 and the buyer intends to reside in the property. Because of the number of exemptions and other requirements relating to this law, it is recommended that the IRS be consulted for more detailed information. Sellers and buyers and the real estate agents involved who desire further advice should also consult an attorney, CPA, or other qualified tax advisor.

"If a taxpayer buys a property owned by a non-taxpaying foreigner and there are capital gains taxes due from the sale of the property, the taxpaying *buyer* will be responsible to pay the tax. To protect the buyer from this potential pitfall, a seller's affidavit is used. The seller signs an affidavit stating whether he or she is or is not a U.S. taxpayer. If he or she is *not* a U.S. taxpayer, at close of escrow the buyer must withhold 10% of the gross sales price from the seller's proceeds and send it to the IRS. The escrow agent will usually perform this task for the buyer.

"Federal withholding occurs for all sales, including installment sales (seller receives a portion of the sale price at the time of sale, and then the balance of the sale price in one or more payments paid by the buyer in the future), along with, exchanges, foreclosures, deeds in lieu of foreclosure (borrower deeds the property directly over to the lender) and other transactions by a 'foreign person.'"

Figure 15.16

f. California State Tax Withholding on Disposition of California Real Property

According to DRE, "In certain California real estate sales transactions, the buyer must withhold 3 1/3% of the total sale price as state income tax and deliver the sum withheld to the **California State Franchise Tax Board**. The escrow holder, in applicable transactions, is required by law to notify the buyer of this responsibility. A buyer's failure to withhold and deliver the required sum may result in the buyer being subject to penalties. Should the escrow holder fail to notify the buyer, penalties may be levied against the escrow

Figure 15.17

holder. Transactions to which the law applies are those in which:

- The seller shows an out of state address, or sale proceeds are to be disbursed to a financial intermediary of the seller;
- The sales price exceeds $100,000; and,
- The seller does not certify that he/she is a resident of California or that the property being conveyed is his/her personal residence."

In other words, if the property is located inside California and the seller lives outside of California, the buyer will need to have an additional 3 1/3% of the sale price withheld from the seller's proceeds and sent to the California State Franchise Tax Board. Again, the escrow agent will usually perform this task for the buyer. The California withholding is for any disposition of a California real property interest, including sales, exchanges, foreclosures, installment sales, and other types of transfers.

> California State Tax Withholding on Disposition of California Real Property: In certain California real estate sales transactions, the buyer must withhold 3 1/3% of the total sale price as state income tax and deliver the sum withheld to the California State Franchise Tax Board.

Chapter Fifteen Summary

The chapter considers the financial analysis of single-family income properties. This includes an investigation of sales comparables, rental comparables, and converting a single-family home into a rental property. A story of wealth building is presented over a sixteen-year period. The chapter looks at an actual single-family rental property and all the factors that go into a purchase decision. The chapter discusses the costs of homeownership, real estate income properties, including single-family homes, duplex, triplexes, and fourplexes, along with large multi-unit residential properties. Lastly, property taxes, capital gains taxes, and exchanges are considered.

Chapter Fifteen Quiz

1. Residential income properties encompass:
(A) tenant-occupied single-family rental homes (a single-family home that has been rented to a tenant)
(B) small multi-unit residential properties containing two (duplex), three (triplex), or four (fourplex) rental units
(C) largest multi-unit residential properties that are comprised of hundreds of rental units.
(D) all of the above are correct

2. Sales comparables can generally be obtained from the:
(A) county recorder in the county where the property is located
(B) county property tax database
(C) local title insurance company's title plant, and/or a local Multiple Listing Service (MLS) database
(D) all of the above are correct

3. A real estate investor usually bases sales price on the market data appraisal method which uses:
(A) sales comparables
(B) double declining balance
(C) quantity survey
(D) unit-in-place

4. Owner-occupied homebuyers are usually buying on:
(A) emotion
(B) generally have lower interest rates and higher loan-to-value ratios than real estate investors
(C) Both (A) and (B) are correct
(D) Neither (A) nor (B) is correct

5. Owner-occupied buyers tend to drive the prices of homes up and down as a function of:
(A) available housing in the local geographic area
(B) employment sources
(C) prevailing wages, and owner-occupied single-family loan interest rates
(D) all of the above are correct

6. Gross rent multiplier (GRM) is defined as the:
(A) Scheduled Gross Income (SGI) divided into the sale price
(B) Effective Gross Income (EGI) divided into the sale price
(C) Net Operating Income (NOI) divided into sale price
(D) Debt Service (DS) divided into sale price

7. Debt Coverage Ratio is calculated:
(A) Net Operating Income (NOI) divided by the Effective Gross Income (EGI)
(B) Net Operating Income (NOI) divided by the annual Debt Service (DS)
(C) Net Operating Income (NOI) divided by the Schedule Gross Income (SGI)
(D) none of the above are correct

8. Operating expenses for an income property include:
(A) fixed expenses
(B) variable expenses
(C) Both (A) and (B) are correct
(D) Neither (A) nor (B) is correct

9. For new home sales and homes that have not been sold for a long time, real estate agents should make their buyers aware of the _____ that will be arriving in the mail in the future and understand that it is part of the property taxes the buyer did not pay in escrow.
(A) special assessment
(B) supplemental assessment
(C) delinquent property tax bill
(D) all of the above are correct

10. According to DRE, "The _____ requires that a buyer of real property must withhold and send to the Internal Revenue Service (IRS) 15% of the gross sales price if the seller of the real property is a 'foreign person.'"
(A) Foreign Investment in Real Property Tax Act
(B) Rumford Act
(C) Holden Act
(D) Unruh Act

Please use this space for notes.

APPENDIX A
DRE Guidelines

According to DRE, the following is a guideline, and nothing more, of defined activities which generally do **not** come within the term "real estate broker," when performed with the broker's knowledge and consent. The following excerpt is directly from the DRE.

"Broker knowledge and consent is a prerequisite to the performance of these unlicensed activities, since without these elements there can be no reasonable assurance that the activities performed will be limited as set forth below.

1. Cold Calling

Making telephone calls to canvass for interest in using the services of a real estate broker. Should the person answering the call indicate an interest in using the services of a broker, or if there is an interest in ascertaining the kind of services a broker can provide, the person answering shall be referred to a licensee, or an appointment may be scheduled to enable him or her to meet with a broker or an associate licensee.

At no time may the caller attempt to induce the person being called to use a broker's services. The canvassing may only be used to develop general information about the interest of the person answering and may not be used, designed or structured for <u>solicitation</u> purposes with respect to a specific property, transaction or product. (The term "solicitation" as used herein should be given its broadest interpretation.)

2. Soliciting Clients

If you are not properly licensed in California, you may not solicit California residents. To do so would be considered conducting activity for which a real estate license is required.

Since the Internet can be read by anyone in any location, advertising a real estate salesperson's services on the Internet would be considered *soliciting* a California resident when read by a resident of this state. If a person conducts an activity which requires a California real estate license, but does <u>not</u> have a California real estate licensee, they could be subject to administrative sanctions such as a Desist and Refrain Order from the California Real Estate Commissioner.

Section 10131 of the California Business & Professions Code sets forth a general description of acts which require a real estate license:
- Sells or offers to sell, buys or offers to buy, solicits prospective sellers or purchasers of, solicits or obtains listings of, or negotiates the purchase, sale or exchange of real property or a business opportunity.

- Leases or rents or offers to lease or rent, or places for rent, or solicits listings of places for rent, or solicits for prospective tenants, or negotiates the sale, purchase or exchanges of leases on real property, or on a business opportunity, or collects rents from real property, or improvements thereon, or from a business opportunity.
- Assists or offers to assist in filing an application for the purchase or lease of, or in locating or entering upon, lands owned by the state or federal government.
- Solicits borrowers or lenders for or negotiates loans or collects payments or performs services for borrowers or lenders or note owners in connection with loans secured directly or collaterally by liens on real property or on a business opportunity.
- Sells or offers to sell, buys or offers to buy, or exchanges or offers to exchange a real property sales contract, or a promissory note secured directly or collaterally by a lien on real property or on a business opportunity, and performs services for the holders thereof.
- If you are now conducting, or plan to conduct, the above activity in California, you need to apply for a real estate broker license.

3. Comparative Market Analysis (CMA)

Making, conducting or preparing a comparative market analysis subject to the approval of and for use by the licensee.

4. Communicating with the Public

Providing factual information to others from writings prepared by the licensee. A non-licensee may not communicate with the public in a manner which is used, designed or structured for solicitation purposes with respect to a specific property, transaction or product.

5. Arranging Appointments

Making or scheduling appointments for licensees to meet with a principal or party to the transaction. As directed by the licensee to whom the broker has delegated such authority, arranging for and ordering reports and services from a third party in connection with the transaction, or for the provision of services in connection with the transaction, such as a pest control inspection and report, a roof inspection and report, a title inspection and/or a preliminary report, an appraisal and report, a credit check and report, or repair or other work to be performed to the property as a part of the sale.

6. Access to the Property

With the principal's consent, being present to let into the property a person who is either to inspect a portion or all of the property for the purpose of preparing a report or issuing a clearance, or who is to perform repair work or other work to the property in connection with the transaction.

Information about the real property which is needed by the person making the inspection for the purpose of completing his or her report must be provided by the broker or associate licensee, unless it comes from a data sheet prepared by the broker, associate licensee or principal, and that fact is made clear to the person requesting the information.

7. Advertising

Preparing and designing advertising relating to the transaction for which the broker was employed, if the advertising is reviewed and approved by the broker or associate licensee prior to its publication.

If a real estate broker's unlicensed assistant prepares a newspaper advertisement, according to the Business and Professions Code the broker is required to read the entire advertisement prior to publication, pay for the advertisement, and place the advertisement himself with the newspaper. A broker may have his unlicensed assistant prepare a newspaper advertisement, however, he must review it prior to publication.

If a non-licensed person wants to place an advertisement in a newspaper, it must be written by the broker (or a salesperson working under the broker's license). In fact, all advertising must be written by a licensed broker or salesperson. Unlicensed individuals may not design and make advertising; however, they can place advertising if the broker (or salesperson) told the person what to write.

8. Preparation of Documents

Preparing and completing documents and instruments under the supervision and direction of the licensee if the final documents or instruments will be or have been reviewed or approved by the licensee prior to the documents or instruments being presented, given or delivered to a principal or party to the transaction.

An unlicensed secretary (unlicensed assistant) in a real estate office can type listings and sales contracts for the salespeople. The unlicensed assistant cannot answer buyer questions about financing or discuss a pest inspection with the sellers.

An unlicensed assistant (unlicensed employee) can type listings and sales contracts for the salespeople; however, an unlicensed assistant (unlicensed employee) of the broker may **not** fill in a pre-typed application regarding a loan for the buyers, explain to the buyers that they need to look into another financial institution because of problems with their *-loan going through, and design and make advertisements.

A. Delivery and Signing of Documents

Mailing, delivering, picking up, or arranging the mailing, delivery, or picking up of documents or instruments related to the transaction, including obtaining signatures to the documents or instruments from principals, parties or service providers in connection with the transaction.

Such activity shall not include a discussion of the content, relevance, importance or significance of the document, or instrument or any portion thereof, with a principal or party to the transaction.

9. Trust Funds

Accepting, accounting for or providing a receipt for trust funds received from a principal or a party to the transaction.

10. Communicating with Principals, etc.

Communicating with a principal, party or service provider in connection with a transaction about when reports or other information needed concerning any aspect of the transaction will be delivered, or when certain services will be performed or completed, or if the services have been completed. For example, a mortgage loan broker's unlicensed assistant may not explain the significance of a document.

11. Document Review

Reviewing, as instructed by the licensee, transaction documentation for completeness or compliance, providing the final determination as to completeness or compliance is made by the broker or associate licensee. Reviewing transaction documentation for the purpose of making recommendations to the broker on a course of action with respect to the transaction.

These 'Guidelines,' when strictly followed, will assist licensees and their employees to comply with the license requirements of the Real Estate Law. They present specific scenarios which allow brokers to organize their business practices in a manner that will contribute to compliance with the Real Estate Law."

12. Unlicensed Assistant
A. Schedule Appointments for the Broker

If an agent has his receptionist (who doesn't have a license) schedule an appraisal for a property, she cannot give the appraiser information concerning the property.

B. Inspections

An unlicensed assistant (non-licensee) may request a pest control inspection and meet the pest inspector at the residence (to gain entry). However, a non-licensee may NOT discuss the inspection with the buyer.

C. Advertising

An unlicensed receptionist cannot advertise (i.e., design and make advertisements) for the broker. However, a non-licensee assistant to an agent who places advertising in a newspaper can only place what the agent told her to write. Therefore, if a non-licensed assistant wants to place an advertisement in a newspaper, it must be written by the agent.

D. Soliciting

A real estate agent hires Jose, an unlicensed assistant, to hand out door hanger fliers in his farm and to make telephone cold calls on Monday and Wednesday evenings <u>soliciting</u> prospective buyers, sellers, and borrowers. This is <u>unlawful</u> for both the agent and the unlicensed assistant.

13. Unlicensed Assistant May NOT Perform the Following Acts

An unlicensed employee of the agent may NOT fill in a pre-typed application regarding a loan for the buyers or explain to the buyers that they need to look into another financial institution because of problems with their loan going through.

If an agent has his unlicensed receptionist schedule an appraisal for a property, she cannot give the appraiser information concerning the property. She can only schedule the appraisal. If she were a licensed assistant, then she would be able to provide information regarding the property.

An unlicensed receptionist cannot advertise (design and make advertisements) for the broker. She can only place what the agent told her to write in the newspaper or other advertising medium.

If a real estate agent has his unlicensed assistant hand out door hanger fliers in his farm area and make telephone cold calls soliciting prospective buyers, sellers, and borrowers, this is unlawful for both the agent and the unlicensed assistant.

14. Access to the Trust Account

Real estate broker, real estate salesperson, or bonded employee will have access to the broker's trust account.

15. Non-Income-Producing Support Activities that Only Can be Performed by the Licensee

Non-income producing support activities can be delegated to other individuals, thus saving the agent's time for high-impact income producing activities. For example, during the holding of an open house, **only a licensee may** engage in the following:

- show or exhibit the property
- discuss terms and conditions of a possible sale
- discuss other features of the property, such as its location, neighborhood or schools
- engage in any other conduct which is used, designed or structured for solicitation purposes with respect to the property

16. **Non-Income Producing Support Activities that Can be Performed by an Unlicensed Assistant**

With the principal's (seller) consent, **an unlicensed assistant may** assist real estate licensees at an open house intended for the public by:

- Placing signs
- Greeting the public
- Providing factual information from or handing out preprinted materials prepared by or reviewed and approved for use by the licensee
- Arranging appointments with the licensee

An unlicensed receptionist (or unlicensed person in general) cannot give an appraiser information concerning a property. This activity would require a real estate license. An unlicensed receptionist/person can schedule an appraisal and/or complete an appraisal request form. However, the person cannot provide any information about the property.

A real estate broker hires Jose, an unlicensed assistant, to hand out door hanger fliers in his farm and to make telephone cold calls on Monday and Wednesday evenings soliciting prospective buyers, seller, and borrowers. This is unlawful for both the broker and the unlicensed assistant. An unlicensed assistant can hand out fliers; however, the person cannot make telephone cold calls without having a real estate license. Additionally, a real estate license is required for a secretary in a real estate office who sells tract homes on the weekends.

A citation issued by DRE may include an order of correction as well as an administrative fine. An order of correction is simply a demand to fix or correct the cited violation(s) within a specified period of time (usually 30 days). To satisfy an order of correction, a licensee will need to correctly identify violations or deficiencies and inform DRE with a Statement of Correction/Compliance that all violations have been corrected and that the licensee is now in full compliance with the Real Estate Law.

In addition to the order of Correction, a citation may also—and will most likely—include an administrative fine assessed for each violation. The range of a fine—or the total of a fine assessed to a licensee—is set by statute at $0 to $2,500. The maximum fine amount for real estate licensees is $2,500 per citation, and fine amounts may vary, depending upon the nature of the violation and other criteria.

For example, answers to the following questions will help determine the appropriate fine: Is this the licensee's first violation of the sort, or is the violation a repeat of similar offenses? Was the violation inadvertent, deliberate, or a result of negligence? Did the violation involve or result in injuries to consumers?

Before a fine amount is assessed, each violation is evaluated according to specified criteria, which helps establish an appropriate fine amount. Persons **unlicensed** by DRE are also subject to citations and fines. Unlicensed activity is currently and has always been a significant challenge for DRE, so issuance of a citation—and accompanying administrative fine—may provide some relief in addressing the problem. Thus, the difference between those persons licensed and those unlicensed is one key factor in how fines will be assessed.

While the maximum fine amount for real estate licensees is $2,500 per investigation, those who are found to be conducting unlicensed activities may face substantially larger fine amounts or, rather, multiple fines tied to the same investigation.

17.   DRE's Citation and Fine Program Now in Action

"The California Department of Real Estate (DRE) recently finalized its authority to issue citations and assess administrative fines to violators of the California Real Estate Law.

Fines apply to each unlicensed act a person not properly licensed with DRE yet found to be conducting real estate activities that require a license may be issued a citation for the unlicensed activity and assessed the maximum fine amount per citation of $2,500. But while the maximum fine amount for a real estate licensee is $2,500 per case or investigation, the maximum fine amount for an unlicensed individual is a $2,500 fine for **each unlicensed act or transaction**.

Calculate the fines that may be assessed against an unlicensed person involved in 100 transactions, for example, and you can see how substantial the cost of operating without a license may become! DRE hopes this citation authority will help deter and discourage unlicensed activity.

A. What to Expect if you Receive a Citation

First, read the citation carefully, along with any notices and details that come with it. The citation will identify the violation(s) you committed, provide information on how to pay the fine, describe any corrective action needed (if necessary), and explain the process for contesting the citation, if you choose to.

If an order of correction is included with the citation, then corrective action will need to be affected within a specific timeframe. Make note of any deadline for making the corrections and instructions for notifying DRE that you are now in compliance.

Finally, regarding the fine, if one is assessed, you will typically have 30 days from receipt of the citation to pay it. There is a review process if you want to contest the citation.

The first level of review is a Citation Review Conference (CRC), which is an informal review of the citation conducted by DRE. Depending upon information that you may submit in mitigation, the citation may be upheld, modified, or even dismissed. If the citation and fine are upheld, then the next level to contest the citation would be a formal administrative hearing before an administrative law judge.

DRE is looking to resolve every citation at the lowest possible level of review; however, in some cases an administrative hearing may be the last resort to remedy the matter. An administrative law judge will review the evidence collected by DRE and uphold the citation or determine that DRE was in error and dismiss the citation. Administrative hearings are expensive, for both DRE and the licensee, so DRE is going to strive to issue citations and assess fines only in cases where evidence is clear and unambiguous. Specific information regarding the review and appeal processes is available on DRE's website and from the Citation and Fine section.

DRE considers the issuance of citations an opportunity to help educate both licensees and non-licensees alike and to encourage and reinforce compliance with Real Estate Law. Given this emphasis upon compliance education, information regarding specific citations issued—and any fines paid—will <u>not</u> be posted on DRE's website, nor will such information be attached to one's individual public licensee website record. The information is <u>still public</u>, however, and may be obtained through a request submitted to DRE pursuant to the Public Records Act. Citations should <u>not</u> be ignored."

Glossary of Terms

#

1031 Exchange: A way to exchange a parcel of real property for a different parcel, while deferring capital gains taxes into the future.

3 Day Notice to Pay Rent or Quit: Eviction notice that lets a tenant know they are being evicted from the premises. The tenant has 3 court days to respond to a 3 day notice. A court day is a day the Superior Court is open.

4-3-2-1 Rule: The front 40% of a retail space is more valuable than areas in the back of the space because of exposure to foot traffic in front of the location.

80-10-10 Loan: A buyer purchases a property with an 80% first deed of trust that is usually made by a conventional lender. The buyer places a 10% down payment and has the seller carry 10% of the purchase price. An 80-10-10 is used to allow the buyer to purchase the property without being required to pay private mortgage insurance.

A

Abandonment: Occurs when a tenant leaves a property without prior notice to the landlord (lessor).

Abstract of Title: A summary of the documents that relate to the title to a parcel of real property. Normally used in other states, however, *not* normally used in California.

Acceleration Clause: A clause in a deed of trust that accelerates the loan balance as due and payable when a loan is in default. Note: an alienation clause/due-on-sale clause is also considered an acceleration clause that makes the loan due and payable when the property is transferred.

Accession/Accretion: Accession is comprised of accretion and annexation. The gradual build-up of alluvium (soil) along a river bank is called accretion. When an adjacent parcel of real property is acquired this is called annexation.

Acknowledgement, Verification, and Recordation: A notary public acknowledges who the person is who is signing the document. The notary verifies the person's identity through a photo identification and thumb print. Lastly, the document is recorded at the county recorder's office in the county where the property is located.

Active Prospecting Methods: Active prospecting methods include open houses and knocking on doors.

Actual Age: The actual age is the property's actual age in years. With good maintenance, a property's effective age can be less than its actual age.

Actual Fraud: When a person intentionally lies to another person who relies on the information to their detriment.

Addendum: Additional pages of material that are added to and become part of a contract.

Adjustable Rate Loan: A loan that has an interest rate that changes with money market rates (cost of money). Usually tied to an index such as the Monthly Treasuries Average (MTA) or London Inter-bank Offered Rate (LIBOR) and the Secured Overnight Financing Rate or SOFR that measures the cost of money and changes over the life of the loan. The SOFR rate measures overnight loans collateralized by U.S. government debt.

Adverse Possession: When a person (adverse possessor) acquires land through possession. It must be open and notorious, uninterrupted for at least five years, there must be a claim of right (reason the person is using the land), and it must be hostile to the owner's intent. In addition, the adverse possessor must pay property taxes for at least 5 years on the land being occupied.

Affixed to the Land: Items that are affixed to the land are considered real property and include a home, personal property incorporated into the land (fixture), and vegetation

After-Acquired Title: Buildings that are built on a property that is already encumbered by a loan will be acquired by the lender if the property is foreclosed in the future.

Agency/Agent: A person who represents another person in the sale or purchase of real property is called an agent. The relationship between the agent and principal is called an agency relationship.

Agent Breaks Promise to Advertise: If a real estate agent promises to advertise a property for sale, the agent must provide the advertising as promised.

Agent Marketing: Occurs when an agent advertises their name toward specific target markets.

Agency Visual Inspection Disclosure (AVID): The real estate agent representing a seller of residential property consisting of one to four dwelling units (or a manufactured home) and any cooperating agent each have the duty to conduct a reasonably competent and diligent visual inspection of the property and to disclose to a prospective buyer all material facts affecting value, desirability, and implicitly intended use.

Agricultural Lease/Rural Lease: The maximum time for an agricultural lease is 51 years.

Airspace: The airspace to a reasonable height above a property is considered real property.

Alienation Clause/Due-on-Sale Clause: An acceleration clause that makes the loan due and payable when the property is transferred (sold).

All-Inclusive Trust Deed (AITD)/Wraparound Mortgage: A loan that wraps an existing first deed of trust with a second deed of trust. It is used when interest rates have increased and the existing first deed of trust is below market level.

Alluvium: Soil and sediments that build up along a riverbank or lake.

Alternative Dispute Resolution: Instead of using litigation through the courts, alternative dispute resolution uses mediation and arbitration. A mediator (mediation) hears the dispute and makes a non-binding decision. An arbitrator (arbitration) hears the dispute and make a binding decision that is called a determination.

Americans with Disabilities Act of 1990 (ADA): A federal fair housing law that prohibits discrimination against people with disabilities.

Amortization: The systematic liquidation of a debt obligation on an installment basis. A fully-amortized loan is fully paid off by the end of the amortization period. Amortization tables are used to calculate the payment needed to pay off the loan balance (with interest) over the life of the loan.

Apartments: One owner owns the property fee simple and rents out the units to tenants. Each tenant has a less-than-freehold/leasehold estate in real property which is possession of the unit for a very short period of time.

Appraisal, Formal: Required by most lenders prior to making a loan on a property.

Appraisal Report: Appraisal reports include a form report and a narrative appraisal report. The form report is called a Uniform Residential Appraisal Report (URAR) and is used for single-family homes. A narrative appraisal report is a lengthy report that is used for commercial properties.

Appurtenant Easement: An easement that runs with the land. Comprised of a dominant tenement whose owner can drive over the servient tenement's land out to a road.

Appurtenance: Runs with the land and is considered real property.

Architectural Styles: Single-family home styles that are used throughout the United States. The most recent architectural style is a modern, contemporary design.

Artesian Waters: Water that springs up from the ground. Usually makes really good beer too.

Assessed Value: The value the county tax assessor places on a parcel of real property. Usually divided into the land value and the building value.

Assignment: When a new person takes over a lease or other document from the existing person. The existing person is no longer responsible for the document.

Auction with Reserve: An auction with a reserve allows the seller to remove the property from the auction at anytime up until the gavel goes down and the property is sold.

Auction without Reserve: In an auction without reserve, the seller must sell the property at the auction as long as the minimum bid amount is achieved.

Automated Valuation Model (AVM): Used by lenders to determine an estimated value for a parcel of real property.

Avulsion: The rapid tearing away of land by water.

B

Backfill: Soil that is filled in around a foundation, retaining wall, or other excavation.

Balance Sheet: Used by businesses to determine their assets, liabilities, and stockholder's equity.

Before-Tax Cash Flow: The amount of money a property provides after all expenses have been paid for the year. Does not include the property owner's income taxes that must be paid on the property.

Beneficiary Statement: When a borrower pays off an existing loan, the lender sends a beneficiary statement to escrow alerting the escrow agent to the amount of funds necessary to pay off the existing property loan.

Bill of Sale: Used to transfer personal property.

Blanket Trust Deed/Blanket Encumbrance: A loan that is placed on several parcels of real property. A release clause (partial release clause) is used to remove a parcel from under the blanket trust deed/blanket encumbrance.

Blind Advertisement/Blind Ad: An advertisement that does not indicate that a real estate agent is selling it.

Blockbusting: Occurs when an agent goes into a neighborhood and informs the residents that minorities are moving into the neighborhood and property owners should sell now before there is a loss in value. Blockbusting is illegal.

Blockchain Technology/Distributed Ledger Systems: A new technology in which things of value or title to real property is placed on many computers located in many different places.

Boarder: Someone who is living in a person's home along with the homeowner.

Breach of Contract: One of the parties to the contract does not complete their portion of the agreement.

Broker Associate/Associate Licensee: A real estate broker who is working under another real estate broker.

Broker Controlled Escrows/Affiliated Business Arrangements: An escrow company that is owned by a real estate broker.

Broker Demand: A broker sends a broker demand into escrow directing the escrow agent to pay the broker's commission at close of escrow (usually paid after confirmation of recording of the grant deed transferring the property from the seller to the buyer).

Broker-Salesperson Agreement: A written document that specifies the relationship between a real estate broker and real estate salesperson.

Broker's Price Opinion (BPO): Real estate broker provides an opinion of value to a real estate lender who is or has foreclosed on a property.

Broker's Protection Clause/Safety Clause/Protection Period Clause: A broker can collect a commission after the term of the listing if there is one of these clauses in the listing agreement.

Building Permit: Used to build a new home or build an addition to an existing home.

Bundle of Rights: The rights of an owner of real property to use, possess, encumber, transfer, and exclude of a thing.

Business Opportunities: A business that is for sale. A clearance certificate is issued by the California Board of Equalization to verify the seller does not have sales taxes due and not yet paid.

Buyer's Agent (Selling Agent): The agent of the buyer.

C

California Association of Realtors (CAR): Industry group of real estate brokers and real estate salespersons.

California Department of Fair Employment and Housing: The entity that hears complaints regarding fair housing laws.

California Department of Housing and Community Development: Handles registration of mobile homes and manufactured homes in California.

California Fair Employment and Housing Act (Rumford Act): Prohibited discrimination is housing accommodations in California.

California Franchise Tax Board: Collects California state income tax.

California Land Conservation Act of 1965 (Williamson Act): A land conservation act that reduces property taxes to below fair market value in return for keeping the land open without development.

California Real Estate Consumer Recovery Fund: A fund used to compensate members of the general public who have uncollectable judgments against real estate licensees.

California Remodel: Tearing a home down to one wall and rebuilding it.

California State Board of Equalization (BOE): Collects sales tax in California. Business buyers may owe sales tax that was collected prior to the time the buyer purchased the business.

Capital Gains/Capital Loss: The increase or decrease in the value of a property from acquisition to disposition.

Cash-on-Cash Return: The return an investor receives on the cash used to purchase the property.

Certified Public Accountant (CPA): A person who passes a rigorous test and commonly prepares income tax returns for the general public.

Chain of Title/Chain of Recorded Title: Every owner who has owned a property all the way back to the Spanish Land Grants in California.

Chattel/Chattel Real: Personal property that exists on a freehold estate.

City Transfer Tax: A transfer tax that is imposed by certain cities in California.

Civil Rights Act of 1866: A civil rights act that was passed in 1866 and largely ignored for over 100 years.

Civil Rights Act of 1968: Landmark civil rights act that assured fair housing in the U.S.

Closing Costs, Recurring: Closing costs that continue to recur, such as property taxes and property insurance.

Closing Costs, Non-recurring: Closing costs that do *not* recur in the future. Examples include escrow fees and title insurance.

Cloud on the Title: Something that causes the property to not have good title and the property owner may have difficulty selling it.

Closing Disclosures: Provided by lenders to borrowers prior to close of escrow.

Collateral: Placing something as security for a loan.

Community Property: Real property owned by husband and wife (or two spouses).

Company Dollar/Office Operating Cash: The money a broker has after paying all commissions to other brokers and salesperson who work under the real estate broker.

Comparative Market Analysis (CMA): Used by real estate agents to help determine a reasonable list price for a property.

Comparison Approach/Market Data Approach/Sales Comparison Approach: Appraisal approach that is used to value single-family homes and vacant land through sales comparables of similar properties that have recently sold near the subject property. Conversely, rental comparables are the rents that are being charged for properties located near the subject property and are used to help value income properties.

Commercial Acre: An acre of land less the amount dedicated for public improvements. The amount of an acre that can be used to build a structure.

Competent: Legally qualified.

Condominium: Each owner individually owns the airspace of their unit fee simple. They also own the common areas fee simple in common with all the other condominium owners in the complex.

Confirmation of Recording: Received by the escrow agent to confirm that the grant deed has been recorded and title has passed to the buyer.

Conflict of Interest: Real estate agent who competes with a principal in the purchase or sale of a parcel of real property.

Coniferous Trees: Trees that lose their leaves all year round.

Conservatorship: Appointed by the courts to handle the affairs of a person who is incapacitated.

Construction Loan: A loan used to construct a building on a vacant parcel of land.

Consultant: A real estate agent is a consultant who provides valuable information to clients.

Consumer Price Index (CPI): Measures inflation and deflation.

Contingency Clause: A Contingency is something that must occur before the buyer must move forward with the purchase of the property. Common contingencies include 72 hour contingencies, appraisal contingencies, financing contingencies, and physical inspection contingencies.

Contingency Removal, Active: Active contingency removal requires the buyer to sign for and actively remove a contingency to a contract.

Contingency Removal, Passive: Passive contingency removal occurs when the buyer does nothing and allows the contingency to be removed by inaction.

Contract: A contract is an agreement to do or not to do something. The five elements of a valid real estate contract include: capacity to contract/not declared incompetent in a court of law, mutual assent, lawful objective, and sufficient consideration. Real estate contracts are required to be in writing, except leases of one year or less.

Contract Rescission (Terminate): To rescind is to terminate. When a contract is rescinded, the contract is terminated.

Contract, Bilateral: A promise for a promise.

Contract, Executed: A contract that has already been completed.

Contract, Executory: A contract that is in the process of being completed.

Contract, Express: A contract that is specified in writing or in oral words.

Contract, Illusory: Occurs when one of the parties is not bound by the agreement.

Contract, Implied: A contract that is formed by the actions of the parties.

Contract, Unenforceable:
A verbal contract to purchase real estate is unenforceable because of the statute of frauds.

Contract, Unilateral: A promise for an act.

Contract, Void: An agreement that is not a contract. An example is a contract to commit a crime is void and has no legal effect.

Contract, Voidable: A contract that can be voided by one of the parties to the contract. A contract signed under duress (threat of harm) is voidable by the party who is under duress.

Conventional Loan: A loan that can be obtained from commercial banks and other consumer lenders.

Corporations: A corporation is a separate legal entity that can hold title to real property. It cannot die and can be set up as a C corporation that is double taxed at the corporate level and dividend level; or as an S corporation that is only single-taxed at the individual stockholder level. Furthermore, a domestic corporation is incorporated within the U.S. A foreign corporation is incorporated in another country.

Cost Appraisal Approach: Values the land using the comparison/market data approach. Then builds a building on the land and uses either the replacement cost (to build a similar building using today's methods) or reproduction cost (built as an exact replica). Replacement cost or reproduction cost is calculated using either the quantity survey method, unit cost in place, or square foot/cubic foot method. The building costs are depreciated through physical deterioration, functional obsolescence, and economic obsolescence.

Counter Offer: Occurs when an offeree (seller) makes a counter offer back to the offeror (buyer).

Cost of Homeownership: Equity is stuck in the home and cannot be used to provide income from other investments.

County Tax Assessor: Assesses each property in the county. Determines the land value and building value separately and then multiplies them by the tax rate (determined by the county board of supervisors or other local entity) to determine the amount of property tax to be paid by each parcel of real property in the county.

Courts (Litigation): Civil courts hear monetary disputes such as commissions. Criminal courts hear criminal complaints against citizens.

Covenant of Quiet Enjoyment: A property owner must not interfere with a tenant's quiet enjoyment of a property.

Covenants, Conditions, and Restrictions (CC&Rs): The breach of a covenant is a minor breach of a promise and is remedied by monetary damages. A breach of a condition is a major breach and is remedied by loss of title to the property.

D

Damages, Compensatory: Compensatory damages return the plaintiff to the position the plaintiff was at before the harm occurred.

Damages, Liquidated: Liquidated damages set the damages ahead of time if the buyer removes all contingencies to the contract and then does not go forward with the purchase.

Damages, Punitive: Punitive damages are punishment damages and are based on the amount of money the defendant has, rather than the severity of the offense.

Death Disclosure: If a person died in a property within the last three (3) years, it must be disclosed by the seller. If the person died from AIDS, the seller must disclose that a person died in the property (for 3 years) but is not required to disclose that the person died from AIDS. However, if the buyer asks the seller a direct question regarding the person dying from AIDS, the seller must disclose this fact to the buyer.

Debt: That which is due from one person or another; obligation, liability (e.g., money that is owed by a borrower to a lender).

Debt Coverage Ratio: The net operating income divided by the debt service.

Debt-Income Ratio: Borrowers may qualify for a new loan by having enough income to indicate a low debt-income ratio.

Deceptive Advertising/Deceptive Ad: Deceptive advertising is illegal.

Deciduous Trees: A tree that loses its leaves in the Fall (Autumn).

Deed, Grant: A deed that transfers legal title of real property from a seller to a buyer. The grantor is the seller and the grantee is the buyer. A grant deed must have a granting clause (e.g., "grants to"), a property description, must be in writing, and must be delivered to the buyer. Recordation presumes delivery.

Deed, Quitclaim: A quitclaim deed removes someone from title to real property.

Deed, Warranty: Used in other states to convey real property. Generally, *not* used in California. Warrants title back to the beginning of the chain of recorded title.

Deed, Special Warranty: Used in other states to convey real property. Generally, *not* used in California. Warrants title back to the time the present owner bought the property.

Deed, Inter-Spousal: Type of grant deed used between spouses.

Deed, Trustee's: Type of grant deed used at a trustee's sale.

Deed, Sheriff's: Type of grant deed used by the sheriff's department to sell seized real property.

Deed, Patent: Type of grant deed used when an individual property owner receives a government patent deeding the property from the sovereign (government) to a member of the general public.

Deed in Lieu of Foreclosure: Occurs when a borrower deeds the property over to the lender, thus not requiring foreclosure proceedings.

Deed of Reconveyance: Given by a trustee to reconvey the basic legal title to a property back to the trustor and thereby eliminates the deed of trust.

Deed of Trust/Trust Deed: Most common security device for real property in California. Comprised of a trustor who is the borrower, beneficiary that is the lender, and trustee that is a third party that holds the basic legal title to the property.

Deficiency Judgment: When a lender forecloses through the courts, the lender may be able to obtain a deficiency judgment that allows for more funds to be recovered by the lender.

Deflation: When the prices of consumer goods decrease.

Deliverability: The property owner has the ability to transfer the property to a buyer.

Demographics: Descriptive variables such as age, sex, etc.

Department of Real Estate (DRE): The California Department of Real Estate (DRE) regulates real estate brokers and real estate salespersons. Headed by the California Real Estate Commissioner who uses an accusation to start a proceeding against a real estate licensee. The Commissioner issues citations and fines for licensed and unlicensed activity.

Depreciation, Tax Purposes: A paperwork loss the IRS allows a property owner to take on their income tax return

Depreciation, Appraisal Purposes: Loss of value for any reason or from any cause.

Desist and Refrain Order: An order from the California Department of Real Estate directing a person to stop from committing an act in violation of the Real Estate Law.

Desk Cost: All of the costs of a real estate brokerage office divided by the number of agents in the office.

Devise: To leave real property by will.

Discounting: Selling a promissory note for less than the face value of the note. The buyer of the note waits until the note is due and then collects the face value.

Doctrine of Appropriation: Allows property owners who own property that is *not* in a riparian or littoral area to be allocated certain shares of water for their use.

Doctrine of Constructive Severance: Example - when a fruit crop is sold while it is still attached to the tree. In this case the fruit crop is considered personal property, even though is it still attached to the tree.

Documentary Transfer Tax/County Transfer Tax: Tax a county receives for transfers of real property. New money in the transaction (down payment and new loans) are taxes at $.55 per $500. Existing loan assumptions are not taxed.

Dominant Tenement: A property that allows the owner of an appurtenant easement (dominant tenement) to drive over another property (called the servient tenement). Also, a person or utility company that has the right to access another person's property is called the dominant tenement.

Down Payment: Money a borrower pays from their own funds toward the purchase of a home. It is added to real estate loan funds that are used to purchase a home.

Draw Down Test: A well tester pumps a well dry and then determines how fast the well rejuvenates itself (water is pumped up to the surface of the ground). If it does not rejuvenate itself fast enough, the well tester may recommend a pressurized holding tank be attached to the well.

Drones: Drones may fly into a property owner's airspace above the home and trespass on the person's real property.

Dry Wells: Holes drilled perpendicular to the surface of the ground that disperse grey water from a septic tank.

Duplex: A two-unit building that is owned by one owner.

Duty of Honest and Fair Dealing: Requirement for an agent to deal honestly and fairly to the other principal and any third parties in a transaction.

Dwelling Units Per Acre: Number of houses that can be built on one acre. Usually based on the zoning for the parcel.

E

Earnest Money Deposit: Money provided by the buyer and usually placed into escrow as a sign of good faith that the buyer is serious about purchasing the property.

Easement: An easement allows someone to use another person's property. The three main type of easements include appurtenant easements, prescriptive easements, and easements in gross.

Easton v. Strassburger: Landmark court case that requires real estate agents to make a visual inspection of accessible areas and note their findings on the real estate transfer disclosure statement.

Economics Life: Economic life is the amount of time the property actually produces income.

Economic Obsolescence: Anything outside the property line that causes a loss of value.

Effective Age: The effective age is the age of the property based on its physical deterioration and upkeep.

Egress: Being able to exit a property onto surrounding roads. Important for retail locations.

Elevation Plan: The front and side views of a single-family home building plan.

Emblements: Growing annual cultivated crops.

Employee: A real estate agent is considered an employee under the Real Estate Law and by the Real Estate Commissioner.

Encumbrances: Encumbrances limit the title to real property. They are divided into money encumbrances (called liens) and non-money encumbrances that are based on use. Examples of money encumbrances (liens) are deeds of trust, mortgages, mechanic's liens, attachments, judgments, taxes, special assessments, and Mello-Roos bonds. Examples of non-money encumbrances include easements, CC&Rs, zoning, encroachments, leases, and setback requirements.

Energy Efficiency Ratio (EER): Measures the property's resistance to heat flow. The higher the EER number the greater the resistance to heat flow into and out of a home.

Equal Credit Opportunity Act (ECOA): U.S. law enacted in 1974 that makes it illegal for a lender to discriminate against a borrower on the basis of race, color, religion, etc.

Equity: Money a person has in a parcel of real property. It is the amount that is left over after loans are paid off during the sale of a property.

Errors and Omissions Insurance (E&O): Real estate brokers generally carry errors and omissions insurance (E&O) to cover their real estate salespersons and themselves against unforeseen problems that occur with a parcel of real property sold by the broker.

Escalator Clause: When a lease includes a provision that increases the rental amount each year to adjust for inflation, this is called an escalator clause.

Escheat: When a person dies without a will and has no heirs, the real property will escheat to the State of California.

Escrow: The deposit of instruments and/or funds with instructions with a third neutral party to carry out the provisions of an agreement or contract. An escrow agent (also called escrow officer or escrow holder) is a third-party intermediary who is the agent of both the buyer and seller during the escrow process. At close of escrow, when all the terms and conditions have been met and the escrow is "perfected", the escrow agent becomes the independent agent of the seller and independent agent of the buyer.

Estate at Sufferance/Tenancy at Sufferance: When a tenant occupies a property and does not pay rent, this is called an estate or tenancy at sufferance. The person suffering is the property owner who is not collecting rent from the holdover tenant.

Estate at Will: An estate at will can be ended by either the lessor (landlord/property owner) or the lessee (tenant). It is commonly seen when an estate for years lease ends and converts to a month-to-month periodic tenancy.

Estate in Remainder: A life estate is a type of freehold estate and its duration is for the life a someone. When that person dies, the property may go to another designated person (estate in remainder). The other person is called the remainder person.

Estate in Reversion: A life estate is a type of freehold estate and its duration is for the life of someone. When that person dies, the property may revert to the previous owner (estate in reversion).

Estate for Years: A lease of a definite duration. An example is a five-year office building lease that starts today and ends five years from now.

Estate from Period-to-Period/Periodic Tenancy: A lease that keeps renewing each period. The most common type of periodic tenancy is a month-to-month lease. The tenant pays the rent on the first of the month for that month. The next month the tenant pays the rent for that month on the first. The tenant can give a 30 day notice to vacate the property, or the landlord can give a notice to the tenant to vacate the property. If the tenant has been living in the property for less than a year, then the property owner must provide a 30 day notice to vacate to the tenant. However, if the tenant has lived in the property for a year or more, the property owner must give the tenant a 60 day notice to vacate the premises.

Estoppel Certificates: Used in commercial leased investment transactions to verify tenant rental information. Each tenant is asked under penalty of perjury to provide the exact rental information regarding their lease. This information is checked against the represented amounts provided by the seller to verify the actual income and lease durations for the property.

Eviction: Used to remove a non-paying tenant from the premises. Usually entails a 3 day notice to pay rent or quit, an unlawful detainer action, and a writ of possession.

F

False Promise: A real estate agent cannot make a false promise to clients. If the agent promises to advertise a home or find an acceptable home for the seller to purchase, the agent must follow through with the promise.

Fee Appraiser: An appraiser who charges a fee to appraise properties.

Fee Simple Absolute: The maximum possible estate in land in which the owner holds unconditional power of disposition; an estate freely transferable and inheritable.

Fee Simple Defeasible: An estate in fee subject to the occurrence of a condition subsequent whereby the estate may be terminated.

Fee Simple Estates: A fee simple estate is an estate of inheritance that can be willed to a person's heirs.

Fiduciary Duty: A duty of Utmost care, integrity, honesty, and loyalty toward the principal.

Final Verification of Condition/Buyer Walk-Thru Inspection: Just prior to close of escrow, the buyer does a walk-thru inspection to verify the condition of the property.

Financing Contingency: Contingency to the contract that allows the buyer to not remove the contingency if the buyer is not able to obtain financing to purchase the property.

Fixed Rate Loan: A loan that does not change its interest rate over the life of the loan.

Fixture: When personal property is incorporated into the land and becomes real property.

For Sale by Owner: A property being sold by the owner without the help of a real estate agent.

Foreclosure: Procedure whereby property pledged as security for a debt is sold to pay the debt in event of default in payments or terms.

Flashing: Metal in the valley of a roof that keeps water from entering the home.

Foreign Investment in Real Property Tax Act (FIRPTA): Foreign individuals who sell real estate they own in the U.S. are required to withhold 15% of the gross sales price to pay capital gains taxes on the sale of the property. A seller's affidavit is used to ensure the seller pays the capital gains taxes that are due.

Foundation: A foundation is used to anchor the house to the land. Footings are the portion of the foundation that hold the house up. California has two major types of foundations: concrete slab and raised.

Fourplex: Four units in one building that is owned by one person. Also called a quadraplex.

Franchise: Successful businesses allow individuals to use their products and methods for a percentage of the individual's gross sales. Thus, the franchisor allows a franchisee to use their business model and are regulated by the franchise investment law.

Fraud: Fraud is merely a nice word for lying. Actual fraud occurs when a real estate agent lies to a principal about a material fact. Negative fraud occurs when the seller or listing agent is aware of a material fact that will affect the value of the property, yet this fact is not disclosed to the buyer.

Freehold Estates: Highest form of ownership in land and is comprised of fee simple and life estates.

Fructus Industriales: Plants and crops that are growing on the land and are not naturally occurring.

Fructus Naturales: Naturally occurring plants that are growing on the land.

Functional Obsolescence: Styling issues within the property line that will affect the property's value.

G

Geographical Neighborhoods (Farm Area): The neighborhood where a real estate agent lives and prospects for clients.

Gentrification: When a neighborhood changes from poor condition to good condition.

Good Title: Marketable title that can be conveyed to another person.

Goodwill: The habit of patronage for customers that increases the value of a business opportunity.

Government Loans: Federal Housing Administration (FHA) loans are insured by the federal government. Department of Veterans Affairs (VA) loans are guaranteed by the federal government. CalVet loans are made on behalf of California veterans and a real property sales contract is used between the veteran and the State of California. Cal HFA loans are special loans used in California. USDA loans are used for rural properties.

Government Patent: When the government deeds a property from the sovereign (government) to an individual, it is accomplished by a government patent. The type of grand deed used is called a patent deed.

Graduated Lease: A lease that increases every year.

Gross Lease/Full-Service Lease: A lease in which the property owner pays all the tenants' expenses that relate to the building.

Gross Rent Multiplier (GRM): A monthly GRM is used by appraisers to appraise small residential income properties. An annual GRM is used by real estate investors and appraisers to help value medium to large size apartment buildings

Guardianship: A person who is appointed by the court to supervise a minor or person with diminished capacity is called a guardian.

H

Halfplexes: One-half of a duplex. Each side of a duplex is separate real property.

Hard Money Loans: A cash loan.

Hip Roof: A roof that slopes on all four sides.

Hold Harmless Clause: A clause in a real estate listing agreement that holds the real estate agent harmless for incorrect information provided by the seller.

Home Inspections: An inspection performed by a professional home inspector that investigates the inside and outside of a property to verify it is in good shape. Additional inspections may include solar heating systems and swimming pools performed by experts in those areas.

Home Mortgage Disclosure Act: Federal law that requires lenders to disclose lending patterns to ensure they are serving the needs of the community and not discriminating in their lending practices.

Homeowner's Association: Condominium complexes and planned unit developments usually have a homeowner's association that is tasked with following and enforcing the bylaws of the association.

Homeowner's Property Tax Exemption: Homeowners in California have a $7,000 homeowner's property tax exemption on the home where they own and live.

Housing Financial Discrimination Act (Holden Act): Prevented discrimination in lending in California.

Hypothecation: Placing a property as collateral for a real estate loan.

I

Image Advertising: Advertising that promotes a real estate broker's business.

Impounds: Lenders that make greater than 80% loan-to-value loans usually require borrowers to pay 1/12th the annual property taxes and 1/12th the annual property insurance each month along with their loan payment. The lender then pays the property taxes and property insurance for the property owner as they become due.

Income/Capitalization Appraisal Approach: Appraisal approach that converts income into value. Capitalization rate is the return a real estate income property will produce if the buyer pays all cash to purchase the property.

Incompetent: One who is mentally incompetent, incapable.

Independent Contractor: Real estate agents are independent contractors for tax purposes. They must collect and pay their own income taxes when they become due.

Industrial Lease: A lease for an industrial property that usually comprises an office in the front of the space and warehouse in the back.

Inflation: An increase in the price of consumer goods caused by too much money chasing too few goods.

Ingress: The ability to enter a retail property from the street. Important for retail tenants to have tenants easily enter from the street.

Insurance Policy: Homeowners insurance usually covers the structure, contents, and liability for the property. An Owner-Landlord-Tenant (OLT) policy is used for income properties.

Interest: Interest is rent charged to borrow money. Simple interest is calculated by multiplying the principal balance of the loan by the interest rate. Compound interest is calculated by multiplying the principle balance by the interest rate, plus interest on the interest that is paid. Nominal interest is the interest rate stated in the promissory note. Effective interest rate is the rate of interest actually paid by the borrower—including fees and discount points. The effective interest rate is also the annual percentage rate (APR).

Interest-Only/Straight Note: A promissory note in which the borrower pays only interest on the principal balance of the loan and does not pay any principal reduction until the last payment when the borrower pays the entire loan amount back at one time.

Interim Occupancy Agreement: Agreement between the buyer and seller allowing the buyer to move into the property prior to close of escrow. A seller rent back addendum can be used if the seller will move out after close of escrow.

Internal Revenue Service (IRS): Federal entity that collect income tax from people in the U.S.

Inverse Condemnation Action: A court action to force the government to purchase someone's property for the fair market value it had before the government did something to devalue it.

J

Joint Escrow Instructions: Instructions to the buyer and seller provided by the escrow agent.

Joint Tenancy: A form of concurrent ownership in which the joint tenants must take title at the same time, with the same title instrument (grant deed), all joint tenants have equal interest, and all have equal possession. There is a right of survivorship when people take title to real estate in joint tenancy. Lastly, if one joint tenant obtains a loan in their own name, the other joint tenant(s) are not responsible for the debt. Lenders know this and insert "joint and severally" into a promissory note to guard against this eventuality.

Joint Venture: When people come together for one specific enterprise.

Joists: Part of a roof or ceiling in a house.

K

L

Land: An inverted pie shape that comprises the point of a triangle at the center of the earth up to the base of the triangle that is the airspace above the surface of the ground—up to as much as the homeowner can reasonably use.

Land Description Methods: Methods used to describe a parcel of real property. The three major land description methods include lots, blocks, and tracts; government survey, and metes and bounds.

Landlord: Property owner (lessor or landlord) who owns a property and rents it to a tenant (lessee).

Late Payment: A loan payment is late after the tenth (10) day after the due date. However, most real estate loans allow the borrower 15 days before the loan payment is late

Leach Field/Leach Lines: Horizontal lines buried underneath the ground that allow gray water to percolate back into the water table.

Lead Sales Agent: Main sales agent in a new home subdivision.

Lease: An agreement between the property owner and a tenant who is paying the property owner rent in return for possession of the property.

Lease-Option: A lease agreement that allows the tenant to purchase the property for a predetermined amount in the future.

Less-than-Freehold (Leasehold) Estate: A tenant's right to occupy real estate during the term of the lease.

Lessee: The tenant in a lease agreement.

Lessor: The landlord in a lease agreement.

Leverage: When a property owner uses a real estate loan to increase returns when a parcel of real property increases in value in the future.

Life Estates: A life estate is a freehold estate that is for the life of a particular person.

Limited liability company (LLC): A way to hold title to real property that reduces liability for a property owner.

Liquidity: The ability to sell an item quickly and turn it into cash. In addition, borrowers may also qualify if they have enough money on hand for a down payment and to pay the monthly debt service.

Listing Agent (Seller's Agent): The real estate agent who represents the seller and lists the property for sale.

Littoral Water Rights: A parcel that is adjacent to a lake or ocean may have littoral water rights to allow the landowner to reasonably use the water.

Living Trust: A way to hold title to real property that avoids probate.

Loan Assumption: A formal assumption occurs when the buyer purchases a property and takes over the seller's existing loan *with* the approval of the lender. Taking title subject to means the buyer takes over the seller's existing loan *without* the approval of the lender.

Loan Commitment: A lender makes a formal commitment to make a loan to a borrower.

Loan Estimate: Provided by the lender to the borrower within a short time after applying for a loan.

Loan Portfolio: The loans a lender keeps and continues to collect interest.

Loan Preapproval/Loan Preapproval Letter: The borrower has provided all documentation to the lender and the lender has run the borrower's credit report. The lender then issues a loan preapproval letter that states that the borrower is preapproved for a loan to purchase the property.

Loan Prequalification: The borrower has merely started the loan process and has not been preapproved for a loan.

Loan-to-Value Ratio: The loan amount divided by the sale price or appraised value, whichever is lower.

Local Building Inspector: Local building inspectors inspect properties to ensure they are built to the Uniform Building Code and/or Local Building Codes.

M

Manufactured Homes: Portable home on wheels that was built *on or after* July 15, 1976.

Market Value: The value of a property in an open and competitive market. Obtained using the willing buyer and willing seller concept. The most saleable properties have good marketability and acceptability by the general buying public.

Material Fact: A fact that if the buyer knew about it, the buyer would not purchase the property. A fact that affects the value of a property.

Mentor: Experienced real estate agent who helps new agents close their first few real estate transactions and collects part of the real estate commission.

Minerals and Mineral Rights: Gold, silver, and other valuable materials that are deposited under the surface of the earth.

Misrepresentation: A false or misleading statement or assertion.

Misrepresentation, Intentional: Occurs when a real estate agent (or principal) intentionally misrepresents information. It is also called fraud.

Misrepresentation, Negligent: When a real estate agent (or principal) unintentionally makes a mistake that harms someone. Negligence and negligent advice fall under negligent misrepresentation.

Mobile Home: Portable home on wheels that was built *before* July 15, 1976.

Modified Gross Lease: A lease that is between a gross/full-service lease and net lease. Usually a result of negotiations between the lessor (landlord/property owner) and lessee (tenant).

Mortgage: A security instrument that is not normally used in California. The mortgagor is the borrower and the mortgagee is the lender.

Mortgage Yield: The percent return a lender receives from a loan.

N

Negative Amortization: The borrower's payment is so low that it does not pay any principal reduction on the loan nor all of the interest that is due. Therefore, the principal balance of the loan *increases* during the life the loan.

Neighborhood Life Cycle: A neighborhood life cycle includes: 1. Growth in desirability; 2. Peak desirability; 3. Stability of time; 4. Deterioration

Net Lease/Triple Net Lease: A lease in which the tenants pay all of the property owner's expenses to operate the property.

Nonprofit and Not-for-Profit Associations: An organization that is not in business to make a profit.

Notice of Default: When a borrower is in default on a loan, the lender will record a notice of default that starts the foreclosure process. A request for notice of default is recorded by the lender on a second deed of trust that notifies the lender when the borrower is in default on the first deed of trust.

Novation: The replacement of a new contract for an old one. A formal loan assumption is considered a novation.

O

Oil and Natural Gas Rights: Property owners who have oil and natural gas located on their property may have the right to extract them from the ground.

Offer: A buyer (offeror) makes an offer to the seller (offeree) to purchase a property. An offer may be terminated by revocation by the offeror, death of either party, rejection by the offeree, or a counter offer by the offeree. Patently frivolous offers are not required to be presented to the seller.

Open-End Mortgage: A loan that allows the borrower to borrow additional funds if needed.

Operating Expenses: The costs associated with operating a real estate income property and are categorized as either fixed or variable expenses. Fixed expenses include items that do not change during the holding period of the property. Examples include property taxes and insurance. Variable expenses include items that change during the holding period. Examples include water, sewer, and garbage bills.

Operational Loss: When an income property loses money during the year it is called an operational loss.

Option: A contract to keep an offer open. The optionor gives an option to the optionee.

P

Panic Selling: Occurs when a real estate agent informs the homeowners in a neighborhood that minority are coming into the neighborhood and the homeowners should sell their properties now to avoid a loss in value to their properties.

Partially Amortized Loan: A loan that is amortized until a certain point in time, then the loan balance is due and payable (balloon payment) at that time.

Partition Action: A court action to force the sale of a property and split up the proceeds to the property owners.

Passive Prospecting Methods: Examples include direct mail and email.

Percentage Lease: A lease that is tied into the gross sales of the business. As a tenant's gross sales increase, so does their rent.

Percolating Waters: Water that bubbles up from an unknown source.

Percolation/Percolation Test: A test to verify the soil can handle gray water percolating back into the soil.

Personal Property: Items that are movable are usually considered personal property.

Pest Reports and Repairs: A pest inspector checks a home for termite damage and dry rot and issues a pest report that can be used by the buyer to ensure the property is clear of termites and dry rot damage.

Physical Deterioration: Occurs when a property wears out.

Physical Life: The physical life is the amount of time the property is standing.

Planned Unit Development (PUD): A group of single-family homes that usually have common areas such as a community swimming pool. Each homeowner pays a homeowner's association fee to pay for the maintenance of the common areas.

Plot Plan: A plan that shows where the house will sit on the lot.

Portfolio Risk Management: Lenders do not want to make too many loans to one risky borrower.

Potability Test: A test to verify water is suitable for drinking. Commonly used for well water.

Power of Attorney: A power of attorney allows one person to sign for (and legally obligate) another person. The person who can sign for another person is called the attorney-in-fact.

Power of Sale: A trustee in a deed of trust is given the power to sell the property if the borrower defaults on loan payments.

Prepayment Penalty: A lender may place a prepayment penalty on a loan, so if the borrower refinances the property during a specific period of time (e.g., 3 years or more), then the borrower will incur a prepayment penalty that must be paid to the (original) lender.

Pressurized Holding Tank: Placed on a well that does not rejuvenate itself (pump enough water up to the surface) fast enough to be used by the homeowner.

Price Appreciation: When a property increases in value.

Prima Facie Evidence: Latin meaning first sight, a fact presumed to be true until disproved.

Primary Mortgage Market: Where loans are made. Types of primary mortgage market lenders include savings banks/commercial banks, insurance companies, private individual lenders, institutional lenders, mortgage bankers, and mortgage brokers.

Prime Tenants: A high-quality tenant in a leased investment property.

Private Mortgage Insurance: Insurance used by lenders to cover high loan-to-value loans.

Private Real Estate Transfer Fees: Developers may place private transfer fees on a property. Each subsequent transfer causes transfer fees to be paid to a third party.

Private Utility: A source of water or other utility that is privately owned and operated.

Probate: When a person dies, their estate may enter probate in which the courts ensure the wishes of the devisor (person who died) are being correctly fulfilled by the executor (person designated to handle the estate of the deceased person).

Promissory Note: A promissory note is evidence of the debt. Important areas include seasoned notes, holders in due course, note endorsements, and promotional notes.

Public Utility: A source of water or other utility that is publicly owned and operated.

Puffing: A statement of opinion that is not considered a statement of fact.

Purchase Agreement: A contract used to purchase a parcel of real property.

Purchasing Power: The amount of money an area has to purchase items.

Purchase Money Loan: A loan used to purchase a parcel of real property

Q

Quantity Survey Method: Under the cost approach, it calculates the value of a building, that is sitting on a parcel of land, considers every unit of material (e.g., board, nail, plaster, brick, etc.) that goes into the construction and totals them up to determine the total cost to build a building on the land.

Quick Move in Homes (Standing Inventory): Existing homes that have been built and not yet sold.

Quiet Title Action: A court action to remove a cloud on the title to real property.

R

Ralph Civil Rights Act: Prohibits violence or threats of violence based on an individual's race, color, religion, ancestry, etc.

Real Estate Broker: A person who is licensed by the California Department of Real Estate to engage in the real estate brokerage business in California. Real estate brokers are generally paid a commission for their efforts. Brokers may also be involved in property management, lending, sale of business opportunities, and other activities.

Real Estate Listing Agreement: Real estate listings include an open listing, exclusive authorization and right to sell listing, exclusive agency listing, exclusive authorization to locate property agreement, net listing, oral listing, option listing, and pocket listings.

Real Estate Owned (REO): When a lender forecloses the loan on a property and then sells the property to a buyer, the property is called a real estate owned or REO.

Real Estate Purchase Agreement (and Joint Escrow Instructions): Used to purchase real property in California.

Real Estate Salesperson: A person licensed by the California Department of Real Estate who must place their real estate salesperson license under a licensed real estate broker.

Real Estate Sales Manager: A real estate salesperson who has at least two years full-time real estate brokerage experience over the last five years can supervise other real estate salespersons in the office.

Real Estate Transfer Disclosure Statement (TDS): A disclosure form that requires the seller to disclose all material facts about the property. Any last-minute changes to the TDS form will provide the buyer with up to five days to terminate the transaction. "As is" sales still require the TDS.

Real Property: Land, buildings, and appurtenances that run with the land. Anything that is immovable.

Real Property Sales Contract/Land Contract/Installment Contract: For example, a seller sells a property to a buyer. The seller extends credit to the buyer and uses a real property sales contract as the security device. The seller becomes the vendor who holds legal title to the property and the buyer becomes the vendee who holds equitable title (possession) to the property. When the buyer/vendee pays off the loan that is evidenced by the real property sales contract, the seller/vendor will convey legal title to the vendee using a grant deed.

Reconciliation: Reconciliation has two definitions under real estate appraisal: (1) when an appraiser reconciles all the sales comparables within the comparison/market data appraisal approach; and (2) when an appraiser reconciles all three appraisal methods (comparison, income, and cost approaches) to determine a final estimate of value.

Redemption Period: If a deed of trust is foreclosed judicially through the courts, the borrower may have a one-year redemption period to come back and redeem the property.

Redlining: When a lender draws a red line around areas on a map where the lender does not want to make loans. This is called redlining and is illegal

Rehabilitation, Restoration, Remodeling, Renovation: Terms to describe different types and styles of rejuvenating a structure sitting on the land.

Reinstatement: During the foreclosure of a deed of trust, the buyer may be able to redeem a property up to five days before the trustee's sale.

Release Clause/Partial Release Clause: Used to remove a parcel from under a blanket encumbrance or blanket trust deed.

Relief Sales Agent: Backup agent to the lead sales agent in a new home subdivision.

Request for Repairs: Occurs when the buyer receives a home inspection and asks the seller to repair certain items in the home.

Retrofitting: Sellers in California must comply with government standards that may include smoke detectors, carbon monoxide detectors, and water heater bracing.

Reverse Mortgage: A loan used by retired individuals to take money out of their home while they are living in it.

Ridgeboard: The highest member of a frame house.

Riparian Water Rights: Land that is adjacent to a river, stream, or watercourse may have riparian water rights for the owner to reasonably use the water.

R-Value: The greater the R-value the greater the resistance to heat flow.

S

Sale-Leaseback/Sale-and-Leaseback: Occurs when a property owner sells the land and building and takes a long-term lease of the premises from the buyer.

Sales Tax: Businesses pay sales tax on a quarterly basis to the California State Board of Equalization.

Sandwich Lease: A type of sublease in which the sublessor is sandwiched between the lessee and sublessee.

Secondary Mortgage Market: A place where lenders purchase loans from primary mortgage market lenders.

Secret Profit: Occurs when a real estate agent purchases one of his or her listed properties at below market value and then resells it at market value, thereby pocketing the profits.

Security Deposit: Tenants give the landlord a security deposit that is used by the landlord to pay for repairs to the unit (not due to normal wear and tear) at the time of move out.

Seller Financing: A seller extends credit to the buyer.

Septic System/Septic Tank: Installed in rural areas to trap solid wastes and allow gray water to percolate back into the watershed.

Septic Tank Inspector: A person who inspects a septic tank for a buyer prior to purchasing the property.

Servient Tenement: A servient tenement must allow the dominant tenement to use their property under an appurtenant easement.

Severalty: Sole ownership is called severalty.

Sewer Lateral: Also called a soil pipe. Carries sewage from the home out to a high-pressure sewer line normally located in the street in front of the property.

Shared Appreciation Loan: A loan in which the lender provides the borrower with a below market interest rate in return for a share of the sale proceeds when the property is sold in the future.

Short Sale: A property is sold prior to a trustee's sale with the existing lender taking less money than the loan amount that is due.

Socio-economic Target Markets: A market segment that is identified using economics and social class parameters.

Soil Pipe: Sewer line that runs from the house to the main sewer line usually in the street.

Soils Report/Soils Engineering Report: A professional report regarding the condition of soil on a parcel of real property. Sometimes called a geotechnical report that makes sure the soil is stable enough to place a house on the property.

Sole Plate: Boards that are parallel and attached to the foundation with bolts. Studs are nailed to the sole plate.

Sovereign Powers of the State: The sovereign (government) has the power to take real property from private individuals; however, it must be for the public good and the landowner must be compensated at fair market value. The sovereign also has the power to tax real property owners. If a person dies without a will and without heirs, the property will escheat to the State of California. Lastly, the sovereign has police power that allows them to designate specific zoning that restricts the use of each parcel of real property.

Special Assessment: A tax that provides for local improvements and is collected in addition to property taxes.

Specific Performance: A lawsuit that forces the seller to sell the property to the buyer based on an existing contract.

Sphere of Influence: Everyone a person knows.

Square Foot/Cubic Foot Method: Under the cost approach, it considers the cost to build a similar building on a square foot basis for residential and most commercial construction; and a cubic foot basis for warehouses.

Standby Loan: A lender is standing by waiting to make a loan for a borrower.

Standing Inventory (Quick Move in Homes): Homes that have been built by a builder and not yet sold.

Statute of Frauds: A law that states that all real estate contracts must be in writing, except leases of one year or less.

Statute of Limitations: How long a person has to take action in court.

Steering: Steering a buyer out of certain neighborhoods because of race is illegal.

Stock Cooperative: A building that is owned by a corporation. Each unit is transferred by transferring stock instead of using a grant deed.

Stock in a Mutual Water Company (Water Company Stock): When a mutual water company services homes in an area, each home is given a share in water company stock that is appurtenant to the land.

Strip Commercial Development/Strip Centers: A strip of retail stores located on a busy street.

Studs: Boards in a wall that hold up a house.

Subagency: A salesperson who is working under a real estate broker is considered the subagent of the principal.

Sublease: When a tenant leases a property from an existing tenant this is called a sublease. The existing tenant who leases the property to a new tenant is called the sublessor. The new tenant is called the sublessee.

Subordination Clause: A subordination clause changes the priority regarding who gets paid if there is a foreclosure. It is used for both construction loans and the refinancing a first deed of trust when there is an existing second deed of trust already on the property.

Succession: When a person dies without a will it is called intestate. The process is called intestate succession.

Successor's Liability: If a buyer purchases a business opportunity, the buyer should get a clearance certificate from the California State Board of Equalization (BOE). This makes sure the buyer is not responsible for sales tax collected by the seller and not yet paid to the BOE.

Supplemental Tax: A bill that is sent to a buyer several months after closing escrow that has the buyer pay the property taxes that were not collected in escrow.

Surviving Contract: When a person dies, a contract will survive the person.

T

Take-Out Loan: A long-term loan taken out after construction of a property.

Tax Base: Every property that pays property taxes in a county.

Tax Lien: If a property owner does not pay their property taxes when they are due, a tax lien will be placed on the property.

Tax Shelter: Limited partnerships have traditionally been considered tax shelters.

Tenancy by the Entireties: Title held by two spouses in states that are not community property states. Normally not used in California.

Tenancy in Partnership: A way to take title to real property that allows several individuals to come together and buy a parcel of real property. Partnerships include a general partnership and limited partnership. A syndication usually has a general partnership and limited partnership and is used to invest in real property.

Tenant: A person who is renting a property from the landlord.

Tenant Screening: Property owners and property managers screen tenants to ensure they pay the rent on time, do not beat up the property, and stay there for a reasonable length of time.

Tenants in Common: A way to take title to real property in which several different owners take title and have only one unity: possession.

Title Insurance: Title insurance insures the title to real property. If a title defect is discovered after close of escrow, the buyer may be able to look to their title insurance policy to pay for their loss. After escrow is opened, the title insurance company usually presents an offer to provide a title insurance policy that is called a preliminary title report. There are two main types of title insurance policies: California Land Title Association (CLTA) standard coverage policy of title insurance and the American Land Title Association (ALTA) extended coverage policy of title insurance.

Title Search: Every person who has owned a property all the way back to the old Spanish Land Grants in California.

Topography: The slope of a lot.

Townhome/Townhouse: A two-story condominium type property that is popular in areas where land is expensive.

Trade Fixtures: Items attached to a rental space that are used in the course of doing business. Even though they are attached to the property, they are considered personal property and are conveyed with a bill of sale.

Triplex: Three rental units in one building that is on one parcel of real property.

Trustee's Sale: Used to foreclose a deed of trust.

Turnkey Property: A property that is completed and ready to move into by the buyer.

U

Uniform Building Code: National standards regarding how a structure must be built.

Uniform Commercial Code (UCC): The UCC regulates merchant to merchant transactions.

Unit-in-Place Method: Under the cost approach, it considers each component (e.g., wall) of the structure and totals up each component to reach a cost to build a replacement building on the property.

Unlawful Detainer Action: A lawsuit filed to evict a non-paying tenant.

Unruh Civil Rights Act: California state law that prohibits discrimination in business establishments.

U.S.A. Patriot Act: Federal law enacted to protect the U.S. from terrorism.

V

Value: The elements of value include demand, utility, scarcity, and transferability.

Value, Principles of: The are several appraisal principles of value that affect the value of real property. They include the principle of highest and best use, conformity, contribution, regression, assemblage, anticipation, substitution, and balance.

Value Variables: Variables of value include price, terms, condition, location, and market timing.

Vicarious Liability: A real estate broker is liable for the actions of his or her salespersons.

W

Walk-Thru Inspection: Final verification of condition by the buyer.

Water Meter: Measures the amount of water a property owner or tenant uses each month.

Well: In rural areas that are not serviced by a public water system, the property owner may drill down to the water table and install a well to bring water up to the surface.

Wills: There are two types of wills: holographic (handwritten) and witnessed. A person who is leaving real property by will may designate an executor (male) or executrix (female) to handle the disposition of the will. The person leaving real property by will is called the devisor and the person receiving real property by will is called the devisee. If a person fails to appoint an executor or executrix to handle the disposition of the will, the court will appoint an administrator.

Wind Turbines: Provides an alternative source of power.

Wood Shingles: Nailed to the sheathing of a home.

Writ of Possession: Courts use a writ of possession to give possession of real property back to the property owner after the tenant has been evicted from the property.

X

Y

Z

Zoning: Public restriction that limits the use of a property to specific uses that will best implement a county's master plan or general plan.

Index

E

S